More Praise for
GODDESS OF ANARCHY

"This dramatic and impressive book vividly brings the tumultuous and tragic life of ex-slave and American revolutionary Lucy Parsons to what should be a large audience. Even those of us who cherish a more heroic view of Parsons's life in struggle will learn enormously from this meticulously researched and learned biography."

— **David Roediger, author of *Class, Race, and Marxism***

"No scholar has done more to illuminate the tangled politics of race and class in American history than Jacqueline Jones. In this deeply researched and powerfully written book, Jones narrates the thrilling life of Lucy Parsons—the infamous labor radical and anarchist who scandalized American audiences with her incendiary critiques of industrial capitalism and government oppression, all the while concealing her own past in slavery. A richly revealing story, brilliantly told. Parsons will get under your skin."

— **Michael Willrich, author of *Pox* and *City of Courts***

Also by Jacqueline Jones

Soldiers of Light and Love: Northern Teachers
and Georgia Blacks, 1865–1873

Labor of Love, Labor of Sorrow: Black Women, Work,
and the Family, from Slavery to the Present

The Dispossessed: America's Underclasses
from the Civil War to the Present

American Work: Four Centuries of Black and White Labor

A Social History of the Laboring Classes:
From Colonial Times to the Present

Creek Walking: Growing Up in Delaware in the 1950s

Saving Savannah: The City and the Civil War

A Dreadful Deceit: The Myth of Race from the
Colonial Era to Obama's America

Goddess
of
Anarchy

The LIFE and TIMES of LUCY PARSONS,
AMERICAN RADICAL

JACQUELINE JONES

BASIC BOOKS

NEW YORK

Basic Books
Hachette Book Group
1290 Avenue of the Americas, New York, NY 10104
www.basicbooks.com

Printed in the United States of America

First Edition: December 2017

Published by Basic Books, an imprint of Perseus Books, LLC, a subsidiary of Hachette Book Group, Inc.

The Hachette Speakers Bureau provides a wide range of authors for speaking events. To find out more, go to www.hachettespeakersbureau.com or call (866) 376-6591.

The publisher is not responsible for websites (or their content) that are not owned by the publisher.

Print book interior design by Jack Lenzo

Library of Congress Cataloging-in-Publication Data
Names: Jones, Jacqueline, 1948– author.
Title: Goddess of anarchy : the life and times of Lucy Parsons, American radical / Jacqueline Jones.
Description: First Edition. | New York : Basic Books, 2017. | Includes bibliographical references and index.
Identifiers: LCCN 2017021023| ISBN 9780465078998 (hardback) | ISBN 9781541697263 (ebook)
Subjects: LCSH: Parsons, Lucy E. (Lucy Eldine), 1853–1942. | Anarchists—United States—Biography. | Working class—United States—History. | Labor movement—United States—History. | BISAC: BIOGRAPHY & AUTOBIOGRAPHY / Women. | BIOGRAPHY & AUTOBIOGRAPHY / Historical. | HISTORY / United States / 20th Century. | BIOGRAPHY & AUTOBIOGRAPHY / Political. | HISTORY / Modern / 20th Century.
Classification: LCC HX843.7.P37 J66 2017 | DDC 355/.83092 [B]—dc23
LC record available at https://lccn.loc.gov/2017021023

ISBNs: 978-0-465-07899-8 (hardcover), 978-1-5416-9726-3 (ebook)

LSC-C

10 9 8 7 6 5 4 3 2 1

To Steve and Henry

Contents

PART 4: THE FALLING CURTAIN OF MYSTERY

Illustrations appear after page 206.

Introduction

THE RADICAL LABOR AGITATOR LUCY PARSONS LIVED MUCH OF her long life in the public eye, but she has nevertheless remained shrouded in mystery. Skilled in the art of rhetorical provocation in the service of justice for the laboring classes, she also offered up a fiction about her origins and denied key elements of her own past. She was born to an enslaved woman in Virginia in 1851, and twenty-one years later married a white man, Albert R. Parsons, in Waco, Texas. Together the couple forged a tempestuous dual career, first as socialists and then as anarchists, urging workers to use all means at their disposal, including physical force, to combat the depredations of industrial capitalism. Their raw rhetoric of class struggle led to Albert's conviction on charges of murder and conspiracy related to the 1886 bombing in Chicago's Haymarket Square, and he died on the gallows in November 1887. Among workers then and successive generations of historians since, Lucy Parsons has achieved secular sainthood by virtue of her widowhood. Yet her career transcended the fate of her famous husband.

By the time Albert was executed, Lucy had gained a national reputation as an orator of considerable strength and power and as a fighter for free speech and free assembly. This reputation would remain intact from 1886 until her death in 1942. More than anyone else in her time (or since), she tended the flame of Haymarket, reminding the public of the miscarriage of justice that resulted from an unfair trial. Her story provides a window into the history of industrial and urban workers through a series of transformative eras that took place from the 1880s through the 1930s. Nevertheless, information about her personal life is as meager as her public persona was fulsome. To adoring audiences no less than curious reporters, she refused to reveal more than the most basic facts about her family, including her husband, Albert, and her two children, Albert Jr. and Lulu. During a six-month speaking tour from the fall of 1886 through the spring of 1887, she traveled to seventeen states and addressed (by her reckoning) forty-three audiences ranging in size from a couple of hundred to several thousand. At her first stop, in Cincinnati, a reporter asked about her background. The thirty-five-year-old Parsons demurred: "I am not a candidate for office, and the public have no right to my past. I amount to nothing to the world and people care nothing for me. I am simply battling for a principle." However, Parsons was mistaken in her claim that the public had no interest in her apart from her message of a looming revolution that would overthrow capitalism.[1]

Public speaker, editor, free-speech activist, essayist, fiction writer, publisher, and political commentator, Parsons was one of only a handful of women of her day, and virtually the only person of African descent, apart from Frederick Douglass, to speak regularly to large audiences. She addressed enthusiastic crowds up and down the East Coast, across the Midwest, and into the Far West for well over five decades. She was a courageous advocate of First Amendment rights, notable for her confrontational tactics and what many considered her shocking language in pursuit of those rights. She had a never-wavering commitment to a free press, and the alternative periodicals that she edited or that published her writings served as a bracing corrective to the contemporary mainstream news outlets that furthered the interests of the powerful. Her stamina over the decades (she was born in a year when the average life expectancy was forty years) speaks to her deep drive: she loved the spotlight, whether that meant center-stage in a hall or a front-page, above-the-fold headline.

Lucy Parsons lived through the Civil War and Reconstruction and engaged directly with the monumental issues shaping the Gilded Age, the Progressive Era, the Red Scare during and after World War I (a political movement with its origins in efforts to silence her during the late 1880s), the reactionary 1920s, and the Great Depression and New

Deal. She demonstrated a remarkable prescience about the vicissitudes of modern capitalism, including the effects of technology on the workplace and the structure of the labor force; the role of labor unions as a countervailing force to corporations; the corrupting influence of money on politics; the inadequacy of the two-party system to address fundamental economic and social inequalities in American life; the cyclical depressions and recessions that hit hardworking people; the lengths to which local police forces and private security companies would go to suppress strikers and violently intimidate their leaders; and the everyday struggles of ordinary people, men and women, to make a decent life for themselves and their families. On countless occasions she defied the attempts of the authorities to silence her, and she remained uncompromising in her denunciations of an economic system that ravaged the unemployed and the white industrial laboring classes. From the early 1880s onward, Parsons held fast to the ideal of a nonhierarchical society emerging from trade unions, a society without wages and without coercive government of any kind.

Neither she nor her anarchist comrades, though, appreciated the larger political significance of many Americans' fierce ethnic and religious loyalties. And she ignored the unique vulnerability of African Americans, whose history was not merely a variation on the exploitation of the working class, but a product of the myth of race in all its hideous iterations. She and Albert lost faith in the power of words to persuade and educate, turning instead to using words to threaten and intimidate, a fatal decision that sent him and his comrades to their deaths. On her own, she favored lurid predictions about the fate that the robber barons, judges, and police would meet should she have her way, a mode of speaking that tarred all anarchists with the brush of violent revolt and alienated reformers working for incremental legislative and regulatory measures. In the Gilded Age, the collective labor actions that she and her allies championed could bring whole cities, or the national rail system, to a grinding halt, but the power of those actions obscured the fact that most American workers rejected radicalism in favor of the chimera of a humane capitalism.[2]

A saint, secular or otherwise, Lucy Parsons was not. Her life was full of ironies and contradictions: She was born to an enslaved woman but maintained a pronounced indifference to the plight of African American laborers, not only those in the South but also in her adopted home of Chicago. She was a frankly sexual being who presented herself publicly as a traditional wife and mother. She extolled the bonds of family, but left behind in Waco a mother and siblings whom she ignored for the rest of her life. She used her children as political props, and rid herself of her son when he threatened to embarrass her in public. She was a labor agitator who had neither the patience for nor an interest in organizing workers, an anarchist who took a long historical view but remained stubbornly oblivious to major political and economic developments that transformed post–Civil War America. She expressed a deep commitment to informed debate and disquisition, on the one hand, and, on the other, an unthinking invocation of the virtues of explosive devices.

A vehement critic of government in all its forms, Parsons used the courts and police to settle personal disputes with creditors, neighbors, lovers, and even blood relations. She preached the need for a united front among the laboring classes and their allies against predatory capitalists, but she famously feuded with many fellow radicals, even those who shared her basic views on power and justice. She glorified the masses as agents of an impending revolution, but believed that in order to launch the revolution, ordinary people needed to master complex texts in the fields of history and political theory. She never grasped that the European tactics and cultural symbols she favored would fail as effective organizing devices among native-born Americans. Her story is a cautionary tale about the challenges of promoting a radical message that would appeal to laborers divided by craft, ethnicity, religion, political affiliation, gender, and ideologies of race.

Newspaper coverage of Parsons chronicles her public performances but tells us little or nothing about her internal doubts and resentments. Editors and reporters from New York to San Francisco, from Georgia to Seattle, from Texas to Wisconsin, followed her obsessively. In what was the nineteenth-century equivalent of the Internet, telegraph operators relayed her speeches, as recorded by journalist-stenographers, across the country, ensuring that readers in remote villages no less than in major cities could partake of what today would be called sound bites—especially her most famous injunction to her followers, "*Learn the use of explosives!*" To her critics, she evoked the destructive power of the Great Chicago Fire of 1871: she was labeled a red-hot firebrand, her words inflammatory, her stubborn resistance to the established order incendiary.

The fact that her ethnic "identity" was indeterminate—she looked neither black nor white—made her all the more intriguing to Americans regardless of political ideology. In searching for an answer to the question, Who is Lucy Parsons? the press described in meticulous (and often contradictory) detail her skin tone and hair texture, the timbre of her voice and the shape of her nose, her style of speaking, and the tragedy that had befallen her family. From Reconstruction through the 1930s, her often-remarked-upon exotic appearance confounded whites curious about her lineage and her "race."

Significant parts of her life—those lived outside the public eye—are unknowable to us. In anticipation of her first national speaking tour, she created a false biography for herself—the story that she was the daughter of Mexican and Native American parents. At the same time, she did little to promote this fiction, and she often mixed up the details—where her parents were supposedly born, for example—when trying to remember them. Though she was of African descent, she did not consider herself black, and went to considerable lengths to deny the circumstances of her birth and her childhood in slavery. And yet she did not attempt to pass for white, either, and certainly a claim of that sort would have been problematic, given her physical appearance. In effect, she rejected a personal historical or ethnic identity in favor of presenting herself as the champion of the laboring classes; that, she thought, was all that people needed to know about her.

Surely Parsons's temperament and her outlook on life were shaped by a series of personal traumas and crises. She and her mother and a younger brother had endured a brutal wartime "middle passage" from Virginia to Central Texas. Parsons was predeceased by her husband and three children, including an infant who died while she was living in Waco. The police in Chicago and elsewhere monitored her every movement, tried to keep her from speaking, and dragged her off the stage when she did. She sparred with some of the most famous radicals of the day, including Eugene V. Debs and Emma Goldman, and maintained fraught relations with her husband's comrades after his death. She survived one devastating house fire only to lose her life in another four decades later.

It is difficult today to fathom some of Parsons's choices, and many of them were troubling even to her friends at the time. What is clear, however, is that as a woman, a former slave, and a radical, she shouldered heavy burdens and faced formidable barriers as she sought to act as a free and independent person. Throughout her long life she would pursue her own interests—sexual, financial, or otherwise—with a certain ruthlessness, even if those interests were inimical to those of her loved ones. She faced public censure by taking lovers, a willful defiance of the prejudices and expectations of friend and foe alike. Although she is presented here as a flesh-and-blood wife, mother, lover, and public figure—and not as a caricature of a heroine of labor—she nonetheless retains an enduring aura of mystery. She deprived her contemporaries, even her most ardent supporters, of a true understanding of herself. We lack a clear written account that would reveal her innermost desires and as a result are left with only hints of the sources of her anger and bitterness, qualities that were on full display throughout her life.

From the time they moved from Waco to Chicago in 1873 until his death, Albert and Lucy Parsons formed a powerful although seemingly improbable partnership, their individual stories tightly intertwined. Together they developed a mutually advantageous, symbiotic relationship with the press, feeding insatiable editors and reporters with the public theatrics and sensationalistic comments newspaper readers craved. During their years together in Chicago, Lucy's story was Albert's story, and vice versa, for they taught and learned from each other, reared two children together, and lectured and strategized together.

However, the story that follows is Lucy's. The first, and until now only, biography of her was Carolyn Ashbaugh's *Lucy Parsons: An American Revolutionary*, published in 1976. Ashbaugh outlined in great detail the trajectory of Parsons's public life, but provided a largely uncritical perspective of her activism. Ashbaugh also failed to locate her subject's origins in Virginia and neglected her formative years in Waco. This book takes a more nuanced approach by integrating Parsons's secret

private life with her high-profile public persona in an effort to understand the struggles she faced as a radical and a woman of color. It also
draws upon the nationwide press coverage of her in order to gauge her
impact as a female agitator.

Although this book focuses on the life of one person born in the
middle of the nineteenth century, it reveals much about our own time.
Parsons and her comrades analyzed America's political economy in
ways that are recognizable and instructive to us now, illuminating the
effects of technological innovation on the workplace, the erosion of the
middle class, the corrosive effects of money and influence on public policy making, and the fecklessness of the two major parties in addressing extreme forms of inequality. At the same time, Lucy Parsons's own
career amounts to an indictment of sorts of the radical labor leaders
who fell back on threats of violence, misread the fears and disdained
the deeply held values of many laboring men and women, and alienated
key constituencies as unworthy and irrelevant to the fight for justice.
In certain respects, then, the story of Parsons's times is the story of our
own.

The pages that follow include several overlapping narratives—a love
story between the former slave and the former Confederate soldier, the
rise and decline of radical labor agitation, the fluidity of the idea of race
as a political ideology and a social signifier, the trajectory of social reform from Reconstruction through the New Deal, and shifting notions
of the relationship between terrorism and the spoken and written word.
Mostly, though, it is an account of one woman, remarkable for her re-
silience and for her ability to reinvent herself. In sum, this book aims
to refute Lucy Parsons's disingenuous claim that "I amount to nothing
to the world and people care nothing for me"—a claim that was false in
1886 no less than it is, or should be, today.

PART 1

An Enduring Civil War

Chapter 1

Wide-Open Waco

ONE DAY IN LATE 1873 A YOUNG MARRIED COUPLE BOARDED A train and left—or, more accurately, *fled*—the small town of Waco in Central Texas, desperately hoping to make a new life for themselves in Chicago. The wife and husband seemed an unlikely pair—she a seamstress, formerly enslaved, age twenty-two, named Lucia Carter, he a Republican Party operative and journalist, formerly a Confederate cavalryman, named Albert Parsons, twenty-eight. They knew all too well that their love was forbidden—for a white man and a black woman in the nineteenth-century South, such a relationship came with the threat of mortal danger.[1]

Lucia was leaving family behind in Waco—her mother and two younger brothers—as well as an industrious freedman named Oliver Benton, formerly known as Oliver Gathings, the presumed father of her deceased infant son. As she moved north she also abandoned her identity as a former slave, changing her first name from Lucia to Lucy, and her surname from that of her stepfather to that of her husband. From this point forward, she would refuse to let her fourteen years as a slave define her or limit her life possibilities. Their names and careers forever and inextricably linked, she and Albert would soon achieve

worldwide fame—and infamy—as anarchists bent on destroying the
political and economic foundations of the United States.

They were a striking couple, turning heads wherever they went:
Albert slight, trim, and dapper, with prematurely gray hair covered
by bootblack, and a carefully trimmed mustache in the English style;
Lucia tall, with wavy black hair. She carried herself with a dignified,
even haughty bearing, impressing those who met her with her striking
good looks, keen intelligence, and fashionable clothing.

The couple's life together began in a high-prairie town situated on
the banks of the Brazos River, a place marked by and destined for inter-
group bloodletting. Waco was founded in 1849 in McLennan County on
a site once occupied by the Waco and Tawakoni Indians. Another tribe,
the fierce nation of the Comanche, persisted in efforts to reclaim their
stolen territory in the vicinity of the settlement as late as 1860. Beginning in 1861 and over the next four years, Waco welcomed slaveholders
from all over the South who were determined to "refugee" their human
chattel out of the reach of both Union forces and Confederate impress-
ment agents. The liberation of the slaves in 1865 entailed the destruction
of nearly half the county's real property value. After the Civil War, a defeated but still heavily armed white male populace carried on a regional
tradition of protracted fighting against successive real and perceived
enemies—the Comanche, the Mexicans, the government of the United
States, and now freedpeople, Republicans, and soldiers of the occupying
Union Army. The county achieved a dubious distinction for how completely civil authority broke down there. Vicious, unprovoked attacks on
freedpeople marked a level of lawlessness extreme even for Texas.

Waco's unsettled nature proved conducive, however, to transgres-
sive behavior and relationships. The town's merchants supplied goods
and services to the area's sheep ranchers, corn and wheat farmers, and
cotton planters and to the cattlemen driving their massive herds north
to Wichita along the Chisholm Trail. The central plaza was dominated
by the offices of men who owned businesses based on credit and land
and traded in cotton, grain, hides, wool, and flour. But the plaza was
also the site of sporadic and at times deadly gunfire. As in the prewar
era, the sons of the planter elite were in the habit of "shooting around

the square and riding and whooping," evading arrest and otherwise having "a little fun," in the words of a local historian. Meanwhile, the many brothels clustered in a nearby red-light district housed dozens of prostitutes, which authorities discreetly referred to as "actresses." Waco was a wide-open town, trafficking in desires of all kinds.[2]

Periodically, local law-enforcement authorities would bow to the pressure of indignant preachers and make sweeps of bigamists, bootleggers, owners of "disorderly houses" (brothels), and enthusiasts of Chuck Luck and other games of chance. Hauled into court, prostitutes, such as Mollie Davis and Frogmouth Lou, among others, would stand trial only to be declared innocent by a jury of twelve men and released to ply their trade until the next raid. Much as the town fathers might rail against sin—the card sharp fleecing the wide-eyed farm boy, the couples living together out of wedlock—this farce of catch and release persisted. In reality, the store owners and other purveyors of goods and services relied upon the business of gullible field hands and cowpokes.[3]

In the early 1870s, a brief period of Republican local and state rule seemed to hold out the possibility that Lucia and Albert could in fact live together in Waco safely as husband and wife. A small number of black and white reformers touted a new "social equality" that signified consensual interracial sexual relations as well as legal marriage, and the couple took advantage of this window of opportunity to marry legally in a state dominated by white supremacists. Albert seemed to have ahead of him a promising, even lucrative career as a political organizer and speaker—and perhaps an elected public official—in the service of the party of Lincoln. However, by 1873 a reenergized neo-Confederate Democratic Party had regained control of the state's political machinery via the ballot box. The Parsonses' move to Chicago in late 1873 was thus a forced relocation reflecting their diminished opportunities as well as the persistent danger they faced in Central Texas. Yet the Waco years profoundly shaped the couple's lifelong roles as antagonists of the rich and powerful. Indeed, in any number of ways their time in Texas presaged their later life outside it—from their commitment to ideas as agents of radical change to their ability to remain unflinching in the presence of those who despised and feared them.

FROM THEIR RESPECTIVE BIRTHPLACES IN ALABAMA AND VIRGINIA, Albert Parsons and Lucia Carter had traveled separate, circuitous paths to Waco, paths forged in the upheaval of mass migrations, civil strife, and the destruction of slavery. Albert Richard Parsons was born on June 20, 1845, in Montgomery, Alabama. His forebears were among the first settlers of New England. Later in life he would invoke his distinguished ancestors, including Congregational clergy and Revolutionary War heroes, as evidence of his thorough Americanness. His father, Samuel Parsons, a native of Maine, had owned a grocery store and shoe and leather factory in Montgomery; together with his wife, Hannah, they had had ten children. Both parents had died by 1850, and Albert was sent to Tyler, Texas, in Smith County, in the northeastern part of the state, to live with his brother William H. Parsons, who was nineteen years his senior. William had fought with the 2nd Dragoons under General Zachary Taylor in the Mexican-American War, when the United States wrested huge swaths of territory from Mexico to expand its southern border. Trained as a lawyer, William edited a newspaper, the *Tyler Telegraph*, from 1851 to 1853, and he took an early interest in Texas Democratic politics. Between 1855 and 1860, he moved his household three times in a southwesterly direction, to Johnson County, then Hill, then McLennan. Albert had fond memories of his own childhood "on the range," where antelope and buffalo lived in abundance. As he later wrote from his jail cell, "My frontier life had accustomed me to the use of the rifle and the pistol, to hunting and riding, and in these matters I was considered quite an expert."[4]

In 1859, Albert, then fourteen, went to live in the village of Waco with his nineteen-year-old sister, Mary, who had married a wealthy merchant. William probably wanted Albert to attend school, which he did for a year. Around this time, William settled his family nearby on a parcel of land on Waco Creek. An avid proponent of southern independence, William published a periodical called *South West* that advocated a reopening of the African slave trade, an extreme position even for the most rabid of late antebellum pro-slavery ideologues. The paper was, in the words of a contemporary, "so hot for secession it had to be handled with a pair of tongs." William also planned to write a book titled "Negro Slavery, Its Past, Present, and Future." Considering his stern defense of "the purity of blood and supremacy" that he said marked whites as "a distinct race," he could hardly have anticipated the day when he would be the brother-in-law of a former slave.[5]

The William Parsons household contained only one enslaved worker, "Aunt Easter," whom William's wife, Louisa, had brought to the marriage. In 1860, Easter was fifty years old and worth $800 on the market for human flesh. By this time the state had a total population of 604,215, of whom 182,566 were enslaved persons and only 355 free blacks. (In contrast, Virginia, with a population of 1,596,318, was home to 490,865 enslaved persons and 58,042 free blacks.) Slaveholdings in Central Texas amounted to a value of $2.7 million, more than the value of the region's land.[6]

Texas was a perennial magnet for southern planters seeking to take advantage of cheap, fertile land suitable for cotton cultivation in the eastern and central part of the state, and among these slave owners was James J. Gathings. Born in 1817 in South Carolina, Gathings and his two brothers had established a plantation near Prairie, Mississippi, in 1839. The enslaved workers they purchased there included Clara Gatherus and her son Oliver (later called by whites Oliver Gathings), who was born in 1832. As an adult, Oliver, by then known as Oliver Benton, would believe himself to be the father of Lucia's first child, and he would consider her his wife. In 1849, the Gathings brothers uprooted their bound workforce of thirty and moved them to Hill County, Texas. After the war, James exemplified the virulent resistance to emancipation and Republican rule that characterized much of Anglo Texas.[7]

The state's large and powerful slave-owning class overwhelmingly supported disunion. A special February 1861 convention passed a secession ordinance by a vote of 166–8, and, unlike their counterparts in most other states, the fire-eaters submitted the question to the voters, who approved it 46,153 to 14,747. This tally underestimates the opposition, however, as some state residents who had been born in Mexico and Germany did not vote, fearing violence should they attempt it, and other men declined to participate in an election they considered unconstitutional, or at least ill-advised. Moreover, support for secession did not necessarily indicate support for the institution of slavery, since some secessionists were seeking only to protest the federal government's apparent failure to quell persistent Indian raids on white settlements throughout the state.[8]

McLennan County voted 586 to 191 for secession, a decisive victory. Soon after hostilities commenced in April, 900 men from the county (out of a total population of 6,200) volunteered to fight on behalf of the newly formed Confederate States of America. Together they composed seventeen companies consisting of both cavalrymen and infantry. In October 1861, William H. Parsons raised a regiment in Waco, the 12th Texas Cavalry, and with his troops set out for Arkansas. During the war he would serve as both a regimental and brigade commander.[9]

Albert Parsons was not in Waco during the great torchlight parades that gave rousing send-offs to local troops in 1861. The year before, William had arranged for him to serve as an apprentice—a "printer's devil"—for the publisher Willard Richardson, owner of the *Galveston Daily News*. Albert found Galveston to be a cosmopolitan place, where he, in his own words, grew from a "frontier boy into a city civilian." The Richardson household consisted of the publisher's family and also a clerk, three printers, and five apprentices, natives of Ireland, Germany, New York, Missouri, and Louisiana, all working in an impressive four-story building befitting the paper's political influence. While Albert learned his craft, he also learned about state politics, for under Richardson's direction the *Daily News* served as a decidedly prosouthern chronicler of the momentous events of the time. Thus began Albert Parsons's lifelong engagement with the printing press and his devotion to the printed and spoken word as a means of advocacy and provocation.[10]

The sixteen-year-old ignored Richardson's prediction that the war would be a short, two-month romp and joined the Lone Star Grays, a Galveston military group, in 1861. Later, of his decision to enlist, Albert would write, "These were stirring 'war times' and, as a matter of course, my young blood caught the infection." In November of that year he found his way to a makeshift fort at Sabine Pass, Texas, where he took up the position of "powder monkey" (carrying powder to the guns) under the supervision of another older brother, Richard Parsons, captain of an infantry company. Discharged in June 1862, Albert caught up with William, who was now leading a brigade of Confederate cavalrymen west of the Mississippi, and received an assignment as a scout. William's brigade fought in fifty skirmishes and battles during the course of the war. Although his men respected and honored him, calling him "Wild Bill," the Confederate Congress declined to promote him to the rank of brigadier general. After the war, he received the title major general from the governor of Texas, who believed that Parsons had rendered services insufficiently appreciated by officials in Richmond. If William's eventual turn toward the Republican Party requires some explanation, his turn away from the former Confederate leadership perhaps does not.[11]

Hardly any clashes between Confederate and Union forces took place on Texas soil, but the state was the site of multiple conflicts pitting secessionists against Union sympathizers, and Anglos against the German Texans and Tejanos (people of Mexican descent living in Texas), whom Anglos considered traitors to the southern cause. Bushwhackers roamed the countryside preying on civilians under the guise of searching for deserters. At the same time, in the words of Nelsen Denson, a former slave, "folks everywhere was comin' to Texas," propelled out of the Deep South by the turmoil of what black men and women called the "freedom war." When New Orleans fell to federal forces in April 1862, planters gathered their enslaved labor forces and headed west, and the capture of Vicksburg in the summer of 1863 hastened the departure of many more from Mississippi, Louisiana, and the Red River Valley region of Arkansas.[12]

Adding to the panic were the efforts of the Confederacy's chief of labor to impress into service fully one-fourth of all the slaves en route to or settled in Texas during this time. Aggrieved slave owners complained that they could not even put down stakes in Texas before their workforces were requisitioned by Confederate labor agents. In response, General John B. Magruder complained that whole plantations were deliberately remaining on the move, and if those "who have not *settled themselves*" continued to stay out of reach, he would have virtually no black fatigue workers (those men assigned to support tasks) at his disposal. The general estimated that during the war owners had brought some 150,000 slaves to Texas (no doubt an exaggerated figure), most of them arriving in the state between July 1863 and July 1864. All over the

South, Confederate commanders expressed dismay that the enslaved laborers who were "refugeed" away from the fighting not only depleted the food-growing workforce but also deprived the army of cooks, teamsters, and trench diggers.[13]

While Yankee troops and Confederate press agents were pushing slave owners out of the Mississippi Valley, the lure of Texas as a rock-solid slave state was drawing them westward. Former slaves interviewed many years later were perhaps echoing their erstwhile owners when they accounted for the mass influx: "Cause nobody thunk dey'd have to free de slaves in Texas," said Patsy Moses. Presumably, Texas was too far away from the battleground and the seat of federal power to fall to Union forces, and too defiant to capitulate. The so-called Texas Firsters, white men imbued with a sense of the state's exceptionalism, counted on the reestablishment of Texas as an independent republic should the Confederacy go down to defeat. And some planters thought the Supreme Court might overturn Lincoln's Emancipation Proclamation of January 1, 1863. In a message of December 8 of that year, the president stipulated that vanquished Southerners must take an oath of allegiance to the Union, and relinquish their slaves "so long and so far as not modified or declared void by the decision of the Supreme Court." Perhaps emancipation would not survive a legal challenge.[14]

During the war, the mere mention of Texas was enough to inspire fear in black people all over the South. The forced trek out of the Deep South, a brutal overland Middle Passage, could take three or four months if the starting point was Baton Rouge, and as long as two years for those leaving from Richmond. Along the way, enslaved people were compelled by their masters to forage for food. They had to keep to back roads and forest byways in an effort to avoid northern and Confederate soldiers. Families were separated, and mothers buried babies along the way. The ill and the elderly were abandoned at the first sign they were unable to endure life on the move. Although some brave souls managed to escape, most chose to suffer through the ordeal with kin and community members.[15]

These forced migrants found no respite in the valley of the Rio de los Brazos (literally, the river of the hands of God), which was overrun with prairie chickens, bears, and panthers and devoid of dwellings, outbuildings, fences, and orchards. Living in wagons and working "from

sun to sun" clearing brush and felling trees, cutting tall grass and plow-
ing tough sod, and building bridges and cabins, men and women who
had previously grown cotton or tobacco found themselves cast back into
the drudge work endured by their seventeenth- and eighteenth-century
forebears. Until well into the 1850s, Indians appeared by moonlight and
raided the new plantations for livestock and horses. During the war, the
predations of deserters from the Confederate Army, cattle rustlers, and
desperadoes made life and labor on the prairie frontier not only back-
breaking but also harrowing.[16]

Between 1860 and 1864, McLennan County officials saw the number of taxable slaves increase from 2,105 to 3,807. The county and the
town of Waco welcomed slaveholding newcomers and apparently asked
few questions of the white men who sought to deprive the Confederacy
of their slaves—or of their own service as soldiers. During the war, the
town embraced a kind of state socialism, using taxpayer money to supply arms and ammunition to native sons in harm's way, to care for soldiers' families, and to bury bodies brought home. The region's support
for the South had its limits, however. In early 1864, the county court
recommended that physicians be excused from the draft in order to
tend to the ill at home in Central Texas.[17]

Missing from the list of doctors so exempted was Thomas J. Taliaferro, a slave owner and physician who had brought at least a portion
of his workforce to Texas in late 1862 or 1863. Taliaferro had joined the
46th Tennessee Infantry in Henry County, Tennessee, in November
1861, when he was thirty-six years old, enlisting as an assistant surgeon.
Later he was captured by Union soldiers and imprisoned in Camp
Douglas, Illinois. Discharged in Chicago in July 1862, he was exchanged
in return for Union prisoners two months later in Vicksburg, Mississippi. His regiment moved to Jackson, where it was reorganized. However, Taliaferro resigned from service and apparently returned home,
either to Virginia or Tennessee, to gather his slaves, soon afterward
striking out for Texas. In early 1863, he bought about two hundred acres
in the north-central part of McLennan County. Taliaferro was not
listed with other Waco physicians on the exempted list, however, perhaps because he had already fulfilled his military obligations or because
the terms of his parole forbade him from rejoining the army.[18]

Among the workers Taliaferro brought to Texas in 1863 were at least four slaves who had been born in Virginia—Charlotte, age twenty-nine; her twelve-year-old daughter, Lucia; her seven-year-old son, Tanner; and another young woman, Jane, eighteen. Since Charlotte was dark-skinned—and, according to at least one Waco white man, "comely"—it is probable that the fairer-skinned Lucia was the daughter of her master (that was the rumor around town) or another white man. Charlotte and Jane both bore children at an early age. Soon after coming to Texas, Charlotte had another son, Webster, and Jane gave birth to her first child, Nellie.[19]

For Lucia, the trauma of a forced march to Texas was perhaps mitigated by the presence of her mother, younger brother, and Jane. It is possible that Dr. Taliaferro worked full-time as a physician, and so spared his slaves the arduous labor of clearing the land. Charlotte had housekeeping skills, and as a young woman, Lucia, too, learned to cook and sew, so she probably never had to work in the fields. Still, she was old enough to remember leaving familiar surroundings in Virginia and enduring long weeks and months on the road, an ordeal that must have haunted her the rest of her life.

WHEN THE WAR ENDED IN THE LATE SPRING OF 1865, THE LAWLESS town of Waco proved an unlikely refuge for freedpeople from the nearby countryside, where white Texans tried to re-create slavery in all but name. In 1866, Taliaferro returned to Tennessee to marry Martha D. Woods. It was perhaps in his absence that Charlotte and Jane resettled their children in Waco, away from the horrific abuse meted out to freedpeople in rural McLennan County. The former slave Oliver Gathings also abandoned the plantation of his owner and moved to Waco. By this time, James J. Gathings had organized a criminal gang that prowled the countryside, shooting and whipping black men, women, and children. An official of the Bureau of Refugees, Freedmen, and Abandoned Lands—a federal agency authorized by Congress in March 1865 to ease the transition from slavery to freedom—alerted his superiors to the crimes perpetrated by the Gathings gang. Another local bureau agent cited the pervasive castrations, burnt limbs, gouged eyes, and other instances of mutilation and murder to suggest that black people might be better off re-enslaved.[20]

The many instances of white-on-black violence were part of a general reign of terror on the countryside. Vigilante "drum-head courts" pronounced guilt upon and then hanged accused offenders because, in the words of one bureau officer, the people "seem[ed] to have lost all confidence in jails and regular trials by jury." Armed with six-shooters, individuals declared themselves the law—sheriff, judge, jury, executioner—and labeled every victim a horse thief as a pretext for whippings and murders. Despite whites' intense demand for their labor, blacks tried to resist signing labor contracts, preferring to work for themselves; but lacking land and credit, they had little choice but to resume planting and picking cotton and hoeing the fields for white landowners, their former masters, only to be cheated out of their wages at the end of the year.[21]

Exhibiting what one Union officer called a "lofty spirit of disdain" toward all Yankees, the white people of Texas defied a federal mandate to reorganize the state government. By December 1865, all of the other former Confederate states with provisional governments had held constitutional conventions and elected new officials. Texas alone failed to elect representatives to Congress that month. The 11th Texas Legislature, which met in August 1866, refused to ratify either the Thirteenth or the Fourteenth Amendments, which together abolished slavery and granted citizenship rights to the former slaves. Although federal troops occupied parts of Central Texas, neither they nor Freedmen's Bureau agents could keep track of all the attacks on blacks by whites, all the "outrages." Whites acted as individuals as well as in groups, which included not only the Ku Klux Klan across the South but also homegrown terrorists such as the Gathings gang, the Families of the South, the Knights of the Rising Sun, and the Fishbackers (led by Bud and Bill Fisher). These whites had a term for raping black women and girls—"splitting" them.[22]

Charlotte no doubt feared for her safety and the safety of her children. Moreover, a new set of "Black Codes" posed a direct threat. An 1865 involuntary apprenticeship law authorized local officials to seize black children and put them to work for white men and women. The following year, the legislature passed "An Act to Define and Declare the

Rights of Persons Lately Known as Slaves, and Free Persons of Color." This law required that all family members toil in the fields, prevented black workers from recovering wages fraudulently withheld from them, and provided for harsh punishments for "vagrants"—that is, blacks not working under direct white supervision.[23]

In moving to Waco, Charlotte sought to protect her family from the white predators on the countryside, from the Black Codes—and possibly from Taliaferro himself. The town offered paid (if ill-paid) employment, a community of formerly enslaved people who were building their own churches and schools, and shelter from vengeful planters and marauding gangs. The family's removal to Waco was thus part of a larger, region-wide migration after the war, when even small towns beckoned to freedpeople eager to escape the constraints of slavery that still prevailed throughout much of the rural South.

POSTWAR WACO ATTRACTED WHITES AS WELL AS BLACKS. IN 1865, after four long years of a soldier's life, twenty-year-old Albert Parsons joined a steady stream of war veterans returning home. He immediately "traded a good mule, all the property I possessed, for forty acres of corn in the field standing ready to harvest, to a refugee who desired to flee the country." He hired a group of freedpeople, and "together we reaped the harvest." With the proceeds, he paid for a semester's worth of tuition at the local Waco University (which later merged with Baylor University and took its name). Enrolled in the preparatory division, he studied spelling, reading, arithmetic, and penmanship. After one semester he left school and took a job as a typesetter, and soon after that another job in the county clerk's office as a deputy clerk. Like other young Waco men-on-the-make, he became a member of the local Freemasons Lodge 92 at the level of "Apprentice Degree." At this point he was probably boarding with his sister and her husband. Albert's acquaintances would variously refer to him as "Colonel Parsons" or "Captain Parsons," honorific terms based on his military service in the war. By early 1867, possessed of the basics of a formal education and a firm, bold style of handwriting, he was well positioned to become a bookkeeper or the manager of a dry goods store and an upstanding member of the Waco business community.[24]

Yet Albert Parsons had far greater ambitions and, as it turned out, a taste for risk, and so he became swept up in postwar politicking. For the outnumbered Unionists in Waco—a few whites and all of the blacks—the immediate postwar years had brought fresh humiliations, as former Confederates continued to lord it over the town, county, and state. One Waco Unionist wrote to the Radical Republican congressman Thaddeus Stevens explaining the vulnerability of all who had opposed the Confederacy: "To the same old persecuting hell hounds of treason, we must now look for that protection to life and property we have been bereft of for six years. Will we get it? Will the kite protect the sparrow, will the lion protect the lamb?" Still, in the spring of 1867, the passage of Congressional, or Radical, Reconstruction mandated the federal military occupation of the defeated South, which meant that in Texas the path to political power would run through the newly organized state Republican Party. Later, Parsons would profess support for "the reconstruction measures securing the political rights of the colored people," citing as the impetus for this new commitment the "love and respect for the memory of dear old 'Aunt Easter,' then dead, and formerly a slave and house-servant of my brother's family, she having been my constant associate and practically raised me, with great kindness and a mother's love." Yet it is not clear that his Republicanism was a principled stance in favor of black rights or an opportunistic move, as it opened up possibilities for him to take patronage jobs and gain a wider influence within the state. He wrote, simply, "I became a Republican, and, of course, had to go into politics." In organizing the fledgling state Republican Party, he joined a few southern-born whites, the vast majority of freedmen, some northern newcomers to Texas, and the state's German population (who made up 5 percent of the total population).[25]

Parsons's regular encounters with German Americans in Texas Republican politics would turn out to be a significant development in his life. Though Texas Germans were not numerous overall, in certain parts of the state—the coastal plain to the east of Waco and the Hill Country to the west, in particular—they played an outsized role in wartime politics. Diverse in terms of their religious affiliation, economic pursuits, and culture, they were bound by a common language, and a goodly number of them had opposed slavery and secession. During the war many had suffered mightily at the hands of their Anglo neighbors, who resented and feared the foreign-born, liberal, free-thinking Unionists. In the Hill Country, most wartime deaths resulted from raids by pro-slavery men on farms owned by German immigrants, some of whom were hanged or shot; it was no wonder that the postwar Republican Party included such a large German American presence. Parsons regularly saw these men at local and state conventions and at rallies, and he probably picked up at least a rudimentary understanding of their native language. Eventually the German connection would determine where Albert and Lucy lived, the parameters of their social life, and even the ideas and political culture they embraced as radicals.[26]

IN 1868, AFTER HER ARRIVAL IN WACO, CHARLOTTE MARRIED Charlie Carter, a Virginia-born freedman who worked at J. B. Baker's brickyard on the east side of the Brazos. (On the marriage certificate her name is listed as "Charlott Taliferro.") Charlie had dropped his slave name, Crane, to take the name Carter, which Charlotte also assumed and in turn gave to her three children. To help support the family, Lucia found odd jobs as a cook and seamstress in the homes of several northern transplants, and her mother also labored as a domestic servant. Yet at an early age the younger woman sought to take control of her own life to create a future bound neither by her former master nor by her mother.[27]

When she was sixteen or seventeen, Lucia became attached to the man formerly called Oliver Gathings, who was thirty-five or thirty-six. He would always maintain that they had married, although there is no evidence that they did so—legally, at least. After the war, the Mississippi-born freedman endured the ridicule of Waco whites by aggressively adopting a new persona—he took the surname of his father, Benton, in place of that of his former owner. On June 19 of every year he put on his best clothes and celebrated Juneteenth to mark the emancipation of Texas slaves on June 19, 1865. Throughout his long life in

Waco, Benton would find a steady stream of handyman's work, making a decent enough living, given the limited opportunities for a black man. He encouraged Lucia to attend the first school for black children in Waco and paid her expensive monthly tuition fees—spending "all his cash balance upon her education," he told one reporter. Perhaps he was also able to indulge her with the fine clothes she loved.[28]

Charlie Carter and Oliver Benton parlayed a postwar Waco building boom into jobs that paid cash, following livelihoods that eluded many black men in the countryside. Although most freedmen in town were limited to menial work, a labor scarcity allowed some to find employment as draymen, waiters, cooks, barbers, blacksmiths, shoemakers, and butchers; these men could earn enough to establish households apart from whites and allow their wives to stay home and their children to attend school. The relative financial stability enjoyed by some black Wacoites spawned a class of leaders from the ranks of preachers, teachers, and skilled tradesman, several of whom became active in the Republican Party. The blacksmith Shep Mullins helped to oversee the purchase of a fourteen-acre tract of land for $75 for a schoolhouse, a key institution for any freed community. One sympathetic observer noted, "The colored are well united and very anxious for acquiring knowledge."[29]

The sight of a black school, no matter how ramshackle, inflamed the local white population. At the same time, literate black and white men and women competed against each other for jobs as teachers, struggling to earn a modest living in the cash-starved postbellum South. One recently arrived New Hampshire native, David F. Davis, started his own Waco school in April 1866, and Lucia Carter became one of his pupils soon thereafter. As schoolmaster, Davis faced challenges both financial and political. He jealously guarded his modest monthly commission from the Freedmen's Bureau. (Asked how long federal support would be needed to support such schools, one Waco bureau agent answered, "Until the present generation of [white] Southerners die.") Davis argued against the use of white women and freedmen as teachers, claiming that both groups were incompetent in the classroom. He faced the wrath of local black teachers, who considered him a meddlesome interloper, and of black and white missionaries, who disapproved of his nonsectarian

brand of schooling. Contentious school politics could mirror Republican politics, with presumed allies competing and feuding with each
other. And in fact, although David Davis and Albert Parsons soon took
their place among Waco's leading Republicans, they were rivals—for
local influence, for the favor of the governor, and perhaps even for the
affections of Davis's precocious pupil Lucia Carter.[30]

While freedpeople worked to secure the rights of full and inclusive
citizenship and to achieve control over their own productive energies
in the town and in the fields, some young black and white women and
men flaunted the social conventions that had been integral to the slave
system. By 1867 or so, Albert Parsons had renounced his Confederate
past—as a teenage soldier, his motivations had been less than principled in any case—and at least tentatively embraced the idea of a new
kind of equality between blacks and whites. He gradually came to advocate a role for black men in the Republican Party, but he was also
alive to the erotic dimensions of the new order.

Later, Parsons acknowledged that sex between blacks and whites
was "sort of a custom in those days [in Waco, during Reconstruction],"
that "such affairs were very common in Texas, and that no one paid any
attention to them in those days." He added, "I was wild when I was
young, and had many escapades with girls." In the town's brothels, for a
price, white men could have sex with black women. Yet Parsons's words
suggest a new, more profound openness in black and white male-female
relations, especially between black women and white men, and he was
not the only white man to disregard long-held customs. Schoolmaster Davis—by all accounts a good-looking man, with "black hair, full
beard, [and] dark complexion"—was in the habit of escorting a young
freedwoman around town, and seemed unfazed by the rumor that he
had fathered a child by another black woman. One Waco resident later
recalled that Lucia herself had "young bloods" running after her day
and night who were attracted by "her hair and her shape." Depending
on their politics, Wacoites feared or welcomed what all perceived to be
the dawning of a new day in Texas, one that broke taboos by making
public what were heretofore private relationships.[31]

The federal government seemed to be the institutional harbinger of
this new day. In March 1867, Congress passed the First Reconstruction

Act, which enfranchised black men in the former Confederate states and moved swiftly to nullify state Black Codes and other discriminatory statutes. The subsequent reorganization of the South into five military districts prompted a fresh wave of violence in Texas. Furious at the emergent Republican Party, whites in McLennan County reacted violently to the appointment and election of former Unionists to political office. Although Central Texas counties were home to only 4 percent of the state's population, between 1865 and 1868 the region accounted for 12 percent of all blacks killed by whites in the state, with most of the murders taking place in 1867 and 1868. One bureau agent summed up the gruesome reality: "The life of a [Union, or northern] white man is worth but little, the life of a Freedman is worth nothing."[32]

On July 10, 1867, the first day of voter registration under Radical Reconstruction, Albert Parsons stood fifth in line with twenty other men, black and white, at the Waco registrar's office. Other men toward the front of the line included well-to-do white men who had been born in Kentucky and Tennessee, indicating they had retained some affinity for border-state Unionism throughout the war. During that initial registration period, the local Freedmen's Bureau agent expressed alarm at the number of armed freedpeople who came marching into town from the surrounding countryside to register, bearing a red flag and frightening the white townspeople. He chalked up their performance not to a contemporary form of politicking (which it was), but to their "love of display." By the time registration had ended in late August, 1,003 blacks and 877 whites had signed up to vote. Now constituting a majority of McLennan County voters, blacks proceeded to elect the thirty-eight-year-old blacksmith Shep Mullins as a delegate to the Texas Constitutional Convention of 1868–1869, and they would send freedmen to the state legislature in 1869. These startling developments, combined with the sight of black men carrying pistols and shouldering rifles, caused Wacoites of all political persuasions to anticipate all-out war if anyone discharged his gun, even accidentally, and yet the imperatives of self-defense would seem to require that black field hands no less than newly elected officials should remain armed and make a "display" of it.[33]

In this feverish environment, black parents showed considerable courage in sending their children to the school opened by David Davis in the spring of 1866, the first of its kind. Forty-nine pupils—twenty-nine girls and twenty boys—commenced their studies in a primitive, windowless structure with a dirt floor and no benches or blackboard. Before long, Davis was boasting to his superiors that "what I have cannot be surpassed, I think, in point of scholarship by any colored school in the South." Still, in December of that year, only twenty-five pupils were attending regularly, at least partly because of the great demand for hands in the cotton fields. It is possible, too, that the Waco Manufacturing Company, a local cotton and woolen mill, had hired large numbers of children among its one hundred employees. Another impediment to attendance was the $1.50 a month that Davis charged, much more than most manual workers and cotton pickers could afford. Lucia Carter was one of a handful of the privileged few, for Oliver Benton paid for her books and tuition and so she was able to attend consistently. (She was probably among the four or five girls over the age of sixteen who were recorded on Davis's monthly attendance sheet for much of 1867 and 1868.) According to a reporter who interviewed Benton, "he was proud of his handsome wife, and aspired to lift her to as high a place as he could."[34]

Davis the teacher had arrived in Waco at the behest of a friend in the Freedmen's Bureau, and he found himself decidedly out of place among white Southerners. A graduate of Phillips Exeter Academy and Dartmouth College, he had worked for the US Army's quartermaster department from 1863 to 1865, coming to Waco at the end of the war. He wrote poetry and followed a brand of spiritualism that set him apart from his southern-born, business-oriented Baptist and Methodist neighbors—he urged his Republican allies to "hug fast to the *vital force*," which would eventually "bury the old ideas." Like Parsons the typesetter, he harbored greater aspirations than his lowly title—in this case schoolteacher—would imply.[35]

Sometime between December 1867 and November 1868, Lucia Carter became pregnant. (Her baby was born between August 1868 and July 1869.) By this time, several older men had come into her life. Her teacher, Davis, apparently developed a close relationship with at least one unnamed freedwoman. In September 1868, when bureau agent Charles Haughn learned that Davis was a candidate for registrar of voters, an appointed office, he wrote to his superiors reporting that "Mr. Davis is a man of good intellect and education, but is not a man of good morals. Mr. Davis has been seen walking in the streets of Waco frequently in the company of a f. w. [freedwoman] and a f.w. here has a child and the evidences are so very strong against Davis that I have not the slightest doubt that the child is his." Haughn said this scandalous state of affairs was public knowledge, and that he had given Davis a chance "to clear his name, but to no purposes." Whether or not Davis was smitten with his pupil Lucia Carter is unknown, but it is certainly possible.[36]

Oliver Benton considered Lucia his wife, and he claimed that her baby was his; if she was not infatuated or in love with Benton, then she was at least beholden to him for her schooling. She was still working on and off as a cook in the homes of prominent white families, furthering her informal education in well-equipped kitchens and well-appointed parlors. One employer was Oscar H. Leland, a native of Vermont, who served as the chief officer for the Internal Revenue Service in Waco.[37]

Although the precise moment when Albert and Lucia first laid eyes on each other is unknown, the small circle of Republicans in Waco provided ample opportunities for them to meet. Trustees of the school she attended were also prominent Republicans, and at least some of them lived near her and her mother in the River Street section of town. Oscar Leland would serve as Albert Parsons's boss once Parsons assumed the role of assistant assessor. According to Wacoites interviewed years later, the youthful Lucia Carter had no trouble attracting attention from men, black and white, who saw her as smart and beautiful. As a teenager, then, she learned the power of her own special allure.

DAVID DAVIS AND ALBERT PARSONS COMPETED FOR INFLUENCE within the emerging Republican Party. Davis had set about organizing blacks for the Republican Party as early as May 1867, appearing at political rallies in Waco. Parsons cast his net considerably wider. He tried his hand at publishing a Republican newspaper, *Spectator*, but, as he admitted himself, it was "short-lived, in a community of overwhelming opposition." He was much more successful as an orator than as an editor. Of his years stumping for the party across the state, he wrote, with some understatement, "My political career was full of excitement and danger." He added, with what would eventually be revealed as characteristic bombast, "The lately enfranchised slaves over a large section of country came to know and idolize me as their friend and defender, while on the other hand I was regarded as a political heretic and traitor by many of my former associates." In his autobiography Parsons vaingloriously referred to the loyalty shown him by "a multitude of ignorant but devoted blacks." He forever remained self-consciously proud of his own formidable speaking skills; despite his small stature (he estimated his weight at 135 pounds at the time), he had the physical endurance and rhetorical capacity to hold a massive crowd in his thrall for hours at a time. Standing on any kind of platform he could find, he would lecture, cajole, and berate his listeners, no matter how hot and humid the day. In the words of one who knew him in his Republican days, he was "an incessant talker."[38]

For the most part, Parsons's white neighbors held their tongues while he became a fixture in the town and in the statewide Republican Party. They hesitated to make too much trouble: federal troops were headquartered in their midst, and by this time the local police force included some black officers, who wore their blue uniforms proudly and carried weapons. At one point, John T. Flint, a banker and railroad entrepreneur, a big man, became fed up with Parsons, accosting him with a five-pound piece of iron cogwheel and causing him to fall down a flight of stairs, bloodying his face. Looking back decades later, white Wacoites described Parsons this way: "A violent agitator, affiliating with the worst class of Negroes, . . . ever ready to stir them up to strife." The *Galveston Daily News*, Parsons's first employer, saw fit to print the charge that "he was always on hand at the gatherings of Negroes, eager for fame and notoriety among them, seeking every opportunity to be seen and heard, parading before them the great wrongs they had suffered and the rights denied them by their political opponents, and inciting them to regard all white people as enemies except such as he would affiliate with them as he was doing." Such an indictment spoke to Parsons's familiarity with black leaders and voters.[39]

In June 1868, Texas Constitutional Convention delegates convened in Austin to rewrite the state's constitution according to federal

Reconstruction mandates. Among those in attendance was Shep Mullins, who by this time had served in a variety of appointed positions, including that of county commissioner. The new state constitution, ratified in 1869, provided for the increased power of the state government, support for black education, and the permanent franchise for black men. These developments lifted Albert Parsons's spirits, and in early 1869 he embarked on a new venture as a traveling correspondent for a newspaper started by his brother, who had settled in Houston—the *Houston Weekly/Daily Telegraph*. The new job allowed Parsons to combine the role of journalist with that of Radical Republican activist.

After the war, William Parsons had made a brief sojourn to British Honduras, where he planned to establish a colony for Southerners hoping to hold onto their slaves. When he returned to Texas he tested the political waters by attending an 1868 conservative state convention. Its avowed purpose was to prevent "the Africanization of the state." Before too long, though, William apparently recognized the potential financial gains to be had by working within a party that promoted the use of taxpayer dollars to subsidize business interests of various kinds. (A Democratic detractor complained that the general had, "all at once, in a twinkling of an eye, flopped over" to the Republicans.) He then initiated contact with state Republican leaders and offered to reach out to former Confederates—"many old army friends"—and, with himself as an example, make the case for a graceful transition from secessionist Democrat to Reconstruction Republican. Egalitarian-minded blacks and whites alike were suspicious of William—especially those who had known him back in the day, when he had defined "Negro subordination" as "the only natural relation of the race . . . the only sphere in which their happiness and destiny can be subserved." Presumably William would promote the notion that, in the words of another white Republican, "the Republican Party is not a black man's party any more than a white." William aimed to use his newspaper as an organ of the conservative (i.e., pro-business, anti–black rights) wing of the Texas Republican Party.[40]

As a roving reporter, Albert Parsons was now in his element, traversing the state on horseback, sending the *Telegraph* periodic dispatches—which he called "Letters from Waco"—and selling subscriptions to the paper. He also worked as an agent for the St. Louis

Life Insurance Company. Apparently during these trips he was combining his role as reporter (and life insurance agent) with that of party organizer—a tricky combination, given his interest in currying favor among the freedmen, on the one hand, and retaining the support of his brother-boss, who was insensitive to the plight of blacks in general, on the other. On his Central Texas speaking tours, he traveled with associates whom he described as "one or two intelligent colored men"— Mullins was probably one of them. Their presence no doubt enhanced his credibility when he spoke to large crowds of freedpeople. Not surprisingly on these trips Parsons found himself "completely ostracized from my former [white] associates": "At noontime or nightfall our fare was only such as could be had in the rude and poverty-stricken huts of the colored people. I ate at their table with them, and slept in the same room as the huts rarely had but one room. This was a degree of self-degradation in the eyes of the whites, which rendered me odious."[41]

Two decades later, Parsons would reminisce about those public meetings in a way that suggested his own high regard for himself, as well as his role as the proverbial outside agitator: "And often have I, amid the rows of slave huts, at night, stood upon a bale of cotton as a platform, and by the faint light of a tallow dip harangued the hundreds assembled around me. What a scene! The stars shone brightly above; a somber, heavy darkness covered the earth's surface—peculiar to Southern swamp regions; the flickering light of the tallow dip; the mass of upturned, eager faces, coal black, with shining eyes embedded in sparkling white, with uncovered heads (but few possessed hats)." Such was his listeners' first school, and he their first teacher of "lessons of political economy." On other days Parsons would speak at the local courthouse, such as the one in Waco, and black men, women, and children would come in from the countryside, riding mules or horses or on foot. Of these meetings, attended by as many as a thousand people at a time, he wrote, "The new-born manhood was aroused and they were stirred with new sensations of independence and self-respect." In his view, he had given hope to the downtrodden, a work he pursued "with the ardor and disinterestedness of an apostle." On the streets of Waco and on the plains and in the cotton fields of Central Texas, Parsons honed his fearless style and felt the exhilaration that flowed from taunting arrogant, well-armed enemies.[42]

On March 1, 1869, Parsons sent to the Houston paper a "Letter from Waco" in which he claimed that the "most intelligent and influential citizens" held Republican sympathies—a dubious proposition, but one calculated to boost the spirits of his beleaguered comrades-in-arms. He reported that Central Texas was in a flourishing condition, with ranchers and farmers prospering. He approvingly recounted a recent incident in Waco in which a black man was sentenced to be hanged for murder, explaining, "Though our sympathies are enlisted in behalf of these erring children of humanity, yet it is a source of gratification and pride also to note these evidences of determination by our people to enforce the law upon the guilty, that innocence may be protected." Reflecting his brother's views, if not his own, he advocated increased state spending on bridges and railroads. At the same time he called upon Democrats and moderate Republicans to "unite to close out" of power "a Radical white man or an unlettered negro." Parsons had either imbibed his brother's brand of Republicanism or was cynically appealing to whites who could not abide the thought of joining a party that included freedmen. Certainly in his perambulations around the state he had spoken to many as a "Radical white man" himself.[43]

In an unusual departure for this budding politician, who at the time was just twenty-three years of age, at the end of the piece he abruptly shifted his focus from politics to herald a different kind of progress he saw in Waco; "solid and substantial buildings" were not the only noteworthy improvements there. He pointed to the domestic pleasures that the town afforded; it was a place now displaying "a refined and cultivated taste." He described "front yards to dwellings, laid off in plots and decorated with shrubbery and flowers, porticoes trellised and ready for the cumbering honeysuckles and morning glory, tastefully painted gate and paling fence and sidewalk, made cool and inviting from the summer heat by the shade from bois de arc and sycamore." These refinements indicated that Wacoites were "'making home attractive,' and by its comfort, beauty and adornment, [they] realise that it is to them the dearest spot on earth."[44]

Such uncharacteristic musings on the virtues of domestic bliss suggest that by this time Parsons had met Lucia Carter. In his autobiography (published in 1886), he claimed that he had indeed met her in 1869—but, he wrote, he had done so while serving as "travelling correspondent and agent" in northwestern Texas for the *Telegraph*. Later, he and Lucia, now called Lucy, would together conspire to offer up the fiction that she had been a "charming young Spanish-Indian maiden" living with her uncle on a ranch near Buffalo Creek in Johnson County. But by locating their meeting in 1869, Albert thereby confirmed, if only indirectly, that they had met around the time he wrote this particular "Letter from Waco." At this point, she was either pregnant or the mother of an infant. Meanwhile, he had changed his residence, boarding in another household, perhaps the better to manage his private life away from the prying eyes of his older sister Mary.[45]

In the fall, as December elections loomed, Parsons's public speeches took on added urgency. He rejoiced at the outcome of those elections: with black men enfranchised and many former Confederates either barred from voting or refusing to vote, Republicans captured virtually all the local and statewide offices. (Texas would be readmitted to the Union the following year.) The Radical Edmund J. Davis was elected governor. Mullins won a seat in the 12th legislative session. David Davis rode to office on this Republican sweep, becoming clerk of Waco's district court. Parsons wasted little time excoriating Davis, charging that the teacher appointed deputies with only a tenuous attachment to the Republican Party. For his part, Davis claimed he wanted "no rebel officers, but a German, a Yankee, a true Southerner, & a colored man"— a none-too-subtle allusion to the rising prominence of not only Albert Parsons but also his brother William, two "rebel officers" now active in state politics.[46]

William Parsons had been elected to the 12th legislative session as a senator from Harris and Montgomery Counties, parlaying his influence as a Houston newspaper editor into political office. That session also included fourteen black senators and representatives (Mullins from McLennan County among them). The election results revealed a deeply divided party, with one faction opposing black civil rights but favoring state-sponsored business interests, and the other agitating for black rights, a statewide public school system, and a crackdown on antiblack violence. Contemplating his potential allies among the new lawmakers, Governor Davis looked favorably on William Parsons, a reliable "railroad man," if one with malleable politics.[47]

It seems remarkable that Albert Parsons could pursue a career in Texas politics at the same time that he was ardently pursuing a young freedwoman in Waco. Certainly the relationship presented profound challenges for both of them; she was already entangled with Oliver Benton, and the birth of a baby further complicated matters. Yet as subsequent events would prove, Lucia and Albert together reveled in their own recklessness.

Chapter 2

Republican Heyday

IN THE EARLY 1870S, CARTER & CO. WAS DOING A FINE BUSINESS, catering to the modest householders and prosperous money-makers of Central Texas. The store, well situated on the main plaza of Waco, was owned by Edward H. Carter and his partner Champe C. McCulloch, and they advertised "cheaper Goods than anybody"—boots, locks, hinges, cutlery, glassware, gunpowder, plows, spades, hoes, chains. On most any day but the Sabbath, Carter & Co. could expect a noisy crowd picking over wares and haggling over prices, cowboys mingling with housewives and plantation managers. Meanwhile, in a storeroom above the din, an enduring love affair was beginning.[1]

The identity of the father of Lucia Carter's baby is a mystery; he might have been David Davis or Oliver Benton or Albert Parsons. The fact that she named the little boy Champ suggests at least the possibility that she wanted to acknowledge the man who allowed her to rendezvous with Parsons in Carter's storeroom—Champe McCulloch, Parsons's next-door neighbor and fellow Freemason. In any case, the spurned Oliver Benton (who later said he had contemplated killing Parsons) on at least one occasion burst in on Lucia and Albert at their trysting place. Benton said he "scourged" Lucia all the way back to his cabin, implying he had cracked a bullwhip on her, but perhaps those claims revealed merely the bravado of a humiliated man.[2]

In the summer of 1870, Lucia's mother, Charlotte Carter, was living in Waco's River Street black neighborhood. Charlotte, now thirty-six, reported to a census taker that her household included one daughter, Lucia (nineteen years old), and two sons, Tanner (fourteen) and Webster (eight). Another apartment in the modest frame building housed Jane Tallavan and her children and Lucia with one-year-old Champ. The census recorded Lucia as a literate mulatto. In Jane and Lucia's unit were also living a freedwoman named Lizzie Murphy, a twenty-two-year-old native of Alabama; Lizzie's two sons, ages five and seven months; and a freedman, James Johnson, a twenty-five-year-old from Mississippi.[3]

Perhaps the suffocating heat of a July midday had clouded the census-taker's judgment; or perhaps, as a nonnative English speaker (he was a German immigrant), he misunderstood Charlotte's description of the family's living arrangements. Although overlapping census districts at times resulted in "duplicates"—a person counted more than once—it was unusual for a census-taker to list the same person twice as a member of two separate households in the same building. That Charlotte reported Lucia as living with her, but the daughter was actually living in a different apartment, with her infant son as well as a man and a woman and two other children, suggests several possibilities—an estrangement between mother and daughter; a desire on the part of the younger woman to establish a household apart from her mother; or a liaison with James Johnson, a lover.

If Champ's father is unknown, so, too, are the circumstances of his birth. Lucia had become pregnant when she was about the same age at which her mother, Jane Tallavan, and Lizzie Murphy had all had their first babies. During Lucia's labor, was she comforted by the presence of the three women, and were others present? Did she have an easy time of it, or hours filled with pain? Did someone pay for the services of a midwife? Or did she bear the child alone, away from her mother and from the man who considered her his wife, but was by now perhaps consumed with suspicion and jealousy? In the summer of 1870, Lucia was living apart from Benton, and she had given the baby the last name

Carter, which had been her own last name since her mother had married Charlie Carter. Charlotte and Charlie were also presumably living apart from each other, as he was not listed as a part of her household, though he was still working at the brickyard east of the Brazos River. (He would remarry in 1888.)

In 1870, Albert Parsons was boarding in the northwest part of town, in a well-to-do area on high ground away from the river, with the family of a Presbyterian minister, the Reverend David C. Kinnard. For all his speechifying, Parsons must have struck Kinnard as a respectable young man; the pastor of the newly formed Cumberland Church would have demanded no less of a boarder (or perhaps he was doing Parsons's well-to-do sister Mary a favor). Next to the Kinnard residence was the impressive dwelling of the Missouri-born merchant Champe C. Mc-Culloch, living with his wife, Emma, and their nine-month-old son, also named Champe. By this time, Parsons was working as an assistant collector for the Internal Revenue Service, a patronage job that rewarded his service to the Republican Party. He would seem to be tempting fate, now that he was not only associated with the despised party of Lincoln, but also collecting taxes in a town that had shown overwhelming support for the Confederacy. Yet Waco did possess a small but vocal knot of northern supporters and sympathizers—former Confederates, such as Parsons, who had deserted the Democrats; Freedmen's Bureau agents and Davis, the Yankee schoolmaster; a couple of hundred black voters as well as bold activists such as Shep Mullins; a few foreign-born and northern migrants who had held their counsel during the war; and, in a soon-to-be-dismantled US Army garrison, forty-nine white soldiers hailing from Western Europe and the southern and northern states who had all been deployed to Waco to keep a fragile peace. Although these groups, according to a Union officer, were initially targets of the "most intense hatred," by 1870 some of them had made accommodations with former Confederates—Davis, for example, had ingratiated himself with local Democrats, and the federal troops were hosting grand balls for their white neighbors at the Masonic Hall on the plaza.[4]

The relationship between Albert Parsons and Lucia Carter soon became an open secret among white and black Wacoites, though little is known about the precise nature of that relationship. For Parsons, the year 1870 had begun auspiciously. Black voters, enfranchised since 1867, were working with German immigrants and other Republicans to challenge the white-supremacist power of the Democrats. After years of delay, the state legislature had finally ratified the Thirteenth, Fourteenth, and Fifteenth Amendments to the Constitution, abolishing slavery, granting the former slaves citizenship rights, and enfranchising black men, respectively. A new state district judge in town, Republican John W. Oliver, was promising a no-holds-barred assault on bands of white criminals and vigilantes. The inauguration of the Radical Republican governor Edmund J. Davis in April had breathed new life into the party and given Parsons a new mission as a political organizer. In Waco, black men were getting jobs as police officers, sitting on petit and grand juries, and receiving appointments as county commissioners. Widely seen as a rising star in the Republican Party, Parsons was skillful at straddling its conservative and radical wings. Yet demographic patterns signaled dangers ahead: the county's explosive population growth meant that soon, in sheer numbers at least, white Southerners would easily overwhelm the small, badly divided Republican Party.[5]

Both William and Albert Parsons gained prominence in the 12th legislative session, a session that saw Republicans using every means at their disposal to bolster the tenuous power they possessed. Soon after he took office, Governor Davis created several new law-enforcement agencies—the Frontier Forces, the State Guard, the Reserve Militia, the State Police, and the Minute Men. Democrats saw all these armed groups as a threatening escalation in state power. In January 1870, Davis appointed Judge Oliver to the 33rd Judicial District in Central Texas, which included Limestone, Falls, and McLennan Counties. Davis exhorted his followers to bring in more white voters. Meanwhile, Albert Parsons began to canvass on behalf of the Union League and the Radical Republican Association, groups of like-minded blacks and those few whites who believed the party's priorities should focus on equal rights for all.[6]

In the late summer and early fall of 1870, Parsons conducted a concerted campaign to reach out and flatter prominent party leaders in an effort to counter the infighting that was pitting Waco Republicans against each other. He reported that too many men were embracing

Democratic prejudices while calling themselves Republicans. In August, he warned the governor that "enemies" skulking about "under the cloak of Republicanism" were seeking to undermine "the united desires of all *genuine* Republicans." In Waco, these false friends were trying to oust the current mayor, B. F. Harris, for malfeasance in office. Parsons also began a correspondence with James P. Newcomb, editor of the Republican *San Antonio Express* and a powerful arbiter in Texas politics. Parsons feared that his "being an Ex Rebel Republican" had compromised his own ability to rectify what he called the *"evils"* that plagued Waco; he cited the local postmaster, who, though "he vociferously asserts his Republicanism," together with other political appointees constituted "an actual encumbrance and dead weight to us." Parsons saved his choicest words for David Davis, the schoolmaster turned district clerk. According to Parsons, to his "chagrin and mortification" Davis was shamelessly larding his office with Democrats. Parsons added, "There is a Republican harvest here but faithful laborers are few."[7]

Parsons set about organizing petitions to Republican officials, declaring in one that "we suffered and born [sic] much from our enemies and unless we get relieve [sic] immediately much more injury will be done." The signatories represented a cross-section of the Waco Republican Party—a merchant born in Poland; a number of freedmen, including Shep Mullins; and southern-born white men, including a saloonkeeper from South Carolina, a stable owner from North Carolina, and Mayor Harris, from Georgia. Parsons's aggressive efforts to curry favor with blacks won him his own Waco "faction," prompting his nemesis John T. Flint to alert the governor that "the Parsons faction here is irresponsible, and if they go into power will offend the sense of justice of all decent men whether Republican or not." In the coming months, Parsons would go out of his way to ingratiate himself with Newcomb, reporting at one point that he had defended the editor against the unkind words of a local Republican official who had called the editor "too vain, conceited, and selfish."[8]

Throughout this period, Parsons seemed to relish battles against both diehard rebel Democrats and the men whom he considered disloyal to his own brand of Republican Party politics. In fact, though, developments in 1871 gave him hope that he would have a chance not only to ascend the party ranks but also to make a substantial living in the course of doing so. He went back to soliciting subscriptions—now for Houston's *Union/Tri-Weekly Union*. In January, he was appointed to the administrative position of first assistant secretary of the Senate for the regular session, which ran from January 10 to May 31. This job he had secured with the help of his brother—now Senator Parsons—as well as through his own successful efforts to gain the favor of party higher-ups. As first assistant secretary he updated the official daily journal of the Senate, recording events, proceedings, and votes. Each morning he distributed two newspapers to lawmakers—one in English, the *Austin Daily State Journal*, and the other in German, the *Austin Vorwarts* (Forward). A quick study, he probably used the *Vorwarts* to practice his German, since an understanding of the language was essential to communicating with a vital Republican constituency.[9]

The 12th legislative session represented the high-water mark of Reconstruction-era Texas Republicanism. Lawmakers funded the state's first public school system, which had been created on paper the previous session but deprived of an appropriation, and chartered black mutual aid societies and social groups. Governor Davis deplored the prevalence of firearms in the state and urged state lawmakers to impose restrictions on gun ownership, a plea that came to fruition in 1871 with a ban on the carrying of pistols outside the home (travelers and those whites living in areas vulnerable to Indian raids were exempt). Yet riven by intraparty factionalism as well as party divisions, most legislators had no appetite for controversy. A proposal to send funds to the people of Chicago in the wake of the catastrophic fire in that city in October 1871 went down to defeat with the argument that Texas citizens should not be taxed "for the purpose of making gifts to individuals."[10]

Nevertheless, Republicans wasted little time enacting measures favorable to business interests. Legislators bolstered commercial development and regional trade by chartering railroads, bridges, toll roads, ferries, canals, dams, waterworks, and fire companies as well as private manufacturing interests. They legislated in favor of stock raisers and bankers; the recording of births and marriages; and foreign immigration into the state (to address a chronic agricultural labor shortage). William Parsons represented the interests of the "Houston Mechanical

Verein" (Union) to shore up his bona fides with a German group back home. He served as chair of Internal Improvements, the political epicenter of the session.[11]

For his support for measures such as "an Act to encourage the speedy construction of a railway through the State of Texas to the Pacific Ocean," William would solidify his reputation as a railroad man. Not all lawmakers were on board: some saw state subsidies to private and public interests, whether railroads or schools, as a form of "black mail" extracted from the people. In the lower house, freedmen expressed their own priorities by pressing for the redistribution of land to the former slaves and measures to protect black suffrage.[12]

As legislative clerk, Albert Parsons made the enviable sum of seven or eight dollars a day (urban workingmen were lucky to earn one dollar a day, while agricultural workers were paid largely in promises). And there is evidence that either he was the beneficiary of his older brother's largesse or that on his own he eagerly sought perquisites from the state legislature to partake of the boom in internal improvements. With partners, he received charters to create a Waco Gas Light Company that would provide gas to streetlights and buildings in the town; to erect toll bridges in Navarro County; and to create a corporation, the Texas Manufacturing Company. Though nothing ever came of these charters, they represented the Republicans'—and presumably Parsons's—conviction that the state could and should provide citizens with opportunities to make money in the private sector.[13]

In the summer of 1871, when his Senate job ended, Parsons went to work for the new Office of Public Instruction (OPI), which had been created to establish a system of free but segregated schools throughout the state. Living in the elegant Raymond House hotel in Austin, he was earning the munificent sum of $125 a month. For a three-month stint at the OPI he made a total of $375, an amount that would one day help finance his move out of Texas. At the end of August he got caught up in an alleged corruption scandal at the OPI; his remarkably generous salary (among other suspicious goings-on) had become grist for the mill of Democrats who considered public education largely a waste of the taxpayers' money. In September, in the run-up to elections that fall, Parsons once again took to the road, addressing large crowds and prompting his detractors to describe him as one of "a set of men notoriously void of character and sent forth to disgust the Republican masses by their idiotic harangues."[14]

In September, Governor Davis recognized Parsons for his party loyalty and raw courage by appointing him a lieutenant colonel in the reviled state militia and sending him to impose order in Bell, Coryell, and Lampasas Counties, where white attacks on blacks were rampant. Forty miles south of Waco in Belton, a freedman, the Methodist minister Romeo Hill, who was also a schoolteacher, observed that for blacks, "the times in Belton is very bad." Hill begged the local bureau agent to reassign him to a school in another district "because these poor white people is so mean we cannot get [a]long here." Hill was no coward—he had registered to vote in 1867—but he feared he would be murdered in his bed. "I don't want to die before my time come," he wrote. Hill, a thirty-eight-year-old native of North Carolina, expressed alarm not only at hostile whites, but also at the freedpeople, who, he wrote, armed with "their gun and knife and pistole," believed that freedom gave them the license to make trouble and do as they pleased. "I cannot teach school hear [sic] in Belton and do it in piece [sic] and I want [to] go [a]way from here," he wrote, adding, "Dear Sir there is no Law here to protect the school."[15]

Governor Davis had sent Albert Parsons to confront the anarchy in Belton—to put in place a new Republican-friendly mayor and city council and install Republican supporters in the local police force. The outcome of Parsons's expedition is unknown, but he later claimed that he was "not an 'ornamental' Colonel," for he had accepted "a most warlike and dangerous undertaking"; in the process, he said, "I became somewhat famous as a champion of political liberty. Beloved by the blacks, I was hated and scorned by the whites"—and this scorn, coupled with the threat of lynching, he embraced.[16]

Meanwhile, Democrats continued to make steady gains at the polls throughout the state. The large numbers of southern white in-migrants added new members to the Democratic Party daily, and furthermore, victory in any particular election usually depended more on who controlled the ballot box than on who won the most votes. The Republicans remained so hopelessly divided that even when their supporters were in a majority they lost elections to the unified Democrats, who, by the end of 1872, had reclaimed the state legislature. Forced now to rely on federal rather than state-level patronage, Albert Parsons was working once again as assistant assessor for the IRS in Austin.[17]

FROM AUSTIN, PARSONS COULD GET TO WACO EITHER BY MAKING the one-hundred-mile trip on horseback in three days or by taking an all-day train, but he knew he risked his life if he returned to the town for any length of time. Political tensions were running high in Waco, owing at least in part to the assertive actions of Judge Oliver. Since his appointment in January 1870, Oliver had used all the powers invested in him—calling out the militia, using black police as ballot-box watchers, declaring martial law, rounding up offenders—in an effort to stem the aggression of whites throughout the 33rd Judicial District. In May 1872, the intrepid—or incredibly foolish—judge had held the entire McLennan County Commissioners' Court in contempt on an indictment for embezzlement and jailed all its members. The local bar association was moved to try to have him declared insane. On May 7, the *Waco Advance* published a broadside titled "Stop the Madman!" Oliver resigned in January 1873 before a grand jury could indict him for corruption.[18]

Albert Parsons understood that the judge's departure signaled not only a marked decline in influence among Republicans in Central Texas but also less-than-favorable prospects for his own political future and his personal life. Nevertheless, the young man was in love, and he took a bold step: he married Lucia Carter on September 28, 1872. He was twenty-seven, she twenty-one. The marriage license was issued in McLennan County, though it is possible that the wedding took place in Cherokee County, to the east of McLennan. (William Parsons would later say that the couple married in Austin, but no evidence exists for that claim.) Albert gave the officiant his correct name, but it was the first and certainly not the last time that his bride would give a public official a different name—she is listed as Ella Hall (in the coming years she would at times give "Ella," at other times "Eldine," as her middle name, and use "Hall" as her maiden name). The couple took advantage of propitious legal developments; they married shortly after a state Supreme Court decision, *Honey v. Clark*, affirmed the Republican interpretation that a section of the new constitution meant that black and white people could marry, briefly opening the way for legal interracial nuptials. Democrats had argued that the section granted former slaves only the right to marry each other. The judge who married the two—no doubt a Republican—neglected to list his own name, though it is possible that it was Waco mayor B. F. Harris, who was a friend of Albert's and was officiating around this time. Weeks later, Democrats would outlaw such weddings.[19]

In fact, by early 1873, the Democrats, now in control of the state legislature, aimed to roll back a whole host of Republican policies and quash the unholy Republican alliance among the freedmen, German Americans, and southern-born white traitors to the neo-Confederate cause. With no more than 5,000 active members, the state Republican Party itself was wracked by internal divisions as well as by voter resentment over the police forces, tax increases, and the growing state debt. Richard Coke, a Waco native and unrepentant rebel, won the governorship in 1873 by a 2-to-1 margin in an election rife with fraud on both sides. One of his priorities was to do away with the various layers of law enforcement created by his predecessor. A Dallas paper bade farewell to the State Police, calling the force "as infernal an engine of oppression as ever crushed any people beneath God's sunlight." The Freedmen's Bureau had ceased to exist, and the last federal troops were withdrawn from the state in 1870. Closer to home, Parsons had lost critical allies— Shep Mullins had died in 1871, and Judge Oliver had retired two years later. Albert's brother William had moved to New York City in 1871 to represent the new Texas Bureau of Immigration (an agency established by the Republican legislature) and serve as a commissioner for the upcoming US centennial celebration.[20]

Whatever hope Albert Parsons might have had for a new day in Waco must have been fleeting. Though they were legally married, he and Lucia could not count on living together openly and in peace. All of Waco knew his wife to be a former slave, and his prospects for lucrative state and federal patronage jobs were rapidly slipping away in the wake of the Democratic onslaught of 1872 and 1873. He had served as a secretary of the state legislature, promoted public-private partnerships to further economic development, charged into the town of Belton with his band of lawmen, and canvassed the state for Republican voters—all thrilling ventures that befitted his temperament and ambition. Yet a future in Waco or anywhere else in Texas promised only peril.

Meanwhile, Lucia faced constraints of her own. In Waco she would have to remain in the shadows and sew and cook for whites. She had glimpsed a life beyond menial labor in her interactions with her school-teacher, her employers, and Albert himself. And her light skin opened possibilities elsewhere that her dark-skinned mother could have never imagined. Although Oliver Benton had the means to indulge her, he could not offer her an entrée into a wider world that was overwhelmingly white. More to the point, perhaps, the attraction between Albert and Lucia was palpable. She was probably not the first, and she definitely would not be the last, woman to be captivated by Albert's public speaking—his eloquence, exuberance, and composure in the face of hecklers and even armed men. For his part, Albert saw his wife as smart and headstrong, a contrast to the illiterate, desperately poor black field-hands he had met stumping across the countryside. So, he might have asked, if Lucia was not downtrodden, was she truly "black"? Facing the choice of a life apart, a life together as perpetual outsiders in Central Texas, or a life together among people who did not know them, they chose the last course—to put hundreds of miles between themselves and the town of Waco.

IN 1873, ALBERT PARSONS ACCEPTED A JOB AS AN EDITOR AND reporter for a new publication in Austin, the *Texas Farmer and Stock Raiser*. On September 10, 1873, he met with other newspapermen in the northern part of the state, in Sherman, and together they formed the seventy-member State Editorial Association. Simultaneously, the group received an invitation from the Missouri, Kansas, and Texas Railroad to accept an all-expenses-paid excursion to visit Chicago, St. Louis, Cincinnati, Louisville, Memphis, Indianapolis, and other cities along the railroad's routes. By entertaining the Texas editors, the railroad men aimed to promote commercial trade throughout the greater Midwest. It would be Parsons's first trip outside the South, and his first visit to the city where he would become infamous.[21]

Around September 12, the group set out, a "precious cargo of Texas brains and influence," according to the *Dallas Weekly Herald*. After stops in Memphis, Chattanooga, and Lookout Mountain, they arrived in St. Louis on the eighteenth, where they were feted in "grand style," enjoying a boat ride on the Mississippi, a trip to the city's fairgrounds, and an evening at the theater. They proceeded to Cincinnati and then on to Chicago on the twenty-seventh, where they set about "enjoying its magnificent sites and partaking of its hospitalities." Their visit to Chicago, a city one hundred times larger than Waco, coincided with the opening of the Inter-State Industrial Exposition. Attracting 20,000 visitors to its formal opening on the twenty-fifth, the fair showcased the city's triumphant rise from the ashes of the disastrous fire two years before.[22]

The exposition was housed in an immense, domed building eight hundred feet long and two hundred feet wide, "the largest and best structure on the continent," according to the *Chicago Tribune*. The paper listed for the edification of its readers the impressive statistics—the number of bricks, linear feet of oak piling, and tons of nuts, bolts, and plates that went into the hall. Here, then, was progress in its most solid, material form. Virtually every local manufacturer, wholesaler, and major retailer exhibited wares; on display were overalls, carriages and cradles, shutters and plows, floral arrangements, and sewing machines. Ordinary folk could admire housewares, wigs, and clothing, while building contractors marveled over new drilling, quarrying, and crushing machinery. Entrepreneurs found labor-saving innovations in mining, agriculture, dairying, and textile production—new machines powered by steam and water.[23]

The truly awe-inspiring nature of the exposition—the size and grandeur of the building that housed it, the seemingly infinite number of products on display—could not completely overshadow the dramatic events that had transpired the week before. On September 23, a banking crisis had rocked New York City when the investment house Jay Cooke collapsed. While the Chicago Exposition highlighted the splendid interconnectedness of the postbellum national economy, the crisis revealed the darker side of the same trend. A decline in demand from eastern railroads reverberated in Chicago, where orders for ties and other timber products fell dramatically. By September 26, the largest

Chicago banks had suspended operations because they feared a run on deposits. The city's boosters sought to minimize the damage; they could hardly have known that the country had started on a steep, downward trajectory into a five-year depression. Back in McLennan County, the price of cotton plummeted.[24]

In December, soon after Albert returned from his trip, came the day of reckoning for the newlyweds, the day they realized they had no future anywhere in Texas. Governor Davis and almost all other Republicans, including those in Waco, suffered a crushing defeat at the hands of Democrats. Within a few weeks the couple decided to move to Chicago.[25]

Albert Parsons went north that winter fully formed, as it were. He possessed the useful skills of typesetting, editing, and writing, and he had thrived off rough politicking and courting controversy with his audacious advocacy for the dispossessed. Self-promotion was his strong suit, and his oratorical gifts gave him an overweening self-confidence that could serve him well or disastrously, depending upon the circumstances. In Texas he had familiarized himself with a political economy that enriched an arrogant few at the expense of the disenfranchised, landless many—a political economy from which, truth be told, he aspired to profit via public office. Chicago beckoned as a new field of labor for him, but it was a field whose outlines he recognized and understood.

En route to Chicago, Lucia relinquished her first name and assumed a new one—Lucy. She seemed to want to erase her past altogether, for she left behind her close kin, Oliver Benton, and the Waco townspeople who knew her to be a former slave. There is no record of how or when, but by this time baby Champ had died; whether this left her grief-stricken or relieved (or both) is unknown. Life in Waco had taught her that a woman's sexual attractiveness could play a critical part in shaping her life's chances. At some point she had also developed a toughness of character that would allow her not only to serve as her own best advocate but also to survive devastating personal crises. She would remain guarded, and circumspect about her true self and her background, especially compared to her garrulous, outgoing husband. In the grand American tradition of self-reinvention, for a while, at least, she became a person without a past.

Lucy's Waco years gave her reason to appreciate the value of a name change. Her mother had shed Taliaferro in favor of the name of her new husband, Charlie Carter, who himself had discarded his slave name. Oliver Gathings considered himself a free, or at least freer, man after he assumed the name Oliver Benton. Jane Tallavan chose a variation on her owner's name—"Taliaferro" was pronounced "Tolliver." In the immediate postwar period, identities remained fluid, especially in a town full of recent arrivals such as Waco, and new names could signal a person's whole new way of being in the world. For his part, Albert Parsons had chosen to shed his identity as a Confederate veteran and become a Republican. Both he and Lucy were learning that a carefully crafted persona, "authentic" or not, could prove useful when either one of them wanted to be heard over the commotion of a hostile world.

Throughout her long life, Lucy would make the most of the fact that no one could tell for certain by looking at her who her parents were or what she had endured in Virginia, or on the coffle en route to Texas, or in wartime McLennan County, or in Waco during the turbulent years of Reconstruction. Albert and Lucy Parsons would never return to Texas, and they never looked back—except when those who wished them harm forced them to do so.

Part 2

Gilded Age Dynamite

❦ Chapter 3 ❧

A Local War

W HEN ALBERT AND LUCY PARSONS ARRIVED IN CHICAGO IN
late 1873, they found a city reeling from depression and a workers'
rebellion. The couple immediately became caught up in a crisis-driven,
nationwide debate about the viability of fundamental American institutions, including industrial capitalism and the two-party political
system.

The path they traveled over the next few years was an extraordinary one, even for these uncertain times—Albert transforming himself
from an aspiring Republican operative in Texas to a leader of Chicago
socialists, the freedwoman Lucy running a small business in an immigrant German community and launching her own career of political
agitation. She read voraciously and continued to imbibe lessons from
her husband about the power of political oratory as a weapon of class
warfare—a weapon useful not only in genteel debates over ideology, but
also in pitched battles fought in the streets by men and women throwing stones against police armed with rifles and cannon.

How to explain Albert's quick embrace of his very public role as
a proponent of socialism? Being a socialist in Chicago was much like
being a Republican in Waco. His foray into Chicago activism called
upon his love of politicking, and he relished the role of outsider in

relation to the powers-that-be. Both Waco and Chicago allowed him to use his gifts as a speaker and journalist and to attempt to manipulate the editors and reporters who controlled the mainstream media. He and Lucy were united in their contrarian natures. In Texas, the radicals were Republican black men and a handful of white voters; in Chicago, they were socialists who challenged the capitalist system as the chief source of the immiseration of the poor. For the Parsonses, it was not a great leap from denunciations of chattel slavery and the planter class in the rural South to denunciations of "wage slavery" and the capitalist class in the urban North.

At the same time, Albert and Lucy were keenly aware of the dislocation they suffered in moving from small-town Texas to the colossus of the Midwest. Chicago was sprawling, noisy, squalid, its air befouled by smokestacks and its clogged streets littered with the excrement of horses—many hundreds of the beasts drawing vehicles that included everything from pie carriers to "Black Marias," police patrol wagons clanging their warning bells. Yet the couple managed to accommodate themselves to a new language, new neighbors, even new kinds of foods at the market and green grocers. Meanwhile, the rent must be paid, so while Albert worked as a compositor for several major newspapers, Lucy sewed to supplement their income. They moved from apartment to apartment almost annually, but they remained on the north side of the city. And they remained together, making a new home for themselves in a German immigrant neighborhood, finding a niche in radical politics, and hosting Monday-night meetings of those who shared their beliefs. Somehow, then, the former slave and the former Confederate soldier adjusted to life in Chicago. And they became caught up in a conflict that seemed to all its combatants a thunderous new iteration of an ongoing civil war.[1]

THE CITY THAT GREETED THE TEXAS COUPLE WAS IN AN UPROAR. By December 1873, the economic downturn that had begun three months earlier had caused severe distress among Chicago's laboring classes; out of a working population of 112,000, an estimated 25,000 had recently lost their jobs, causing untold misery among some 125,000 family members in a city of 400,000. As winter set in and starvation and disease spread, a small group of socialists pressed for jobs and immediate relief from the Common (City) Council. On Sunday, December 21, the 400 members of the immigrant German Socio-Political Workingmen's Union, and members of other immigrant groups, organized a mass meeting in Vorwaerts Turner Hall on Twelfth Street on the Near West Side of the city. Demanding "Work or Bread," a series of speakers delivered the same message about the best way to address the deepening crisis: "It consists in the energetic union and concentration of the workingmen into one solid organization." Furthermore, they declared, the city must provide jobs, food, and shelter for the afflicted, especially since the council had consistently acted "in the interest of a few capitalists, landholders, and professional politicians."[2]

The following evening, under a cloudy sky with the threat of snow in the air, 10,000 workers formed a procession and marched in mournful silence through the streets from Turner Hall east to City Hall, where the council was meeting. Meanwhile, large numbers of policemen, deployed strategically, watched nervously for the first hint of violence. The hushed crowd, in its immensity—with workers hailing from all over the United States and Europe, and representing a variety of trades— exuded a sense of menace to Chicago's powerful propertied classes.

Aldermen dismissed the marchers' demands and suggested they appeal to the city's Relief and Aid Society, a charity in possession of an estimated $600,000 in unspent money that had been raised on behalf of the victims of the Great Chicago Fire three years before. Under pressure, the society released some funds to the needy in early 1874, but leaders of the group were reluctant to help any able-bodied person: indeed, in their view, people so lacking in self-respect as to apply for aid automatically rendered themselves unworthy of it.[3]

Later, Albert Parsons would write that he first took up the "labor question" when he heard critics charge that the Relief and Aid Society had, instead of aiding the poor, further enriched the wealthy. "I found that the complaints against the society were just and proper," he reported, noting that he had seen similarities between the Chicago elites, who condemned the Workingmen's Union as a motley mob of "communists, robbers, and loafers," and former slaveholders in Texas, who had portrayed the freedpeople as dangerous subversives of the established order: "It satisfied me," he wrote, that "there was a great fundamental wrong at work in society and in existing social and industrial arrangements."[4]

Of his move from Waco, Albert wrote only, "I decided to settle in Chicago." Since there was no larger migration out of Texas and into Illinois during this time, he and Lucy apparently found their way north on their own. Still, they were hardly the only ones drawn to this fastest-growing of American cities: between 1870 and 1890, the Chicago population would swell from 112,000 to 1.1 million people. During his visit in September 1873, Albert had probably met a number of German immigrants—perhaps through contacts supplied by his brother William, who had represented the interests of Houston German social groups when he was a Texas state senator. In Chicago, much of the trade-union organizing revolved around the Turners, a German men's athletic club with radical political leanings; it was the club's three-story frame building on Twelfth Street that served as the headquarters and meeting place of Chicago socialists. Perhaps Albert relied during the move on the help of a Republican he had met in the course of politicking in the Hill Country, someone with a hospitable friend or cousin in Chicago who could ease the Parsonses' way into the city's North Side German-immigrant community, where they settled immediately upon arrival.[5]

Or it is possible that during his initial trip to the city Albert had heard that the largest newspapers had a deficit of printers. In the aftermath of the 1871 fire, Local No. 16 of the National Typographical Union (NTU) had offered to find jobs for two hundred of its members in other Midwestern cities, and it was perhaps the departure of at least some of these who made room for him. In any event, on his arrival, he wasted little time applying for membership in Local No. 16, and he found work as a compositor for the *Chicago Times*, the *Chicago Inter-Ocean*, the *Chicago Tribune*, and the *Chicago Daily News*. The NTU admitted him formally in April 1877.[6]

When they arrived in Chicago, the couple rented units 25 and 26 at 157 Fifth Avenue (now Wells Street), rooms that possibly included not only a residence but also a workspace for Lucy, and sometime before 1875 she opened her own seamstress business. Albert's substantial savings, his steady work as a printer, and Lucy's sewing gave them a modicum of financial security for their first three and a half years in the city. Still, they lived in at least four different places during that time, eventually settling in the 15th Ward, an area on the North Side still in the process of rebuilding after the fire. The site of a former German farming colony, the neighborhood had streets named Schubert, Mozart, Frankfort, and Rhine.[7]

By 1873, Chicago had expended enormous amounts of labor, capital, natural resources, and political will and imagination to rebuild itself after the conflagration that began on the late Sunday night of October 8, 1871. The fire killed 300 people, consumed 18,000 buildings, including much of the downtown business district, and leveled 2,100 acres. Yet remarkably, within a year, a public-private partnership had succeeded in scouring the visible effects of the disaster from the cityscape. When the Parsonses arrived, they saw temporary shanties built to house the homeless still in use, but they also saw neat rows of new wooden cottages for workers and impressive new downtown office buildings. The great department stores were selling an abundance of tastefully displayed ready-made goods. Prairie Avenue and Lake Shore Drive were sites of a post-fire building boom among the city's great magnates— Marshall Field (retail sales), George M. Pullman (railroad cars), Potter Palmer (hotelier), Cyrus McCormick (farm machinery), and Philip D. Armour (meatpacking).[8]

The magnificent residences of such men contrasted mightily with the city's vast neighborhoods of low-lying tenements. Mary "Mother" Jones, a labor organizer who began her career as a seamstress in Chicago around this time, took note of "the poor, shivering wretches, jobless and hungry, walking along the frozen lake front" in winter, and the overworked mothers from the West Side bringing their babies to the lakefront for a breath of cool air in summer. The elites' conspicuous wealth provided the gilt for the age, testifying to the city's role as a thriving rail and water entrepôt trading in lumber, meat products, beer, and farm machinery. Here was the Central Texas crossroads of Waco written on a gigantic scale.[9]

Yet recovery from the fire exposed deep social fissures within the city. Many thousands of native-born migrants, together with many thousands of foreign immigrants, had come to Chicago to partake of the so-called Great Rebuilding. The newcomers came full of hope only to seek in vain for adequate shelter, however, now that hastily erected factories and sprawling warehouses had devoured whole residential neighborhoods. They squeezed into high-priced, poorly ventilated barracks, basements, and hovels surrounded by open sewers that were clogged with kitchen slop, human excrement, and animal carcasses. The high death rate, a product of poor sanitation and smallpox and cholera epidemics, exceeded that of London, Paris, and Liverpool. In their first summer, Albert and Lucy encountered the unbearable stench emanating from the polluted Chicago River—although it may have seemed little more than a meandering cesspool, it nevertheless served as a vital commercial artery for lumber and ore, with boats and barges headed toward Lake Michigan—as well as from the fetid stockyards and slaughterhouses overtaking the South Side.[10]

To some extent, the plight of the poor reflected the drop in demand for manufactured goods due to the depression. At the same time, widespread homelessness resulted from larger processes of mechanization and other forms of labor displacement that threatened to shrink the ranks of the employed even when times improved. The construction derrick was the symbol of the city's rebirth but also of builders' rush to replace workers with labor-saving devices. Other groups lost their jobs to new technologies. Machines now did the tasks of sausage-casing workers. The appearance of the refrigerator car in 1874 threw many butchers out of work. The widespread use of the typewriter replaced male bookkeepers with female stenographers, who, for less pay, could record four or five times as many words per minute. Sewing machines forced speedups among factory seamstresses. Cheap labor in general further depressed wages and increased unemployment. Convicts even took the place of some boot and shoe workers, and young boys began to do the jobs of many adult male wood-carvers. Meanwhile, the vast majority of meatpackers, machine factory operatives, and sweatshop workers endured fourteen-hour days in dirty, dangerous conditions. Nevertheless, despite the fact that more and more people were living under Chicago's bridges and sleeping in police stations, the city fathers counseled the poor to practice "self-dependence."[11]

The Parsonses' emerging new politics reflected the German radical tradition as it unfolded in teeming Chicago. Socialists decried the quest for profits that they believed despoiled the life-chances of the masses. The symbols of a future reckoning were everywhere—not only in the mechanical innovations featured at the 1873 Industrial Exposition, but also in the swelling ranks of the jobless and homeless—the "tramps" composing a mighty, footsore "army." Through no fault of their own, these men and women were now superfluous, victims of businesses that were moving, inexorably, toward labor-saving machinery and "efficiency." According to socialists, this process would eventually displace a substantial proportion of the laboring and middle classes together. However, such a transformation was not to be resisted, for it was the spark that in time would ignite a far-reaching popular revolt. The downtrodden laboring classes would finally fight to receive a full share of the fruits of their own labor as their miserable condition became untenable at last.[12]

Lucy and Albert Parsons would come to view the city as a perfect example of evolutionary capitalism—the historical process by which businesses grew into trusts, monopolies, and syndicates, shedding workers along the way. In fact, this view of the grand sweep of the past, present, and future found support not only among German theorists, such as Karl Marx, but also among a diverse group of American thinkers and businessmen at the time. The home-grown American writer Edward Bellamy, and captains of industry such as Andrew Carnegie and John D. Rockefeller (steel and oil magnates, respectively), heralded the seemingly relentless march to corporate bigness. Carnegie and Rockefeller saw gigantic companies as more efficient than their smaller counterparts, the means by which capital could be channeled into philanthropic enterprises for the good of all. For their part, socialists disagreed among themselves about the inevitable and ideal future—whether it would be organized around a strong central government that would absorb and control the largest monopolies, or around a cooperative commonwealth of small voluntary associations.

If socialists and robber barons could agree on the inevitable processes of workplace innovation and business consolidation, they could not agree on the scope and meaning of the personal suffering wrought by these processes. Laboring men and women in Chicago felt the immediate effects of the crash of '73. Railroads moved to cut their labor forces and reduce wages, and businessmen and their allies in the press suggested that the most effective way to help the unemployed was to close the taverns and billiard halls, saving workers as a group $28,000 a week in "squandered" wages. In fact, the pro-business *Tribune* saw the disaster as a blessing if only the irresponsible laboring classes would cut back on frivolous spending: "There is a silver lining to every cloud; adversity is a good school; its lessons are abiding, and, while the entire people are alike temporarily prostrated, all must endeavor to take the brightest view of the situation, and conform their habits to the change in circumstances." Meanwhile, Democratic and Republican Party leaders, preoccupied with cultural issues such as the morality of Sunday-afternoon *Biergarten* outings, and with municipal patronage jobs, the spoils of electoral victory, showed little concern for those who were becoming "prostrated," temporarily or otherwise.[13]

In Chicago, European immigrants took the lead in offering an alternative to the two major political parties and organizing the demonstrations of late December 1873; the Workingmen's Union put forth speakers who addressed the crowds in English and German, with a smattering of Swedish, Polish, and French. Indeed, in the early 1870s, 45 percent of Chicago was foreign-born, and among the voting-age population, immigrants predominated. A vast divide separated the well-to-do—mostly native-born Protestants who believed that, with a bit of effort, every person could control his or her own destiny—from the laboring classes, especially the immigrants, who tended to favor collective action to address perceived wrongs. The Germans (Catholic, Lutheran, and atheist) in particular assumed a lively, visible presence in Chicago—even their parades and picnics gave expression to the labor radicalism favored by many.[14]

In August 1874, Chicago businessmen organized the Citizens' Association (CA). Its members believed that government existed solely to protect private property, and not to cater to the interests of what the CA called the "baser elements of the people." City Hall employed and represented too many people who had no property to protect, these businessmen argued, and in fact, "this city is governed, for the most part, by unfit and unworthy men, in an undignified, uncultivated, and demoralizing manner." Elites disapproved of workers who took to the streets in protest—a time-honored tradition, especially among trade unions. The laboring classes saw mass rallies as a vital expression of the people's will, while the Citizens' Association saw them as a mockery of the democratic process, which they believed mandated that individuals cast their ballots privately in the service of property interests. The mass marches in late 1873 undermined the ideal of the storybook Victorian Christmas, when families should be gathering together in their snug little cottages, and not shamelessly parading through the streets, proclaiming their own poverty and desperation.[15]

By 1874, it was apparent that the city's Republicans and Democrats had become unequal to the task of resolving a volatile mix of ethnic, class, and ideological conflicts. Elites, most of whom favored the Republican Party, remained firm in their conviction that individuals must rely on their own resources—a curious view for men who themselves formed fraternal-based businesses and gigantic combinations, as well as the Relief and Aid Society and the Citizens' Association, in pursuit of "good government." Abetting this larger effort to protect private-property interests were newspaper publishers, who rationalized and promoted a pro-business view of the world, and law enforcement officials, who apprehended and brought miscreants to justice, whether lone burglars or mobs of immigrant "communists." For their part, the Democrats attracted a mix of ethnic and working-class groups but remained focused on capturing patronage jobs rather than upending the capitalist order.

As Albert Parsons knew full well from his Texas days, the Republican Party promoted robust partnerships with business that included state-sponsored subsidies to railroads in the form of land grants and tax rebates. At the same time, throughout the country, small voluntary associations were emerging as a countervailing force to these potent alliances between politicians and capitalists. Many of these groups stressed harmony rather than competition among like-minded people; they included the National Grange of the Order of Patrons of Husbandry, usually referred to simply as the Grange, established in 1867 and intent on freeing farmers from their dependence on middlemen, such as grain storehouses; the Knights of Labor, organized in 1869, which was devoted to small producers and the laboring classes; and the Greenback

Labor Party, which had been determined since its formation in 1873 to expand the currency and thus lessen the burden of debtors who had been victimized by predatory lenders. Lucy and Albert Parsons arrived in Chicago at a time when the Anti-Monopoly Party was organizing farmers and miners in the Illinois countryside, and when the newly formed Workingmen's Party of Illinois appealed to city dwellers. In the summer of 1874, the British-born Elizabeth Morgan helped start a Chicago branch of the Sovereigns of Industry, an urban variation on the rural Grange. The Sovereigns' call to arms amounted to a rallying cry for the age: "You have but to combine, workingmen and women! And a great and immediate benefit is yours."[16]

These proto-political associations shared a basic set of impulses and ideas with the small utopian experiments that had emerged in the antebellum period, communes representing a wide range of beliefs about gender roles, religion, the division of labor, and leadership structures. In general, prewar homegrown anti-capitalist communities embraced the peaceful tactics characteristic of voluntary associations prone toward moral suasion rather than legislation or force as a means of attracting support. Nevertheless, by the postbellum period many native-born Chicagoans were beginning to develop an aversion to anything that smacked of communism and socialism, political ideologies that were now conflated with revolution and domestic terrorism. Karl Marx's *Capital: Critique of Political Economy* was published in 1867. Four years later thousands of French workers took to the streets in Paris in demonstrations on behalf of justice and equality in a sixty-four-day uprising called the Paris Commune; authorities suppressed the rebels only by massacring many hundreds of them. For Chicagoans, "communist" became an epithet signifying foreigners' contempt for American values as well as any instance of collective action on the part of the poor. Native-born Americans especially expressed a visceral hatred for and fear of "communists" of any kind.[17]

IN CHICAGO, NEITHER ALBERT NOR LUCY WAS IN FACT A MEMBER OF the toiling masses, a group consisting of factory workers and unskilled laborers, 70 percent of whom were foreign-born. Most of the men in

this group worked in manufacturing, meat processing, and the building trades, whereas a majority of wage-earning women found jobs as
domestic servants. Printers—such as Albert—represented only 1,826 of
all 96,000 male workers, and seamstresses—a group that now included
Lucy—only 1,686 of all 16,000 female workers. Although both of the
Parsonses were employed in jobs that were vulnerable to mechanization, neither had to contend with long hours inside a sweatshop firetrap
or a foul-smelling slaughterhouse, or outside in the elements. Lucy in
fact ran a small shop, probably consisting of herself and a helper or two.
In the coming years their close comrades would all come from the ranks
of either skilled tradespeople or small, independent entrepreneurs, men
and women who possessed pride of craft and realized that a traditional
way of life was rapidly disappearing in the wake of piecework and mass
production.[18]

It should also be noted that the Parsonses did not live, work, or organize among black people, who at the time of their arrival in Chicago
numbered 4,000 or so—barely 1 percent of the city's population. Before
1874, blacks had remained clustered block by block in the wards along
the lake, interspersed among various ethnic communities; however, a
fire that summer forced them to disperse to other parts of the city. The
black men of Illinois won the right to vote in 1870 after the passage of
the Fifteenth Amendment (three years after their Texas counterparts
were enfranchised), but made up only 800 voters in the city's total voting population of 50,000. The party of Lincoln largely ignored them,
and the Democrats completely shunned them. White labor leaders
looked down on workers who were paid by the task, which most black
workers were; for their part, the 1,500 black cooks, laundresses, and underemployed manual laborers found the call for an eight-hour day irrelevant to their work lives. Yet neither Lucy nor Albert could have been
completely oblivious to the presence of black people, since the local papers were filled with lurid stories about blacks' alleged proclivities for
rape and murder ("The Rochester Horror") and their supposedly bizarre customs and superstitions (witchcraft and "Voudouism").[19]

Had the Parsonses taken an interest in the city's small community
of former slaves, they would have heard thrilling tales of fugitives finding
their way north and banding together to foil the designs of slave catchers

before the Civil War, and of hardworking families making heroic efforts
to piece together a living for themselves. Yet both husband and wife and
their socialist comrades remained preoccupied with white craftsmen and
factory workers, the urban proletariat. Living in a self-sufficient, clois-
tered, virtually all-immigrant neighborhood, they drew upon European
traditions of class struggle that had no room for African Americans.
And most white workers, regardless of ethnicity, saw the black man primarily as a potential strikebreaker, a menace to their own livelihood.
Albert's steadfast indifference to Chicago's black population suggests
that his earlier efforts on behalf of black Texans for civil rights had been
purely opportunistic, a way for him to advance within the Republican
Party, rather than the result of strongly held principle.[20]

Lucy probably kept her distance from Chicago's blacks for more
personal reasons. From the time she arrived in the city, she would go
to great lengths to deny her own African heritage. As a newcomer to
Chicago, where no one knew her mother, she achieved at least partial
success in this effort, as many observers could not determine her precise origins from the color of her skin or the texture of her hair. Taking
up the cause of long-suffering black domestics would have resulted in
calling attention to herself and risking derision or worse. Nevertheless, ignoring workers who shared her African ancestry only brought so
much protection. Throughout her life, those who were openly hostile to
her politics would point to her copper-colored complexion and quickly
label her a "nigger."

Albert and Lucy cast their lot with the mainly foreign-born radicals. Given the shortage of native-born socialists, German immigrant
leaders were grateful to discover in the gifted orator from Texas a devoted comrade who could reach English speakers. When Albert joined
the Social Democratic Party (SDP) in March 1876, both he and Lucy
forged bonds with several men who would shape Chicago's labor politics in the coming years. George A. Schilling, a twenty-six-year-old
German-born cooper, wrote for the Chicago-based *Arbeiter Zeitung*
(Workers' Paper). Level-headed and compassionate, he would prove a
steadfast advocate of the city's laboring classes for the next sixty years,
and together with Albert he helped to found the English section of the
SDP. Thomas J. ("Tommy") Morgan, twenty-nine, an English-born

machinist, had arrived in Chicago with his wife, Elizabeth, in 1868. A long stint of unemployment after 1873, when he lost his job with the railroad, had radicalized him. The bilingual August Spies, a twenty-one-year-old German-born upholsterer who had come to the United States in 1872, loved the theater and had a flair for the dramatic; with his light brown hair and blue eyes, he played the gregarious "ladies' man" and enjoyed dancing and lunching at fashionable restaurants.[21]

Together these socialists expressed faith in the ballot box as a re-demptive force in bringing about a peaceful, more democratic society. To outsiders, though, they seemed to welcome widespread poverty and suffering as engines of radical change, on the theory that, as Schilling put it, "wholesale hunger and destitution . . . would furnish the surplus steam—discontent—that would blow the capitalistic system to 'king-dom come'" by rousing the sluggish masses to act. Indeed, socialists walked a fine line by, on the one hand, exposing the intense suffering of the poor, and, on the other, pronouncing economic hardship and even starvation as necessary and inevitable stages on the road to revolution.[22]

Lucy had not yet become a public figure in her own right, but hints of her personality emerged in two lawsuits she initiated around the same time that Albert was gravitating toward the SDP, one in June 1875 and the other a year later. In the first, she hired a young, up-and-coming white attorney, Alfred S. Trude, and sued Henry M. Taylor in circuit court, presumably for money he owed her for sewing services. (Whether she won or lost the case is unknown.) The following summer she hired another lawyer, George W. Know, and took her downstairs neighbor to court. The suit alleged that Mrs. Putnam "keeps a house of ill-repute, that she cuts off the former's [Parsons's] water supply, and when expostulated with makes threats to do bodily injury." In the court record, Lucy is identified as "a colored woman, who is married to a white man of that name, a compositor in the *Times* office." (The court reporter probably knew Albert, hence the editorializing about Lucy's race and her marital status.) The judge apparently sided with Lucy and told Mrs. Putnam that if anyone else made a complaint against her, "she would be summarily dealt with." These cases indicate that Lucy had the nerve, and the discretionary income, to haul two white people into court with the aid of lawyers.[23]

By late 1876, the Social Democratic Party had merged with the Workingmen's Party of Illinois to form the Workingmen's Party of the United States (WPUS). Albert Parsons had represented Chicago at its founding convention in New Jersey earlier that year. The first corresponding secretary of the Chicago branch was a twenty-four-year-old architectural draftsman named Philip Van Patten from Washington, DC. Van Patten later claimed that he owed his leadership position in the WPUS to the fact that the Chicago socialists had "difficulty in getting anyone who could write correct English." Not only were most labor radicals German, but German thinkers such as Marx, Friedrich Engels, and Ferdinand Lassalle set the agenda for the group. (Lassalle advocated ballot-box socialism, which called upon all citizens to exercise their right to vote.) Van Patten was no rhetorician, however, and so for a long time, Albert Parsons was "practically the only public English speaker we had," as Parsons himself later wrote; it was Parsons who spoke first at any socialist meeting or rally, usually followed by August Spies in German.[24]

Early on, Lucy assumed a prominent role in debates over strategy and theory during the weekly meetings of the WPUS, which stretched from Monday night into the early hours of Tuesday. And she read widely—local newspapers, popular magazines, and books of history and dense political theory. The fruits of her study would become abundantly clear in a couple of years, when she would burst onto the Chicago scene as not only a debater and a lecturer but also a writer of poetry, prose, and social commentary. By that time she had developed a distinctive voice and the vocabulary of a well-educated, highly sophisticated observer of life and interpreter of texts.

Albert soon became a regular on the speaking circuit, traveling throughout the Midwest to promote socialistic principles. On one of his trips, to Indianapolis in 1876, he delivered a July 4 oration marking the country's centennial celebration. It began, "We hold these truths to be self-evident," and detailed the inalienable rights of men, including "Life, Liberty, and the *full proceeds of their Labor*." The crimes of "the Bearers of the Ruling System, the Aristocrats of Capital," were enumerated, including this one: "They brought the last civil war on our country to abolish black slavery, but left wage slavery as it was, while augmenting its ever-increasing cruelty."[25]

During that visit to Indianapolis, Albert joined the Knights of Labor, and, with Schilling, he founded Chicago's first local Knights assembly upon his return. Organized by workers as a secret society, the Knights hearkened back to a time when yeoman farmers and small producers beholden to no one—not bankers, employers, or railroad men— had formulated the founding principles of American citizenship. On the surface, at least, the Knights' romance with the past would seem to be at odds with the socialists' focus on the future and on the relentless forward march of history, from feudalism to capitalism to socialism, from slavery to wage slavery to freedom, variously defined. However, neither Albert nor Lucy hewed to an ideologically pure socialist party line, and they cared little for doctrinal consistency. They saw no contradiction in simultaneous membership in a WPUS branch and a Knights assembly.

In 1877 and for the next four years, Albert began to run regularly for public office as a socialist—once for county clerk, twice for state assemblyman, and three times for alderman from the 15th Ward. As early as May 1876, the Chicago press took note of him; the *Tribune* would thereafter routinely refer to him as a communist demagogue—again, a term that for many conjured up violent European revolutionaries. His notoriety in the mainstream press was a boon to his political career, but it also put him squarely in the crosshairs of law enforcement officers who were becoming anxious about socialists attracting huge crowds.[26]

The police detective Michael J. Schaak, for one, was convinced that the December 1873 demonstrations marking the onset of the depression had served as a mere "pretext for many a diatribe against capital." Before long, undercover police became a fixture at the meetings held at Turner Hall, which were believed by Schaak and his colleagues to be a vipers' nest of communists, drunkards, and thieves. In the winter of 1876, the detective began to single out Albert Parsons, Van Patten, Schilling, and Morgan as socialists gaining prominence "at large gatherings" regardless of the type of those get-togethers. Schaak understood, if imperfectly, that picnics, New Year's Eve celebrations, dances, and musical entertainments were, as much as demonstrations, the underpinnings of a radical German political culture that gave expression to a way of life as well as a way of thinking about the world. Indeed, German-immigrant socialism boasted its own festivals, schools and nurseries, volunteer militias, and charity leagues—providing for a veritable *Deutschtum* (Germany-away-from-home). Because the English-section socialists could claim nothing comparable in the way of a community that fused activism and ethnic culture, Lucy and Albert looked to their German-speaking comrades for sociability and a sense of belonging. The Parsonses would remain native-born, non-German anomalies within the socialist community, even as they became more active in it.[27]

THE GREAT RAILROAD STRIKE OF 1877 COST THIRTY-FIVE CHICAGO workers their lives and wounded an estimated two hundred. Lucy would later write that the strike proved to be a turning point in her life, opening her eyes to multiple forms of injustice and to the realities of structures of power. She also took to heart the attention (both admiring and disparaging) that Albert received during the strike by virtue of his speaking abilities. She saw the potential of the masses to cripple the city's economy, and the potential of the women protesters to unnerve the respectable classes. Assuming a leadership role in the uprising, Albert was eager to rally union members and the unemployed alike; but although he escaped with his life, he lost his job, and from that point onward found himself the constant target of suspicious authorities. Neither the city of Chicago nor his household would ever be the same.

The summer of 1877 marked the first time a US president mobilized federal troops to quash a strike. In Chicago, with its throngs of demonstrators and cadre of WPUS provocateurs, a six-day mass protest that was held a week into the strike convinced elites that the city had entered a period of civil rebellion; this development struck them as more threatening to their businesses and buildings than even the Civil War or the Great Chicago Fire of 1871. The prospect of armed conflict and evocations of Civil War militarization led workers as well as law enforcement authorities to believe that the resolution of bitter class conflict could come about only through bloodshed. Chicago police were determined to preempt challenges to their authority, a tactic that turned peaceful assemblies into riots, minor street skirmishes into pitched battles, and generalized labor unrest into a wider, years-long war of words, bullets, and the hangman's noose. Mayor Monroe Heath exhorted the forces under his command to dig in for the long haul.

At the national level, the six-week strike grew out of the attempt (predictable, according to the WPUS) on the part of industrialists to consolidate their holdings and shore up flagging profits by reducing labor costs. After 1867, railroad owners over-expanded and over-speculated, and the depression of 1873 left them scrambling to cut operating expenses. On June 1, 1877, Pennsylvania Railroad officials told their employees that their wages would be cut by 15 cents an hour (down to 13.5 cents), a total reduction of a substantial $8 a week. The news prompted the *Tribune* (under the editorship of the business apologist and former abolitionist and Unionist Joseph Medill) to offer a rhetorical shrug of the shoulders, opining that "there is no help for it," as wages would rise when times got better and not before. Meanwhile, employers deserved the sympathy of the public, for they "are suffering as well as employees." Certainly the owners' "suffering" was of a different order compared to that of their workers, however. The behemoth railroad industry, capitalized at $5 billion, employed 200,000 people and maintained 79,000 miles of track, arteries carrying the lifeblood of American commerce. On July 21, in response to the wage cuts, West Virginia railroad workers walked off the job. That same day, Pittsburgh strikers torched 39 buildings and destroyed 104 locomotives and 1,245 passenger cars. Three regiments of the local militia, 1,000 federal troops, and a battery of artillery from Philadelphia were deployed to quell the strike, and 20 people were killed. The whole nation seemed to be on edge; people were eager for news by the hour in a way that had not been seen since 1861.[28]

In Chicago, what began as a job action among rail switchmen swelled to a general strike among the skilled and unskilled. Over a week, the WPUS tried to harness the tremendous collective outrage among railroad workers into a massive labor-organizing drive. On the evening of Saturday, July 21, an estimated 1,000 men and women gathered in a vacant lot on the corner of Twelfth and Halsted Streets, chanting "We want work, not charity." A *Tribune* reporter covering the event noted with astonishment that "the printer Parsons" made a speech "which would have done credit, for force and eloquence, to a man of much greater pretensions." Albert Parsons held forth, questioning the manhood of those in the crowd who watched their wives being reduced to prostitution and their children to starvation. In response, "many a tattered coatsleeve came up to its owner's eyes, many a fist was clenched, and teeth were shut hard together," although Parsons seemed conciliatory, and "did not allude to carnage and incendiarism as a means to that end."[29]

On Monday the twenty-third, in front of a packed crowd at Sack's Hall at the corner of Brown and Twentieth Streets, Parsons again took the podium, to the cheers of the crowd. This time he excoriated the city's newspapers, singling out his employers at the *Tribune* and the *Sunday Times* by name as the mouthpieces of the great industrialists. As he had the day before, he tried to shame his listeners, now saying, "If the proprietor has a right to fix the wages and say what labor is worth, then we are bound hand and foot—slaves, and we should be perfectly happy, content with a bowl of rice and a rat a week." With these words, he compared his audience to the freedpeople of the South and the exploited Chinese on the West Coast, both insults to white men's sense of their own manliness. Ironically, this racist appeal echoed his speeches to crowds of Texas freedmen—the demand that they seize their rights by reclaiming their manhood and defying their "masters."[30]

That evening, at a mass meeting on Market Square, Parsons addressed an estimated 30,000 listeners. Calling upon the "Grand Army of Starvation" (a phrase that evoked the Grand Army of the Republic, a fraternal order of Union veterans), he urged them to join the WPUS: "Enroll your names in the Grand Army of Labor, and if the capitalist engages in warfare against our rights, then we shall resist him with all the means that God has given us." Parsons pledged that in opposition to armed capital, "his thought, his voice, and his arm should be raised for bloody war." According to a reporter, "his speech bordered on the inflammatory, but he left the crowd to fill in gaps." And so it did, responding to the names of railroad men with "We'll hang them."[31]

On Tuesday Parsons reported for work at the *Times* only to find that he had been "discharged and blacklisted by this paper for the meeting that night." Of his coworker printers, he said (probably wrongly), they "admired secretly what they termed 'my pluck,' but they were afraid to have much to say to me." At noon, he was with Van Patten in the Market Street office of the *Arbeiter Zeitung* when two policemen came in and seized them and took them to the local police station. There, according to Parsons, the chief of police, Michael Hickey, "in a brow-beating, officious, and insulting manner," grilled him about where he came from and whether he had a family. Hickey warned him, "Parsons, your life is in danger. I advise you to leave the city at once. Beware. Everything you say or do is made known to me. I have men on your track who shadow you. Do you know you are liable to be assassinated any moment on the street?"[32]

Meanwhile, workers were shutting down the Baltimore & Ohio and the Illinois Central Railroads. Parsons stayed away from the crowds, but that night he ventured out to the *Tribune* compositors' room "to be near the men of my own craft, whom I instinctively felt sympathized with me." Suddenly he was accosted by the head of Local No. 16's executive board and three other men who proceeded to drag him out of the office and down the stairs. Before depositing him on the sidewalk, one drew a gun and put it to his head, saying, "I've a mind to blow your brains out." Parsons recalled that his fellow workers "expressed great excitement and threatened to strike" to show their solidarity with him, though they seemed mollified when *Tribune* owner Medill personally assured them that he had had nothing to do with the assault on the outspoken orator. Within a few weeks Parsons would sue the *Tribune* for the libelous charge that he was responsible for "originating and perpetuating the disturbance"—the recent unrest among Chicago workers. The paper's fabrications had left him jobless and "liable to be wounded and even killed, by the people of Chicago, for being a rioter and a conspirator."[33]

On Wednesday immense numbers of men and women continued to rove the streets, with smaller groups coming together at specific workplaces to liberate the "wage slaves," only to scatter when police arrived. The air was filled with a Babel of languages and the strains of the French national anthem, "La Marseillaise." It was no wonder authorities were convinced that the republic was under siege. That morning without warning the police had burst into Turner Hall and broken up a meeting of furniture workers who had been discussing the strike. One cabinetmaker had been shot to death, and others suffered beatings and cracked skulls at the hands of club-wielding police; the walls of the hall were splattered with blood. Seen within the broader context of the strike, this clash was relatively minor, but the unprovoked nature of the attack had a lasting impression upon Chicago's workers, especially the German Americans. They were now convinced that, no matter how peaceable their meetings, they would remain vulnerable to ambushes from authorities.[34]

That afternoon, in the "Battle of the Viaduct" four blocks away, heavily armed police and National Guardsmen fought with as many as 10,000 demonstrators. One reporter described what he considered to be a most "disgusting" scene—an "unsexed mob of female incendiaries," hundreds of them, their hair loose and their dresses tucked up to their waists, doing battle with the police. He wrote, "Some were young, scarcely women in age, and not all in appearance." With their "knotty hands" and their "brawny, sunburnt arms," these "Amazons" hurled rocks, sticks, wooden blocks, and obscenities at officers. By the end of this bloody day, at least eighteen victims, all of them workers, had died. One socialist noted, "Chicago's workers never viewed the police in the same light as they had prior to this hour."[35]

That week saw an unprecedented mobilization of armed city, state, and federal forces as well as of private interests. In the words of one observer, "The city was alive with warlike preparations." Police, organized in "platoons," joined forces with the 9th and 22nd United States Infantry, regiments of the Illinois National Guard and Illinois State Militia, several companies of cavalry, and the Ellsworth Zouaves and other veterans groups. The mayor deputized 5,000 civilians as law enforcement agents, and leading businessmen and other "respected members" of the Chicago Board of Trade hastily formed a "Law and Order League." Individual employers paid private security forces and armed their clerks and bookkeepers to take to the streets in the service of public order. The US secretary of war called up six companies from Omaha and four from St. Paul and sent them to Chicago. Chicago editors hoped that prominent Civil War officers, including three generals (Philip Sheridan, George R. Crook, and John Pope), would be diverted from fighting Snake, Sioux, and Apache Indians and sent to this newest "seat of local war." Meanwhile, the streets echoed with the crack of gunfire and a barrage of artillery.[36]

All summer, industrialists and newspaper editors had goaded lynch mobs and the police, calling for workers to be poisoned with arsenic or strychnine, hanged from telegraph poles, blown apart by hand grenades, dragged before firing squads, or force-fed a "rifle diet." (In 1875, the *Tribune* had urged authorities to dispense with due process for communists, who were, apparently, criminals by definition: "Judge Lynch is an American by birth and character. Every lamp-post in Chicago will be decorated with a Communist carcass if necessary.") Reporters used military metaphors to chronicle the efforts of police and military in pursuit of "this formidable army," a "tramp army" in "rebellion." On July 27, Mayor Heath reported that calm had been restored. Though the campaign was won, however, the war was far from over.[37]

The Citizens' Association reacted to the summer uprising by creating a committee devoted to domestic "military" affairs and pressing the city to create a volunteer militia, which the association would support. The militia was now as essential as firefighters and police in protecting the property of the business community. In 1878, the CA presented the city with a Gatling gun, a newly developed continuous firing machine; 600 breech-loading Springfield rifles; 4 twelve-pounder Napoleon cannons; and enough ammunition and rounds of canister and case shot to equip a small army. The group paid the expenses that had been incurred by two regiments of the Illinois State Militia during the recent fighting. Authorities also began to keep an eye on the small immigrant-sponsored volunteer militias, most of which had begun as fraternal associations but now took on a sinister cast. Chief among these was the German Lehr und Wehr Verein (Education and Defense Society), founded in 1875 with thirty men. Albert Parsons would admit that indeed he and other workers "had entered upon a warfare" during the July 1877 demonstrations—but, he said, it was a war "against starvation wages and overwork," and not against any particular elected official or employer.[38]

Parsons invoked the Civil War, saying, "My enemies in the southern states consisted of those who oppressed the black slave. My enemies in the North are among those who would perpetuate the slavery of the wage workers." Indeed, the strikes of that summer brought to the fore critical questions that the Civil War had failed to address in any meaningful way. If workers were indeed constrained by the iron law of wages, then wherein lay their freedom, their independence as citizens? Condemning "wage slavery" as a labor system equivalent to the one supposedly abolished by the Thirteenth Amendment, Parsons held that workers were staging a revolt against industrial masters, and chafing at chains that thwarted their desires and denied their basic rights as Americans. In contrast, Joseph Medill and other Chicago leaders believed that workers and employers shared fundamental interests—they were *"Partners in business"*: employees freely offered their labor, and they received the market-based compensation due them.[39]

Parsons and his comrades considered the events of the summer "the First Declaration of War" on peaceable civilians, a time when the full weight of the US military was brought to bear on unarmed men and women exercising their constitutional rights of freedom of assembly. Certainly the strikes radicalized not only large numbers of ordinary Chicago laborers but also men and women who would gain fame in the annals of American labor history as leaders, including the seamstress-turned-organizer "Mother" Jones and the socialist Eugene V. Debs. Samuel Gompers, who would go on to found the American Federation of Labor, later claimed that the upheaval "was the tocsin that sounded a ringing message of hope to us all."[40]

Looking back on the events later, Lucy Parsons wrote that "it was during the great railroad strike of 1877 that I became interested in what is known as the 'Labor question.'" She became convinced of the worthlessness of the two major parties; the Republicans and Democrats, she believed, would continue to lie and prevaricate in order "to remain in power at all hazards . . . [and] build up a powerful machine; one strong enough to crush all opposition and silence all vigorous murmurs of discontent." Her future writings and speeches echoed the themes that her husband had stressed during the uprising of 1877—the call to "manliness" among white workers; the plight of wage slaves who were no better off than chattel slaves; the conviction that the historical conflict between capital and labor had evolved into all-out war.[41]

The fact that nearly three dozen workers lost their lives during the Great Strike forced Albert and Lucy Parsons to contemplate the meaning of violence in forestalling or furthering the class struggle. Must the toilers languish in their misery and wretchedness and expect to be slaughtered by agents of the capitalists? Should men refrain from protecting themselves and their families against the forces of tyranny? Did not heavily armed city police, state militia, federal troops, and private security forces pose a dire threat to workers' collective action in general? One imperative seemed certain: the laboring classes must somehow defend themselves in a way that would not only repel but also forever discourage further deadly attacks from capitalist aggressors. Albert and Lucy Parsons both stood at the ready to command a grand army of laboring foot soldiers, sluggish though the masses might prove themselves to be in anticipation of the coming revolution.

Chapter 4

Farewell to the Ballot Box

IN THE LATE 1870S, LUCY TOOK ON MULTIPLE ROLES THAT, combined, would test her physical and emotional stamina and also thrust her into the public sphere. She became a regular writer for the radical press and a labor agitator deemed by mainstream newspaper editors to be worthy of coverage, all the while contending with the new demands of motherhood and providing the family's main source of income. After five years in Chicago, she emerged out of Albert's shadow and took her place next to him in the columns of newspapers and at labor-organizing meetings. And she began to see herself as a leader in her own right, prepared to do battle against misguided comrades no less than against the lackeys of capitalism. Eventually, the couple would chart a dangerous new path together away from electoral politics and toward the idea that the laboring classes were incapable of voting—or, for that matter, reading or reasoning—their way to a better world.

After the summer of 1877, now that no newspaper would hire Albert as a typesetter, Lucy faced greater responsibilities as breadwinner. She expanded her sewing shop into "Parsons & Co., Manufacturers of Ladies' and Children's Clothing," with her husband as business partner and agent, and the two opened a "factory" at 306 Mohawk Street. While she oversaw production, he spent some of his time soliciting orders for uniforms from hotels, restaurants, and laundries, and for a few years, at least, he noted later, "[I] sold suits for a living." In fact, although Albert might have earned what little money he did make from selling suits, he was spending most of his energies promoting socialism, running for office, and speaking wherever and to whomever he could. Of his ability to reach all kinds of listeners, whether in an elegant parlor with Methodist clergy or in a crowded union hall with carpenters, one friend remarked, "No audience or circle of people ever in any way disconcerted him."[1]

In losing his livelihood as a printer, Albert had become not only "a martyr for the cause," according to his comrades, but also an object of intense interest on the part of Detective Michael Schaak, Police Chief Michael Hickey, newspaper reporters on the beat and their powerful editors, and even Allan Pinkerton, head of the notoriously lethal private security force. Pinkerton saw the massive strikes of the summer of 1877 as only an expression of workers' "greed, avarice and fiendishness," and he singled out as responsible for the bloodshed "a young American communist named Albert Parsons," a man of great "viciousness and desperation." According to Pinkerton, Parsons seemed "to possess a strange nature in every respect"—he lived openly with a "colored woman, whom he has at least called his wife," and he possessed "a devilish ingenuity in the use of words which has permitted himself to escape punishment."[2]

Parsons worked mightily to put his "devilish ingenuity in the use of words" to good use. Believing that workingmen must express their grievances forcefully at the ballot box, he regularly ran for local office between 1877 and 1880 (never successfully). He also helped to found the Chicago Council of Trade and Labor Unions, a confederation of a dozen (all-male) socialist unions. Around this time the WPUS changed its name to the Socialistic Labor Party (SLP). Parsons became assistant editor of the group's paper, The Socialist, and, in 1879, its editor. This lively weekly of news, editorials, poetry, serialized fiction, letters to the editor, and a column of quotations from "enemy capitalists" chronicled the daily struggles of ordinary Chicagoans—for example, those in the meatpacking industry, where men did jobs impervious to mechanization, including the stickers, who thrust razor-sharp knives into animals' throats; the scrapers, who rubbed their fingers raw cleaning the hair off hides; and the scalders, who toiled over cauldrons of boiling liquid. It was on the pages of this periodical that Lucy Parsons made her debut as a purveyor of biting social commentary.[3]

In April 1878, Albert lost his bid for county clerk, although he garnered 8,000 votes and the socialists managed to elect one of their own to the Common Council. Some workingmen eschewed radicalism but cast their ballots for SLP candidates as a protest vote, a statement against the Republicans and Democrats who promised so much before an election but inevitably failed to deliver on their promises afterward. The SLP adopted the slogan, "Go to the polls and slaughter them with ballots instead of bullets, O!" Before long, however, it became clear that the socialists could not ride to victory on the backs of protesters. In the late 1870s, Albert and Lucy changed course: they condemned the ballot box, and in a bid to shock the masses out of their torpor, resorted to more extreme rhetoric. Several years of frustrating engagement with the local election system convinced them that workers must use means other than the vote to advance their own interests. Turning on many of their colleagues, the Parsonses rejected partisan politicking and governmental authority and became anarchists.[4]

CHICAGO TRIBUNE REPORTERS FOUND ALBERT PARSONS FASCINATING; he made good copy. One who approached him for an interview at his office at No. 7 Clark Street "had no difficulty getting him to talk." The result was a series of high-profile newspaper stories in 1878 about the small cadre of Chicago socialists, including an article titled "They Are Arming to Resist Illegal Interference with their Meetings." As usual, Parsons was eminently quotable: "Force, as represented in strikes or armed mobs, we denominate gut revolutions, to use a strong word—a revolution of the belly." He denied that socialists aimed for the redistribution of private property, and indicated that he and his fellow workers would use violence only for defensive purposes: "We intend to carry our arms with us, and if the armed assassins and paid murderers employed by the capitalist class undertake to disperse and break up our meetings, as they did in such an outrageous manner last summer, they will meet foes worthy of their steel." To the *Tribune*, the ideas of this slight young man, with what Pinkerton called such a "strange nature," demanded a rebuttal in the form of a lengthy editorial, "What Communism Really Means."[5]

As Albert began to devote his full energies to the SLP, Lucy was making her first foray into labor organizing. In the summer of 1878 she joined with like-minded women, who were, like her, in their mid- to late twenties, to found Chicago's Working Women's Union (WWU) No. 1, a group that aimed to bring all women, but especially servants, department store clerks, and seamstresses, into the socialist fold; together these groups represented about 15 percent of all Chicago workers. Now twenty-six, Lucy was forging a public persona of her own, although the WWU was a creature of the Council of Trade and Labor Unions, and Albert often attended its meetings. In her early work with the WWU, Lucy defied convention merely by appearing in public, for by this time she was in her last trimester of pregnancy, and this was an age when pregnant women, regardless of class, were usually confined to the home.[6]

Socialists claimed to welcome all wage earners, but in fact many tradesmen considered women and children the mere pawns of cost-cutting employers. German American radicals dismissed calls for women's suffrage and other forms of gender equality, which they associated with native-born Americans and thought, in any case, to be irrelevant to the class struggle. The WWU, meanwhile, ignored the plight of black working women, although in 1878 the SLP finally admitted two "swarthy sons of Africa" into its ranks.[7]

The leaders of WWU No. 1 were an illustrious lot, and within a few years several would become prominent members of the Knights of Labor. The group's first president, Alzina Parsons Stevens, born in Maine, had worked as a youngster in a Lowell textile mill, where she lost part of a finger to a machine. Later she followed the trade of printer; as a member of NTU Local No. 16, she had probably met Albert Parsons at union meetings. Elizabeth Rodgers, a native of Ireland, was the wife of George Rodgers, an iron molder. A mother (eventually of eleven), she advanced the novel idea that housekeeping was a form of productive, albeit unwaged, labor. The Sovereigns of Industry member Elizabeth Morgan, a native of England, had as a child toiled for up to sixteen hours a day in a mill in Birmingham, England. Her husband, Tommy, had joined the Chicago socialists in 1873, four years after he and his wife had moved to the city. By 1877, the Sovereigns had disbanded, and Elizabeth turned to labor organizing alongside her husband.[8]

Lizzie May (or Mary) Hunt Swank, another WWU leader, would become a lifelong friend of both Albert and Lucy, and she was one of the very few women—perhaps the only woman—with whom Lucy developed a deep relationship. Swank did little to dispel the popular image of herself as the petite piano teacher from Ohio who, incongruously, promoted an angry, militant brand of labor radicalism. One reporter marveled, "From her meek appearance one would never guess she was a fire eater and a blood drinker, . . . a blatherkite [i.e., spouter of foolishness] orator and a writer of inflammatory slush for anarchic publications." However, if Lucy and Lizzie ever shared late-night confidences, they no doubt discovered some surprising parallels in their lives, secrets that both sought to suppress.[9]

Born in Linn County, Iowa, in 1851, Lizzie May Hunt began teaching school and giving piano lessons at the age of fifteen. Within two years she had married a Union veteran and grocery store owner, Hiram J. Swank of Bolivar, Ohio. In July 1869, the couple had a son, born around the time of Lucy's first child, Champ. They named him Raphael Ashford Swank. A second child, Gladys, followed in 1873.[10]

Within five or six years, however, Lizzie and her mother, Hannah Hunt, had both left their husbands and were living together in Chicago. Although Lizzie eventually remarried (as did her father and her first husband), it is possible that neither her first marriage nor her parents' had been formally dissolved. At some point (probably in the early 1860s), Hannah had joined a small Ohio free-love community called Berlin Heights, founded on the principle of "a woman's absolute right to self-ownership." Perched four hundred feet above Lake Erie in Erie County, Berlin Heights had thirty dwellings that housed two hundred residents who rejected conventional notions of monogamy, marriage, and divorce. Neighboring churchgoers were uncertain whether to laugh at the women in bloomers, the men by their side, up to their elbows in the washtub, or to condemn this shocking, if short-lived, den of iniquity and lust.[11]

Sometime before 1880, Lizzie moved to Chicago with Gladys and joined the household of her mother and siblings. In the mid-1870s,

Hiram had taken Raphael west with him to a Colorado mining camp, but the boy died soon thereafter. Although Lizzie told an interviewer in the early twentieth century that her first husband and her children had long since died, in fact Gladys was still alive; she married in 1892 and lived in Chicago until her death in 1924. Lizzie was never a widow; Hiram had married again.[12]

Lizzie Swank would go on to write critiques of marriage, an institution she considered the tomb of happiness. She expressed her ambivalence toward romantic love, motherhood, children (and grandchildren), and male-female relations in general, leaving the details of her own life out of her nonfiction work and referring only indirectly to her own tribulations in a novel. In losing a firstborn, abandoning the father of a first child (and, in Swank's case, two children), and building new lives for themselves in Chicago, Swank and the famously reserved Lucy Parsons had more in common than was immediately apparent.[13]

Within the space of a few years of moving to Chicago, Swank had labored as a seamstress in a factory, in a sweatshop, and at home. The grueling conditions she endured prompted her and her sister to lead one of the first strikes among Chicago needlewomen (around 1880), when they protested the owner's fraudulent pay practices. The owner changed his practices—but only after firing the two of them. Swank continued to write long exposés about the abuses young women suffered at the hands of their bosses. Making little more than $5 or $6 per week despite putting in ten-hour days, these workers were barely able to support themselves. The growth of large shops subjected ever more of them to the tyranny of the clock. In 1870, nine factories employed 491 workers, but ten years later, nineteen factories were employing 1,600. Fashionable women took advantage of desperate seamstresses who, in Swank's words, "can frill and flounce and hem and stitch in marvelous fashion, who can set stitches in a gown which would drive the most captious feminine critic wild with delight and admiration." In 1881, Swank joined the SLP.[14]

THE WORKING WOMEN'S UNION GATHERED EVERY OTHER SUNDAY afternoon in "open meetings"—more like a high-minded salon—to come up with ways to attract young women to the group. The leaders spent much time debating and discussing labor economics. At one meeting, in response to the question, "Can Women Live on their Present Wages?" an elderly servant stood to say, "The worst feature of the question was that girls working at the present wages could not keep up appearances, go about dressed neatly, and live comfortably and be honest and virtuous." Still, there were other, more heated discussions, about the eight-hour-day movement, for example, with some arguing that shorter hours would provide women with more time at home, and others claiming that such an effort would further depress wages.[15]

Official SLP policy discouraged women from taking "men's" jobs (that is, any job in which men predominated) on the theory that the work would harm mothers and their capacity to rear children, and also that the women's low wages would undercut those of men. Plank number 7 of the SLP platform called for the "prohibition of the employment of female labor in occupations detrimental to health or morality." *The Socialist* engaged in decidedly un-revolutionary rhetoric when it called for women to withdraw voluntarily from wage-earning drudgery so they could assume "their rightful position as the sovereign queen of a good man's household and at the same time ensure that 'good man' has a chance to work and the right to the fruits of his labor." Presumably, then, women could continue to labor in their own homes as seamstresses, though not in shops as tailors or machine operatives; or in other women's homes, as domestic servants and cooks, though not in hotels as waiters or chefs.[16]

Lucy knew firsthand the tribulations of those who engaged in women's work, paid or unpaid, and she was a prominent member of the WWU, at times presiding over meetings. Yet competing claims on her energies suggest that her devotion to the organization was not wholehearted, and in fact, she lacked the patience to go into individual small workplaces and convince the women there that their best interests lay with the WWU, as other members did. She was also busy helping Albert with his political campaigns each spring and fall. In all likelihood, it was she and Lizzie Swank who sewed the colorful slogan-banners that adorned every large socialist event—"Our Civilization: The Bullet and the Policeman's Club" and "No Masters, No Slaves."[17]

Lucy was also active in planning and publicizing the "monster picnics" that had become a significant part of her family life. These large gatherings struck her as more satisfying and more useful to the cause than the tedium of small-bore outreach to workers, one person at a time, often in the presence of a hostile boss and panicked coworkers. A celebration of Whitsunday (Pentecost) on June 16, 1878, showed how socialists tried, with mixed success, to harness large pleasure outings to their own purposes. At the "great demonstration," Albert interrupted the afternoon entertainment to lecture the crowd and defend socialism as a genuinely American movement. Still, his listeners consisted of only a small knot of the sympathetic, or the curious. Most young people barely paused from dancing and flirting, while others visited with friends or enjoyed the merry-go-round. He competed with popcorn vendors for the attention of the crowd.[18]

Late 1878 marked the beginning of Lucy's lifelong career as essayist, editorialist, and investigative journalist when *The Socialist* published a series of her letters to the editor. These pieces obliquely evoked her own ordeal in bondage. They also suggested her eclectic taste in reading, including poetry, fiction, and current news, and revealed a rhetorical style and substantive focus all her own, yielding florid indictments of capital and melodramatic descriptions of suffering women. In one letter, she dismissed the notion of "harmony of employer and employed (master and slave)," arguing that it was as unlikely as harmony between the "robber and the robbed." She asked, "Oh, when will ignorance be dethroned, and reason and justice reign supreme? When will the masses learn that property is his and his *only* who has produced it—earned it?" She also denounced the unjust treatment of impoverished Union veterans, out of work and out of luck, condemned to the poorhouse and scorned by a new "slavocracy"—city officials and employers: "But alas! What must be their heartfelt humiliation and burning indignation when they are denied by a bloated aristocracy, a cruel money-ocracy, the commonest right that should be accorded the yellow cur that runs the streets—the *right to live!*—and [instead] find themselves alluded to in the columns of a hireling, venal press as 'mendicants,' 'relics from the late carnage,' 'unfortunates,' etc. But then, what else can they expect from *A speculating, thievish clan, / who rob alike on sea and strand.*" The heroic liberators of the slaves were now either enslaved themselves, bound by the wage system, or cast out on the street to scrounge for scraps like animals.[19]

Unlike Albert, who wrote in grand terms about socialist theory and the shifting structure of the labor force, Lucy engaged with popular magazines. In one *Socialist* piece she responded indignantly to a recent *Scribner's* article, "Hints to Young Housekeepers," with its condescending proscriptions for the duties, clothing, and even food allowance appropriate for cooks and servants. Her days as a domestic in a slaveholder's household, and later for employers in Waco, surely informed her critique of cruel mistresses who would keep young women in "the bondage of aristocracy." In another piece, she took the same magazine to task for fawning over British lords and ladies, admonishing its readers: "Hear, ye who love republican institutions, with what a gush of sophistry the aristocracy greets the 'royalty' of old monarchy-ridden Europe, whose history has floated down to the present generation in the blood of the work-people—and the end is not yet!" No doubt she was the only contributor to *The Socialist* who had been born a slave, and one among the few who possessed only the bare bones of a formal education.[20]

On September 29, 1879, Lucy gained the attention of Chicagoans outside radical labor circles when a *Tribune* reporter offered an account of a speech she had given the day before at the socialists' weekly meeting in Uhlich's Hall. It is possible that this short notice, "The Regular Weekly Meeting of the Socialists," marked the first time any newspaper had quoted her: "Mrs. A. R. Parsons spoke at some length, and held the attention of her auditors closely to the end." She called for legislation "which should wipe out the private and exclusive ownership of the land." Impressed by her confident demeanor, the reporter noted, "She avowed herself as being very ultra in her views, and expressed the belief that, should she give expression to her extreme views, she would be annihilated," a characteristic bit of hyperbole on her part.[21]

The fact that Lucy was speaking at all indicated she was a woman possessed of considerable determination and physical strength, for just two weeks earlier, on September 14, she had given birth (at home, under the care of a neighborhood midwife) to a baby, Albert Parsons Jr. The birth certificate, which gives the child's race as "Negro," is notable because it is possibly the only public document for which Lucy provided accurate information about her background: she listed her maiden name as Carter, and her place of birth as Virginia. Perhaps she felt she could not risk falsifying an official state form. She also gave her full married name as Lucy E. Parsons, with the "E" in subsequent years standing for either Ella or Eldine.[22]

Clearly, the birth of the baby added to Lucy's responsibilities. Meanwhile, Albert traveled, solicited subscriptions to *The Socialist*, and campaigned for a new group, the Eight-Hour League. He appeared before a congressional hearing held in Chicago by a select committee of the House of Representatives in late 1879. The committee was looking into the "cause of the general depression on labor and business." It was perhaps there that he first met forty-year-old Dyer Lum, a bookbinder by trade and a Union veteran as well as secretary to the committee that sponsored the hearing. Lum, a descendant of the illustrious abolitionist Tappan family, was given to an idiosyncratic brand of individualistic socialism that could veer toward spiritualism. Beginning in 1880, he and Albert worked together to promote the eight-hour day.[23]

When the WWU collapsed in late 1880, the local press gleefully chronicled its internal contradictions and unfulfilled promise. Like other SLP-sponsored gatherings, WWU meetings attracted curious reporters bent on describing for their readers the pronouncements of those with "communistic proclivities," as well as any trouble within the group (for example, attempts to recover the modest funds from a treasurer who had allegedly embezzled them). Exposed as interlopers and asked to leave, reporters would then denounce the proceedings as "secret," implying a conspiracy afoot.[24]

At its demise, the group had little to show for its efforts. A special meeting called in November 1879 on behalf of sewing women, "who are invited to attend," and presided over by Lucy, had attracted twenty people, fifteen women and five men. Of those, only one or two were needle-women. Lucy dispensed with the planned program and suggested the group instead address the well-worn adage "Union is strength." Several months later, the group was still discussing "the feasibility of organizing a sewing girls' union," and leaders were still reading aloud essays designed to rally "the slaves of Chicago." One member delivered a paper "in which [she] recited some of the cruelties practiced upon the working women at the present day, whose condition, she claimed, to be no better than negro slavery." Invited to stand and tell their own stories, the handful of working women in attendance chose instead to remain in their seats. Mid-Sunday afternoon meetings held no appeal for the WWU's target audience. Exhausted after toiling six days a week for pennies, most young women were not inclined to listen to well-meaning ladies engaging in political debate. Later, Lizzie Swank described the challenges of organizing young women, who typically hoped to marry and quit the workforce as soon as possible, and native-born workers, who often shied away from collective action. Pride played a role in their hesitancy: "They preferred to bear their privation alone, and allow others to think they were comfortably situated, quite well off, and needed no one's sympathy," Swank wrote. She encouraged the founders of a similar group in Denver but also offered advice: "A great deal of tact and genuine sympathy is necessary to deal with all the cases you meet. 'Patronage' will not do—I have seen too much of that tried in this city."[25]

By 1880 Albert Parsons had won the deep admiration of his socialist comrades, both German- and English-speaking. In 1879, they had sent him to an SLP convention in Allegheny City, Pennsylvania, where the delegates nominated him as their candidate for president of the United States. Parsons declined the honor, pointing out that he was too young to serve (though throughout his life he would shave three years off his age, claiming a birthdate of 1848). The Illinois state legislature had created a bureau of labor statistics, a key demand of the socialists, and its research would bolster his argument about the effects of a transformed industrial economy on the state's most vulnerable workers. In January 1880, he represented Chicago at a Greenback Labor Party (GLP) conference in Washington, DC, and that June he and Lucy served as delegates to the national GLP convention held in Chicago. (The Parsonses eventually broke with the party because it refrained from condemning "those lordly pirates called capitalists.") In May, the Knights of Labor and socialist unions founded the Trade and Labor Assembly (TLA), with Albert taking the helm. The TLA was dominated by German immigrants; the SLP still lacked meaningful support among English-speaking workers.[26]

Furthermore, the SLP's principled stance against cheap labor often spilled over into a deep animus for the most exploited workers. A

Socialist piece, probably written by Albert, detailed the plight of black sharecroppers, who were forced to subsist on "stinking lard, mouldy flour, spoiled meat, and other refuse," but it also denounced the exodus of blacks out of the South and into the north as an implicit threat to wage-earning white Chicagoans. The writer argued that blacks should remain where they were and "secure to themselves the whole fruit of their toil by utilizing their political liberty in the right direction." Of course, by this time, among southern blacks "political liberty" was in short supply, as Albert well knew. Even more striking was a strident rallying cry among Chicago socialists, "The Chinese must go!" At a "monster meeting" in May 1879, members of the TLA resolved, in support of their West Coast counterparts, "that in answer to the California war-cry of 'The Chinese must go,' we echo the universal watchword of American workingmen: 'Not only the Chinese, but Chinese institutions [i.e., indentured servitude] must go.'"[27]

Despite pandering to the prejudices and fears of Chicago's white workers, the socialists saw their organizing efforts sputter and stall. The depression that began in 1873 and lasted for six years took a tremendous toll on organized labor nationwide. Membership in trade unions throughout the country declined from 300,000 to 50,000 in the course of the downturn. In Chicago, recent strikes by coopers, cigar makers, and shoemakers had failed, with the last group intimidated by employers who threatened to import Chinese workers from the western states. In August 1879, *The Socialist* ceased publication after just eleven months, depriving Albert of his modest weekly income and both him and Lucy of a platform for their ideas and observations.

It was in this context that, after three years of mounting regular campaigns for elective office, Albert began to reconsider the ballot box as a means of socialist revolution. He had come to believe that workers' long hours and pitiably low wages effectively disfranchised them; they had no time to devote to the political process, or even to cast their votes on election day. His string of failed campaigns meant that the electoral process was inherently corrupt, he thought, depriving him and other socialists of the support they clearly deserved: "My experience in the Labor party had also taught me that bribery, intimidation, duplicity, corruption, and bulldozing grew out of the conditions which made the working people poor and the idlers rich, and that consequently the ballot box could not be made an index to record the popular will until the existing debasing, impoverishing, and enslaving industrial conditions were first altered." The spring 1880 municipal and state elections further convinced him that officials had "counted him out," not even bothering to record the votes cast for him. He and Lucy began to argue that all forms of government, propped up by the façade of a democratic process, were illegitimate and inherently coercive—"that every law and every Government in the last analysis was force, and that force was despotism, an invasion of man's natural right to liberty."[28]

Stuffed ballot boxes were not the only source of frustration for the Parsonses. Many workingmen seemed resigned to hardship, caring nothing about politics. And yet certain vital constituencies, such as Irish immigrants and native-born whites, had become convinced that the voting booth was a more effective vehicle for change than the weak and fragmented unions were. They favored throwing their support behind one of the two major parties' political machines. Some socialists, seduced by partisan patronage, endorsed mainstream candidates; too many, according to Albert, "doggedly, the most of them, hugged their idols of Democracy or Republicanism, and fired their ballots against each other on election days."[29]

In the spring of 1879, Carter Harrison, a Democrat, had won the mayoralty in an upset vote that reflected his aggressive appeal to German socialists, including at least a portion of those living in the Parsonses' 15th Ward. In the prior fall's state elections, the SLP had elected a state senator and three state representatives, with their supporters casting 12,000 votes out of a total of 57,000, suggesting a substantial bloc of votes that no serious candidate could afford to ignore. Once in office, Harrison instructed the police to temper their approach to strikers and to tolerate public appearances by militia groups, such as the Lehr und Wehr and the Bohemian Sharpshooters. His successful appeal to white workers, even radicals, ushered in a period of Democratic dominance in Chicago politics that lasted until the end of the century. Predictably, however, the mayor's concessions to labor failed to impress Albert Parsons, whose own political fortunes had suffered proportionately.[30]

Parsons would run for office one last time, in November 1880; after that, the Parsonses' decision to renounce the party system altogether meant that for the rest of their lives both would refrain from voting—not only in local, state, or national elections, but, as a matter of principle, even in meetings of comrades. They remained wary of yielding decision-making to a majority and believed instead that the ideal way for any group to resolve any question was to talk its way to consensus. As editors and orators, Albert and Lucy shared the conviction that well-read, well-informed leaders must prod the masses, and not wait for at least half of them to act.

In the December 7, 1878, issue of *The Socialist*, Lucy expressed the generalized disgust for electoral politics that both of them felt with a poem titled "A Parody," modeled after Lord Byron's "Darkness" (1816). In his poem Byron had described an apocalyptic landscape, scorched and smoking: "The world was void / The populous and the powerful was a lump / Seasonless, herbless, treeless, manless, lifeless— / A lump of death—a chaos of hard clay." Lucy began her poem with Byron's words—"I had a dream, which was not all a dream"—and told of men wandering "aimless, homeless, hopeless," weeping, lying prostrate on the ground while the "the cries of their hungry children / And the prayers of their despairing wives fell like curses upon them." In this dystopia, a dream and not at all a dream, each man suffered alone, "And each sat sullenly apart, gorging himself in gloom." People were starving on this "cheerless earth," watered by the blood of tramps and the tears of children.[31]

As they calculated their support among the masses, Albert, Lucy, and other SLP members played a numbers game that alternately buoyed and deflated them. Socialists could organize picnics that attracted many thousands of men, women, and children. Trade unionists could summon 7,000 workmen to march in their parades. In 1879, a three-day July 4 celebration sponsored by the Eight-Hour League brought an estimated 50,000 men, women, and children into the streets to watch a grand procession, with onlookers appearing in every window and door along the way. *The Socialist* noted that "a new and striking feature" of the event was the presence "of a large body of *ladies*—the wives and daughters of workingmen," who also marched through the streets.

A WWU float was festooned with white and pink fabric and ribbons and banners that read, "No rights without duties, and no duties without rights," and, "When woman is admitted into the council of nations war will come to an end, for woman more than man, knows the value of life." At the head of the mile-long procession flew the Star-Spangled Banner alongside the "gory-red banner of the Socialists," according to the *Daily Inter-Ocean*. Lively spectacles such as this one over and over again renewed the Parsonses' faith that the revolution was at hand, while convincing the authorities that a general strike was just a parade away from shutting down the entire city.[32]

Yet at its height in 1879, the Chicago SLP could claim only 870 members, and the English-speaking section a mere 150. And these small numbers produced not a tightknit band of fearsome stalwarts, but a querulous group rent by personality conflicts and disagreements over ideology and strategy. Weekly meetings devolved into rancor as the English-speakers clashed with the Germans. Albert objected to Morgan's support for fusion with the Greenback Labor Party and to Morgan's argument that the eight-hour movement was a piecemeal, largely meaningless reform. Philip Van Patten had by this time moved to Detroit, the national headquarters of the SLP, but from afar he took to denouncing the increased visibility of Chicago's Lehr und Wehr, which he considered unnecessarily provocative. Van Patten also persisted in supporting electoral action in direct opposition to Parsons. The SLP English section was dissolving even as an infusion of energetic young refugees from Otto von Bismarck's Anti-Socialist Law of 1878 galvanized the Germans. Feuds took on a bitter, highly personal tone. Van Patten wrote darkly of coming expulsions of party apostates, telling George Schilling, in August 1880, "Experience has taught me that if you do not crush a sworn enemy he will assassinate you. I have had too many lessons in these difficulties to underestimate an enemy's power." Other socialists, not capitalists, were the "enemy."[33]

Points of contention among SLP members seemed infinite in their permutations, as disagreements over various issues metastasized and ultimately tore the group apart—members argued about the viability of the Knights of Labor (which some said moved too slowly to support striking workers), the distinction between economic organization and political action (trade unionism versus partisan political activity), and the divergent goals of state socialism and a cooperative commonwealth. In November 1880, Albert decided to venture once more into the political arena and run for state representative from the 6th District, despite the fact that Schilling and Morgan and others were backing a different socialist candidate named Christian Meier. Both Meier and Parsons lost, garnering 3,418 and 495 votes, respectively. In a letter to Van Patten, Elizabeth Morgan excoriated Albert Parsons for his betrayal: "We all feel like doing anything to beat that D[evil]. of Parsons. We are all death on that man and he knows it." If Albert was having second thoughts about his role in Chicago politics, this election put those doubts to rest. As a means to a workers' revolution, the ballot box was a sham.[34]

During these years the media thirsted for evidence of violence-prone schemers, finding threats to the social order in German parades and picnics, and making it nearly impossible for socialists to convey their ideas to a wider audience beyond their immediate ethnic neighborhoods. Although Albert remained a much-sought-after interviewee among reporters and their editors, he was at the same time dismissed as "The Communist Parsons," his ideas reflexively labeled "foreign"—associated with the city's Germans, Bohemians, Poles, and Scandinavians, and outside the bounds of American tradition and culture. Socialists hailed their red flag as a symbol of equality—"the blood flowing in the veins of every human body, rich or poor, white or black"—while the media pointed to the same banner and conjured the blood of innocents flowing in the streets after a radical takeover. In March 1879, immigrant workers gathered in large numbers to raise money for the Arbeiter Zeitung and celebrate the Paris Commune of 1871; the event garnered the headline "The Reds." Held at the cavernous Exposition Building, the event drew, according to the Tribune, thousands of thieves from the dives and slums of the immigrant wards and "the worst specimens of female depravity." A speech delivered by Parsons, "but a small man," received short shrift. Featured in the lengthy descriptions of the event were pointed references to various ethnic military companies composed of men who "strutted about in their uniforms with belts, cartridge boxes, bayonet scabbards and breech-loading Remingtons."[35]

The press and the police expressed trepidation over the designs of immigrant rifle companies—the Lehr und Wehr, in particular. Founded in Chicago in 1875, the group of volunteers grew out of the conviction of recent immigrants that defense of the republic—the new fatherland, the United States—necessitated an armed citizenry. Chicago had spawned a host of ethnic military companies during the Civil War, so this development was not entirely alien. The Lehr und Wehr carried new Springfield and Remington rifles, and its members drilled every week in parades followed by music and drinking—more merry-making than menacing. In 1878, however, the cautious Van Patten was worried about a growing public perception that the group was drilling for revolution and not for pure enjoyment; he urged its members "to avoid any military display and instead ridicule the authorities by appearing in a manner as innocent as that of a religious procession," advice the members rejected. Some of these militias dispensed with weapons altogether and drilled exclusively in the spirit of camaraderie. John F. Waldo, a printer who belonged to a group of native-born radicals called the International Rifles, described it as "the International Rifles without the rifles." In 1879, the state legislature moved to outlaw such militias altogether.[36]

At the end of 1880, the Parsonses faced a troubling reality. Since arriving in Chicago, Albert had joined Typographical Union No. 16, lectured huge crowds of restless strikers, and helped cobble together the Trade and Labor Assembly. Yet he had received no support from his No. 16 comrades during that fateful week in July 1877. He was a much-sought-after speaker at rallies and picnics, and had received endorsements from the powerful *Arbeiter Zeitung*, such as: "A. R. Parsons has suffered hunger and want for his convictions and is an independent character, who will not be taken in tow by other persons to be guided to other goals." Yet he consistently lost his election campaigns in the 15th Ward, presumably a hotbed of socialist fellow-feeling. Chicago's laboring classes remained fragmented, with employers and even union leaders pitting native-born against foreign-born, skilled against unskilled, women and children against men, wage-earners against "tramps." For her part, Lucy had helped to launch the Working Women's Union, with high ideals, only to see it languish, thwarted by the indifference of the women who could most benefit from its message.[37]

Even the socialists' modest reformist platform seemed utopian. At an August 30, 1880, meeting (dubbed the "Chicago Commune" by the *Daily Inter-Ocean*), the delegates nominated Albert as their candidate for Congress (he declined to run) and also put forth a platform that must have struck newspaper readers as so much wishful thinking— maximum-hour labor legislation, "the inspection of food, to the end that all impurities therein might be detected," the creation of a national bureau of labor statistics, the abolition of child labor in factories, compulsory schooling for all children under the age of fourteen, and redistricting of political wards on the basis of population growth. These demands, which within a generation would gain a favorable hearing from Progressive reformers and politicians, remained associated in Gilded Age Chicago with communists, the "tumultuous mob."[38]

Still, at the end of the decade, the depression had begun to lift, and for a few years, at least, workers saw reason to hope that the upturn would bring a more generous hourly wage, or the chance for them to open their own small shops. Albert continued to preach to the socialist choir via the *Arbeiter Zeitung*, using an urgent tone: "Who would not employ force, if all peaceable ways have failed to get one's right? It is only power, which sustains the throne of the despot. Only power can maintain the existing systems and forms of Government.... Everybody should join the glorified red flag of liberty and equality as a lifelong fighter and make a determined stand for the rights of humanity." Taking stock of their frustrated ambitions, their electoral and organizing disappointments, fueled by what they believed were stolen elections, and the dismal outlook for socialist reform, the Parsonses now shifted course to address more directly what they considered the grand hoax of the American voting system.[39]

EVEN AS THE PARSONSES BEGAN TO CULTIVATE A MORE RADICAL outlook, they were settling into their immigrant neighborhood. Striding through her Larrabee Street neighborhood on the way to her workshop, Lucy Parsons cut a striking figure—tall, with an erect carriage, and with brown skin and black hair, she seemed out of place in a neighborhood that was overwhelmingly German, with a few Swiss, Austrian, Swedish, Hungarian, and Irish families. Almost all of the native-born residents of the North Side were children, the offspring of immigrant machinists, house painters, carpenters, tinsmiths, white washers, tailors, bookkeepers, firemen, and wagon makers. By the early 1880s, Lucy and Albert had probably achieved a high level of fluency in the German language, not only to communicate with core socialist activists, but also to survive in a largely self-contained community where most of the storekeepers hailed from German-speaking states. They no doubt gathered regularly with their comrades in one of the nearby *Biergarten*, family-friendly eating and meeting places.[40]

Larrabee Street consisted mostly of two-story frame tenements, two or three families in each dwelling, interspersed with saloons, grocers, and workshops. The Parsonses' neighborhood was one of solid, working-class, two-parent families, with almost all of the wives keeping house and a few taking in laundry or sewing. Residents could hardly keep from whispering about the peculiar couple—a slight, well-dressed white man and his attractive wife of indeterminate origin—who had settled among them. Later, according to an 1887 article in *Knights of Labor*, a weekly publication put out by the organization, a neighbor recalled them as "a very queer-looking couple." They lived on the second floor of a dwelling with a sign that read "Mrs. A. R. Parsons, fashionable dressmaking," though it was clear that more than sewing transpired there. After 9 in the evening men and women would arrive and take their places on the wooden benches at the back of the neat, well-furnished apartment; Lucy told her curious neighbors that Albert was teaching English to immigrants. Still, the article said, "the demeanor of the lady was so well-bred and dignified that she commanded the respect of all with whom she came into contact, so that gradually even the horrified gossips became used to the queerly matched pair and ceased to pay any particular attention to their actions."[41]

The neighbor remembered Lucy as "a thorough lady in her manners and . . . much respected despite her dark complexion," and the couple "seemed devotedly attached to each other." In the process of moving from Texas to Chicago, Albert and Lucy had forged a relationship of mutual dependence and affection. Lizzie Swank, who saw them frequently and knew them both as well as anyone did, described it as "a long period of uninterrupted and happy companionship."[42]

The family expanded on April 20, 1881, with the birth of Lulu Eda, perhaps named for a daughter of Albert's brother William H. Parsons and his wife, Louisa, a child who died in 1868 at the age of six. Lulu Parsons was identified as "Niger" on her birth certificate, which gave her father's occupation as "clothier." Lucy listed Virginia as her place of birth, but reported her full maiden name as Lucy Ella Hull (partly echoing the name on her marriage license, Ella Hall). By this time, she was the mother of two children under the age of two, and questions remain about how she and Albert divided household tasks and child rearing. Did they leave their son and daughter in the care of one of their employees during the frequent nights they stayed out late at political meetings, or did they take the children with them? Did Lucy have to adapt her southern-style cooking to ingredients found in German-owned grocers? Could she count on any help lugging water from a nearby well or scrubbing floors and clothes? Did she, with her love of fine clothes, ever peruse the collection of French kid gloves at Marshall Field's downtown department store? Did she miss her mother or mourn the infant Champ whom she had buried in Waco? Certainly, her persistent habit of reporting different maiden names and middle names for herself suggests that she wanted to obliterate any traces that would allow Chicagoans of any stripe to trace her back to Dr. T. J. Taliaferro and his other slaves.[43]

In 1881, Lucy's intensified duties as mother and breadwinner did not prevent her from joining Knights of Labor Local Assembly 1789. Founded in September, the local was in fact a reconfigured Working Women's Union, all female and "mixed"—that is, composed of workers in a variety of occupations as well as middle-class activists and intellectuals. However, she objected to Local 1789's "mixed" nature and its emphasis on political action; she thought it a poor vehicle to further working-class solidarity. Before long, 1789 would founder on the same issues that had hindered the WWU—the predominance of middle-class reformers and the difficulty of organizing young sewing women.[44]

Around this time, Albert and Lucy worked to bring more members into the TLA. They planned periodic outings, each of which would begin with a procession wending its way through the city. The "grand demonstration" of Sunday, August 21, 1881, culminated in a picnic at Ogden's Grove on the North Side. It drew an estimated 10,000 workingmen and their families and featured twenty unions affiliated with the TLA, including typographers, blacksmiths, seamen, tin and iron sheet workers, cigar makers, bricklayers and stone masons, plasterers, iron molders, and silver gilders. At the same time, the size of these events masked the organizational weaknesses of socialist unions. The Parsonses would remain disappointed by the large socialist-sponsored outdoor gatherings that yielded so few new converts to the cause.[45]

In early 1881, Philip Van Patten anticipated the impending breakup of the Socialistic Labor Party. He knew that an impatient group of SLP members, whom he labeled "anarchists" (they called themselves the "Socialist Revolutionary Club"), had decided to dispense with the idea that politics was the surest course of action to achieve a class revolution. Van Patten defended state socialism, maintaining that workers must invest the state with the protection of rights and the distribution of property. He charged that anarchists, in denying *all* governmental authority, also denied the authority of the people. Anarchists provided no mechanism, no structure, for social change, insisting on chaos as a matter of principle: "A single discontented, ignorant, spiteful or dyspeptic member could block all business!" Lobbing the harshest charge of all, he argued that the anarchist, in his extreme individualism, resembled no one so much as "the grasping capitalist" who defended "the barbarous plundering of one another that makes men all claws and stomach, like the crab or the devil fish."[46]

In a significant departure from their previous brand of activism, Albert and Lucy Parsons eagerly accepted the label "anarchist"; it possessed a shock value that they craved. Yet they were hardly doctrinaire, and anarchism, like other political philosophies, encompassed a wide range of views. Later, Albert would write, "We are called by some Communists, or Socialists, or Anarchists. We accept all three of the terms." For the time being, at least, the distinctions among these three ideologies mattered little to them (though soon enough those distinctions would incite self-destructive internecine warfare among radicals). Albert defined anarchism as "the elimination of all authority in social affairs; it is the denial of the right of domination of one man over another. It is the diffusion of rights, of power, of duties, equally and freely among all the people." He and Lucy could simultaneously champion trade unions as the seeds of a new order and the Knights of Labor, the Eight-Hour League, the WWU, and anarchism. Others argued that these various associations all operated from wildly divergent assumptions, and offered contradictory strategies for economic transformation. To the Parsonses, though, anarchism primarily represented a renunciation of mainstream political parties; in their view, no true anarchist would ever cast a ballot for any kind of candidate.[47]

Founded in London in 1881, the anarchist International Working People's Association (IWPA)—at times called the "Black International"—inspired Albert Parsons and the upholsterer August Spies to form a Chicago chapter of the group two years later. The association took as its guiding principle an idea developed by the German anarchist Johann Most—"propaganda by deed" (*attentat*), a burst of violence that would awaken the masses from their slumber and impel them to overthrow their masters. Most proposed that that jolt might conveniently come in the form of dynamite; the powder was easy enough to make, to carry, and to conceal, and it leveled the field of battle between employers and employees, police and street demonstrators. He said the mere mention of it should be enough to instill fear in the cold hearts of capitalists.[48]

By late 1883 the IWPA claimed 2,000 members in the United States, with a few hundred in Chicago divided into English, German, and French sections. Albert and Lucy Parsons joined the English (or American) group, consisting at first of just five other people (a number that would grow to ninety-five in early 1885). For the time being, at least, they cared little about the small numbers, believing that a handful of devoted members could serve as *avant couriers*, advance messengers, for the cause. Nationwide, Easterners dominated the IWPA, and in Chicago, German immigrant craftsmen predominated. Together the couple attended Sunday "mass meetings" of the IWPA, and they hosted discussions each Wednesday night in their apartment.[49]

For the Parsonses, the turn toward anarchism came at the expense of some old friendships (with Morgan and Schilling, for example) as they embraced a new circle of activists. Lizzie Swank remained a loyal friend, as did her soon-to-be husband William Holmes, an English-born teacher who lived in Geneva, Illinois, west of Chicago. August Spies became the editor of the *Arbeiter Zeitung* in 1884 and turned it into an anarchist publication. Spies and Albert Parsons would soon control, respectively, the city's German and English-language anarchist press. Active in the English-speaking section of the IWPA was Samuel Fielden, a self-employed stonecutter and teamster. Born in England, he had started work as an eight-year-old in the cotton mills, which he termed the dwelling place of the devil, "his satanic majesty"; he arrived in Chicago in 1869 and became an itinerant Methodist minister and a lifelong champion of the working poor.[50]

In March 1883, the Parsonses met Johann Most himself when he visited Chicago for the first time. (The conversation was probably in German; Most was uncomfortable with English in its written or spoken form.) By now the thirty-seven-year-old writer and newspaper editor had achieved international notoriety; he had been in and out of jail in the course of his exile from Germany, at first living in France, and then moving from France to England and, in 1882, from England to the United States. He was lucky to have escaped with his life after calling for workers to massacre capitalists and assassinate heads of state throughout Europe. A medical procedure in his youth had left him with a misshapen jaw, and some saw in his physical disfigurement a reflection of his own disregard for human life.[51]

Most expressed contempt for all kinds of labor reform and all kinds of labor unions. Substantive differences separated him from the Parsonses, who, together with Spies, believed that unions and Knights assemblies were "the embryonic groups" of an ideal cooperative society. George Schilling wrote that he considered Most "so exceedingly authoritarian that I have never regarded him as a consistent opponent of the state." The Parsonses appropriated Most's heightened rhetoric, which was shocking in the extreme even to socialists, but neither Albert nor Lucy showed much concern for the finer points of the German theorist's ideology.[52]

The IWPA's defining manifesto, approved at a convention in Pittsburgh in October 1883, contained boilerplate SLP rhetoric and a call for "equal rights for all, without distinction to sex or race." Written by Parsons and Most, among others, the document began with wording from the Declaration of Independence but went on to quote Thomas Jefferson's justification for armed resistance to tyranny. And the rhetoric was raw: The dispossessed masses owed their fate to "a system that is unjust, insane, and murderous." The IWPA called for a new American revolution: "By force our ancestors liberated themselves from political oppression, by force their children will have to liberate themselves from economic bondage. 'It is therefore your right, it is your duty,' says Jefferson, 'to arm!'" Albert began writing for a radical San Francisco paper, *Truth*, which was running articles with headlines such as "Dynamite: Plain Directions for Making It," and "Dynamite Will Be Used in America."[53]

The Parsonses were convinced that anarchy emerged from conglomerates that strived for efficiency—anarchy was, then, the "inevitable end of the present drift and tendency of things," Albert wrote. Ultimately, by eliminating workers, these businesses slowly destroyed themselves, for the jobless could no longer buy goods. The couple saw anarchy as a "science" because current trends could predict outcomes, and those trends could be proven by marshaling statistics related to output, unemployment, and company profits. (Albert titled a major 1887 essay *Anarchism: Its Philosophy and Scientific Basis*). The solution to the "labor question," flowing from easily verifiable facts, was nothing more or less than "a scientific subject."[54]

Nevertheless, the dearth of radical literature in English would continue to frustrate members of the American group. The IWPA sponsored a library, but its holdings were almost exclusively in German. Not surprisingly, then, the Parsonses, Lizzie Swank, and William Holmes took advantage of a new English-language paper published in Denver, *The Labor Enquirer*, which provided a suitable outlet for their essays, letters, and dispatches from Chicago. Joseph R. Buchanan, its socialist editor, supported the Knights of Labor, but remained critical of its leader, Terence V. Powderly, whom Buchanan considered too accommodationist. The *Enquirer* included Lucy's denunciations of venal employers and retrograde two-party politics. Swank wrote exposés detailing the plight of starving needlewomen. Holmes defended the poor from charges that their "extravagance was the only thing preventing them from climbing out of the desperate straits they found themselves in." Albert Parsons wrote a summary of the proceedings of the first Illinois State Labor Convention and criticized the delegates' faith in useless reforms and the political system (the two parties, he said, were each only faintly veiled "agents of private capital").[55]

Meanwhile, Lucy felt pressed to make money. In 1884, the Parsons family was living on the thin edge of distress, with Albert contributing only sporadically to the household income. The demand for clothing in Chicago was increasing exponentially, but so, too, were the numbers of garment workers—25,000 women and 5,000 men were now employed in the industry, which included wholesale clothing houses, some 500 small shops and factories, and custom dressmakers and tailors. A family of four needed $60 a month just to make ends meet, leaving nothing for small pleasures or modest savings accounts. And with two children to care for, Lucy had her hands full.[56]

The year 1884 was notable for a series of failed strikes nationwide, and another recession had followed the four-year economic recovery beginning in 1879. In April, Albert took the podium at Uhlich's Hall and denounced the suppression of a recent strike in Cincinnati. Last on the program was "Mrs. A. R. Parsons," who, according to the *Tribune*, "spoke in the same spirit as those who had preceded her," but also maintained that the lesson from Cincinnati was "that the women should take an interest in the wage-workers' cause." The following month, Albert and Johann Most shared the stage at Turner Hall, where in "blood and thunder harangues" they applauded the collapse of several Wall Street firms.[57]

In June 1884, Albert withdrew from the TLA, taking twelve unions with him, because he felt the parent group lacked revolutionary fervor. He formed a new federation—the Chicago Central Labor Union (CLU), which consisted of an estimated 12,000 members, rivaling the TLA—and began to embark on lengthy "agitation trips" throughout the Midwest to proselytize for the IWPA. His oratorical abilities had only increased over the years; he could speak for two to three hours

and for at least a portion of that time hold the attention of the unini-
tiated as well as true believers. Drawing from history, poetry, political
theory, and the day's headlines, he impressed listeners as erudite yet
genial, down-to-earth and approachable. On the afternoon of July 4,
1884, he was standing before a crowd (of 3,000, he later claimed) in Ottawa, Kansas, declaring that "to be forewarned was to be forearmed,"
and that the workers "must be prepared to meet force with force."[58]

Within a few months he would begin to edit his own newspaper,
a venture launched with contributions from respectful listeners like
those in Ottawa. The only English-language IWPA periodical in Chicago, *The Alarm* would give both Albert and Lucy a broad forum for
their ideas as they rejected traditional politics and followed a new, more
radical path compared to that of even the socialists. Already widely appreciated for his fiery speeches, Albert would take his place among anarchist leaders admired for their journalistic flair; and Lucy, his writing
partner and an increasingly public presence in her own right, would
share equal responsibility for this new publication and the catastrophic
whirlwind it wrought.

❦ Chapter 5 ❧

A False *Alarm?*

B Y THE MID-1880S, ALBERT AND LUCY PARSONS HAD DEVELOPED
mutually advantageous relationships, not only with several reporters for major Chicago newspapers, but also, remarkably, with the
plainclothes policemen and private security agents who had become
a ubiquitous presence at International Working People's Association
gatherings. Reporters covered the Parsonses assiduously, providing detailed accounts of their speeches as well as exclusive interviews with
them. An old newspaper hand himself, Albert understood that editors
had a voracious appetite for sensational copy. For her part, Lucy proved
herself a rhetorical provocateur of the first order, a distinction that
would garner her a rapt audience of friends and foes alike. Together
they hoped to use the mainstream press as the medium through which
they spread a startling new message about the power of dynamite far
beyond the tiny subscriber base of *The Alarm*. In this effort, they succeeded spectacularly—and disastrously.[1]

Albert went out of his way to cultivate the police department's undercover detectives, who routinely posed as ordinary workers, hoping
to learn more about the presumed anarchist threat. Members of the
small IWPA American Group had no trouble identifying poseurs in
their midst. The interlopers, believing they had actually insinuated

themselves into anarchist circles, would leave a meeting and return to their precinct captains with breathless tales of conspiracies and dynamite plots. At one gathering, a man hired by what the anarchists called the "Pinkerton army" listened raptly as Albert proclaimed (presumably for the agent's benefit), "I say to you, rise one and all and let us exterminate them all; woe to the police or militia who they send against us." Albert pretended to take these poorly disguised spies into his confidence, using them as message-bearers to the city's establishment, all in an effort to make the IWPA seem more powerful and menacing than it was, or ever could be.[2]

These carefully calibrated, symbiotic relationships among anarchists, reporters, and police officers were on full display during the dedication of Chicago's magnificent new Board of Trade building on April 28, 1885. Built at a cost of $2 million, the LaSalle Street structure took the form of a pavilion backed by a ten-story building that housed 110 offices. To celebrate the opening, the building was "bathed in a sea of electric light," welcoming 5,000 delegates representing city exchanges from all over the country. The glittering affair included speeches delivered by dignitaries and an elaborate repast that cost an extravagant $20 per person.[3]

The IWPA organized a protest demonstration that evening at nearby Market Square, one that revealed their strategy of creating a public spectacle while also manipulating journalists and undercover men. Standing on a salt barrel, Albert took the lead in exhorting the crowd (which, according to a reporter, included 1,000 men and 6 women), and declared, "A new board of thieves is to be opened to-night. It is time this thing is stopped. These robbers fatten off our toil." He advised his listeners to "buy a Colt's navy revolver, a Winchester rifle, and ten pounds of dynamite, and learn how to make and use dynamite."[4]

After the speeches, the crowd formed a procession, twelve people abreast. At the front was Oscar Neebe, who was American-born but of German descent, the co-owner of a yeast company and office manager for the *Arbeiter Zeitung*. He was flanked by Lucy Parsons, who carried a red flag, and Lizzie Swank, carrying a black one. Heading toward the Board of Trade, the organizers led the marchers in singing "La Marseillaise" and shouting "Vive la Commune!" As the crowd neared the new building, they cried, "Blow it up with dynamite." Meanwhile, 600 officers formed an impenetrable cordon around what the anarchists called "the robbers' roost." Diverted from their destination, the marchers returned to Market Square. News reports contrasted the elegance of the proceedings inside with the ruckus outside, complaining of how the motley crowd had been "permitted to make the night hideous by their cries on some of the downtown thoroughfares." The *Chicago Tribune* fumed that laborers in the building trades had benefited from work on the construction of the building, and decried the ungrateful demonstrators of this "unreasoning, ignorant, inconsistent association."[5]

However, the end to the procession was not the end of the story. The IWPA entourage, which included Albert and Lucy Parsons, August Spies, Samuel Fielden, Michael Schwab (a mild-mannered, bespectacled, German-born bookbinder), Lizzie Swank, and William Holmes, retreated to the offices of *The Alarm* and *Arbeiter Zeitung* (*AZ*) in Greif's Hall at 107 Fifth Avenue. The small group represented the core of the two papers: Schwab was business manager of the *AZ*, and Lucy Parsons, Swank, and Holmes were regular contributors to *The Alarm*, which Albert, of course, owned. Fielden was treasurer of the American Group of the IWPA. There, on the second floor in the *AZ* office, Albert leaned out a window and continued his speechifying, declaring that "it was only a matter of time before the working men would have to assert their rights by dynamite and pistol." He urged the poor to raid stores such as Marshall Field's for clothing and other necessities.[6]

Soon after Albert finished speaking, Marshall H. Williamson, a reporter for the *Chicago Daily News*, appeared in the office and asked him about the evening's events. According to Williamson, Parsons confided that he and his comrades had planned to blow up the trade building with dynamite, but were surprised by the size of the police presence, and so postponed their attack for another day. Parsons showed the reporter a dynamite cartridge containing some reddish powder, and also a fifteen- to twenty-foot-long coil that looked like a fuse. Parsons and Spies proceeded to explode a fulminating cap in Williamson's presence—"to show me it would go off, I presume," he said later—and claimed that they had stockpiled dynamite, rifles, and revolvers. The reporter added, "Their manner of warfare would be to throw their bombs from the house tops and tops of stores, and in that way they could annihilate any force of militia that could be brought against them without any harm to themselves whatsoever."[7]

As Williamson was leaving the building, he ran into two men he recognized as undercover police officers, Thomas L. Treharn and Jeremiah Sullivan, mingling with the crowd. Williamson suggested the two go up to the second-floor office and talk to Parsons. Securing an audience with Spies and Parsons, Treharn and Sullivan presented themselves as comrades inspired by the night's dramatic events. They, too, were shown the cartridge with what looked to be a fuse, and concluded it was a stick of dynamite. They quizzed Parsons about his failure to carry through with the scheme that night, but he shrugged off the question, saying, "Oh, the blood hounds were there to prevent as usual." He then boasted that he was in possession of devices that "could knock a hundred of them [police] down like tenpins," and that he had enough fuse that a man a block away could detonate a charge sufficient to destroy the targeted building. Sullivan later acknowledged that Fielden might have known that he was a policeman; and if Fielden knew, then the rest of the IWPA did as well. But the highly scripted performance that unfolded that night in the *AZ* offices satisfied all participants and illustrated a systemic dynamic of mutual back-scratching—Parsons and Spies got a ready audience of would-be infiltrators who served as a conduit to the city's press and police, furthering the strategy of scaring and shocking these groups; and the reporter and undercover cops got a private showing of the anarchists' incendiary devices and a helpful lecture about how such devices would someday be used.[8]

After the failed strikes of 1884, the Parsonses and their fellow anarchists escalated their rhetoric, threatening death to the capitalists by dynamite or other means, at the same time the *Alarm* and *AZ* editors were periodically taking pains to show off suspicious-looking objects they claimed were bombs. Together these efforts formed a well-orchestrated attempt by the IWPA to create a dark narrative of a small but bold band of anarchists who were poised to bring the establishment to its knees. Presumably, in the face of this imminent threat, businessmen, mainstream politicians, and newspaper editors would prove more responsive to the demands of workers, and the proponents of dynamite would not need to engage in violent deeds after all. This narrative of potential violence in fact produced just the opposite result: the determination among elites to extinguish the ideas—and if need be, the lives— of the would-be dynamiters.

ALBERT PARSONS PUBLISHED THE FIRST ISSUE OF *THE ALARM* ON October 4, 1884. It was one of seven anarchist periodicals in Chicago, but the only one in English. He chose the title from a quotation by the philosopher Edmund Burke: "I love clamor when there is an abuse. The alarm disturbs the slumber of the inmates, but it awakens them to the dangers that threaten." In the pages of *The Alarm*, and on tours throughout the Midwest, Parsons preached an increasingly militant form of anarchism, promoting "force—physical force, the only argument that tyrants ever could or would listen to." He predicted that "a storm is brewing which will break ere long and destroy forever the right of man to govern, exploit, and enslave his fellow-man." Workers must "agitate, organize, revolt!" And also subscribe to *The Alarm*.[9]

The paper's first year and a half of publication coincided with the depression-driven Great Upheaval, a nationwide ferment that swelled the ranks of organized labor. The Knights of Labor grew exponentially, adding 1,000 members a week in 1885 and claiming an estimated 700,000 by mid-1886. In boomtown Chicago, both the Trade and Labor Assembly and the Central Labor Union welcomed new constituent unions. Anarchists interpreted these developments as a sign that the masses, now finally stirring from their slumber, more than ever required the guiding hand of activist-ideologues. Although Parsons eventually turned on his own union, Typographical Union No. 16, he remained deeply invested in the CLU as well as the Knights of Labor. In October 1885, a national umbrella group called the Federation of Organized Trade and Labor Unions met in Chicago and announced the opening of a dramatic, months-long campaign for the eight-hour day, which would end with a massive demonstration the following May. The anarchist IWPA belatedly sought to take the lead in this effort, even though some of its members perceived it as a misguided sop to reformers.[10]

The Parsonses took stock of the Great Upheaval, and within their household, serving up clamor was hardly Albert's exclusive province.

On the first page of the first issue of *The Alarm* appeared "To Tramps, the Unemployed, the Disinherited, and Miserable," an essay written by Lucy. Before long, the "Tramps" essay would become a staple of anarchist propaganda, distributed at "indignation meetings" near and far, along with other tracts, such as Victor Hugo's "Message to the Rich and Poor." Produced as a broadside for 12 cents per 100 copies, and resold at 5 cents apiece, "Tramps" spoke directly to the estimated 35,000 unemployed men in Chicago, casualties of a downturn that was overwhelming private charities and adding daily to the number of the homeless. The 1,000-word-long piece helped solidify Lucy's notoriety, but more tellingly, its publication also set her and Albert on a path to a fatal reckoning. If "Tramps," like *The Alarm*, was a call to arms among the workers, it was also a cause for deep alarm among the ranks of Chicago's powerful.[11]

In "Tramps," Lucy Parsons addressed the legions of famished men trudging through the streets of windswept Chicago. The city fathers blamed them for bringing misfortune on themselves, for wasting their wages on drink, and for ignoring basic principles of "economy" in their own homes. In fact, she wrote, these men had toiled for up to sixteen hours a day, but could eke out only the meanest existence: "With all your squeezing, pinching, and economizing, you never were enabled to keep but a few days ahead of the wolves of want." Meanwhile, shop and factory owners lived luxurious lives in "voluptuous homes," and carelessly invoked the mantra "overproduction" as a reason for firing a faithful employee. Long harnessed to "an iron horse," the worker was now "turned upon the highway a tramp, with hunger in your stomach and rags upon your back." Parsons urged these men to ignore the hypocritical capitalist who offered them only the salve of religious faith—the idea that the poor would receive their reward in heaven. And she dismissed the fear that presenting "a petition in too emphatic a manner, will mean certain death at the hands of the oppressor. So hearken not to them, but list!"[12]

Parsons aimed to take her audience from despair to a triumph that was at once intimate, grand, and existential. She reminded her readers of the "bitter tears and heart-pangs of your loving wife and helpless children." Tramps must resist the urge to throw themselves "into the cold

embrace" of Lake Michigan. Instead, they should hasten to the homes
of the rich, and "awaken them from their wanton sport at your expense!
Send forth your petition and let them read it by the red glare of destruction." To strike against the ruling class required neither planning
nor collective action: "You need no organization. . . . In fact, an organization would be a detriment to you; but each of you tramps who read
these lines, avail yourselves of these little methods of warfare which Science has placed in the hands of the poor man, and you will become a
power in this or any other land." To wit, *"Learn the use of explosives!"*[13]

"Tramps" folds late nineteenth-century Victorian literary devices
into a gothic horror story of betrayal and revenge. The language is florid.
The starving wife and child were stock figures of contemporary sentimental fiction; but here, in contrast to a conventional story of a desperate father redoubling his search for work, he commits premeditated
murder by lobbing a bomb or stick of dynamite through the window
of a Prairie-district mansion. Parsons observed that machines ("iron
horses") were allowing bosses to produce more and pay their workers
less, a persistent theme for IWPA speakers and writers in the mid-
1880s. By this time the Chicago chapter of the association had set its
sights on unskilled laborers—not just skilled craftsmen—as incipient
"revolutionists." Moreover, the idea of the transformative power of dynamite, a product of Science with a capital S, would become a hallmark
of subsequent issues of *The Alarm*. At the same time, the tramp in this
piece is remarkable for his autonomy. Both Lucy and Albert remained
committed to labor unions as the building blocks of a cooperative commonwealth; but here, in "Tramps," a single, aggrieved victim acts on
his own to bring justice to an immoral world. In fact, neither of the
Parsonses was particularly dogmatic when appealing to the masses, yet
both resorted increasingly to explicit threats in their speeches and writings. As a so-called bloodthirsty woman—and, furthermore, a woman
of color of indeterminate origin—Lucy seized the attention of Chicagoans of all stripes and played the press well.[14]

The publication of "Tramps" marked her more robust participation in labor agitation generally. When speaking to crowds or giving
interviews to alternately intrigued and horrified reporters, Parsons resisted moderating her language, to the point that she seemed to aspire

to sheer outrageousness. At the same time, her distinctive prose style set her apart from other self-proclaimed anarchists of the time; in fact, she brought to anarchist propaganda a literary sensibility uncommon among writers for *The Alarm* and *Arbeiter Zeitung*, its German counterpart.

Indeed, this former slave had grown into a confident writer who delighted in her own voice. In April 1885, she followed her "Tramps" sensation with an article titled "Dynamite" in the Denver-based *Labor Enquirer*. She rejected the idea that anarchists were only "a lot of thirsty blood-drinkers, who go up and down this broad earth, howling themselves for gore." Instead, she claimed, they aimed to install a whole new "free society" that flowed from "the good judgment of the people" and not the dictates of government. The "dear stuff (dynamite)," which put power in the hands of the people and fear in the hearts of the bosses, was critical to this effort: "Thus the 'terror' becomes a great educator and agitator." The emerging "dynamite era" enacted a new principle: "The more oppressors dead, and the fewer alive, the freer will be the world."[15]

In an *Alarm* article from the summer of 1885, titled "Our Civilization: Is It Worth Saving?," Parsons answered her own titular question in the negative. Alluding to recent inventions such as the telegraph, the telescope, and electricity, she noted, "We have stolen the lightning from the gods and made it an obedient servant to the will of man; have pierced the clouds and read the starry page of time." Although the dizzying heights of Chicago's skyscrapers proclaimed the city's progress, in their shadows lived the "the young girl offering her virtue for a few paltry dollars" as well as other miserable, degraded toilers. Why was labor not credited for its part in building wealth? "Is it not that a few idlers may rot in luxury and ease—said few having dignified themselves as 'upper classes'?" Echoing "Tramps," she ended with a rhetorical flourish that was part challenge, part recrimination, demanding that the downtrodden workingman boldly enter "into the arena with those who declare that 'Not to be a slave is to dare and DO.'"[16]

In another piece, "The Factory Child," Parsons offered a deeply felt, poetic meditation on the ravages of capitalism as visited upon its youngest victims. She contrasted the carefree life of the privileged boy or girl, whose "giddy laughter and wine-bibed mirth rings out within soft silken-hung walls," with the plight of the "little factory serf," his (or her) eyelids "flooded with hot, burning tears," and body wracked by "twitching nerves and aching limbs [that] refuse to be calmed after the long strain of the day's drudging." And yet in their torment these little ones go unnoticed: "Oh! Factory child, what sage has sung thy song correct?" Someday, "brave hearts and strong arms will annihilate the hell-born system which binds you down to drudgery and death." Yet this new day depended upon men of courage: "Be men! Dare and *do!*"[17]

In "A Christmas Story," published in December 1885, she drew upon a popular late nineteenth-century form of social criticism that provided an outsider's perspective on a corrupt society rotting from within. Foreigners from a distant, isolated, and seemingly backward isle marvel at the wonders of the modern American city with its material abundance, including "marble halls where banquet boards were spread and lovely women came and went, fairy-like, all bespangled with precious jewels and gems of greatest worth" (no doubt a nod to the Board of Trade opening the April before). A sanctimonious preacher of the gospel soothes his wealthy listeners, invoking the goodness of the meek and lowly Jesus while ignoring the "pale-faced, care-worn and hard-worked people who seemed to have no time nor desire to stop and enjoy the beautiful displays in the show windows as the well-dressed ones whom we had during the day seen doing so." Ultimately, the outsider concludes that the government of such a place "is simply organized fraud and oppression"; it is the residents of this so-called advanced society (and not his own) who are the "barbarians" in need of lessons in how to live a decent life.[18]

In "Communistic Monopoly" from March 1886, Parsons provided a critique of state socialism in the form of a dream transporting the writer to a land of "Communist anarchy," where associations of people—"monopolies"—make decisions for everyone else. Shopping for shoes and dresses, the bewildered dreamer finds only limited styles because the huge distribution departments worship at the false idol of efficiency, and produce goods en masse regardless of individual consumers' tastes. As portrayed here, communism allows for social groupings of all kinds, including religious ones, and so permits Christians to sustain "the church with all its nunneries, monasteries and theological factories where men and women were trained to become the teachers of superstition and stupidity." Such diverse, inherently tyrannical foundational institutions would inevitably lead to conflict, according to Parsons, in contrast to "an individualistic state of society," which would give free rein to people's idiosyncratic needs and desires.[19]

As a literary stylist, Parsons was noteworthy among the writers for anarchist periodicals. Several common elements run throughout her writing regardless of the topic of the piece or its genre—news reportage, analysis, or fiction. Beginning in the 1870s, she showed a particular interest in imaginative renderings of political ideas as well as in contemporary gender relations and in violent rhetoric intended to startle readers regardless of political persuasion.

Compared to the dry and predictable articles offered up by other writers (including the statistics-laden pieces written by her husband), Lucy Parsons's work was descriptive and colorful. She exploited melodramatic themes and took considerable care in fashioning her prose. Parsons's tramps are not merely hungry; they suffer from "pangs of hunger now knawing [sic] at [their] vitals." They do not merely work; they are "harnessed to a machine that was harnessed to steam." She speaks directly to the reader, questioning his manhood and taunting him: "Oh, working man! Oh, starved, outraged and robbed laborer, how long will you lend attentive ear to the authors of your misery?" In "Factory Child" she employs repetition to emphasize her grief and outrage: "Toil on, toil on, thou victim of private capital. One day thy tears will be dried; one day thy chest will cease to heave." She was also adept at bringing vividly to life the juxtapositions that implicitly formed the core of radical thought: socialists and even moderate reformers appreciated her descriptions of emaciated workers set against a backdrop of Chicago skyscrapers, the ill-clad children gazing upon storehouses stuffed with moldering food and moth-eaten clothing. Her articles had a strong narrative thread; these are stories in which, over time, characters suffer, learn, and finally redeem and avenge themselves.

With the parting salvo in "Tramps"—*Learn the use of explosives!*—Lucy Parsons invited and received the scrutiny of authorities, who were already preoccupied by the potential of dynamite in the hands of radicals. In February 1885, she was speaking at regular weekly IWPA meetings on Wednesday nights, prompting papers in places as far away as Cleveland, Ohio, and Macon, Georgia, to take note. As the *Cleveland Leader* reported,

> Mrs. A. R. Parsons, a "lady" of Chicago, is a dynamiter woman. She made a very fiery speech, berating her hearers as cowards, unworthy of the name of manhood, because they allowed the aggressions of capital to continue. If they were men, as they claimed to be, she said they would blow up every house on the adjoining avenues before they would submit to it. If they were afraid to do this, however, they need not look for a captain, for she would fill her apron with dynamite and lead them along the avenues of the city where the rich reside, destroying as they went.

That same month, the American Group leader Samuel Fielden was speaking to Ohio audiences consisting of what a *Cleveland Leader* reporter called "the local dynamiters, Socialists, and would-be murderers," and distributing the "Lucy E. Parsons handbill." Several papers quoted from "Tramps" at length as an example of "the gospel of murder and dynamite," a "rank production" of "the colored female socialist of Chicago." The *Illinois State Journal*, based in Springfield, reported that Parsons had said, "Dynamite is our savior. We don't want a better savior. Let us learn how to make it, and then not spare its use." Similarly newsworthy was a speech in which she urged the use of "little dynamite bombs" to ensure that of aggressive National Guard troops, "very few would be left to report at headquarters when the muster roll was called." She assured listeners and readers alike that "death had no terrors for her."[20]

In their embrace of dynamite, the Parsonses and other Chicago anarchists were seizing on a particular historical moment. For years, the German anarchist Johann Most had been promoting the gospel of terror—the *attentat*—but recent events were sending shockwaves through major cities in the United States, Europe, and Russia. In 1881, anarchists had used handmade grenades to assassinate Czar Alexander II. The Irish Republican Brotherhood, or Fenians, conducted a four-year series of dynamite attacks on British military barracks, gas-works, canal viaducts, and the London Underground. The attacks cul-minated on January 24, 1885, with the detonation of three bombs in the House of Commons chamber, Westminster Hall, and a banquet room in the Tower of London. The *New York Times* sent a reporter to an IWPA meeting that night, and he had taken note of Lucy Parsons, whom he described as "a negro woman, wife of the rabid white Social-ist, A. R. Parsons." "She had often wanted to be a man," the reporter wrote, "but since she had heard that it was a woman who had blown up the Parliament Buildings in London, she would not swap places with any man in the country." Meanwhile, Chicago shuddered: in Feb-ruary alone, the *Tribune* published eighty-eight articles dealing with dynamite.[21]

Following the example set by the *Labor Enquirer*, *The Alarm* offered ringing affirmations of the power of dynamite as the perfect weapon. Articles focused on the manufacture and deployment of explosive de-vices of various kinds as well as directions for street-fighting and calls for martyrdom and the execution of Chicago's business leaders. In pieces such as "Bombs! The Manufacture and Use of the Deadly Dy-namite Bomb Made Easy," the appeal was straightforward: "One man armed with a dynamite bomb is equal to one regiment of militia, when it is used at the right time and place." Albert waxed eloquent about the potential of explosives to achieve "the equilibrium," the diffusion of power, with this ultimate deterrent to evil: "It is the abolition of au-thority; it is the dawn of peace; it is the end of war, because war cannot exist unless there is somebody to make war upon, and dynamite makes that unsafe, is undesirable, and absolutely impossible." Dynamite, in fact, was both a harbinger and an agent of progress, he said, the climax of a historical process: "Gunpowder brought the world some liberty and dynamite will bring the world as much more as it is stronger than gun-powder. No man has a right to boost himself by even treading on an-other's toes. Dynamite will produce equality."[22]

From the Great Railroad Strike of 1877 onward, the Parsonses and other anarchists and socialists wrote and spoke often about the need for the laboring classes to defend themselves against armed authori-ties: when the police, or militia, or federal troops used force to break up peaceful assemblies, the masses must respond in kind. Yet by 1885 the anarchists' invocation of violence had gone well beyond the rationale of immediate self-defense. For his part, Johann Most urged followers to plant bombs in (or torch) such places as ballrooms, banquet halls, and churches. Yet curiously, considering their eagerness to parse the doctrines of various political ideologies, few, if any, Chicago anarchists seem to have devoted much serious thought to the larger implications of a strategy based on terror. How could one be certain that only the capitalist, and not innocents, would fall to a stick of dynamite, no matter how careful the assailant's aim? Was it credible that the death of a single employer could impel his Board of Trade colleagues to embrace anarchistic principles? At one IWPA mass meeting, a speaker asserted, "We believe in, if necessary, sacrificing 1,000,000 lives to-day, to save uncounted millions who otherwise must be sacrificed to the demon of greed." The Alarm reworked the ratio: "It is clearly more humane to blow ten men into eternity than to make ten men starve to death." Yet the Chicago anarchists' failure to think past their own words suggests that the alarm they raised about their intentions was a false one; these men and women sought primarily to be heard and heeded within the cacophony of the city's labor politics.[23]

According to the anarchists, if talk of dynamite had the potential to terrify elites, it also had the potential to galvanize the laboring classes by showing them that these radicals had evolved out of the "talking" phase into *doing*. Lizzie Swank observed that words alone seemed unequal to the task at hand. Glorifying dynamite offered a rhetorical strategy meant to impress upon ordinary people their ability to change the world: "You can talk much more effectually to ignorant and careless working people when you tell them that they have the power to enforce their claims, than if you merely point out their wrongs and tell them what ought to be," Swank wrote. Dynamite—not as much the material but the *idea* of it—amounted to the ultimate weapon of the dispossessed.[24]

In the words of one contemporary, this focus on dynamite amounted to loose "bomb-talk," a sign of weakness and desperation on the part of news-media-savvy anarchists, but largely harmless in fact. Regardless, it is probable that both Lucy and Albert felt validated when, by the spring of 1885, the Chicago press had begun to associate both of them with the making, using, and praise of dynamite. The police detective Michael Schaak reported that his agents had infiltrated "secret" IWPA meetings where Albert was demonstrating methods for assembling what he (Albert) called "the dear stuff dynamite" in a little tin box that could be carried around in an unobtrusive handbasket and used to level hundreds of houses. The description of this incident and others, however, suggests that Parsons was fully aware that an undercover agent was present, and that he intended to impress upon Chicago authorities that he and his comrades were prepared to move beyond street skirmishes with the police into a more deadly phase of class warfare. Writers for *The Alarm* understood, and seemed to welcome, the panic their words instilled in the public at large. Dynamite could only become a viable weapon if its potential was widely appreciated by both the laboring classes and their enemies.[25]

To their friends, the Parsonses appeared to be a devoted couple and loving parents living a wholly respectable life. Both took pride in their appearance—Lucy wore fashionable dresses, and Albert dyed his hair and kept his mustache nicely trimmed. He remained attentive to the particular outfits worn by members of his audiences, whether shiny silk and satin or grease-stained cotton. Lucy at times cited the love of fine clothes as a universal impulse thwarted by a cruel capitalist system. The couple's attractive dress and prim demeanor now conveniently helped to dispel the popular stereotype of the bewhiskered, slovenly, foreign-born anarchist. How could this portrait of a couple basking in the love of family, and even in bourgeois domestic contentment, be reconciled with their public calls for murder and mayhem? In the end, both Albert and Lucy begged to be taken at their word—specifically, their conviction that a spectacular act of killing was necessary to ignite a revolution. And so they promoted that criminal message with impunity, and with breathtaking naïveté.[26]

With the launch of *The Alarm*, Albert began to spend more time out of town, not only to make new converts to the cause, but also to solicit new subscriptions. As editor, he earned a paltry $8 a week, less than the average Chicago workingman, who made $2 a day. Intended as a weekly, after just a few months the paper became biweekly; printing it more often was too expensive. Non-English papers grabbed a greater share of the anarchist readership. Two German weeklies, one German daily, one Bohemian weekly, and one Scandinavian weekly made Chicago the center of the anarchist press in the country. By early 1886, the *Arbeiter Zeitung*, edited by the German immigrants Spies and Schwab, had a circulation of 3,600, while *The Alarm* reached perhaps 2,000 to 3,000 subscribers in Chicago and the Greater Midwest (a generous estimate, to be sure, but some of these readers no doubt passed their copies on to friends).[27]

Every once in a while, *The Alarm* would carry a small ad for "Mrs. Parsons, Dressmaker"; the word *kleidermacherin* (lady dressmaker) appeared in German script. Located at 377 West Indiana Street, Parsons's dressmaking business catered to the immigrant community, which in turn provided her with her social circle. When she wrote "Tramps," she was thirty-three years old, the mother of a five-year-old son and a three-year-old daughter. She was just beginning to assume the persona of what the press mockingly called "Citizeness Parsons," an evocation of the murderous female French revolutionary of 1789, or the American Louise Michel, the defiant "Red Virgin" of the 1871 Paris Commune. Parsons accommodated reporters with pithy if frightful quotations, as she did on the occasion of a strike by Lemont, Illinois, quarry workers in the spring of 1885: "Let every dirty, lousy, tramp arm himself with a revolver or knife and lay in wait on the steps of the palace of the rich and stab or shoot the owners as they come out. Let us kill them without mercy, and let it be a war of extermination without pity." Her peculiar talents—the ability to marry extreme rhetoric with a woman's sensibilities, and a mother's at that—served her well as orator, performer, and, eventually, national celebrity. Yet such boldness could be self-indulgent, as she seemed determined to say anything so long as it might turn up as the next day's headline.[28]

Drawing upon European revolutionary ideals and icons, the IWPA tended to relegate women to symbolic roles. The group sponsored *tableaux vivants* and parade floats that featured "lady liberty"—"a woman costumed as the Goddess of Liberty bearing aloft the red flag," *The Alarm* said, "while a proletariat armed with a flaming sword and his cartridge box inscribed with 'dynamite' stood beneath." Parsons, however, was a real woman, not a goddess, and she pushed the IWPA toward a greater acceptance of women in the public sphere. In August 1885, *The Alarm* published a piece titled "Brave Marching Women," noting that a large IWPA procession on a Sunday the month before had featured a novel sight—seven women serving as honor guards and marching with a large silk banner. "It was a thing unique," noted the writer, and it no doubt impressed upon the thousands of spectators "that if Communism can attract the gentler sex to such a degree they will take part in public demonstrations, and in obedience to their convictions dare to face public scorn and possibility of disorder and arrest by the organized powers of society, there surely must be some quality in Communism which challenges respect." Most of the marchers were mothers, the same article noted, and their presence belied the popular image of anarchists as "creatures of the baser sort—rough, disorderly, animated by the impulse of destruction for plunder's sake alone, and at war with the best interests of society." In a story the day after the procession, the editors of the *Tribune* highlighted the participation of "Mrs. Parsons, the female agitator." Yet the paper's chief concern seemed not to be the presence of the women but the absence of the American flag: of the 2,000 or so participants, the paper said, there was "no other class of people who parade[d] without the national flag."[29]

In an effort to attract the attention of ordinary onlookers as well as the authorities, Parsons was developing a fine sense of the flamboyant. That Sunday was not the first time that she had marched in an IWPA parade; to mark Thanksgiving in 1884, she and Lizzie Swank had each carried a flag—the red, for universal solidarity among working people, and also the black, the symbol of hunger and starvation, apparently in the first time it was borne aloft on American soil. Their performance that day was notable because the procession wended its way through a wealthy neighborhood, where the two women halted before one mansion after another and then gleefully pulled doorbells, groaned, and shouted threats to the residents—a shocking breach of street-demonstration decorum, even for anarchists.[30]

Not content to serve a decorative function at parades, Parsons also became a prominent speaker at the huge weekly Sunday-afternoon lakefront meetings held during the summer of 1885. These picnic-rallies

drew thousands to enjoy the cool breezes off Lake Michigan and listen to a predictable lineup of anarchist English and German-language
speakers, including the Parsonses, August Spies, and Samuel Fielden.
The events confounded the police because the crowds consisted of families as well as political orators. ("Wives and children," observed one reporter, "always diversify the Anarchistic assemblies.") The mainstream
papers ridiculed the lakeshore "sour-headed cranks" who railed "against
the people and property of this city, as well as against the laws of the
state and the country." Still, the lakefront gatherings became predictable over time, and the audiences became inured to talk of the *attentat*; one reporter for the *Daily Inter-Ocean* opined that the speakers told
their audiences over and over again "go arm yourselves"—and "away
they would go, to arm themselves with beer, and the next Sunday the
whole thing would be gone over again in substance and form."[31]

By that summer Lucy Parsons was determined to speak at virtually
all IWPA-sponsored events, despite the fact that they were customarily
masculine affairs; even male anarchists only grudgingly admitted women
to indoor mass meetings because their presence demanded that the men
refrain from smoking, an activity that might offend the "ladies." At rallies of strikers, the few women present were likewise deemed a novelty.
Such gender conventions made Parsons's frequent public appearances
and heated rhetoric all the more remarkable. During the bitter Chicago streetcar strike of July 1885, the organizers refrained from calling
upon her to speak at a Sunday rally, though she was eager to address the
crowd. At a regular American Group meeting the following Wednesday night, she excoriated the employees who remained indifferent to
the plight of their fired coworkers, "like whipped curs kissing the hand
that smote them." She complained about the slight she had suffered a
few days before, pronouncing the strikers' gatherings "wishy-washy hog
wash." If workers were indeed denying they had pushed streetcars off the
tracks, she exclaimed, "What rot! They're either knaves or fools—knaves
if they derailed the cars and failed to own up to it, and fools if they left
any splinter of any car the company has got."[32]

To a large degree, Parsons declaimed freely; the opposition to
her speaking at an outdoor meeting during the streetcar strike came
from the workers themselves, not from the police. In this respect she

benefited from Victorian policing methods and faced neither official harassment nor arrest. Later, some critics would complain of the protective shield of womanhood that allowed her to continue to speak with impunity—in the words of one attorney, "By her talk and other means of instilling their devilish sentiments into the minds of the people, she could at all times escape arrest and do tenfold more harm than good. They could quell the men, but woman-like, she would have her say."[33]

CHICAGO'S GREAT UPHEAVAL SPURRED ALBERT AND LUCY TO exploit the rising resentment among white workers during the depression months of late 1884 and all of 1885 and at the same time devote themselves to seemingly never-ending fundraising efforts for *The Alarm*. Each week brought a round of regular events—the lakefront meetings on Sunday afternoons, Monday-night drills among members of the armed American Group, and sporadic strategy sessions of *The Alarm's* subscription committee (led by Lucy Parsons and Lizzie Swank). Lucy frequently presided over the three-hour-long Wednesday-night debates, reports, and book discussions ("How the Working People Are Robbed") held at the American Group offices at 54 Lake Street. The IWPA sponsored orations, theater events, concerts, dances, and day-long outings to places such as Sheffield, Indiana. Lucy helped to choreograph the "monster" rallies that marked American holidays such as the Fourth of July and Thanksgiving, now appropriated by the anarchists as occasions to denounce the United States. She continued to sew banners that proclaimed "Workingmen, Arm Yourselves!" and "Down with the Throne, Altar, and Moneybags."[34]

The couple found time to take weekly rambles with Swank, when Albert would entertain the two women. He was "an excellent mimic [who] would, sometimes, where he thought no one would be hurt, 'take off' the eccentricities of people in a very laughable manner," Swank later remembered, calling the walks "memorable incidents." In November 1885, Swank married her comrade, the thirty-four-year-old, British-born William Holmes, the American Group recording secretary and a prolific writer for the *Labor Enquirer*. She moved to his home in Geneva, west of Chicago, where he taught school, and continued to write for *The Alarm* and other radical publications.[35]

Lulu and Albert Junior at times accompanied their parents to meetings, and they must have become accustomed to falling asleep at home as American Group meetings stretched late into the night around them. By this time Junior was attending the Kosciusko public elementary school nearby; his mother lamented that patriotic songs such as "Hail Columbia, Happy Land," and "Yankee Doodle" were part of the curriculum. The children went to the regular IWPA picnics at Ogden's Grove, the Sunday lakefront meetings, and other social gatherings. Yet it is possible that, as their mother became more visible as a speaker (at times sharing the podium, or salt barrel, or wagon, with her husband), the children found themselves placed in the care of a neighbor or a friend. Both parents were spending more time outside the home.[36]

Between October 1884 and May 1886, Albert embarked on a series of "agitation trips" that took him as far east as New York and Maryland, as far south as Kentucky, and as far west as Nebraska. He spoke in large cities such as Kansas City, Cleveland, and Cincinnati and stopped for a day or two in small company mining towns. It would later become apparent that Lucy's reaction to Albert's out-of-town trips was not resentment that he was gone from home so much, but dismay that she was not sharing in the excitement, in his travails as well as his triumphs. Indeed, his detailed accounts of his exploits while spreading the gospel of anarchy only seemed to whet her own appetite for adoration from the crowds. One day, his tours of the mid-1880s would become road maps for her own.

Parsons had always relished his role as outside agitator. By the mid-1880s, he was so familiar to the laboring classes of Chicago that he could no longer count on reaching a pool of new listeners. Moreover, with *The Alarm*'s Chicago subscription base static (and small), he needed to attract a stream of new readers if the paper were to survive. It is possible, too, that the predictability of his weekly routine of IWPA obligations, combined with the inevitable commotion of a household with two children under the age of six, propelled him out of Chicago and into towns and cities where he could look forward to greeting old

comrades and meeting new ones. Once again he would feel the exhilaration of speaking to a crowd of rapt listeners. Leaving the editorship
of the paper to Lizzie Swank Holmes (presumably Lucy had her hands
full with her sewing business and the care of the children), he was gone
for weeks at a time.[37]

Parsons's out-of-town trips proceeded most smoothly when he
could rely on the hospitality of local labor leaders. Drawing on IWPA
connections, he often stayed in the homes of German immigrants,
and spoke in Turner halls throughout the Midwest. He also sought to
leverage his membership in the Knights of Labor, the Typographical
Union, and the American Group sections of the IWPA into invitations
to speak. (These ties could be unpredictable, however; for example, the
"conservative workingmen" of Saint Joseph, Missouri, loudly objected
to the Knights sponsoring this well-known "communist.") An enthusiastic host could provide a suitable venue for his speech, quickly print
and distribute announcements—surreptitiously, if necessary—and find
him a back-alley escape if he was confronted by persons less than enthusiastic about his visit. After a long day speaking and dodging police,
Parsons would unwind with his hosts, and (as he apparently did in Topeka) tell them how to make dynamite bombs, reminding them to keep
the room well ventilated while assembling the pieces.[38]

Still, even his glowing reports chronicling his own remarkable suc-
cesses contain hints of the difficulties he faced. In some cases, the largest local venue charged an exorbitant afternoon or evening rental fee,
devouring any money he might have made. Often he labored under conditions that were less than ideal—there was the day he spoke in Springfield, Ohio, in February on a skating rink that was "cold as a dead man's
feet," or the day in July when he spoke in a stifling lecture hall in Topeka. In some outdoor spaces Parsons had to compete with the fire-and-
brimstone sermons of nearby itinerant evangelists, or the fulminations
of temperance activists. And he at times had to work to counter his
own unprepossessing appearance as a slight, earnest, well-spoken man;
he was the first to admit that he did not look "very dangerous." At a
speech in Canton, Ohio, he inquired of his listeners whether they were
prepared to use navy revolvers, long knives, Winchester rifles, or dynamite; he swore that "before I would see my child standing barefoot in

the snow and crying for bread, I would sink everything down into the deepest abyss of hell and damnation." The sheer force and number of his words must somehow compensate for his kindly, nonthreatening demeanor.[39]

On the road, Parsons delivered his standard speech with the same rhetorical strategies he used at "monster" rallies in Chicago, but in the space of just two hours or so, it was difficult for him to convey the full logic of the idea that "the existing social order has outgrown its usefulness, if it ever had any." And not all audience members warmed to his grim conviction that "wage bondage" admitted of only three options for workers—to suffer as slaves, as objects of charity, or as prisoners in jail. Parsons seemed intent on dashing the modest hopes of workers who might want a better paycheck, or a better life for their children: "Here in Cleveland, in America, not Ireland, Russia, Italy or despotic Europe, but right here in Ohio, beneath the 'Stars and Stripes,' over twenty thousand American sovereigns in one small city were perishing of hunger and cold," he said to an Ohio crowd.[40]

Soliciting the attention of the press, both sympathetic and hostile, he no doubt reveled in reports that labeled him and other IWPA interlopers as "Dynamiters"; at the same time, his long-winded speeches might be distilled to the headline "He Counsels Murder" (as was the case in Cleveland). Both inside and outside of Chicago, newspapers followed his perambulations through the Midwest, assuming that their readers would take an interest in—or be outraged by—what he had to say when addressing workers in a faraway state or town. In March 1885, the *New York Times* featured Parsons's trip to Cincinnati, highlighting his prediction that "the final outbreak against law and order" was nigh and identifying him as the "husband of a negress," presumably a sure way to discredit him. The *Chicago Tribune*, too, was keeping close track of Parsons as he traveled around the country waving the red banner of revolution.[41]

Parsons fully deserved his reputation as a rousing public speaker, full of energy and moral righteousness, and his friends admired him as a sparkling conversationalist with a deft sense of humor. Yet his railings against law and order in mid-1880s Chicago seem at odds with his former role as a Texas political operative. He had transformed himself from a Republican loyalist to a self-proclaimed anarchist, but he remained a proud outsider, embracing a cause that was couched in different terms at different times—but that was ultimately consistent—to bring enlightenment to his benighted listeners, to bolster their sense of manhood, and to instill in them the courage to destroy their oppressors. He was a knight-errant, traveling from the Reconstruction era to the Gilded Age, spreading "freedom."

During one of his trips to Pennsylvania coal country in Pennsylvania, Albert wrote a letter to Lucy describing her as one "whose whole being is wrapped up in the progress of the social revolution." More broadly, the thread running throughout her life was her fierce determination to rise above the circumstances of her birth. An avid reader with eclectic tastes, within ten years of first stepping into a schoolroom she had become a writer and orator of some distinction. Wife, mother, seamstress, essayist, reporter, and agitator, Lucy Parsons eschewed the identity of a black person or a freedwoman. Notably, she lacked her husband's warmth and his sense of ease in the world. She had worked too hard becoming "Citizeness Parsons" to tolerate people who struck her as patronizing or superficial. She and Albert always retained the courage of their convictions, but questions remained: Could they blast the laboring classes out of their sluggishness by spreading the gospel of dynamite? Were they themselves even true believers of that gospel? Or, more likely, were their threats merely rhetorical, idle, and the alarms they raised simply false?[42]

❧ Chapter 6 ❧

Haymarket

B Y THE MID-1880S, SEGMENTS OF THE LABORING CLASSES HAD demonstrated in a most convincing fashion their ability to upend whole sectors of the economy and wrench concessions from mighty captains of industry. Working together, railroad workers, in particular, could disrupt interstate trade, mail delivery, and passenger travel, and in the process threaten a range of businesses, from banks and large manufacturers to farmers and other small producers. In Chicago, trade groups protesting longer hours and lower wages were constantly walking off the job and "slugging" (physically assaulting those who refused to join them). Such protests, combined with routine, highly politicized parades and picnics and a robust anarchist press, created a charged atmosphere in Chicago. Many city elites were convinced that workers in their collective capacity possessed the power to destroy the very fundamentals of the American economy: the cherished institutions of state, church, and representative democracy. Radical labor leaders seemed ever poised to light the fuse and throw the bomb that would ignite a tinderbox of working-class resentment and anger, with the subsequent explosion leaving the city in a smoldering shambles, surpassing the horrors of the fire of 1871.[1]

To a great extent, the fears of the Chicago business community were overblown, for workers remained badly divided among themselves along the lines of competing craft, ethnic, religious, and racial loyalties. Lucy and Albert Parsons exacerbated the bitter internecine feuds among Chicago's laboring classes in the mid-1880s, heaping contempt on more conservative elements with a kind of disdain they usually reserved for the bloated plutocracy. An 1885 Labor Day celebration sponsored by the Chicago Federation of Organized Trades and Labor Unions banned all banners except for the American flag, essentially excluding all anarchists and thereby eliciting scorn from *The Alarm*. Unwilling to furl their red or black flags, members of the IWPA decided to march on their own, and later sneered at the competing 8,000-person-strong "meaningless affair." The federation had passed a number of resolutions objectionable to the IWPA, including "praising the ballot and denouncing the bullet," as well as insulting foreigners and hailing America as "a free republic." *The Alarm* described the rival march this way: "The Voluntary Slaves Exhibit Themselves Before Their Delighted Masters."[2]

Yet the anarchists' rhetorical provocations were out of all proportion to their actual strength. The IWPA remained a small group— with perhaps 12,000 members throughout the United States, and no more than 3,000 of those in Chicago by early 1886. Of the fifteen IWPA groups within the city, only one, the American Group, was composed of English-speakers, probably no more than a few dozen people at most. During the 1880s, Chicago's population doubled, from about 500,000 to 1 million, and labor organizations of all kinds, including trade unions and local assemblies of the Knights of Labor, grew in membership and strength. However, by mid-1886, of the city's total population of 800,000, no more than 52,000 to 85,000 belonged to a union of any kind. No single trade could boast that all of its members were organized.[3]

Albert and Lucy Parsons remained convinced that the IWPA was composed of *avant couriers*, and that absolute numbers of anarchists, socialists, or trade unionists counted for little. This was just as well, for despite their exhausting round of weekly activities, American Group members had won few converts. In fact, the IWPA held virtually no appeal for native-born American workers, who recoiled at the constant paeans to dynamite and bloodshed in general. Many radical immigrant agitators, anarchists and socialists alike, persisted in distancing themselves from incremental efforts to make the workday shorter and the workplace safer, claiming, for instance, that the fight for an eight-hour day was a waste of time and a distraction from the impending revolution. In this respect, Albert Parsons, who served as the head of Chicago's Eight-Hour League, was the exception who proved the rule. Even he, however, vastly overestimated the revolutionary potential of the Chicago laboring classes.

The Parsonses and their comrades possessed a keen sense of the inexorable historical transformations of the day, including the great industrialists' insatiable quest for higher profits and reduced production costs via technological innovation. IWPA members understood that machines were replacing humans, supply was outstripping demand, and businesses were consolidating, swelling the ranks of the poor, who were now forced to fend for themselves. At the same time, the anarchists did not possess any real insight into the values of diverse groups of white male American-born workers, many thousands of whom were afflicted with deep prejudices against women, African American, and Chinese immigrant workers. Machine operatives and manual laborers in Chicago shared certain hardships—the grueling conditions of everyday life, including long hours for little pay, dependence on their wives and children for the family's income, and crowded and expensive housing, but much divided them as well. And for all their prescience regarding mechanization's ills, the anarchists could not foresee the dramatic growth in the number of jobs, and also in different kinds of jobs—in other words, the capacity of the American economy to expand and to absorb (albeit imperfectly), the many millions of immigrants arriving in the country from the 1880s onward.

The anarchists also underestimated the power that the promise of upward mobility held for many workers—not spectacular mobility, Carnegie-style, but incremental mobility, especially among native English speakers. More significant perhaps was the promise of intergenerational progress—the bricklayer's hope that his son might someday become a building contractor, the waiter's hope that his son might someday own a small restaurant. In fact, anarchists worried that workers who escaped into the middle classes would doom their movement, dependent as it was on the long-term loyalty of suffering toilers. Albert and Lucy never grasped the power of symbols such as American or red flags either to animate or disgust the native-born laboring classes—a group the Parsonses conceived of narrowly, as urban white wage earners exclusively, with all others dismissed as a cheap-labor threat to working-class solidarity.[4]

Lucy Parsons was among the chief architects of the anarchists' escalating attacks on industrialists and conservative union leaders. She did not suffer fools gladly, and the fools, in her view, included not only Democratic and Republican trade unionists but also socialists and fellow anarchists who disagreed with her. For someone who pressed for working-class solidarity in the face of overweening capitalist power, over her long career she consistently ridiculed and dismissed other radicals to a surprising degree. As one Chicago anarchist noted, "if you started talking with her chances are you would get a beautiful slap in the face with her words. She could just brush you off, insult you, bulldoze you—that was Lucy."[5]

If the white laboring classes had little use for the anarchists, one influential group in the city did take this fierce little band seriously, hanging on their every word, written and spoken, and believing completely in their almost otherworldly power. This group, of course, consisted of wealthy businessmen and the law enforcement establishment. Police detectives read each new issue of *The Alarm*, and plainclothes officers attended every Wednesday-night and lakefront meeting and mass rally and picnic. If and when class warfare actually did break out in Chicago, the authorities would have no trouble locating the source of the bloodshed, and they would ensure that justice would be swift toward the offenders—or their proxies in crime. And in that way the city's small coterie of anarchists would finally secure their place in history.

ALBERT'S EVENTUAL BREAK FROM HIS OWN LOCAL CHAPTER OF THE National Typographical Union reveals his estrangement from aspirational, English-speaking trade unionists in general. In his first years in Chicago, Parsons had been the proud owner of a union card, but by mid-1885 he was using the pages of *The Alarm* to excoriate NTU members and their acquiescence in the wage system. The union identified with the so-called respectable skilled laboring classes; these workers infused their identity with a commitment to temperance in alcohol consumption and to other forms of self-improvement, unapologetic antiforeign and antiradical tendencies, and a belief in the possibility of upward mobility. In their own words: "Now printing can boldly throw down the glove and challenge comparison with any and every trade or profession for sobriety, respectability, the calling to high places of trust and honor, as it has ever been able to do for education, intelligence, genius, and the rare dowry of brains." Parsons opined that Local No. 16 was not a true labor union at all, but rather "a mere make-shift, a place where cliques, rings, and selfish schemes are fostered, and it becomes an instrument for the hopeless enslavement of the worker to his capitalistic task-master." Here his animus toward the local seemed to stem not only from broad ideological differences with its members but also from his bitter memories of those members who had abandoned him when he was blacklisted after the Great Strike of 1877.[6]

The American Group readily adopted immigrant-ethnic iconography, art, history, and ideology. Of necessity, and with apparent genuine enthusiasm, Lucy and Albert partook of the rich pageantry that drew on European radical traditions. At the same time, the American Group also looked to American history for inspiration and for a guide to the future. Albert (more often than Lucy) invoked the words of American historical figures such as Thomas Paine and Thomas Jefferson in an attempt to portray radicalism as a homegrown impulse; after all, blood flowed freely during the American Revolution, that seminal revolt against tyranny. English-speaking anarchists also presented themselves as the new abolitionists, working in the tradition of Wendell Phillips, William Lloyd Garrison, and John Brown, on the cusp of another momentous conflict. Philip D. Armour, the meatpacking industrialist, and George Pullman, the manufacturer of the Pullman sleeping car, were the new slaveholders, and they wielded the lash of hunger that lacerated the back of the wage-slave. Yet most native-born workers found this analogy highly offensive. IWPA speakers and writers charged that Chicago men and women were "slaves" if they worked for wages, voted in elections, obeyed the law, and professed allegiance to the United States. Among immigrants, the epithet "slave" might have served as a bold rallying cry, but among white, American-born men, to be compared to enslaved blacks, or to Chinese "coolies"—or cowardly "dogs," for that matter—registered more as an insult and less as a call to arms. This attempted fusion of European and American radical traditions won few converts.[7]

The anarchists' ideal of a transnational, universal struggle among workers went well beyond the waving of red and black flags to make pointed attacks on organized religion, the ballot, secular and religious holidays, and the system of government generally. Promoting a European anticlericalism manifested in "free thinking," IWPA speakers and writers, including both of the Parsonses, went out of their way to denigrate religious faith of any kind. They objected to the idea that "God has a grudge against all humanity, in consequence of a little difficulty he had with our ancient parents," as *The Alarm* once put it. The clergy were hucksters peddling superstition, Christian charity a hoax and a distraction. Yet denominational affiliation (or lack thereof) represented a profound signifier among the major labor organizations in Chicago, with the Central Labor Union dominated by atheists, the Trade and Labor Assembly by native-born Protestants, and the Knights of Labor by Irish immigrants and other Catholics. The Parsonses had little understanding of the fact that although some clergy were arguing that a shorter workday would provide more opportunities for dissipation, others were claiming that such a day was part of a benevolent God's plan to improve the lot of man on earth. To Albert and Lucy, religion came in the form of either the Salvation Army preacher competing for souls on the lakefront, or the priest urging his congregants' forbearance in this worldly vale of tears.[8]

Members of the IWPA took pride in appropriating American holidays for their own purposes and mocking venerated American heroes: Thanksgiving, for instance, was a day to reflect on this "Thankless Day." In late November 1884, the IWPA circulated a handbill that included sarcastic suggestions for the upcoming holiday: "You are to give thanks because your masters refuse you employment; because you are hungry and without home or shelter, and your masters have taken away what you created, and arranged to shoot you by the police or militia if you refuse to die in your hovels, in due observation of Law and Order." Lucy wrote a dramatic account of the proceedings that dreary, cold day for *The Alarm*, pronouncing the holiday generally as "a lie—a stupid, hollow mockery—a sop thrown out by the ruling classes to tickle the pates of their ignorant dupes and slaves that they may, with better security, continue to rob them."[9]

The anarchists, in keeping with the conviction of European radicals that the secular state was just as hierarchical, authoritarian, and corrupt as they believed the Vatican to be, charged that church and state represented "twin relics of barbarism" and "the fountain of all evil." In dismissing voting as a pernicious charade, the Parsonses managed to alienate the workingmen who considered the suffrage a sacred, hardwon right and the ballot box the site of a broader equality. Anarchists ridiculed believers in the ballot, "that capitalistic humbug," as dupes and fools. In April 1885, Lizzie Swank Holmes took to the pages of *The Alarm* to chide a black man who resented that "the dregs and scum of Europe and America" could vote, while he could not. The woman suffragist was equally misguided, according to Swank Holmes: "Her brother slaves have had the ballot for more than a hundred years and are worse off now than at the beginning [of the nation]."[10]

Proposals to ameliorate the harsh life-circumstances of the poor found no favor with the IWPA. Until the momentum for the eighthour day built in early 1886, *The Alarm* included regular denunciations of that movement and other forms of "rancid reform pap," such as minimum-wage and maximum-hour legislation. At times, even Albert Parsons had to seek some middle ground between, on the one hand, his dogmatic anarchist comrades, and, on the other, the mass of workers who were focused on bread-and-butter measures. Pressed from the left, he couched the fight for the eight-hour day as a revolutionary project, the first step in a process that would eventually yield a six-hour day, and then a four-hour day, and so on, until wage slavery must of necessity disappear altogether. At the same time, many native-born skilled workers believed that incremental change could flow from personal transformation—through forgoing alcohol, moving to another place or another job, or acting collectively to boycott or strike against

employers. The anarchists' constant calls for street-fighting, assassi-
nating, and dynamiting—all strategies they considered "brave and
humane"—sounded alien and frightening, even when uttered by that
mellifluous American Albert Parsons.[11]

More generally, though, the anarchists' message was one of unmitigated pessimism—the middle class would sink into poverty, they said,
millions of tramps would freeze to death, machines would take over the
workplace, and the United States would remain as despotic as the most
backward European regime. In a growing city and country, this scenario of misery and decay failed to move many workers. Nevertheless,
according to Albert, to quarrel with the inexorable march to anarchy
was "silly and vain." For their part, members of the Socialistic Labor
Party referred to their anarchist rivals as "the dynamite assassins." One
cynic charged that the amount of beer consumed at an IWPA picnic
could have been better used to pay for the funerals of a dozen children
who had starved to death.[12]

Mother Jones, herself possessed of impeccable radical credentials,
objected to the anarchists' harsh language and theatrical tactics, which
she believed did more harm than good. All proponents of the shorter
working day suffered from guilt by association: "The employers used the
cry of anarchism to kill the movement," Jones wrote in her autobiography. "A person who believed in an eight-hour working day was, they said,
an enemy to his country, a traitor, an anarchist. The foundations of government were being gnawed away by the anarchist rats." Jones recalled
that on Christmas Day in 1885, the IWPA organized a march among
"poverty-stricken people in rags and tatters" out of their neighborhoods
and into the Prairie Avenue mansion district, where they waved the
black flag and railed against their oppressors. She wrote, "I thought the
parade an insane move on the part of the anarchists, as it only served to
make feeling more bitter. As a matter of fact, it had no educational value
whatever and only served to make the police more savage, and the public
less sympathetic to the real distress of the workers." Anarchist leaders,
with their constant talk of murder and dynamite, were tainting a rea-
sonable drive for the eight-hour day: "Such speakers cause every spark
of sympathy to disappear and bring us into disrepute."[13]

THE FAST-MOVING EVENTS OF 1885 AND EARLY 1886 LEFT THE IWPA scrambling to keep up: after years of agitating, workers in Chicago and throughout the nation were organizing strikes and boycotts, and joining labor unions in record numbers. New statewide trade unions sprang up in the state of Illinois, and the anarchist Central Labor Union and the socialist Trade and Labor Assembly both grew in terms of constituent groups and overall numbers—increasing, by March 1886, to twenty-four groups with 28,000 members, and fifty groups with 20,000 members, respectively. IWPA members watched, delighted at the upwelling of collective action, but largely disapproved of the upstarts' tactics. They felt the groups were neglecting to do the necessary work of educating and organizing workers before having them take part in spontaneous walkouts.[14]

Employers, too, began to modify their strategies for dealing with restless workers, further confounding the anarchists. More and more companies were concluding that the violent strife that flowed from wage reductions could only be avoided by introducing labor-saving machinery. And in Illinois and throughout the Midwest, employers were recruiting local or southern African American men as strikebreakers, replacing one group of exploited workers with an even more destitute one. Mine owners in Ohio's Hocking Valley, and quarry owners in Lemont, Illinois, were among those introducing blacks as scabs in 1885. Although Albert appeared and spoke at rallies among white strikers in both places, he never mentioned these black workers in his speeches or in his reports published in *The Alarm*.[15]

The most dramatic development, and no doubt to the IWPA the most aggravating one, was the meteoric rise of the Knights of Labor, especially after the summer of 1885, when it conducted a series of successful strikes against railroads owned by the financier Jay Gould. The workers won a remarkable victory: they managed to get Gould to back down and not only reverse wage reductions but also refrain from firing workers who belonged to the Knights, thereby demonstrating an astonishing collective power equal to that of one of the country's largest railroad barons. By the late spring of 1886, Chicago boasted twenty-six local Knights assemblies and 10,000 members. Albert still belonged to Assembly 1307, a "mixed" group that included both skilled and un-skilled workers, but within the American Group and the IWPA at large he was in a distinct minority as a Knight.[16]

Although Chicago justly claimed to be the center of labor mili-tancy in the country, the city's record for 1885 and early 1886 was far from triumphant. The McCormick Reaper strike of April 1885 and the streetcar strike in July of that year both ended in defeat for the workers. In the spring of 1886, the eight-hour campaign competed for the atten-tion of the estimated two-thirds of Chicagoans who were churchgoers with a series of massive religious revivals led by Baptists and Catho-lics; the well-known preacher Dwight Moody made headlines, but the spate of revivals also featured lesser-known figures such as Sam Jones and Sam Small, who presented themselves as "Two Soul-Saving Sams." Evangelists denounced the anarchists not only for their godless anti-Americanism but also for patronizing the *Biergarten* on Sundays. To a degree, the religious revivals and the eight-hour rallies competed for workers' time, energy, and loyalties.[17]

In 1885, labor politics remade partisan and police-department pol-itics. Although generally able to maintain the support of mainstream trade unions and the city's elites simultaneously, Mayor Carter Harri-son angered the former group in the summer of 1885 when he appointed John Bonfield as inspector and secretary of the police department. Bonfield, who shared with businessmen and Pinkerton security forces a deep and abiding fear of labor radicals, used the police to crush the streetcar workers in July (and he was not averse to roughing up strik-ers himself). Of his penchant for breaking up peaceful meetings, he said, famously, "The club today saves the bullet tomorrow." The near-ubiquitous presence of Albert Parsons and August Spies at outdoor rallies, where they lectured crowds about the need for force, prompted the police department to install more efficient means of communication among officers, beef up their surveillance of routine weekly meetings as well as "monster" demonstrations, and call for more and better arms. Detective Michael Schaak spoke for law enforcement officials when he claimed that radicals deserved no free-speech rights because "socialism places itself beyond the pale of moral forces."[18]

In this tense atmosphere came signs that Lucy was eager to start her own agitation tour. The March 6, 1886, issue of *The Alarm* carried the announcement that "Mrs. Lucy Parsons, of Chicago," was to speak on the occasion of the fifteenth anniversary of the Paris Commune in St. Louis, Missouri, on the 13th of that month. A few weeks later, the paper reported that she had canceled the trip due to illness, but now that she had recovered, she "contemplates making a tour of Socialistic propaganda in that section soon." Lucy's itinerary was to have included the cities where Albert was well known—not only St. Louis, but also Kansas City, Leavenworth, and Saint Joseph. She planned to leave as soon as he returned from a series of extended trips that stretched over a three-month period, beginning in January. Perhaps she, like Albert, was becoming bored of a routine that consisted mostly of talking to a small knot of American Group members on Wednesday nights, and much larger, but less engaged, crowds on Sundays. Or she realized that her oratorical abilities matched those of her celebrated husband, and hoped to make her mark on the IWPA. The couple had begun to assemble a collection of newspaper clippings from the many places where Albert had spoken; before long, radicals in these places would soon welcome the remarkable Mrs. Parsons as well.[19]

Around this time Lucy wrote a piece for *The Alarm* responding to a March 17 massacre in Carrollton, Mississippi, a small town one hundred miles north of Jackson. Two black brothers, Ed and Charles Brown, sought to have a white man arrested for attempting to murder them. When the Browns and their supporters appeared in the county courthouse for a hearing, several dozen white men stormed in and opened fire, killing ten blacks on the spot and fatally wounding thirteen more. The white assailants were never prosecuted. One of only a handful of *Alarm* pieces devoted to southern blacks, this one, titled "The Negro," begins with a lament: "Who has stood upon the sea-shore and watched the weird dash of the ceaseless waves and has not become tired of the monotonous sameness?" Parsons then turned to her own fatigue born of a never-ending struggle: "Who but a devoted soul in this labor movement does not at times become tired—a weary tiredness, verging on a disgust at the apparent sameness and monotony of the wage system as depicted by those engaged in the noble work of exposing the hideous inequalities of the present economic system?"[20]

After this introduction, Parsons considered the plight of black men and women in Carrollton and throughout the South—"defenceless, poverty-stricken, hemmed about by their deadly enemies . . . these our fellow-beings are murdered, without quarter." She rejected the argument that racial prejudice was the cause of injustice: make no mistake, she wrote, the black man was terrorized because he was poor and dependent, not because of the color of his skin. In this, one of her only direct statements on racial ideologies, she suggested that southern white terrorism sprang from the lack of legal protection accorded to blacks, not from any inherent characteristics of their "race." Here she was partly right: blacks were uniquely vulnerable in the late nineteenth-century South because of their historical liabilities in the eyes of the law, first as enslaved workers, and then as disenfranchised, landless laborers. Parsons, however, adopted a Marxist analysis, saying that black people constituted a subset of the poor generally, and that the pernicious idea of "race" should have no place in anarchist thought or action.[21]

This view allowed her to hold blacks responsible for their own liberation: "And to the negro himself we would say your deliverance lies mainly in your own hands." Tilling the same soil as their enslaved forebears, blacks must foreswear both politics and prayer, and instead wreak revenge on white landowners. If their profound humiliation was not incentive enough, then they should "look in the tear-stained eye of your sorrowing wife and hungry children, or think of your son, who has been sent to the chain-gang or perhaps murdered upon your doorsteps." Grasp what weapons are available, she urged black men—"the torch of the incendiary," the only argument that tyrants and capitalists understood. In this case, though, Parsons was wrong in her suggestion that the Carrollton blacks were passive; the Browns and others had tried to defend themselves on the streets of the town and in the courtroom, where, according to one report, they came armed with "every conceivable kind of firearms, double barrel breech-loading shot guns, Winchester rifles, pistols of all calibers, including the long horse pistols, with their immense balls." Still, whites overwhelmed them with their numbers, brooking no defiance.[22]

It is unclear why Lucy Parsons decided to forgo a regional speaking tour in the spring of 1886. It is possible that the eight-hour-day movement was gaining momentum, and that she and Albert saw in it the bright promise of revolution right there in their hometown. What is clear is that as soon as the opportunity to agitate widely presented itself, she would be ready and eager to avail herself of it.

AS EARLY AS THE WINTER OF 1885–1886, CHICAGO AUTHORITIES HAD gone on high alert in anticipation of the upcoming May 1 demonstration on behalf of the eight-hour day. In late December, parties unknown deposited a tin can filled with explosive material on the doorstep of a local judge; later detonated at a nearby police station, "the infernal machine . . . caused consternation among the force," according to a report in *Labor Enquirer*. The wealthy members of the Commercial Club ordered a $2,000 machine gun for the 1st Infantry Regiment and formed a Committee of Safety, which employed its own security force. Detective Schaak stepped up surveillance of "anarchists and hot-headed strikers."[23]

In March, the IWPA called a mass meeting to denounce a lockout of McCormick Reaper strikers and to celebrate the spreading labor actions against Jay Gould's Missouri Pacific and Texas and Pacific Railroads. Both Lucy and Albert addressed the crowd. In uncompromising terms, Lucy criticized the Knights' support for arbitration, issuing the ultimate indictment of the group—that it "stood for law and order." Albert, too, faulted the Knights for their timidity, but at the same time he offered at least half-hearted praise for their ability to organize all kinds of workers in such large numbers; the Knights were socialists, whether they knew it or not, he suggested. The ideological differences between husband and wife might have been subtle, but Lucy was staking out her own more radical critique of the Knights and their program.[24]

The May 1 issue of the daily mainstream paper the *Chicago Mail* greeted the long-anticipated (or dreaded) day with the pronouncement that Albert Parsons and August Spies should be held "personally responsible for any trouble that does occur." On that day, a Saturday, an estimated 300,000 workers went on strike at 13,000 workplaces nationwide. Chicago marked the day with a march of 80,000 people down Michigan Avenue, with Albert and Lucy, together with their children, at the head of the march—whether they claimed their place at the head by acclamation of their followers or simply by assuming that position on their own is unknown. Hopes ran high: as many as 45,000 employees, including 35,000 meatpackers, had recently won a shorter workday without going on strike. Still, the outpouring of laboring humanity could not mask raw conflicts within the crowd: that morning the *Arbeiter Zeitung* had attacked the Trade and Labor Assembly, calling its members "miserable creatures . . . more despicable then we can find words to express."[25]

Albert left Chicago that evening, taking an overnight train to Cincinnati, where on Sunday he spoke to a huge rally in favor of the eight-hour day. He did not return until 7 or 8 the morning of May 4, and so the fateful events of Monday, May 3, transpired without him.[26]

That afternoon, employees of the McCormick Reaper works clashed with police on Blue Island Avenue and Twenty-Second Street, not far from the plant. Earlier that year, the company's owner, Cyrus McCormick Jr., had locked them all out; he decided to install more machinery and hire strikebreakers, and thereby rid himself of union labor altogether. Some of the workers had been reinstated, but others—the molders, for example—remained locked out of the plant. The 1,300 men now on strike were divided, with more than half belonging to the Knights, 250 to the Metal Workers Union (affiliated with the Central Labor Union), and 300 to no union at all. August Spies was speaking to the lumber-shovers when the shift changed, and pickets began to attack scabs streaming from the factory. The police, who had been standing by, beat the pickets with their clubs and then opened fire, killing two and wounding many others. Enraged, Spies hurried to the AZ office and printed a handbill in German and English calling for a mass meeting the following evening (Tuesday) at Haymarket Square on Randolph Street, between Desplaines and Halsted Streets: "Good speakers will be present to denounce the latest atrocious act of the police, the shooting of our fellow workmen yesterday afternoon." The AZ printer Adolph Fischer added a line—"Workingmen, arm yourselves and appear in full force," but Spies hastened to cut it for the majority of the handbill's print run.[27]

Meanwhile, that Monday, groups of workers throughout the city were moving from one shop to another and pulling people out of work. Women joined the walkout, prompting the *Chicago Tribune* to report that hundreds of "shouting Amazons" had quit work early that day and, led by "two tall Bohemians," were canvassing garment shops along the way and urging others to join them. Laughing, singing, and accompanied by a brass band, the garment workers called for better pay (the fourteen-year-olds earned 75 cents to $1 a week for 55 hours of work) and shorter days (their current stint was eleven hours). A Knights organizer paused long enough to tell a reporter, "We are not red-flag or Socialistic people, and we have no use for Spies or the *Arbeiter Zeitung.*"[28]

On Tuesday, May 4, the strike that had begun on Saturday entered its fourth day, with groups as diverse as laundresses, lumberyard and glue-factory workers, Jewish male cloak makers, and high school students joining in the protests. Men armed with pick handles and clubs, who continued "slugging" scabs, ran up against troops from the 1st Infantry with bayonets leveled.

Albert had arrived home from Cincinnati between 7 and 8 a.m. that day and promptly fallen asleep. The details of his day's activities thereafter remain in dispute. However, he, Lucy, and Lizzie Swank Holmes would later tell a similar story: that Lucy roused him at 10 in the morning to tell him that she and Lizzie wanted him to call a meeting of the American Group for 7:30 that evening to discuss tapping into the long-dormant energy of young seamstresses. (Swank Holmes had come to Chicago that morning from Geneva, Illinois, where she lived with her husband.) Lucy had addressed a large meeting of sewing girls on Sunday night, and she said (as Albert later recounted), "I think we ought to help those sewing girls to organize and join the eight-hour movement, because they work harder than anybody; these great tailor machines are very hard to work." Sometime that morning Albert wrote the announcement: "American Group meets to-night, Tuesday, 107 Fifth Avenue. Important Business. Every member should attend. 7:30 o'clock sharp. Agitation Committee." Questioned later, he was vague about who actually hand-delivered the ad to the *Chicago Daily News*, which carried the notice in its afternoon edition.[29]

The major participants also agreed on the details related to the Parsonses' early evening hours. After eating dinner together at their apartment, Lucy, Albert, Albert Junior, and Lulu, together with Lizzie, headed to the offices of the *AZ* and *The Alarm* on Fifth Avenue. First, though, sometime between 7:30 and 8, they stopped at the corner of Halsted and Randolph Streets (about half a mile from their residence), the site of the planned Haymarket Square protest. There they ran into two reporters, Edgar E. Owen from the *Chicago Times* and Henry E. O. Heinemann from the *Tribune*, who had both heard about the rally, but now, in the early evening, could find no evidence of one. People were milling around, but no one seemed to be in charge. Albert engaged in genial banter with the two men, jokingly asking Owen if he was armed. Replying that he was not, the reporter inquired of Albert, "Have you any dynamite about you?"—a question the whole group seemed to find amusing. Lucy said, "He is a very dangerous-looking man, isn't he?" The reporters asked Albert if he was going to speak at the Haymarket, but he told them he had made other plans. After this brief exchange, the Parsons party took a streetcar east to 107 Fifth Avenue, which housed the *AZ* and *Alarm* offices.[30]

The Parsonses, with their children in tow, and accompanied by Lizzie Swank Holmes, arrived late to the meeting, at 8:30. About a dozen people were in attendance, including Samuel Fielden. The discussion had been in progress for only about twenty-five minutes when a messenger arrived to say that the Haymarket meeting lacked for speakers, and that August Spies wanted Albert to address the crowd. The rally had started about half an hour late, with an estimated 3,000 people on hand. Albert agreed to go, and with Lucy, Lizzie, Fielden, and several others from the meeting, set out for Haymarket Square. The Parsonses may have arranged for someone else to take their children home from the offices, although later, both parents denied having made such arrangements, instead saying that they had taken the children with them to Haymarket Square. This detail about the whereabouts of the children that night turned out to be one of some import.[31]

When the Parsonses and the other members of their group arrived at the square around 9:15, Spies quickly wrapped up his remarks, and Albert mounted a makeshift speaker's stand, an empty wagon parked near the square, at the mouth of a passageway called Crane's Alley. Lucy and Lizzie sat on a spring seat in a nearby wagon. Albert spoke for about forty-five minutes, giving his classic stem-winder. Later asked if he had heard Parsons that night "go over and over, going into a thousand facts and figures, in regard to laboring men," the journalist Heinemann replied, "That is Parsons, yes." G. P. English, a stenographic reporter for the *Tribune*, judged Parsons's speech "pretty much the same thing" as "his ordinary talk." English, who had covered Parsons's speeches for years, had instructions from his editor "to write out the most incendiary parts of the speeches." At the end of his talk Parsons exclaimed to his listeners that if they did not want to see their wives and children perish from starvation or murder, then "in the interest of your liberty and independence, arm, arm yourselves!" Still, English found the speeches that night "a little milder" than usual.[32]

With the exception of Bonfield, who was observing the crowd, the police were nowhere in sight—nearly two hundred officers were waiting in the Desplaines police station, only half a block away, in case they were needed. Together with Bonfield, Mayor Harrison eyed the crowd and anticipated trouble. Still, Harrison found nothing particularly noteworthy in the speeches. As Parsons concluded his remarks, the mayor indicated to the inspector that all seemed to be in order, and the police would probably have no cause to intervene. Harrison left for home, and Bonfield walked the short distance back to the police station.

Albert finished at about 10 p.m., when Fielden took to the speaker's wagon and began to talk. Before long, however, rain clouds moved in from the north, causing many in the crowd to disperse. Albert and Lucy and Lizzie, as well as Adolph Fischer, the *AZ* typesetter, retreated to a tavern in nearby Zepf's Hall, about half a block from the speaker's stand. Fielden continued to speak to a dwindling number of people on the square, estimated at five hundred or so. At about 10:20, he began to denounce the legal system that undergirded the capitalists' power, urging his listeners to "keep your eye upon it, throttle it, kill it, stab it, do everything you can to wound it—to impede its progress." Though this was boilerplate anarchist rhetoric, his words prompted two under-cover detectives to run to the station and alert Bonfield. Together with a captain, the inspector led his contingent of eighty men on a rapid clip down the street, scattering the crowd before them before stopping and confronting Fielden. Bonfield ordered him to stop speaking and climb down from the wagon, and Fielden protested, "But we are peaceable."[33]

Suddenly, someone in the nearby alleyway threw a round object with what one observer called a "slender tail of fire." The metal cas-ing filled with dynamite and lit by a fuse landed in front of the police column and exploded. A tremendous explosion ripped through the square, felling some police and causing others to draw their pistols and begin firing wildly into the crowd. One officer, Mathias Degan, died immediately; another six police and at least four civilians would later succumb to their wounds. The square now took on the appearance of a battlefield, with the dying groaning and writhing on the pavement. The injured numbered at least sixty-seven, probably more, as many of the workers sought aid in nearby storefronts and homes, never to be counted. Most of the wounds came from bullets, not bomb fragments, but whether from the guns of police or men in the crowd is unknown.[34]

The Parsonses and Lizzie Swank Holmes saw none of this; they were in the nearby saloon. Albert later said that upon hearing a loud noise he thought that perhaps the Illinois regiments had trained their Gatling gun on the demonstrators, and so he quickly ushered the two women to the back of the building, where they waited in the darkness for about twenty minutes. Finally, when all was quiet, they emerged into the street and hastened to the Milwaukee Avenue viaduct. Lizzie gave this account of her words to Albert at this point in the events: "I do not know what has happened, or whether there is any further dan-ger, but we may be sure some kind of a conflict has occurred. Everybody knows you and they all know your influence. If any of our boys are in danger you are. Whatever has happened, leave the city for a few days at least. We can't spare you yet, and in the excited condition the people must be in[,] we do not know what might happen to you." When he hesitated, she recalled, she used "many other arguments to induce the brave, home-loving man to depart before he at last consented." Albert accepted a loan of $5 for his travels from Thomas Brown, a member of the American Group who had attended the meeting early in the evening and now stood close by. He was about to go, but, according to Lizzie, he spoke to his wife before leaving: "Before he turned away he said, 'Kiss me Lucy. We do not know when we will meet again.'" Lizzie said "there seemed a sad, almost prophetic, tone in his voice; so hurriedly, and with what unexpressed feelings none can ever know, their parting, the end of a long period of uninterrupted and happy companionship, took place." Lizzie offered to see him off at the train depot, and the two disappeared down the street. Lucy headed back home to the Parsonses' apartment on West Indiana Avenue, where Lizzie would join her later that night.[35]

THE FOLLOWING DAY—WEDNESDAY, MAY 5—LUCY HAD TO CONTEND with the harsh glare of the media, but she seemed prepared. That morning, police began a hasty, indiscriminate roundup of men suspected of the bombing, a crackdown that would eventually net two hundred individuals. A Chicago vigilante committee warned, "Spies, Parsons, and Schwab [Spies's *AZ* colleague] and others of their kind, beware! The rope does its work quick. The massacres of our brave policemen must be avenged." The *Tribune* added Fielden, the speaker at the time of the bombing, to the list of prime suspects, berating municipal authorities for allowing these men "to pursue their frenzied course without the slightest interference." Like a deadly snake, the monster of anarchy had struck with stunning ferocity.[36]

The police ransacked the Parsonses' apartment, and Lucy later claimed that the officers had cruelly taunted their son, demanding he tell them where his father was hiding. She might have chosen to shrink from the intrusion—the menace of it all—but instead, when the men left, she and Lizzie Swank Holmes hurried to Fifth Avenue and the offices of the *Arbeiter Zeitung*. There they found another raid in progress. Michael Schwab and August Spies had been working on that afternoon's edition of the paper, but now, they, together with the entire twenty-three-person staff of the *AZ*, were placed under arrest. Oscar Neebe, who was also present at the time, later recounted what he called "another lot of ruffians" who ran up the steps and saw the two women writing at a desk. One of these officers demanded of Lizzie, "What are you doing there?" before grabbing her. Then "she protested as an American woman, and as she protested he said: 'Shut up, you bitch, or I will knock you down.'" Apparently, Lucy "was called the same name by the officers. They called her a black bitch, and wanted to knock her down; and they said they would not let us publish any paper; they would take the types and material and throw them out of the window." Subsequent newspaper reports indicated that a search of the *AZ* office had yielded dynamite sticks, fuses, blasting caps, and a kind of lead type that matched fragments of the bomb, and that Albert's desk upstairs contained gunpowder and a fuse in addition to a six-foot-long "brass cartridge that is used in heavy bombing."[37]

Officers arrested the two women and took them down to the central police station. Lizzie was held until Saturday. Lucy spent only a brief time behind bars, since the officers were planning "to shadow her, hoping she would make some appointment with her husband, so that the latter could be captured." The search for Albert had commenced, with officers looking up and down Lake Street (the site of the American Group headquarters) and its vicinity and going from door to door, from basements to attics. Soon there were reported sightings of him in Chicago, wounded; in Dallas, disguised; in Pittsburgh, hiding out with immigrant sympathizers; and in Cleveland and St. Louis.[38]

Over the next few days, Lucy found time to write an account of the bombing for *Labor Enquirer*. Although she had not witnessed the moments before the bombing herself, she offered her own recollections of that night at Haymarket, when the "minions of the oppressing class were marching up to one of the most peaceably assembled meetings ever held in this country by any class of people to discuss questions concerning their own interests." Had the anarchists wished to destroy their enemies completely then, she wrote, they could have done so easily, so "thoroughly disorganized and demoralized" were the police. She reported on the last few days' "reign of terror . . . which would put to shame the most zealous Russian bloodhound." The authorities had quickly suspended the anarchist papers and were now conducting home invasions of everyone "who has ever been known to have raised a voice or sympathized with those who have had aught to say against the present system of robbery and oppression." She added: "This organized banditti have arrested me four times; they have subjected me to indignities that should bring the tinge of shame to the calloused cheek of a hardened barbarian." Though they might try to intimidate her, "they simply challenge my contempt." By this time she was well aware that, as a reporter put it, she was "under the strictest surveillance, and wherever she goes or turns an officer is on her track."[39]

Newspaper editors quickly responded to the public's eager demand for news about the fugitive Parsons and his enigmatic wife. As early as May 6, two days after the bombing, stories began to surface about Albert, Lucy, and their courtship in Texas. The *Dallas Morning News* ran an article about Albert's Radical Republican days, when he "levanted with a colored woman, who is the present Mrs. Parsons, and who occasionally helps him out by making street speeches." That same day the *Waco Day* featured a piece on Albert titled "His Early Career in Waco—Learning the Rudiments of Agitation," which portrayed him as "argumentative, as cranky, as discontented and as little disposed to hard work as ever" and recounted his run-ins with the local Democrats who now controlled the city's politics. The Waco reporter also went into detail about his "liaison with a colored woman (rather bright color) known as Lucy Gathings" and described her "husband" (formerly Oliver Gathings, now Oliver Benton) who was still living in Waco. Taken by the sudden infamy of a native daughter, the reporter noted that she was "quite intelligent for her opportunities" and that her socialistic speeches "are intelligently worded." Apparently, at least someone in Waco had been following the careers of both Lucy and Albert in Chicago.[40]

The Waco paper's story was picked up by a number of papers in Illinois, Texas, and beyond, and before long reporters were referring to the absconded anarchist's wife as a "mongrel," or as one who looked like "an ordinary plantation 'nigger.'" Perhaps, opined the Dallas paper, the anarchists were aiming to produce "a single family through the intermarriage of the races," and "with the mule thus produced and an equal division of the fruits of industry the anarchist expects to bring order out of chaos."[41]

Intrigued by the reports from Texas, the *Chicago Daily News* sent a reporter to interview Lucy on the evening of May 7; he found her at home, "reticent and defiant." Denying any knowledge of her husband's movements, she seemed rather inclined to talk about herself. Based on what she told him and what she looked like, the reporter wrote that she was thirty-three years old (taking two years off her true age), a native of Texas, and "of Mexican and Indian descent with a possible trace of Ethiopian blood in her veins." Describing her appearance and manner to his readers, he noted: "She is of a swarthy complexion, darker than an ordinary mulatto, but without the olive tint of the half-bred Ethiop. Her hair is abundant and rebellious, waved but not kinky. She has the high cheek bones of the Indian strongly marked and a long, pointed chin. Her eyes are as black as ebony. She is tall and angular. She is a self-possessed speaker and a fluent one." The interviewer informed his readers that her "socialistic harangues" revealed her to be "the most violent and vindictive of all the orators of that persuasion." Asked if she still maintained that "the ambition of her life is to fire the engine that shall run the guillotine to cut off the heads of capitalists," she replied coolly, "That is my religion." The reporter concluded, "She is a remarkably strong willed and determined woman of a fair education and no ordinary ability."[42]

With her husband in hiding, Lucy immediately set out to fashion a new life-story for herself, one that would introduce her to a nationwide audience as the daughter of Mexican and Indian parents. She now claimed, "My ancestors were here before any Europeans. They went forth to meet Cortes when he landed on the Pacific slope." With this one deft stroke, she sought to deflect attention from her blackness and also repudiate the idea that all anarchists were suspect because of their foreignness. She became a new person, the captivating orator, the Mexican Indian wife of the famous Haymarket conspirator. And only a few knew better for certain—those Wacoites who remembered when Albert the Confederate veteran met Lucy the former slave.[43]

❦ Chapter 7 ❧

Bitter Fruit of Braggadocio

SOON AFTER HE LEFT ZEPF'S HALL THAT TUESDAY, MAY 4, ALBERT
Parsons took a late-night train to Geneva, Illinois, the hometown
of Lizzie Swank Holmes and her husband, William Holmes. Geneva,
located about thirty-five miles west of Chicago, resembled a New England village; there, according to Lizzie, all the residents knew each
other, and "poetry, music, painting, and classical literature dwell peace-
fully in every household." The couple found Geneva at once serene and
infuriating, for despite its laudable egalitarianism—with few poor and
none rich—the residents knew little and cared nothing about the great
struggle raging not far away in Chicago. Lizzie was indignant that Geneva authorities refused to allow homeless men to tarry within the
town's borders. In an homage to Lucy's famous propaganda piece, she
suggested that tramps could either slink away in shame, "or stay—have
you a match about you?" William predicted the downfall of the smug
denizens of Geneva—"*there will be eternal war; war to the Knife*—to
extermination," he wrote. "Let the day come quickly that shall see the
beginning of the end."[1]

Geneva was too small not to notice a newcomer who was now being
hunted as a notorious fugitive, so Parsons quickly set about disguising
himself. He shaved his mustache, stopped dyeing his prematurely gray

hair, grew a beard, and donned ill-fitting clothes, effecting a complete transformation from dapper city gent to rough-hewn rural workman. By May 10 he had moved on to Waukesha, Wisconsin, a town of 5,000 just west of Milwaukee, where he found lodging with Daniel Hoan, a subscriber to *The Alarm*. Under the name of Amos Jackson, Parsons worked in Hoan's well-pump factory and picked up odd jobs as a painter and carpenter. He regaled the neighborhood children with stories of his boyhood on the Texas frontier and took daily hikes over the rolling hills, stopping every once in a while to drink from a spring and admire the lovely vista of lake and meadow. After months on the road speechifying, he now enveloped himself in the idyll that was Waukesha.[2]

For years Parsons had presented himself to the world as a "revolutionist," but he slipped easily into his new Waukesha persona. Boarding with the churchgoing Hoan family, he even addressed their congregation on a couple of occasions, preaching a bland socialism of "liberty, fraternity, equality, for our oppressed and down-trodden fellow man." Later he would tell the Hoans that he fondly recalled their happy "Sabbath" outings. He also quoted from the Bible the family had given him—passages from the New Testament condemning "the pulpits of mammon" and the hypocrites who would embrace Jesus on the one hand and pursue their own greedy ends on the other. To the Hoans' neighbors he was the funny little "Mr. Jackson," who, reverting to Parsons the Wacoite, loved "the perfume of wild roses, clover, cherry, apple and many beautiful flowers in fragrant bloom."[3]

Soon Parsons would shift again, now presenting himself to a curious public as the descendant of rock-ribbed Yankee preachers and Revolutionary war heroes, a patriot devoted to traditional American values of freedom of assembly and speech. He would deny that he had ever advocated the use of force generally or dynamite particularly, and he would disavow articles in *The Alarm*, whether he had written them or not. In this sort of backtracking he was not alone; Lizzie Swank Holmes, too, disowned her own writings, proclaiming, "The theory of anarchy is opposed to all idea of force." In contrast to her husband and her friend, Lucy Parsons felt no need to prevaricate about her political beliefs in the wake of the Haymarket bombing—although she certainly did dissemble about her origins.[4]

A few days after Albert's disappearance from Chicago, Lizzie informed Lucy that he was in Waukesha. In the meantime, Inspector John Bonfield and Detective Michael Schaak had enlisted the aid of the private security chief William Pinkerton (his father, Allan, had died the year before) in making hundreds of arrests, conducting warrantless searches, and shutting down radical labor presses. Mayor Carter Harrison expressed reservations about these tactics, but his concerns went unheeded. Businessmen such as Marshall Field, George Pullman, and Cyrus McCormick Jr. charged that the mayor and his administration had tolerated the anarchists for far too long. The *Chicago Tribune* and other papers initiated their readers into a cult of the dead policemen, now martyrs to the cause of law and order. The wave of repression made national news, with the *New York Times* approving the crackdown on what it called "Anarchy's Red Hand" and reporting "a preconcerted plan on the part of Spies, Parsons, and Fielden" to lure the police into a Haymarket trap and murder them all.[5]

In Chicago, a grand jury convened to consider the evidence and proceeded to indict thirty-one men as accessories after the fact for the murder of police officer Mathias Degan, who died on the spot that night. Eight of the suspects were slated to stand trial—*Arbeiter Zeitung* editor August Spies; coeditor Michael Schwab; office manager Oscar Neebe; the printer Adolph Fischer; a recent newcomer to Chicago and suspected bomb-maker, the carpenter Louis Lingg, who was active in the Central Labor Union; a known militant, George Engel; and the American Group members Samuel Fielden and Albert Parsons. (Of the eight defendants, only Parsons and Fielden were neither German-born nor of German descent.) The prosecution believed that the person who threw the bomb was Rudolph Schnaubelt, the husband of Schwab's sister, who had disappeared and was never apprehended. State's Attorney Julius S. Grinnell constructed a case that posited a meeting in the basement of the *Arbeiter Zeitung* offices on the evening of May 3, the day before the bombing. Supposedly, Fischer, Engel, and others met there to plan an attack on any police who appeared in the course of a rally they had called for the following night at Haymarket Square. The exploded bomb was, according to the prosecution, the culmination of groundwork laid over many years by IWPA speechmakers and *AZ* and *Alarm* writers. The defendants—who, except for Lingg, were all orators, editors, or both—stood accused of murder and conspiracy.

By this time the Chicago papers were doing their best to whip their readers into a frenzy. In late May, the *Chicago Times* had already reached a verdict: "Public justice demands that the assassin A. R. Parsons, who is said to disgrace this country by being born in it, shall be seized, tried, and hanged for murder." The paper also indicted someone who had not been charged: "Public justice demands that the negro woman who passes as the wife of the assassin Parsons, and has been his assistant in the work of organized assassination, shall be seized, tried, and hanged for murder." Considering Lucy's own straightforward calls for workers to use dynamite and thereby wreak havoc on the capitalist system, it is worth noting that she escaped the police dragnet and, ultimately, any charges related to the Haymarket bombing.[6]

Unbowed and uncowed, Lucy Parsons had the freedom of movement as well as the nerve to play at least a supporting role in the great drama that was the Haymarket trial. By mid-June, with Albert still hiding in Waukesha, she had met at least twice with defense lawyers to devise a strategy for the trial. (If the defendants had been truly principled anarchists, they would have refused counsel, arguing that the state-run proceedings were inherently corrupt.) The legal team of four was headed by Captain William Black, a corporate lawyer and Union Army veteran. Together he and Lucy discussed the merits of having Albert return to Chicago to surrender to authorities. (Sigmund Zeisler, another member of the defense team, later described Lucy as "well-educated and ladylike, though somewhat temperamental.") Black favored an unannounced, highly choreographed appearance by Albert: the fugitive would show up on the first day of the trial, astounding officials who would now realize that an innocent man stood before them, since presumably no killer would turn himself in voluntarily. Thus forced to reexamine their prejudices against one defendant, the general public would have to reexamine their prejudices against all of them, and the prosecution would come under immense pressure to drop all charges. Lucy agreed to this plan and sent word to Albert, who made preparations to return.[7]

On the morning of June 21, the day after his forty-first birthday and the day the trial proceedings were to begin, Albert arrived in Chicago and, as planned, made his way to the home of American Group member Sarah Ames, where he showered, shaved off his beard, and cut his hair, using bootblack to restore it to its preternaturally dark color. Lucy met him there for a brief reunion before the two of them took a hansom cab (together with a reporter for the *AZ*) to the county's criminal court building. There, according to the *Tribune*, they found Black nervously "stalking up and down the sidewalk in the sun." As Albert Parsons and William Black ascended the steps of the building and walked into the courtroom, there was "considerable stir and craning of necks," as people whispered and then shouted, "Parsons has come into court!" Asked where he had been hiding, he replied, "O, I've been out West to a watering place." As he took his seat next to the other defendants, Lucy sat "smilingly watching the proceedings." She told reporters, "He's been more than 500 miles from Chicago, and so thoroughly disguised that his own mother wouldn't know him."[8]

Clearly shocked at Parsons's sudden appearance, State's Attorney Grinnell nonetheless quickly recovered his composure and ordered that he be taken into custody so he could stand trial with the other defendants. Black had not anticipated this development; it was, he told Grinnell, "not only most ungracious and cruel, it is also gratuitous." The whole scene confounded the defense. Instead of accepting accolades from all sides as a hero and effecting the release of his co-defendants, Parsons spent the night in the Cook County jail, in company with his old friend August Spies. Later, he would explain his return in patriotic terms: "I thought I could safely trust the sober, second thought of the community and the love of fair play, which I think is characteristic of the American people."[9]

LUCY—"JAUNTILY ATTIRED," ACCORDING TO THE *TRIBUNE*— attended every day of the trial, including jury selection; from June 21 through July 15, nearly 1,000 men were examined during the voir dire, a preliminary part of the proceedings in which witnesses and jurors are evaluated for competency. Eventually the process seemed so time-consuming that both the defense and the prosecution agreed to authorize a special bailiff to complete it. Judge Joseph E. Gary proved decidedly welcoming of jurors who expressed an initial bias against the defendants, but then, under questioning by Grinnell, assured the court that they could evaluate the evidence in an impartial way. In the end the jury consisted primarily of native-born middle-class men, clerks and proprietors of small businesses. Factory hands and other wage earners were conspicuous for their absence, as were immigrants and union members.[10]

Within a few days of Albert's return, Lucy had abandoned her dressmaking business, at least temporarily, in order to capitalize upon what she believed would be Chicagoans' newfound appreciation for anarchist ideology. Like Albert, she welcomed the opportunity to give interviews to all who asked. In the early evening of June 22, a reporter found her at home at 245 West Indiana Street (pressed for funds, she had moved to a cheaper place after the events of May 4) "in a pleasant, well-furnished flat," sipping a beer and reading the paper. Parsons recalled the disrespectful treatment she had suffered at the hands of the officers who had ransacked her apartment and rummaged through her clothes the month before. She ridiculed the notion that a handful of anarchists would be accused of "terrorizing an entire city, if not the world." At one point she went to the back of the flat, and, shoving aside a wardrobe, opened a trap door in the floor and took out a framed picture of her husband taken on May 1. "My husband is good looking, don't you think? But oh! The horrid pictures of him they did print." She said she would be following the example of Spies's friends and relatives, who were raising money selling his likeness. (The *Cleveland Plain Dealer* published a story titled "How the Negro Wife of Parsons, the Anarchist, Will Support Herself," the headline suggesting that she had an uphill climb to convince the public of her new biography.) Parsons maintained her husband's innocence but also said that "our cause will never be a cause until we have a few martyrs to write about. That is what we need." She had no doubt that the defense would be adequately funded: "As it is, I have been very liberally supported by my admirers—I don't mean personal admirers—rather sympathizers."

The reporter suggested it was she and not her husband who had written *Alarm* articles published under his name, a point she did not dispute.[11]

Many other supporters of the defendants shared Lucy's belief that the movement needed martyrs. Once incarcerated, Albert was often compared to nineteenth-century abolitionists, and especially to John Brown, who had been executed for his raid on the federal arsenal at Harpers Ferry, Virginia, in 1859. Brown had died so that the slaves might go free, just as Albert Parsons would (if necessary) die for the righteousness of the anarchists' cause. Yet few of his supporters then or since paused to consider that the analogy might be as troubling as it was telling: Brown had an indisputable history of domestic terrorism, hacking pro-slavery men to death on the Kansas frontier.

Once the jury was seated, the trial began; with the court in session every day of the week except Sunday, it stretched from July 16 until August 11, for a total of fifty-four days. By modern standards the courtroom seemed a carnivalesque affair. The judge was surrounded by a coterie of well-dressed female acquaintances to keep him company, the wives and children of the defendants mingled with the lawyers before and after the day's events, members of the jury played cards during the proceedings, and a crush of curiosity-seekers and reporters filled the tense, stiflingly hot courtroom.[12]

Meanwhile, the city was in an uproar, consumed by the tragedy of the policemen who had died at Haymarket. Of the wounded police, most were in critical condition. Not unexpectedly, many Chicagoans—and not only members of the Citizens' Association and the Board of Trade—had been quick to condemn the defendants. Workers, including many socialists and Knights of Labor members, distanced themselves from the accused men in no uncertain terms. Even Boston anarchists charged their Chicago counterparts with "falsely sailing under anarchist colors, committing murder, arson, and mob violence." Right after the bombing, *Labor Enquirer* editor Joseph Buchanan made what was at the time a bold statement, saying that he did not intend "to defend the actions of the wild men of Chicago," but "neither do I unqualifiedly condemn" them. After all, he wrote, "there can be no effect without a cause," and certainly the arrogance of capital presented abundant cause. Few shared William Holmes's conviction that Haymarket would bear anarchist fruit by stirring the American people, and thus bringing into focus a revolutionary imperative heretofore only dimly appreciated by the masses.[13]

In presenting the case before the grand jury back in May, Grinnell had claimed that the identity of the bomber was irrelevant, and that a suspect need not have attended the Haymarket rally in order to be found guilty. Detective Schaak proposed that "the core of conspiracy" revolved around a generalized "moral responsibility" for the carnage; Spies, Fielden, Schwab, and Parsons, though not connected directly to the alleged May 3 secret meeting, had nonetheless paved the way to mayhem with their "seditious utterances." The taint of treason—the crime of trying to destroy the US government—hung over the trial as part of the sixty-nine-count indictment.[14]

Testifying at the trial were 118 witnesses, including 54 members of the Chicago Police Department as well as defendants Fielden, Schwab, Spies, and Parsons (but not the hot-headed and unpredictable Lingg). Testimony brought up many angles—that Johann Most's books were sold at IWPA picnics and that *The Alarm* had published parts of the bloodthirsty 1871 Russian-anarchist manifesto *Catechism of the Revolutionist*; that there had been secret codes and secret meetings among the alleged conspirators; that Spies had boasted about the nitroglycerin pills in his possession; that receipts and orders for dynamite purchases and a mysterious package with a greasy substance had been discovered in Parsons's desk in his *Alarm* office after the bombing; that some of the defendants had been involved in an aborted attack on the Board of Trade Building in April 1885; and that defendants had made endless calls for assassination and violent resistance in their anarchistic writings and speeches. A reporter for the *Daily Inter-Ocean* told of covering the lakefront meetings, where Albert Parsons had urged his listeners to arm themselves with pistols and dynamite; and where Lucy Parsons, asked what kind of pamphlets she was distributing, would say only that "she was doing missionary work."[15]

At the end of the trial, Judge Gary summarized the case against the men by making it clear that their words—written and spoken—had encouraged the bomb-thrower, whoever he might be: they had furthered the conspiracy "by general addresses to readers and hearers; by every argument they could frame; by every appeal to passion they could make; advising, encouraging, urging, and instructing how to perform acts *within which* the act of throwing the bomb was embraced." Here, then, was the horrible culmination of the Parsonses' provocative speeches, newspaper articles, pamphlets, and boasts to reporters and undercover police: they had convinced the state of Illinois that they were willing and capable of causing death and destruction. To the prosecution, the fact that only Spies and Fielden were actually in the square when the bomb was thrown was irrelevant; the groundwork for the crime had been laid at Sunday-afternoon lakefront gatherings, in the columns of *The Alarm*, and in Lucy's tirade to tramps.[16]

Although they were by no means equivalent in terms of political power, the prosecution and the defense proceeded to mount similar charges against each other. Each accused the other of representing a very few individuals who nonetheless wielded extraordinary power by virtue of the resources available to them—money and influence, on the part of elites, and dynamite, on the part of the anarchists. Each side supposedly had bypassed the ballot box in favor of more extreme and direct measures to further their own despicable agenda. They had revealed themselves to be "unmanly" (that is, lacking in moral character), and they needed martyrs (the dead policemen, the defendants) in order to stoke the rage of their fanatical supporters.[17]

ALTHOUGH HE WAS CONFINED TO THE COOK COUNTY JAIL, ALBERT Parsons saw no reason to slacken his efforts to defend himself and spread the gospel of anarchy. He sent letters to editors of local papers and began working on his biography, which had been solicited by the new Chicago weekly publication *Knights of Labor*. He also wrote directly to Grand Master Workman Terence Powderly, the head of the Knights and a bitter critic of the defendants. In early July, members of the Chicago Knights District Assembly (DA) 24 had denounced the anarchists "as advocates of 'riot and murder,'" and demanded that Parsons be expelled from the organization. The prisoner, confined to cell 106—as he put it, "Behind Bastile [sic] Doors"—ignored the protests of DA 24, whose members claimed that it was "an organization of peace," and instead stressed that he had been a Knight in good standing, devoting much of his time to work as a union organizer. He also highlighted his New England roots—the fact that his "ancestors helped frame that declaration [of independence], and sacrificed and fought to maintain it." In a bow to the Knights' religious sensibilities, he ended with a quotation from the book of James: "Go to, now, ye rich men, weep and howl for your miseries that shall come upon you" (5:3). Desperate times demanded Bible verses.[18]

Certainly it was a great injustice that all eight men were tried together. The degree of alleged culpability for each varied, even taking into account witness testimony that was less than trustworthy. Although the evidence clearly revealed that none of the eight men had actually thrown the bomb, the prosecutors were able to tie Lingg, Spies, Fischer, and Engel more closely to the crime than the other defendants. A search of Lingg's residence had turned up bomb-making materials, some of which matched the fragments of shells extracted from the bodies of dead and wounded police officers; but although Lingg was a "practiced bomb-maker" (in the words of one defense lawyer), he was not present at Haymarket the night of May 4. On the stand, August Spies admitted to having shown off dynamite bombs to reporters who had visited the AZ office; like Parsons, he had hoped to frighten the powers-that-be into thinking the anarchists were armed and ready to fight. Witnesses (though not necessarily credible ones) placed Adolph Fischer and George Engel at the secret May 3 evening meeting where presumably the plot for the next day's violence had been hatched. The plan, according to the prosecution, had been to lure the police into Haymarket Square like so many lambs to the slaughter.[19]

There was no such evidence against Parsons because he had been en route to Chicago from Cincinnati the night of the supposed May 3 meeting. Still, Black believed that the prosecution and the judge feared Parsons because of his "boldness and eloquence," and that they might be inclined to treat him harshly for that reason. Trial testimony revealed a difference of opinion on that score. Some of the reporters who regularly covered Parsons made it clear that they considered his long-winded tirades to be little more than bombastic, self-important rantings combined with mind-numbing recitations of statistics. Clearly, however, neither the prosecution, nor the judge, nor the jury granted

him special dispensation because he was native-born; in fact, some observers were convinced that because of his New England lineage and
distinguished forebears, he should have known better.[20]

Black was convinced that the evidence absolved all of the men of
the charge of throwing the bomb that killed officer Mathias Degan.
The attorney believed that he and his co-counsel had proved that the
defendants were more "Braggadocio" than action. Nevertheless, Black
considered himself a realist. As the trial progressed, he predicted that
Neebe would be acquitted, that Spies, Lingg, Fischer, and Engel would
be found guilty and executed; and that Parsons, Schwab, and Fielden
would be found guilty and sent to prison.[21]

Lucy figured in the proceedings as a presence in the courtroom
throughout the trial and therefore a fixture in daily news accounts, and
as a de facto unindicted co-conspirator by virtue of her inflammatory
writings over the years. Prosecutors introduced a number of *Alarm* articles into evidence, including one, "Dynamite: Instructions Regarding Its
Use and Operations," which dealt with Johann Most's book *The Science
of Revolutionary War*. Also read into evidence was People's Exhibit Number 18, Lucy's "To Tramps" piece of October 1884, and her article on the
1884 Thanksgiving procession and the unfurling of the black flag. Over
the objections of the defense, the prosecution argued that *The Alarm*
consisted of pieces that were "editorials, others extracts from other papers, but they are all in the same line. We desire to show that the whole
paper is devoted to that subject [i.e., dynamite] and nothing else."[22]

In all, the prosecution presented to the jury sixty-two *AZ* and
forty-one *Alarm* articles. From the latter publication were culled exhortations to "*Learn the use of explosives!*" ("To Tramps"); to wage "war
with all means"; and to "get dynamite, get dynamite!" Other articles
contained sayings such as "One man armed with dynamite is equal to
one regiment of militia," and "we say a vigorous use of dynamite is both
humane and economical." Some pieces voiced support for recent assassinations in Europe: "We rejoice over and applaud this noble and heroic
act." *The Alarm* published calls for arson, street-fighting, and the dis-
obeying of laws in general.[23]

Several witnesses placed Lucy at the Haymarket meeting, sitting with Lizzie Swank Holmes in the wagon some distance from the

speaker's wagon, and then later (the two of them together) in Zepf's
Hall. Yet during the trial, and consistently thereafter, the defense argued that Albert Parsons would never have taken his wife *and two little
children* to the Haymarket that night had he known or even suspected
that the square would erupt in dynamite and gunfire. Both parents
would also pursue this line of reasoning after the trial, arguing that
the presence of their children in the wagon with Lucy and Lizzie ex-
onerated Albert of the charge of conspiracy, since had he known what
was going to transpire in the square, he would have left the children at
home. Black tried to pursue this line of defense when he questioned
witnesses. Called to the stand on August 6, Lizzie Swank Holmes was
identified in the court record as the "former assistant editor, *Alarm*,"
but her halting, tentative courtroom performance contrasted with her
seemingly fearless anarchist writings.[24]

Black asked Swank Holmes whether or not she had accompanied
"Mr. and Mrs. Parsons and their children" to the American Group
meeting at the *AZ* offices that night. When she answered in the affirmative, he repeated, "And the children?" to which she replied, "Yes." For
his part, Albert testified that after dinner on the fourth, "I left my house
in company with Mrs. Holmes, my wife and two children." Other witnesses remembered Albert taking Albert Junior and Lulu downstairs to
a saloon to get a drink of water after the meeting there disbanded, and
before he and Lucy headed off to Haymarket. A number of witnesses
said they saw the children with their parents en route to the meeting
at the newspaper offices, but none testified to seeing the children at the
Haymarket rally or later that evening. On the stand, Albert did not
mention the children's presence at Haymarket; they dropped out of his
narrative of that evening after the party arrived at the newspaper offices.
It seems clear that someone who left from the offices must have taken
the children with him or her; nevertheless, for the rest of their lives,
both Albert and Lucy would invoke the image of Junior and Lulu sitting
in the wagon at Haymarket as proof of Albert's innocence.[25]

On August 9, as part of his testimony, Albert reprised his Haymarket speech, reconstructed (he said) with the aid of notes. Relish-
ing the grand stage that the courtroom afforded him, he delivered a
forty-five-minute oration. In it he described the struggles of the miners

throughout the Midwest; the "compulsory idleness" among the poor; the main newspapers' determination to persecute him; and the homicidal class biases of the two major political parties, the federal government, and the legal and judicial establishment. He decried the railroad magnates and newspaper editors who advocated shooting workers or poisoning and blowing them to bits with hand grenades, all part of a larger war initiated by private security agents, vigilante groups, city police officers, Illinois National Guard units, and US Army regiments. He admitted that he had said the *Chicago Times* "was the original dynamiter in the interest of monopoly in this country, and of throwing bombs," but denied that he was a proponent of the use of dynamite. If anyone was to be blamed for the bloodshed, it was Police Inspector Bonfield and his men.[26]

Taken as a whole, the trial transcript reveals several omissions, contradictions, and inconsistencies related to Albert Parsons's comings and goings on May 4, all issues ignored by the prosecution, which was preoccupied with more sensational evidence. For his part, Albert gave an incomplete accounting of his movements during the day of the bombing and then that evening—his stop at the Haymarket, and then on to 107 Fifth Avenue, and back to the Haymarket, followed by a brief stint at Zepf's, and to the depot to purchase a last-minute train ticket out of town.[27]

Contrary to the story offered by the Parsonses and Swank Holmes, the hastily called and quickly ended meeting of the American Group almost certainly dealt with some issue other than the impoverished needlewomen of Chicago. Later, Albert, Lucy, and Lizzie implied that Albert himself had placed the ad about the meeting in the *Chicago Daily News*, but under oath, he was vague, noting, "At least I wrote the notice, and it was carried to the office by some one." Lizzie arrived in Chicago from Geneva on Tuesday morning, so the story later promoted widely that she and Lucy had led the previous day's demonstration of sewing women cannot be true (and indeed, Lizzie did not mention it in her published reminiscences about May 4). In any case, the ad mentioned nothing about sewing women, and the meeting itself transpired in a space other than the American Group's traditional gathering place, its headquarters on East Randolph. One witness testified that an organizational meeting of female garment workers was indeed underway that night—but at Foltz Hall, and under the sponsorship of some group other than the IWPA.[28]

Albert, Lucy, Lizzie, and the children did not arrive at the American Group meeting until 8:30 p.m., an hour after it was scheduled to start. The party had stopped first at the Haymarket, sometime between 7:30 and 8, where Albert had bantered with the reporters Owen of the *Times* and Heinemann of the *Tribune*. On the witness stand, William Snyder, the head of the IWPA, told of his irritation that the Parsonses had kept everyone else waiting at the *AZ* offices, a breach of etiquette considering that Albert had written the ad that called for people to gather at "7:30 sharp." Snyder was elected chair of the meeting, but had to be informed of its purpose (as did others there). During testimony, the defense sought to quash questions about the substance of the meeting. Other witnesses did report that those in attendance were asked to appropriate money from the treasury of the American Group to support an organizing drive among the sewing girls led by Lucy and Lizzie. The fact that no needlewomen were present at what was called an organizational meeting was not surprising; still, it was curious that only three women attended—Parsons, Swank Holmes, and a Mrs. Timmons. Presumably such a timely undertaking, ignited by the eight-hour-day demonstrations, would have claimed the energies of other women associated with the American Group, the reliable Sarah Ames among them. Samuel Fielden testified that people at the meeting allocated $5 to publish and distribute a handbill related to the sewing girls, the only business that any of the participants conducted.[29]

Perhaps most curious is Albert's seemingly spontaneous decision to go into hiding and stay there for six weeks. Flight in and of itself was no proof of guilt, but it is likely that Albert, Lucy, and Lizzie all knew that someone had planned some kind of action for the Haymarket that night, and that Albert needed the ruse of his children's presence there in order to dispel suspicions that he was privy to the information.

The May 4 narrative that Albert told after the trial in his writings and a series of interviews included patent falsehoods, such as his contention that he had not left Chicago for Geneva until May 5 or later, and then only because in the day or days following the bombing he saw that "many innocent people who were not even present at the meeting were being dragooned and imprisoned by the authorities, and not courting such indignities for myself I left the city, intending to return in a few days." During her testimony, Swank Holmes was not asked about urging Albert to take his leave of the city or going with him to the train station to buy his ticket; nor did she offer any information on the subject. Thomas Brown, an IWPA member who had attended the American Group meeting, had walked with the Parsonses to Haymarket from the meeting, and after the bombing he had lent Albert $5 for his travels. He later described to the police his final conversation with Albert: the two had been standing on the corner of Kinzie and Desplaines Streets in the company of Lucy and Lizzie. Albert had expressed uncertainty about what he should do next. According to Brown, "he said he had no money, wanted some money, to get out of town with, thought he better be away for a day or two, or a little while, until the thing had blown over."[30]

In his courtroom testimony, Albert either denied altogether that he had urged workers to use force against their capitalist tormentors or claimed that he had always seen dynamite only as a defense against trigger-happy, club-wielding police, not as an offensive weapon. His speeches and his previous articles in *The Alarm* of course told a different story, one that much of the public found convincing. That he and Lucy chose to promote the fiction about their children's presence at the Haymarket Square that night suggests that they both were desperate to counter his history as an angry anarchist agitator with the sentimental narrative of his loving care for a son and daughter.

ALBERT AND LUCY FOUND SOME UNANTICIPATED SUPPORT AMONG the courtroom observers during the trial. William H. Parsons, Albert's older brother, had traveled to Chicago from his home in Virginia to reunite with him and hear him testify. Later the former general would claim that he had lost track of Albert in 1871, and had not laid eyes on him again until he entered the Chicago courtroom. William, now himself a member of the Knights of Labor, had served as a representative of Texas on the commission to celebrate the 1876 national centennial. He had worked as a lawyer and writer and a promoter of Mexican economic development, and was now an employee of the US Treasury

Department. He told a reporter for the *Tribune* that he had come to Chicago "to be near his brother in this perilous hour," and contradicted recent reports that the extended family had "repudiated and disowned" their kinsman, for, according to William, they knew him to be "a man of integrity and of profound political convictions." Though he himself was not an anarchist, and he had not followed Albert's career closely, William declared that he intended to stand by Albert because "blood is stronger than water," and "from brotherly sympathy"—and also because their sister had asked him to do so. He was convinced that Albert was innocent, "as he has not murder in his heart."[31]

Albert derived hope not only from his brother's outspoken and unconditional support but also from the instructions that Judge Gary gave the jurors on August 19: that they must establish a link between the defendants' writings and speeches and "the consummation of the crime"— that is, the throwing of the bomb. The jury took just three hours to deliberate and arrived at a verdict at 7 that evening. The following morning, when the court reconvened to hear their decision, a cordon of police stretched across the main entrance to the building. In the courtroom, police stood in a line to form a barrier between the defendants and the spectators. Albert went up to a window and waved a red silk handkerchief to the crowd of spectators gathered on the street below. Lucy found herself seated between two police officers—one on either side of her—with another two immediately behind her. The foreman then read the verdict: the jury had found seven of the men—Parsons, Spies, Schwab, Fielden, Fischer, Lingg, and Engel—guilty of murder, and it was recommending the death penalty (formal sentencing, however, would not take place until October). Neebe, who was nowhere near Haymarket Square that night and did not even learn about the bombing until the following day, was nonetheless found guilty by virtue of his association with the *Arbeiter Zeitung*; the jury recommended that he serve fifteen years in prison. One reporter described Albert as looking "disconsolate and broken down" but still possessed "of his Texas nerve," and Lucy as "sharing her husband's gritty spirit" but looking "haggard." She left the courtroom for a minute, then returned to confer with William Parsons about an appeal.[32]

Defense lawyer Black was stunned, finding the verdict "a profound and universal surprise." He would have to live with the fact that he had urged Albert to turn himself in, a decision that he now believed to have been a terrible mistake. Attorney Zeisler declared the verdict "against anarchy and not the anarchists on trial." William Parsons predicted that the defendants would be vindicated, since the police had broken the law by trying to break up a peaceful meeting. He believed that the right of peaceable assembly had been on trial. Supporters of the defendants immediately cited a large number of irregularities during the trial proceedings: the obvious biases of the jurors and the fact that they had not been properly sequestered; the unapologetic bias of Judge Gary against the defendants; the fact that the trial had taken place too soon after the bombing and too close to the police victims' homes to ensure a fair hearing for the eight men; and the failure of the prosecution to prove who threw the bomb.[33]

After the trial, reporters were eager to hear from Detective Schaak and other authorities about a possible role played by women in the Haymarket bombing. Rumors abounded that the names of Lucy Parsons and Lizzie Swank Holmes were among those on a list of hundreds of anarchists who would soon be arrested. The day after the verdict was rendered, Schaak assured reporters that his work to defeat the anarchist scourge had just begun. Pressed about whether any future arrests would include "the women," Schaak exclaimed, "Why not the women! Some of them are a good sight worse than the men," to which the reporter added, "Then Mrs. Parsons and Lizzie Holmes will of course be arrested." Schaak replied that no good card player ever tipped his hand to his opponent, and that his next moves would be revealed only in due time. His coyness was enough to spawn headlines such as "Secret Meeting of the Chicago Female Anarchists."[34]

The verdict constituted a bitter irony for the defendants. For years—ever since the Great Uprising of 1877—Albert Parsons and his comrades had sought to convince the city of Chicago that, although their numbers were small, they represented a potent threat to the American economic system. By convicting the eight men of conspiracy to murder, jurors confirmed that view—that a handful of men who boasted about the virtues of dynamite could indeed wreak havoc on a whole city, and deserved the ultimate punishment as a result. In that sense, Lucy's "To Tramps" article was prophetic, highlighting as it did a lone assailant whose one bomb could reverberate throughout Chicago and beyond.

ALTHOUGH ALBERT AND LUCY WERE DISPIRITED BY THE JURY'S verdict, they anticipated a more favorable outcome during the sentencing phase in October or after the case had been appealed to higher courts. There was still time to write, speak, and agitate. However, less than a month after the verdict came down, the couple found themselves distracted by a wholly unexpected development—a public airing of their courtship seventeen years earlier in Waco. On September 15, 1886, the *St. Louis Globe-Democrat* published a "Special Dispatch" from the Central Texas town under the headline "Mrs. Parsons' Negro Husband." The article informed readers that the day before, Mrs. M. A. Cooper—the wife of a well-to-do Waco grocer—"induced Oliver Gathens (colored) to go to Stapley's photograph gallery" to have his picture taken so that his likeness could be distributed to Cooper's friends in Chicago. Referring to Oliver Benton with a misspelling of his former surname, Gathings, the story stated that "the face is that of a very good-natured negro." Mrs. Cooper aimed to have Lucy "look upon the face, if she reads the Chicago papers, of the husband [she] deserted in Waco to become the mistress of Albert R. Parsons."[35]

An enterprising reporter had interviewed Lucy's mother's (former) husband, Charlie Carter (he described himself as Lucy's "step-father"), who was still living in East Waco and working in a brickyard. Benton was described as "a negro—not light-colored, either." It had been about twenty years since he and Lucy had lived as husband and wife, he claimed. Benton told of the couple's child, now long dead, and his solicitous treatment of his young wife—paying her school tuition and buying her textbooks "to elevate her to as high a place as he could." Albert Parsons, in Benton's words, began "attracting her attention and drawing her away."[36]

Readers were assured, however, that "there is nothing of the 'Hostler Joe' in his [Benton's] composition," a reference to the main character in a sensational poem, "'Ostler Joe," written by journalist and reformer George Robert Sims in the spring of 1886. The poem tells the story of a humble, hardworking man named Joe who is seduced by the beautiful Annie, a woman "who lured men's souls to the shores of sin with the light of her wanton eyes." Joe weds Annie, and together they have a son. Yet soon she abandons her family for a stranger with a "tempting tongue." The villain whisks her off to London, where "her beauty won men's homage, and she prospered in her shame." She proceeds to discard one lover after another and make a spectacle of herself: "Next she trod the stage half naked, and she dragged a temple down / To the level of a market for the women of the town." She eventually returns to America, where, consumed by her own sinfulness, she falls ill. The loyal Joe rushes to her deathbed and forgives her. The poem, with its vivid description of a fallen woman, became a favorite of dramatists at the time.[37]

The *Globe-Democrat* reporter was correct that Benton had not remained eternally faithful to the mother of his first child. A gardener and general laborer, he was now married to a woman named Della, and they had started a family. Lucy's mother, Charlotte, was still working in Waco as a cook, domestic servant, and laundress. By this time, Lucy's brothers, Webster and Tanner, had either changed their names or moved to another place.[38]

The *Globe-Democrat* reported that as Albert's "wife and ally" in the cause of anarchism, Lucy "has achieved a kind of fame that has gone throughout the world. All her utterances, and especially her speeches at the anarchist gatherings, are wired throughout the country as fully and eagerly as though she were a Louise Michel or a Petrolouse of the Paris commune," a reference to a real woman, and women in general, who fought on behalf of the French uprising. Though the author might have exaggerated Lucy's public reputation at this point, he was correct in labeling her lifetime trajectory "a queer whirligig career." In Waco, "old negroes here who knew her when she was humble Oliver's contented wife still talk of the pretty mulatto that Albert Parsons stole away, and wonder if she ever thinks of Oliver now." The *Globe-Democrat*'s article was picked up by the *New York Times*, the Chicago papers, and others around the country, and even the *Anglo American Times* for the edification of Americans living in London.[39]

Within three days another dispatch from Waco reached the St. Louis paper. This one, published alongside a woodcut of Oliver Benton, recounted the schadenfreude that had gripped white Wacoites now that Albert Parsons, "the radical scalawag," had met his downfall. Waco whites also seemed eager to ridicule the lowly "Gathens," who was in the habit of donning "tony clothes" and generally acting above his station. His decision to discard the surname of his owner in favor of that of his father was an act of personal liberation that the white community refused to recognize or honor.[40]

Appended to this story was a brief notice that several Chicago reporters had approached Albert in his cell for comment on the earlier report, "and have all received from him a flat denial of the story, and a statement that his wife was of Spanish-Indian descent, born and raised on the Western frontier of Texas, and that she had never been near Waco." Recent efforts to locate Lucy at the apartment on West Indiana Street had been futile; she and the children had been evicted, since she had apparently not paid rent in the four months they lived there. She in fact had moved her shop, with the sign "Parsons & Co., Dressmakers," to 785 Milwaukee Avenue.[41]

Not to let the matter end there, on September 19 the *Globe-Democrat* carried a story that recounted dramatic developments the day before. A Chicago reporter had finally located Lucy and presented her with a letter from Waco, together with Oliver Benton's photograph, and she had agreed to let him accompany her to the jail and solicit her husband's response to the allegations. After "carefully scanning" the picture, Albert said, "Yes, that is Gathings; I know him. I was raised in Waco, and was in those days very popular among the colored people there. I had something to do with his wife or the woman he lived with." He continued, "Well, it was sort of custom in that town in those days. I was wild when I was young, and had many escapades with girls. Of course, Gathings did not like what I did." Lucy urged Albert to elaborate, saying: "Now, don't go beating about the bush. Tell the whole story as it is. I won't rest under this false imputation any longer." According to the reporter, "Thus adjured, Parsons said that he had lived with the woman who was known as Gathings' wife; but that he left her some time before meeting the present Mrs. Parsons in Austin. . . . This was positively all there was to it and his wife knew no more of Gathings than the child unborn." A Chicago reporter representing the *Tribune* was apparently the source of this story, or at least present for the interview. On the twentieth the *Tribune* added a detail provided by Lucy— that Albert's paramour at the time was twenty years older than she. Lucy said that, as his wife, she was "not accountable for any wild oats Mr. Parsons may have sown before me." Albert embellished the fiction: "He said he found [Lucy] a pure and beautiful and talented young orphan girl in the wilds of Texas and married her, and that she ever has been noble, pure and true." He added, "She is Indian and Spanish, and has no African blood in her veins."[42]

This exchange in a cellblock of the Cook County jail represented one more chapter in a press campaign to feed the public's hunger for details about Albert and Lucy Parsons. Beginning with the lengthy article in the *Waco Day* shortly after the Haymarket bombing on May 6 and continuing for the next four months, papers in Chicago and elsewhere seized on gossip about the pair and about Albert's extended family near and far. (The headline in the *Day* on May 8 was "Beast Parsons: The Sneaking Snarl from Some Moral Morass in Which He Hides; Miscegenationist, Murderer, Moral Outlaw, for Whom the Gallows Waits.") Meanwhile, both Lucy and Albert apparently considered all publicity about the two of them good publicity. Appealing to a variety of journalists, he presented himself as a defender of all-American political values. Lucy submitted to interviews that helped her promote a counternarrative to the inconvenient story of her Waco origins: she was preparing to introduce herself to a larger national and international audience as a person of Spanish and indigenous descent. The reaction of a *Kansas City Star* editor suggested some of the potential pitfalls in this strategy, contrasting her attempt to pass "as a dusky descendant of the extinct race of powerful Aztecs" with the facts of her life—that this "notorious woman is probably a straight case of an illegitimate mulatto." The writer concluded, "She is not responsible for her being, but she can not escape her environments."[43]

Lucy created her identity as a Latina at a time when very few Mexican Americans lived in Chicago, and the city had no Mexican American press to confirm or deny her claims—for instance, by testing her knowledge of Spanish or demanding specific information about her forebears. In the coming months, as she and Albert fought to overturn his conviction, she would seek to construct her own "environments" and create a new life-story for herself. In this effort she enlisted the powerful newspapers that had vilified her husband and his codefendants. Whether Lucy Parsons helped or hurt her husband's cause in the process would remain an open question.

❦ Chapter 8 ❧

"The Dusky Goddess of Anarchy Speaks Her Mind"

O N SATURDAY, OCTOBER 8, 1886, A BONE-TIRED LUCY BOARDED A late-night train bound for Cincinnati. Looking out the window into the darkness, Chicago receding into the distance, she felt a welter of emotions wash over her. She had endured three drama-filled days in the courtroom of the criminal court building, and listened as Judge Gary that morning had pronounced a final sentence on her husband and the seven other defendants. Now she was embarking on a grueling, weeks-long, multistate speaking tour to raise money for the appeal of the guilty verdicts and to expound upon anarchy to cynics and skeptics. Her challenge was to present herself as the fierce widow-in-waiting, unyielding to the forces that threatened to obliterate radicalism and destroy her family. Albert had given his blessing: after the jury's decision, he had written from his cell to her, saying, "You I bequeath to the people, a woman of the people." She, his "darling wife," must continue the fight "where I am compelled to lay it down." With her children being taken care of by friends, Lucy would tell audiences: "The boy is in Wisconsin, the little girl in another state, the father is in jail in Chicago

161

awaiting an ignominious but glorious death, and the mother, broken in health if not in spirit, is before you."[1]

The afternoon before, Albert had launched into the speech of his life, a speech to save his life. Seven weeks after he and his codefendants had been convicted of conspiracy to murder, Judge Gary permitted the men to address the court and explain why they believed that he should not sentence all but one of them to death, as the jury had recommended. Beginning with August Spies on Thursday morning, each of the prisoners in turn chose not only to defend himself against the charges but also to tell his own story, this time to a vast audience that numbered in the hundreds of thousands, if not millions. The courtroom was packed to capacity with two hundred people—politicians, judges, newspaper reporters and editors, and well-dressed curiosity-seekers, men and women. The prisoners' close kin, including Lucy and the children, were there. And a crowd of an estimated one thousand had gathered outside the courthouse to await the climactic sentencing. Albert and his comrades knew full well that they were in fact speaking not only to Chicagoans but to all those who would read the latest dispatches published in the largest city newspapers and picked up by smaller outlets all over the country. For him, the courtroom afforded a grand stage, and he was prepared.[2]

Parsons spoke last. He had spent weeks getting ready for the day, and now he was primed for the occasion, his hair and mustache neatly trimmed, his suit well-pressed, with a boutonniere in the lapel. Occasionally he referred to his notes, speaking for two hours on Friday afternoon and another five hours and forty minutes on Saturday—a display of stamina that was remarkable even by his own standards. Over the nearly eight hours that he spoke (almost half of the total time consumed by all eight speeches), he sought to enlighten an audience that was alternately enthralled—here is a man doomed to be hanged!— and bored (on Saturday, some of his famished listeners took a lunch break, while he forged on). As he had countless times before, Parsons reiterated the crimes committed by American capitalists; one reporter rightly termed his speech a bit of "stump speaking." When he charged that nefarious agents of Wall Street had actually planted the Haymarket bomb, murmurs of surprise rippled through the courtroom. Finally, he ended with his now familiar account of what he said happened on

May 4. That fateful evening, he claimed, he took his wife and two little children to Haymarket Square: "Your honor, is it possible that a man would go into the dynamite-bomb business under those conditions and those circumstances? It is incredible. It is beyond human nature to believe such a thing, absolutely." At 3:15 p.m., he collapsed, utterly depleted, with the words, "I have nothing, not even now, to regret."[3]

In the weeks running up to the hearing, Judge Gary had had an opportunity to review the transcript of the trial and to consider the affidavits of those who aimed to impeach the prosecution's star witnesses. On October 7, he announced that he had rejected the defense attorneys' arguments for a new trial. So it came as no surprise that he seemed unmoved by the prisoners' speeches. As soon as Parsons took his seat, Gary announced that he found that the men had "advised murder" as a means of political resistance, and that the bomb-thrower, whoever he was, had committed a heinous crime "in pursuance of such advice." The judge sentenced Oscar Neebe to jail for fifteen years, but ordered the other seven "to be hanged 'til you are dead." The execution was to be carried out on December 3. Before the prisoners could be led away, Lucy rushed up to her husband, threw her arms around his neck, and kissed him passionately—"vehemently," according to one observer—on the lips.[4]

Despite the theatricality of the moment, the condemned men considered Judge Gary's decision neither wholly unexpected nor final, and they were already planning the next phase of their defense. Later that day, Lucy visited Albert in his cell to say goodbye; she would not see him for several weeks. Lawyers had advised her that an appeal to the Illinois Supreme Court would cost an estimated $12,500, and she hoped not only to raise those funds but also to enlighten all of America "upon this all-important judicial murdering operation in Chicago": the people themselves must sit in judgment and arrive at their own verdict on the Haymarket bombing. As she stood in the Cook County jail, she was overcome with fatigue, not only by the intensity of the past three days in Judge Gary's court, but because, she told a reporter, "she had worked her fingers off dressmaking night and day for the past four weeks to keep body and soul together." By this time she had made arrangements for the care of the children while she was gone. Albert Junior would be staying with Daniel Hoan's family in Waukesha, and Lulu with another family (unnamed) in Chicago. Lucy roused herself enough to give the reporter some quotable material, saying, in the reporter's words, that "there was work to be done. Her husband's voice was silenced perhaps forever, and the world must hear from her now. Their cause was worth fighting for and dying for." The next night, Sunday, she was speaking to a crowd of four hundred at Cincinnati's Druid's Hall.[5]

As Lucy sought to defend her husband in the wider court of public opinion, union leaders in Chicago were reconfiguring the labor movement, in part in response to the Haymarket convictions (which at least some now had decided were unjust), and in part in response to the actions of Democratic politicians who they believed had once again betrayed the interests of working people. Prominent socialists and Knights of Labor in the city as well as around the country were arguing that, whatever their rhetorical indiscretions, Parsons and the other defendants had been tried under blatantly unfair conditions with a judge and a jury that were openly hostile to them. Many also charged that the major prosecution witnesses were guilty of perjury, and that the state's attorney had been determined to put the idea of anarchism, as much as the men who propounded it, on trial. Furthermore, all laboring people, men and women, unorganized and organized, lived under a death sentence, one arbitrarily enforced: the sophisticated weaponry wielded with reckless abandon by law enforcement authorities gave credence to the argument that workers needed the means to defend themselves during peaceful rallies no less than violent strikes.

On Monday, September 5, Labor Day, before the verdicts had been rendered, Chicago socialists, who had once been wary of the anarchists, had sponsored an outing to Sheffield, Indiana, with the explicit purpose of raising money for the defense. Three thousand people listened as Lucy, the featured speaker, quoted Thomas Jefferson—"Resistance to tyranny is obedience to God"—and urged all to defy the court; otherwise they were "unworthy to be called men." She ended by imagining a scenario both mournful and full of promise: "It is your duty and I demand of you to echo the crash of those seven scaffold traps by a counter crash that all this country will hear and hearing tremble. You know that it is for you and our glorious principles that these men now suffer in their cells. See that their prosecutors do not go unrewarded." Despite the violent repression of labor radicals in the wake of Haymarket, Lucy Parsons refused to moderate her language of revenge.[6]

During the late summer and early fall, white workers of diverse ethnicities and ideologies coalesced into a new political party that was national in scope, the United Labor Party (ULP). In Chicago, the ULP aimed to challenge the Republicans and Democrats, including Mayor Carter Harrison, who was responsible for the original appointment of labor's archenemy, Inspector John Bonfield. The new party grew out of a meeting on August 21—the day after the conclusion of the trial—that brought together 251 delegates representing 47 trade and labor organizations and 41 Knights of Labor assemblies. Many prominent Knights dissented from the view of their national leader, Terence Powderly, who had denounced the doomed anarchists—including Parsons, himself a long-term Knight in good standing. The beginning of Lucy's lecture tour in October coincided with the annual General Assembly of the Knights in Richmond, Virginia, where delegates voted in favor of "mercy" for Parsons and his comrades; an indignant minority countered that the Chicago men were in fact deserving of a just verdict of innocence, rather than mercy, which amounted to little more than pity for the presumed guilty.[7]

Intending to bridge the enduring gaps between anarchists and socialists, Knights and conservative trade unionists, and immigrants and the native-born, the ULP positioned itself as a third party fully committed to the white workingman. Its municipal and county platforms called for the eight-hour day, a strong public school system, the public control of utilities and transportation, the abolition of child and convict labor, the outlawing of land speculation, and an end to private security forces such as the Pinkertons. At the helm of the Chicago ULP were the socialists George A. Schilling and Thomas J. Morgan, who were determined to weld disparate, often warring factions into a formidable force in city and county politics. Seeking to heal the fractious relations that had caused them to break with the anarchists years before, they became outspoken in Albert's defense, and tolerant, if not always enthusiastic, about Lucy's new prominence as a public speaker. Although she had long expressed an unwavering hostility toward political action of any kind, the indomitable "Widow Parsons" would nevertheless prove useful to the ULP; the party came to understand that her searing rhetoric would continue to amaze, delight, and inspire workers in a post-Haymarket world, where widespread anti-labor sentiment threatened to extinguish the spark of radical speechifying.[8]

BETWEEN OCTOBER 1886 AND JANUARY 1887, LUCY PARSONS MADE three extended trips. The first, from October 10 to November 25, 1886, took her (in order) to Cincinnati, Louisville, Cleveland, New York City, Jersey City and Orange (New Jersey), Philadelphia, back to New York City and Jersey City, Paterson (New Jersey), New Haven (Connecticut), Baltimore, Pittsburgh, and back to Cleveland. The second, during the month of December, included trips to St. Louis, Omaha, Kansas City, back to Omaha, and Saint Joseph (Missouri). In January 1887 she lectured in Detroit and Buffalo. Three weeks into the first tour, on November 2, the Illinois Supreme Court announced that it would consider an appeal from the defendants, and on the twenty-seventh of that month that court issued a stay of execution, investing her fundraising efforts with urgency and purpose.

Although Parsons would revel in the adulation of the crowds she addressed on all three tours, raising money (for her rent, as well as for the defense) was uppermost in her mind. Just before she began the first tour she approached the owner of the Chicago Vine Street Dime Museum, a collection of "freaks" and other curiosities, suggesting that he pay her a salary and tap into the current public obsession with all things Haymarket. She would sell portraits of herself, her husband, and his comrades, plus copies of their speeches, to patrons of the museum. The price of admission would buy any man, woman, or child the opportunity to meet the famous Mrs. Parsons and engage her in conversation. Nevertheless, the museum's proprietor concluded, according to the *New York Times*, that "the case of the anarchists was not of that healthy nature which would make the wife of the leader of the revolutionists a good and talking feature in a dime museum, and Mrs. Parsons's offer was refused."[9]

On the road, Lucy collected—or had her hosts later send her— newspaper articles covering her lectures, which she presented to her husband when she returned to Chicago. His scrapbook, filled with such reports, some of them identified by publication and date and others not, some of them neatly cut out and others torn with jagged edges, serve as an illuminating chronicle of Lucy's fast-paced tour—and more. Included in the scrapbook is a November 20 article disputing her "Montezuma Princess story" and claiming that she was actually the daughter of an enslaved woman and a Mexican peon, the servant of a couple living in Houston. It is possible that both Parsonses welcomed speculation about Lucy's background, for such questions bolstered attendance at her lectures and thus filled the coffers of the defense fund.[10]

Aware of her growing stature as a featured speaker in the city's labor circles, the *Chicago Tribune* cautioned all Americans against granting Lucy Parsons the kind of respectful hearing that a man in a similar situation would be denied: she deserved "no more consideration by reason of being a female." In fact, the editors declared, after her Labor Day oration in Sheffield, that "if Mrs. Parsons thinks she is another Joan of Arc she should make an effort to un-deceive herself. She is only a very ordinary blatherkite. The country is not in the mood to hear the gospel of hate and murder preached any longer, even by a woman." This warning was picked up by national publications, including *Harper's Weekly*, which opined that authorities in Chicago "feared this one woman more than all the chief Anarchists combined. By her talk and other means of instilling their devilish sentiments into the minds of the people, she could at all times escape arrest and do tenfold more harm than the men." Other publications used Parsons's own denunciation of the law against her: "Lucy Parsons, you are right—one of the imperfections of our laws is that which allows women like you to rant and rave all over the country." It is true that the "dusky representative of Anarchy," this "sanguinary Amazon," the "quadroon anarchist of Chicago," caused a sensation wherever she went. People who would never see her face or hear her voice could nevertheless form an opinion about Parsons, "one of the most notorious women" in America. Meanwhile, Chicagoans followed her tour via the *Tribune* and other local papers, and the Citizens' Association saw fit to keep tabs on her, listening with apprehension as, in the words of one headline, "The Dusky Goddess of Anarchy Speaks Her Mind."[11]

An eclectic collection of individuals and groups sponsored Lucy's lectures and played host to her while she was on tour. She spoke at resorts, in saloons, and at lecture halls, in modest venues as well as in storied places such as Cooper Union and Clarendon Hall in New York City. In the Midwest she often followed in the footsteps of her husband, and appeared in Germania and Turner Halls, or under the auspices of branches of the International Working People's Association or Knights of Labor assemblies. The price of admission, from 5 to 25 cents per person—ladies free sometimes—helped to pay for the hall rental and her travel expenses and added to the defense fund. In some cities her visit was arranged by a woman's organization, such as a *Frauenbund* (German women's society), which was connected to a local socialists' group, or the Ladies of the Golden Rule, an auxiliary of a secret benevolent society, the Knights of the Golden Rule. Prominent local anarchists—such as Joseph Labadie and Sam Goldwater in Detroit— hosted and introduced her, and in the process showed the world that they could withstand and even thrive in spite of the public vitriol aimed at radicals in the aftermath of Haymarket.[12]

Certainly Parsons's reputation preceded her as she made her way through small towns and large cities. One sponsor in a small town in Pennsylvania (probably Allegheny, near Pittsburgh) panicked at the possibility that she might cancel her appearance and seek a larger venue: "Alles ist hier vorbereitet," he wrote, meaning that everything was in a state of commotion in anticipation of her visit. And she received commensurate press coverage: her speech at New York's Cooper Union in November 1886 was covered by all the city's major papers—the *Sun*, the *World*, the *Evening Journal*, the *Times*, the *Star*, and the *Tribune*.[13]

More generally, Parsons tapped into a vibrant 1880s reform impulse that had only grown wider and deeper since she and Albert had first stepped foot in Chicago—a sensibility that animated not only anarchists and socialists but also suffragists and supporters of Henry George, a writer and politician who promoted the idea of land reform as a way to eliminate poverty. (His 1879 book *Progress and Poverty* was a late nineteenth-century bestseller.) In New York Lucy was introduced by Cynthia H. Van Name Leonard, a noted suffragist, socialist, and philanthropist, the first woman to run for mayor of New York City (on the National Equal Rights Party ticket, in 1888), and the mother of the famous actress Lillian Russell. Parsons also exhibited her characteristic recklessness in New York City when she made her "headquarters" at the home of the widow of Charles W. Zaddick, who had boasted of sending dynamite to Chicago's anarchists. Zaddick had died in a recent explosion, reportedly of a blast by a bomb of his own making.[14]

Securing a venue could prove a formidable barrier to Parsons, as she had to contend with proprietors who refused to rent their hall to her as well as authorities trying to intimidate people from attending. In some instances she encountered silent sentries of uniformed police who blocked the entrance of the place where she was scheduled to appear, or stood watch over the crowd as she talked. Routinely, undercover police ("like thieves in citizens' clothes," she sneered) monitored her actions and words. In Buffalo, her hosts identified themselves only by numbers, so fearful were they of a police crackdown. The reporter covering her visit there noted that the "committee of arrangements" consisted of "Nos. 3, 19, 9, 23, and 7, for they refused to give their names." In Cleveland, the handbills had all been printed and the circulars all distributed, but the hall's owner, disapproving or scared, refused to allow her to speak. Parsons promptly located a chair, placed it in the middle of the street, and stood on it to address the crowd.[15]

In most places she could count on an aggressive marketing campaign for her upcoming talk, billed variously as "The Nineteenth Century and What It Has Done for the Masses," or simply "The Chicago Trial," or "LABOR PROBLEM!" Printed circulars and handbills and notices in local papers heralded her arrival. Kansas City residents were informed, on one handbill, that "everybody should avail themselves of this opportunity to hear the most Talented and Eloquent Woman of her Age." Another notice, in New Haven, said, "Mrs. Lucy E. Parsons will appeal this case to the Grand Jury of the American People! Workingmen, give your brethren fair play!" More elaborate announcements included testimonials from the mainstream press lauding her for her message, courage, beauty, wit, poise, mode of delivery, or some combination of these. By the end of her tour in the spring of 1887, one circular advertised her upcoming appearance in Bordeau's Hall, Iron Mountain, Michigan, by listing a dozen such extracts from papers in major cities in as many states: "She is a very fluent talker and worked the audience into the highest pitch of enthusiasm and excitement" (Pittsburgh's *Daily Dispatch*); and "Mrs. Parsons is a woman of commanding appearance, has pleasant features, and a good command of the language" (Milwaukee's *Evening Wisconsin*). Many of her lectures were standing-room-only affairs.[16]

By and large, Parsons stuck to her routine—a standard, two-and-a-half-hour speech (some days delivered once in the afternoon and again at a different venue in the evening), followed by a passing of the collection plate, and culminating with sales of Albert's images or printed speeches. She almost always began her address by declaring, "I am an anarchist," mocking the stereotype of the wild-eyed, shabbily dressed, unshaven immigrant bomb-thrower. After describing the starving, homeless masses, the products of a cruel system that rewarded the exploitation of children and punished hardworking men and women, she went on to give a full-throated defense of the Haymarket prisoners. She told the story of the May 1 strikes, and recounted the night of the bombing: "Do you think that if Parsons intended to murder he would have taken his wife, two other ladies and his own children there?" She asked the audience, "Is that the way a man acts when he is going to throw bombs?"[17]

For the most part, Parsons downplayed the finer points of anarchist ideology in favor of a more universal appeal that stressed workers' need for self-defense. She refrained from ridiculing the United States and its legal institutions, a signature theme in *The Alarm*. Indeed, she could sound downright patriotic: "Free speech must be maintained or all the blood it took to float the Stars and Stripes would have gone for naught."[18]

Still, she liked to embellish her message with color—literally and figuratively. Reporters often highlighted her description of the red flag of anarchy: "But the red flag, the horrible red flag, what does that mean? Not that the streets should run with gore, but that the same red blood courses through the whole human race." During lectures she took out a scarlet silk handkerchief, and, with a dramatic flourish, said that no matter whether she died on the gallows or in her bed, she wished it to be her shroud. She would laugh and taunt the audience, urging calm:

"This is our color," the color of revolution. In Cincinnati she was pleased that even "conservative trade unionists . . . applauded my utterances to the echo, and accepted my definition of the red flag with *rapture*." (It was no coincidence that headline writers at times termed hers a "red-hot" or "bloodthirsty" speech.) Her hosts appreciated the symbolism and festooned lecture halls with large red flags; some arranged for little girls to present her with bouquets of red roses. Women came to the lectures wearing red ribbons in their hair, the men red neckties. These colorful displays added to the entertainment value of her appearance. Backdrops included large red flags or portraits of the Chicago eight, or German anarchist assassins. Bands played "John Brown's Body" and "La Marseillaise," and choral groups such as the Communist Singing Society performed a "revolutionary hymn."[19]

Parsons could also depart from her prepared remarks, playing to the crowd and commenting on local news of note. In New York soon after the Statue of Liberty was unveiled in late October, she seized on the occasion to point out that in the city over which "Bartholdi's big girl casts her light," less than one-half of 1 percent of the people owned their own homes. (When Cynthia Leonard introduced Parsons as the true "Liberty Enlightening the World," the audience erupted in cheers.) In Cincinnati, Parsons made pointed comments about the reactionary stance of the local Law and Order League and contrasted the soft, pampered babies being wheeled by their nursemaids in the city parks with the impoverished children of factory hands in the same city.[20]

Only rarely did Parsons offer a hint of her childhood or background as a younger woman, though at times she recited a fictitious origins story that reporters reproduced in detail:

Mrs. Lucy E. Parsons is the daughter of Senora Marie del Gather, a Spanish-Mexican lady, and John Waller, a civilized Creek. She was left an orphan at the age of three years in charge of her mother's brother, a Mexican ranchero and farmer, of Texas, where at her uncle's house at 16 years of age, A. R. Parsons, himself a mere youth but a travelling correspondent of the Houston Telegraph, first met and became enamored with her. This was in 1869. Having been raised by her uncle, she always bore her mother's and uncle's name.

Parsons explained that her interest in anarchy stemmed from her "taking sides with the opposition against the proprietors of a factory in the South, where a number of children were employed." She had championed them when they requested a twelve-cent raise per week. Parsons said she "gained the enmity of whites and was forced to leave the place" because of her agitation against the factory—perhaps an allusion to the Waco Manufacturing Company.[21]

Her lectures provided generous amounts of crowd-pleasing bluster and invective. Those who expected to hear a pathetic wife begging for her husband's life and invoking the names of her soon-to-be fatherless babes were sorely disappointed. She declared, "I don't come here to plead for my husband. No couple ever lived more happily together than we have, but when it comes to principles we revolutionists sacrifice everything. I now give him up to the cause for which we have struggled so long side by side." And the "cause" she put forward in no-holds-barred terms. She sought to use gender conventions to good effect, claiming credibility as a wife and mother when she disputed the argument that anarchism "would rend the fabric of the family home"; and she could draw upon her own maternal feelings when describing the young workers who never saw the light of day or a blade of grass. Yet she also departed from that sentimental script to declare that she would never apologize for her actions or those of her anarchist comrades.[22]

Claiming that she herself would have thrown the bomb in Haymarket Square, had she possessed one when the police charged the meeting, Parsons lauded "the missiles of today" as an improvement over weapons of war in the past. "Science" had advanced beyond the bow-and-arrow stage and given the worker the gift of dynamite, she said (often to loud applause): "You want to take advantage of it." She excoriated the jury in the Haymarket trial "as a waltzing, fiddling, card-playing jury that reached a verdict in three hours, making six widows and numberless orphans." The meatpacker Philip Armour she termed "a slaughterer of children as well as hogs," John Bonfield "that chief of sewer rats." Chicago police were "the scum of the sewers and gutters, and as bloodhounds, worse than those trained in Russia for blood-work." She denounced as "dumb as oysters" the churches that sided with the capitalists. Should anyone doubt her courage, "she would have no more compunction wiping a detective off the face of the earth than a fly," one paper reported, paraphrasing her, and, should anyone doubt her intentions, another quoted her saying, "I will take the red flag of the Commune and plant it all over New England in mills and factories."[23]

Parsons could salt a single speech with language rarely heard by ladies in public, let alone uttered by them, condemning the "damnable judicial murders about to take place in Chicago," and the "damnable capitalist" who refused to rent her a hall while she "left [Albert] to go to the scaffold" and "[went] forth to herald the damnable wrong to the American people." More than one reporter found her statements "at times positively indecent," though it is not certain that the women in the audience invariably "hid their heads in shame," as some men charged. Most people who attended her lectures associated her with vitriolic hyperbole, and they expected no less.[24]

At the same time, Parsons's assertive command of the room, no matter how large or small, took many by surprise. She would interrupt herself to point out and ridicule men whom she suspected of being plainclothes detectives, admonish the crowd to refrain from interrupting her with applause, "as it bothered her," and demand that yapping dogs be removed from the hall. She asked the rowdies to cease their talking: "Keep quiet, won't you? There's no need to make a disturbance. I only ask the courtesy of a stranger to be heard." She instructed members of the audience to stop smoking: "My dear sir, you with the big pipe at the door, must bear in mind that smoking is strictly prohibited in this room while I am talking." In Detroit, she "remarked that smoking violated the atmosphere of the hall, and in any event it wasn't good manners, and several cigars went out with celerity." Most of the men of the day were accustomed to debating politics through the haze of tobacco smoke, but Parsons was not about to defer to the custom.[25]

She felt no hesitation in demanding that the men remove their hats and treat women in the audience with courtesy: "Are there not some Chesterfields in the audience who are gallant enough to give up their chairs to the ladies?" Still, in other cases her demand for respect from the crowd took an unexpected turn, as when she demanded angrily of one woman, "Put out that crying baby." She sought to disabuse those who believed her black dress was in fact widow weeds, saying that she favored the color because it was flattering on her. (Indeed, she displayed no sense of false modesty, sending the *New York World* a picture of herself to refute the idea that all anarchists were "so hideous" that they could cause every watch in the hall to stop.) She was, in fact, a walking contradiction in terms, mesmerizing rapt admirers and hard-bitten reporters alike. In Allegheny, Pennsylvania, she allowed herself a melodramatic moment, and with tears running down her cheeks pictured for the crowd her husband bound and with a noose around his neck; but then, "pausing for a moment[,] she turned to her followers on the stage, and in an entirely different tone said, 'Get ready to take up the collection.'"[26]

LUCY PARSONS WAS HER OWN PERSON, AND TRY AS THEY MIGHT, no one could affix predictable labels to her or define her background with any precision. Her physical appearance and manner of speaking inspired in listeners a wide range of emotions, from scorn to admiration, but she always seemed quite unlike any woman they had ever encountered. Although Parsons was not the first or only sensational female speaker of the last quarter of the nineteenth century (a period bracketed by the free-love proponents Victoria Woodhull and Emma Goldman), she was unique as a woman of color with an aura of mystery. When reporters saw her for the first time, virtually all of them wrote at some length about her dress and hairstyle, the contours of her face, and her enunciation, hoping to divine from such tangible evidence not only her character but the circumstances of her birth. Although some editors sent a stenographer to record her speech verbatim, few assigned a sketch artist to her lectures (and the few images produced varied wildly in quality). Most newspaper readers had to rely on descriptions provided by reporters, white men who struggled to convey their own assessments of Lucy Parsons the person, who might or might not be the sum of her parts—a woman, a person of color, an anarchist, an orator, a wife and mother. These various roles often seemed at odds with each other, shattering reporters' expectations. In Buffalo, "the detective and a crowd of reporters in the doorway were watching for Mrs. Parsons, but the good-looking, well-dressed mulatto walked by them so quietly and demurely that her identity was not known until she had got into the hall." These men were expecting a more formidable-looking woman. And even the most "fear-laden" of her listeners had to admit that she was appealing in multiple ways.[27]

Parsons's rhetorical strategies—her use of sarcasm and vibrant imagery, her off-the-cuff interactions with listeners—enthralled audiences, and those qualities, combined with her physical attractiveness, could prove quite alluring, even titillating, to the men in the room. The incident in Orange, New Jersey, when, on the afternoon of Sunday, October 24, she muscled her way into Central Hall, is an apt example. She had enlisted the help of her host in breaking the hinges of the door and yanking it open. Once inside, she came face to face with the hall's disapproving proprietor, W. H. Latimer. Parsons ran past him across the stage, flung open a window, and urged the crowd below to enter the building. His words unheeded, Latimer shoved a musket in the hands of a fifteen-year-old, telling him to keep the waiting crowd at bay, and then rushed off to the police station. There he managed to secure a phalanx of police officers, but, presented by Parsons with a receipt for $2 for the hall's rental deposit, they refused to interfere, and with no further delay she proceeded to speak before the crowd of two hundred.[28]

Widely reported in newspapers (and in some cases featured on the front page), this incident earned Parsons some grudging praise from her opponents, for her "pluck." A long article in the male "sporting" magazine *National Police Gazette* of November 6, apparently submitted by a detective who had been on the scene, noted that "Mrs. Parsons was equal to the occasion." During the confusion, she had exhorted members of the audience to remain in the hall despite the police intimidation: "Are there not men among you? Will you let them put you out like slaves when I have hired a hall and have a contract for it? Stay where you are. Don't move for them." Added the reporter, "She looked positively handsome as she stood trembling with excitement and gazed around her" before beginning her lecture on what she termed "the history of the greatest crime of the century." This description suggests the degree to which Parsons's public image was being eroticized and commodified for the benefit of a nationwide male audience.[29]

Parsons was, by most accounts, "a woman of commanding appearance." The *New York Times* reporter who covered her speech at Clarendon Hall provided a description:

> She has a handsome oval face with arched eyebrows, a large, full but well shaped mouth, showing a set of white, even teeth, while speaking, and a softly rounded chin. The mahogany hue of the face, with its covering of crinkly black hair, and the large nostrils, conveyed the impression that some of her ancestors were of African birth. This impression was strengthened by a side view which revealed a depression of the bridge of the nose. The forehead is prominent and the head large. She has a symmetrical figure and is of about the medium height. She was dressed in black. She spoke in a positive way, in a full, clear voice that was heard with distinctness throughout the hall.

This observer added that her inflection and pronunciation of certain words "gave evidence that her youth had been spent in the South."[30]

Although reporters generally agreed on this quality of her voice, they struggled to convey to readers her skin color and hair texture, physical qualities that routinely went unnoticed in white speakers. Her skin was variously described as "exceedingly dark," "brown-like" in tone, and "neither black nor yellow, but just between," and most often as a shade of copper—dull copper, the color of a new penny, a copper tint, or "coppery." Some reported that her hair was "fluffy, silken," others that it was coarse, "kinky and unmanageable." Despite her protests, she was labeled variously a Negro, a "quadroon," or a "light-colored negress."[31]

Some reporters, however, thought that Parsons could not be black, noting, of her speech, "there is no trace of the florid style which almost always characterizes an African"; rather, she exhibited a self-restraint "for which the American Indian is noted," confirming her claim that she was "of mixed Mexican and Indian origin." Some observers cited evidence for whatever they wanted to see: "Her dark, swarthy complexion indicates her Spanish birth. A long face, aquiline nose, and a pair of sharp black eyes are set off with a head of jet black hair."[32]

Predictably, reporters tried to connect Parsons's "racial" heritage, as "revealed" by her appearance, to her intelligence, or lack thereof. One who labeled her a Negro also said, "Her dense ignorance of the rules of grammar and her efforts to indulge in metaphors were laughable," an assessment contradicted by virtually all other listeners, including the one who wrote that, although her "intelligence was unexpected . . . she spoke fluently, used very fair phraseology, and had a voice that was pleasantly musical, even when she was excited by the threatened police interference." One noted that despite being a "Negro-Mexican," "she has read a good deal, and is well enough informed to talk intelligently and with considerable originality on many subjects."[33]

Parsons's manner of dress provided some measure of gravitas and ruled out any descriptions of her as lacking in good fashion sense. She always appeared in a form-fitting black gown, either plain or embossed in black velvet. The *New York Times* gave front-page coverage to her talk in Philadelphia on October 30—calling it "the biggest demonstration of Anarchists" held in that city—and the reporter admiringly described her becoming outfit, a richly trimmed black satin dress with a Berlin twill jacket, boots with French heels, and a "Gainsborough black hat with a half dozen handsome black ostrich feathers." Her long hair was worn with bangs and a fashionable topknot on her head, and she eschewed makeup and used tasteful accessories—a corsage of red and white roses, a gold pin fastening a black lace scarf, or (her most distinctive piece) a necklace with a gold charm in the shape of a tiny gallows. Some remarked on her colorful jewelry: "Her nose is of the flat or negro type. Her whole face has a strong suggestion of Aztec blood. With her heavy ear rings, [and] topaz buttons[,] she has an air of old Egypt about her." She was "a modern Cleopatra, a veritable African queen."[34]

Just as reporters attempted to reveal Parsons's character through her physical appearance, they sought to comprehend the nature of her often raucous, foot-stomping, cheering audiences, usually a mix of working-class men and women and well-to-do intellectuals and reformers. The sympathetic *Advance and Labor Leaf* of Detroit claimed she attracted "an unusually intelligent looking crowd," but the hostile *Cincinnati Enquirer* puzzled over the "strange-looking people" in the audience: interspersed with "the tangle-haired, wild-eyed variety of anarchist" were well-dressed women, some of them in attendance with their children.[35]

According to the pseudoscientific ideologies of the day, the shape of a person's head or brow revealed character traits, and some reporters judged her audiences accordingly. In the Omaha hall, where all of "Bohemia town" had turned out to hear her, few men were wearing linen, and the smell of stale beer, tobacco, and garlic hung in the air; there were found "roughly clad, sullen browed men, who sat heavily in their chairs," in the words of a reporter. In Buffalo's Harmonia Hall, of the "sharp-featured, thin-haired, uneasy, carelessly dressed workmen," one reporter asserted that, "in many cases low brows and scraggly beards were observed, both indicative of limited intelligence and lack of force of character."[36]

No doubt the presence of African American men or women would have made audiences seem even stranger, but there is no indication many of them ever attended, and Parsons never noted their absence. Transcripts of her speeches during her tour of 1886–1887 indicate that she exhibited a seemingly perverse indifference to the escalating state-sanctioned assaults on the bodies and rights of black southerners. She was aware of the Carrollton, Mississippi, massacre of March 1886, and, as an avid newspaper reader, she certainly knew that southern whites were killing many dozens of blacks annually in bloodfests meant to torture the victims and serve as grisly warnings for all people of African descent. In her lectures, Parsons exposed the immense power of local law-enforcement and judicial authorities, and she derided the cowardly ineffectiveness of the two main political parties in protecting the most basic rights of the white laboring classes. These two themes were pertinent to blacks' unique vulnerability; but in fact, with the exception of routine references to Haymarket, her speeches were the same as those that she or any other labor radical might have given five or ten years before. In most areas of the country, the class struggle had no room for black people, though it is worth noting that at that very moment black workers in Richmond, Virginia, were pressing the white Knights of Labor for full and equal participation in the labor movement.[37]

Not surprisingly, many editors of the largest newspapers bristled at Parsons's message and the excitement she caused when she came to town. In Omaha, one editor wrote, "She addresses men as slaves. The American citizen knows that he is not a slave. He knows that he is living under the most kindly and the most liberal government that the sun shines upon." Parsons was dismissed as a brazen fraud who spouted "loud-mouthed treason" and endangered the sanctity of the family. She should be banned, or, failing that, her talks boycotted, for "she has a tongue like a lash. She has a temper like a scorpion, and a moral nature that has been turned awry."[38]

Observers on the extremes of the political spectrum could agree that she hindered the cause of labor reform. For example, some Henry George supporters in New York dreaded her appearance, fearing that she and other representatives of the "dangerous classes" would tar their own cause with the red brush of anarchism. One workers' paper agreed that she had her facts right, but disputed her conclusions, since, it claimed, the people had "peaceful means at their disposal every time the polls open[ed]," and they must "attend to the duties of citizenship": to destroy the system was "not the way to repair it." The argument that Parsons was doing her husband's cause no good found expression in the *Omaha Republican*, which suggested that lawyers for the Haymarket defendants should summon her home to Chicago, since her treasonous rantings would only tighten the noose around her husband's neck: "She is doing the prisoners more harm than all other influences combined," the paper said. "The incoherent lunacy to which she gives vent disgusts people. She should be muzzled." Other editors urged their readers to "give her a fair hearing and judge of her accordingly." The *Kansas City Times* disapproved of her message, but said "it greatly admire[d] her pluck and magnificent poise."[39]

BY MOST MEASURES, LUCY PARSONS'S SPEAKING TOUR OF 1886–1887 was a rousing success. Initial reports suggested that she had raised as much as $100 a day for the prisoners' defense fund, sending as much as $750 a week back to Captain Black and his associates, though that sum apparently represented funds commingled with donations from socialists and anarchists all over the country. (An event in Philadelphia that attracted an audience of 1,000 people brought in $125; most audiences were smaller.) Parsons delivered dozens of speeches and made her case against a jury that rendered its verdict without knowing the identity of the person who wielded the murder weapon, the Haymarket bomb. In the process she upheld the principles of free speech and assembly and defied authorities who would silence radical labor agitators and their allies. Nevertheless, newspaper editors, politicians, and police chiefs remained convinced that her speeches were designed to incite violence. In Cincinnati, for example, one paper called her a "red-mouthed anarchist" and said her words were "well calculated to stir up the worst feelings of a mob, and if blindly obeyed to leave this city in ruins."[40]

Parsons garnered extensive coverage in newspapers all over the country. Henceforth, she was a celebrity speaker in her own right, no longer merely her husband's surrogate relegated to second-tier status or a supporting role at workers' gatherings. Much later, the radical agitator Elizabeth Gurley Flynn would pay homage to Parsons, writing about how her speeches were delivered "in a beautiful melodious voice, with eloquence and passion," and about her pioneering efforts, which caused union men to become accustomed "to listen[ing] respectfully to a woman speaking for labor."[41]

An assessment of Parsons's tours must rely almost exclusively on published newspaper accounts of her speeches, leaving out as a matter of course many facets of her trip. Reporters could not have known about the long, lonely nights Parsons spent in hotel rooms, or the missed train connections, or the slights and indignities she endured as a woman of color traveling by herself. Moreover, what might have been a triumphant return to Chicago in the spring of 1887 instead plunged her back into the harsh reality of family life—a husband in prison, the children to be gathered up, a landlord clamoring for rent money she did not have. And Lucy Parsons had to confront the reality that her own blossoming reputation was built upon her husband's impending death.

LUCY PARSONS'S SPEAKING TOUR, 1886–1887

October 1886	11–13	Cincinnati
	14	Louisville
	15	Cleveland
	17	New York City
	20	Jersey City
	24	Orange, NJ
	30	Philadelphia
November 1886	4–5	New York City
	7	Jersey City
	8	Paterson, NJ
	17	New Haven, CT
	20	Baltimore
	22	Pittsburgh
	24	Cleveland
December 1886	12	St. Louis
	18	Omaha
	21	Kansas City
	22	Omaha
	31	Saint Joseph, MO
January 1887	15–28	Detroit
	31	Buffalo
February 1887	17	Milwaukee
March 1887	10	Cincinnati
	11	Columbus

❧ Chapter 9 ❧

The Blood of My Husband

IN EARLY 1887, CHICAGO POLICE BEGAN TO MONITOR VIRTUALLY ALL of Lucy Parsons's public appearances, whether she was addressing a crowd of picnickers in Ogden's Grove or selling her husband's likeness and writings on a city street corner. The authorities faced a dilemma in dealing with the notorious publicity-seeker: they could either place her under arrest whenever she exhorted the laboring classes to defend themselves with dynamite, and in the process risk adding her name to the list of eight presumptive martyrs now holding court in Cook County jail; or they could ignore her and endure the wrath of those Chicagoans who demanded the silencing of all critics of capitalism and other basic American institutions. For the time being, at least, the police left the fiery orator free to speechify, on the theory that either she would soon tire and burn herself out, or that the labor leaders, mortified to be associated with her, would extinguish her flame. Meanwhile, in the journalistic equivalent of police surveillance, the city's dailies were sending out reporters to follow Parsons in hopes of recording her next outrageous statement or sensational outburst. Indeed, the ambitions of reporters and police converged when both groups disguised themselves to gain access to anarchist meetings; a *Chicago Tribune* reporter covering one of her speeches lost his fake beard when he was forced to flee from an officer who thought he looked like a rabble-rouser.[1]

Parsons loved the heightened notoriety and, honing her flair for the dramatic, declared that her enemies portrayed all anarchists as blood-thirsty fiends, who hatched their terrible plots and drank sour beer from the skulls of capitalists' children in dank subterranean chambers. It is true that her critics indulged in hyperbolic attacks: one anonymous letter-writer called her a "disgrace to your Sex and Humanity," a woman "born of wolfish proclivities, a frequenter of dens of thieves and murderers," and said she should "be throttled at once and left above ground as warning to others of the same ills." However, though she might revel in such hyperbolic personal attacks, Parsons was becoming increasingly anxious over the impending execution of her husband. Her distress now merged with public spectacle as she frantically sought to call attention to his incarceration by attracting publicity to herself.[2]

Lucy and Albert were not only famous anarchists but also husband and wife and the parents of Albert Junior and Lulu. Their family now came together on "murderers' row," where the condemned men were kept in adjacent cells. The jail remained a beehive of activity, with next-of-kin, reporters, celebrities, and curiosity-seekers crowding each other in the hallway outside the "cage," an iron-mesh enclosure where the prisoners were held during visiting hours. From October 1886 through March 1887, Lucy spent most of her time on the road, returning to Chicago for two weeks at a time in early December and January and in late February and early March. She made a point of visiting Albert every day that she was in the city, though prison regulations at times interfered with her plans. Their reunions, recounted in detail by reporters, were invariably described as "most affectionate." Hoping to meet with her husband upon her return from a particularly eventful trip to Columbus, Ohio, in late March, Lucy ran afoul of the rule that prohibited such visits on Sundays. Albert protested loudly, "They think they got us where they can jump on us, but they'll be sorry for it one day. I'll live to be Sheriff of Cook County, and mark me, I'll make 'em dance to my music."[3]

Reporters were eager for quotable quips such as this one, and so they hovered outside the "cage" throughout the day and into the evening, hoping to overhear conversations between prisoners and visitors.

Lucy and Albert declaimed loudly and gestured broadly when they wanted their words to appear in the paper. If the couple preferred privacy, they drew their chairs together, bent their heads in close to the cage, and whispered to each other. The fervid atmosphere of the jail, with seven men (all the defendants but Neebe, who was facing fifteen years in prison) condemned to die and their loved ones alternately stoic and hysterical, provided much human-interest fodder for the dailies. (Again, though, press manipulation ran two ways: a *Chicago Herald* reporter named Maxwell E. Dickson would bring Albert poetry to read, and then "furnish first-page stuff for the *Herald*," reporting that the prisoner "had been consoling himself with poetry," without any evidence that he had even looked at it.)[4]

In the fall, a narrative emerged in the mainstream press that Lucy Parsons the defiant female dynamiter had been replaced by the sorrowful wife and mother, and that she had "completely broken down." Yet this narrative might have been a product of either wishful thinking on the part of the police or an editor's desire to keep readers engaged in an ongoing melodrama. Lucy had likely decided on her own that she must keep her name in the headlines, even if it meant presenting herself as a distraught widow-in-waiting. Perhaps Albert's only chance of swaying the Illinois Supreme Court justices or gaining a pardon from the governor, Richard Oglesby, would come through her ability to rouse sympathy for herself and her children. Yet she failed to pursue this goal with her customary political savvy and self-awareness, instead seemingly going out of her way to baffle and repel supporters and to confound the public in general. Indeed, some observers saw in her behavior a self-destructive streak that endangered any chance for clemency that her husband and the other prisoners might have had.[5]

THE PARSONSES WERE NOT THE ONLY COUPLE ON WHOM THE PRESS fixated. The dashing August Spies, at times compared to Lord Byron, carried on a presumed romance, of necessity quite Victorian in its restraint, with a woman named Nina van Zandt, a twenty-five-year-old graduate of Vassar College possessed of intelligence and wealth. Van Zandt proved to be a favorite with the papers, which eagerly covered her proxy wedding to "the amorous editor" on January 20, 1887. Lucy found the titillating stories annoying and distracting; asked her opinion of the marriage during her speaking tour, she snapped, "I do not know or care. I am not travelling to discuss Miss Van Zandt." Reporters compared the two women on their looks and fashion sense and discerned a distinct coolness in the women's relations with each other. For his part, Chicago police captain Schaack said that van Zandt's love for Spies "could only have been the product of a disordered mind."[6]

Junior and Lulu likely did not return to Lucy's care until after she returned from her tour for good at the end of March. Predictably, the family suffered from Albert's imprisonment. On December 23, 1886, when Lucy was somewhere between Omaha and Saint Joseph, Missouri, Albert heard from Lizzie Swank Holmes that Lulu was ill. Of the five-year-old Lulu, Swank Holmes wrote, "She is with the kindest of people, indeed she could not be taken better care of any where as they have the means and ability and willingness to do anything in the world for her." Lizzie had visited Lulu and reported that they had a warm meeting, but that the girl barely spoke to her. Concerned, Albert telegraphed his friend Dyer Lum to check on Lulu. Lum, a frequent contributor to *The Alarm* (he would become Albert's successor as editor of a resurrected version of the paper in 1888), had been living in Lucy's apartment while she was away. He went to see Lulu and assured Albert that she was recovering as well as could be expected from scarlet fever.[7]

Albert entertained a stream of guests, some of them bearing fruit and other gifts—Lucy brought him cigars and grapes—and for the most part he welcomed the attention of the reporters always milling around outside the cage. When he was in town, General William Parsons accompanied Lucy to see his brother. Other visitors included a young lawyer named Clarence Darrow, who had just moved to Chicago looking for work. He found Parsons to be a "bright, talkative fellow," the author of "brainless" speeches that were nonetheless deserving of First Amendment protection. Joseph Buchanan, editor of Denver's *Labor Enquirer*, had moved both himself and his paper to Chicago in February 1887, and he frequently went to the jail to talk with Parsons. One unexpected visitor was the newspaper editor James P. Newcomb, Parsons's Republican mentor from his Texas Reconstruction days. Newcomb, the brother-in-law of State's Attorney Julius Grinnell, who had prosecuted the case, remembered Parsons as "a very impulsive man." He told the prisoner to his face that he considered the verdict a just one. For the benefit of reporters standing nearby, pencil and notebook in hand, Newcomb also ridiculed Lucy's story of her Native American origins, saying that Waco had many black people, but "no Indians with whom she could claim relation."[8]

Of all the prisoners, Parsons seemed to adjust to life in prison best, bearing up under intense public scrutiny with calm courage, according to observers. His amiable demeanor, clear eyes, firm handshake, and love of animated conversation betrayed no trace of depression or existential angst, in contrast to some of the other men, and he did not seem to be losing weight. Buchanan later wrote that Parsons exhibited a "cheery manner that never once left him." Allowed to greet his family outside his cell on occasion, he gave the children piggyback rides up and down the corridor. He took advantage of the twice-a-day exercise periods and kept up a disciplined writing schedule, firing off angry letters to the major Chicago papers and to the Knights' Grand Master Workman Powderly. Parsons reminded Powderly that he had spoken before an estimated half-million laboring men over his career, and disputed the idea that anarchism "is destructive of civil liberty." He also wrote a brief autobiography, which would be published in the October 16, 1886, issue of Chicago's *Knights of Labor*; he assured his readers that "anarchists do not advocate—or advise—the use of force," making no note of the glaring contradiction between this assertion and his past statements. With only a penknife he whittled two small wooden vessels, a tugboat and a steamer, extraordinary for their detail; at least one of them was later raffled off at 10 cents a ticket and brought in $147.47 for the defense fund. He read the morning papers regularly and kept up a scrapbook of clippings from Lucy's speaking tour and other articles about Haymarket. He tidied his cell, and he tried to curry favor with his keepers and with the deputy sheriff, Canute R. Matson.[9]

The guards developed a grudging respect for Parsons and granted him small privileges, such as allowing him to keep an easy chair in his cell, and allowing Lucy and the children to visit him outside the cage. Grateful for access to him, reporters wrote favorably of his self-discipline and love for his wife. The *Chicago News* provided a breathless account of one of the couple's meetings: "His anarchist arms were thrown open, and into them glided the sylph-like form . . . , her head rested on his bosom for an instant, then their lips met in conjugal salute," adding, "a more affectionate couple the turnkeys hadn't seen for a long time." In an interview with a reporter for the same paper, Parsons went out of his way to say that he and the other prisoners had received courteous treatment, "and have every comfort and attention that one can reasonably expect when under sentence of death, etc. We realize the fact that we are in jail, and not stopping at a hotel, and therefore do not expect to have things quite our way." For the time being, at least, he would make peace with these agents of a corrupt capitalist state—and perhaps pass along to them a cash token of his appreciation for their seemingly solicitous behavior.[10]

Parsons relished his new role as the resident oracle of Chicago labor politics. Soon after the first convention of the United Labor Party in September 1886, the *Chicago Times* ran a story under the headline "What Parsons Thinks," quoting him at length. From his cell, though, he could only watch as striking workers suffered a series of setbacks. In the fall of 1886, the meatpackers were forced to return to a ten-hour day, though they had won shorter hours the spring before, and the following May the building trades suffered a crushing lockout. Still, he felt vindicated when several of his former socialist comrades took the Knights in a direction that contrasted mightily with the policies of the parent body as shaped by the conservative Powderly. For Tommy Morgan and other socialists, the Haymarket trial amounted to an attack on free speech: the police might deprive workers of guns, "but they can't keep us from shooting off our mouths," Morgan said. In the early fall of 1886, the Illinois legislature had passed anti-conspiracy and anti-boycott legislation in reaction to the bombing. These extreme measures gave the ULP a boost as embattled workers rallied behind the party in opposition to mainstream politics. During the November county and state elections, the party won 25,000 out of 92,000 votes cast, sending seven men to the lower house of the legislature and one to the state senate. Of the six judges the ULP endorsed, five were elected. A substantial amount of support for these candidates came from Chicago's northwest, the immigrant community that incubated the Parsonses' radicalism. Even some anarchists there were voting for the ULP.[11]

Despite the strenuous exertions of Morgan, Schilling, and others, the ULP soon foundered. In the city, as in the rest of the country, the ULP appealed by and large to currency reformers and German and English socialists, failing to dislodge most native-born workers from their traditional loyalties to either the Republicans or the Democrats. Irish American Democrats, for instance, felt sympathy for the police killed in the Haymarket blast, most of whom were their compatriots.[12]

For Albert and Lucy Parsons, the moribund labor party served to illustrate the futility of political action, though the Knights of Labor retained a strong presence in Chicago through 1887, and its leaders cast a favorable light on the Haymarket prisoners and their families. Bert Stewart, the editor of the organization's vibrant weekly, *Knights of Labor*, promoted socialist ideas and provided favorable and extensive coverage of the cellmates. The paper also gave over considerable space to Lucy, with enthusiastic feature stories highlighting her supposed life-story ("Mrs. Lucy Parsons: The Spanish Wife of A. R. Parsons"), her speeches, and her triumphant speaking tour. The paper included a drawing of her, and reprinted her letters to Albert. In them, she gleefully quoted a New York newspaper urging that "Parsons be let out as a compromise to get Mrs. Parsons to stop talking."[13]

LUCY PARSONS ENDED HER SPEAKING TOUR IN MARCH 1887 WITH trips to Cincinnati and Columbus. She was, by her own admission, suffering from physical and emotional exhaustion from all the travel. Her decision to return home for good after visits to Michigan, New York State, Wisconsin, and Ohio from January to March of that year might have been her plan from the beginning. Or perhaps she missed her husband and children, and felt she could do more good in Chicago in any case. It is also possible that her experience in Columbus, where she was briefly jailed for disorderly conduct, convinced her that each day on the road she risked incarceration at the whim of a mayor or local police chief.

Arriving in Columbus on March 8, she learned that her hosts had rented the armory for her for the next day. When the hall's agent realized that it was she who was to speak, he rescinded the agreement. Outraged, Parsons quickly made her way to the office of Mayor Charles C. Walcutt, where she found him "much the worse for drink," and sur- rounded by twenty-five police officers. When she tried to argue with the mayor, he stopped her in mid-sentence and said, "I don't want to hear anything from you. There will be no meeting in that hall tonight." He then ordered his "sleuth-hounds" to "take her down." An officer ripped off her shawl, the better to grasp her arm, and dragged her down- stairs to the "ranch," a narrow corridor leading to "small, dark, filthy, ill-smelling dungeonlike cells." Shoved into the passageway, she found sympathy among the prostitutes; they tried to cheer her up, saying that as a first-time offender charged with disorderly conduct, she was bound to get off easily, with bail at $10, a fine of $5 (or, in lieu of cash, a watch). She spent the night in an "insufferably hot hole" with leering guards posted outside her cell.[14]

The next day, in anticipation of a courthouse hearing, reporters, police, and her supporters packed the building's lobby. Accompanied by two lawyers, Parsons paid her $100 bail with money that had been telegraphed to her by friends in Cincinnati and Chicago, on the under- standing that she would return on April 13 to stand trial for "obscene lan- guage," among other charges (she would fail to keep the court date). At some point she exclaimed to the crowd gathered outside, "Your liberty is ended, American citizens. The right of free speech is refused." In print she berated the "petty tyrant of a Mayor" who abrogated a hall rental contract and trumped up charges to throw her in jail. She professed shock that the police had treated her so disrespectfully, and disgust that she had been made to sleep on a stone floor and suffer other indignities that offended her womanly sensibilities. "As for the vile libel about my using 'obscene language,'" she wrote primly, "the thousands of my friends who know me in this and other cities, can bear witness that no language is ever used by me unbecoming to a lady." The indictment claimed she had used "hot and angry words" against the officer who arrested her.[15]

The arrest made the front page of the New York Times and major Chicago dailies (the Tribune reported that she "acted more like a wild beast at bay than a human being"). A guard at the Cook County jail

in Chicago took it upon himself to give a reporter a telegram she had
sent to Albert. It read, "Arrested to prevent my speaking. Am all right.
Notify press. Lucy," an indication that she considered her troubles in
Columbus something of a publicity coup. And indeed, Lucy made good
use of her short stint in jail; afterward, she wrote a lengthy account in
the form of a letter to the city's *Sunday Capital*, a piece that was reprinted in labor periodicals and other papers. The editors of the *Capital*
signaled their sympathy toward her when they condemned her "unnecessary arrest" as judicial overreach; although they abhorred communism and anarchism (and "Mormonism and Mahomedanism," for that
matter), they believed she had a right to speak. Still, despite some positive publicity, in the end the incident offered a cautionary tale: if hall
rental contracts could be broken with impunity, and if the authorities
could arrest her for disorderly conduct, by continuing the tour she was
gambling that the mayor in the next city would show more forbearance.
And for the rest of her life, she showed a determination to avoid overnight stints in jail at all costs; presumably, the physical discomforts that
came with incarceration were too great for her to bear willingly.[16]

The fallout from Lucy's Columbus appearance and jail time angered the Knights' leader, Powderly, who represented the many workers and union leaders reluctant to express their misgivings about the
peripatetic Mrs. Parsons in public. Powderly was queried by Albert's
Denver supporters: "Have you not sworn to protect his life, reputation, and family?" More specifically, "Why did you not step to the front
to defend his helpless wife when she was in jail for the cause of labor
and she was denied the right of free speech and jailed for opening her
mouth by the drunken mayor of Columbus, Ohio?" Powderly replied
(in comments published in a "secret circular"), "My answer is because
she is not his wife; because they only live together, and are not married,
and because it is not my business to look after any woman of bad reputation, white or negro who tramps around the country as she does."
Powderly also claimed that Albert's brother William had provided him
with proof-positive evidence that "the Chicago men are assassins."[17]

Back home, Lucy encountered a "press of admirers" who wanted
to shake her hand and congratulate her for raising so much money for

the defense of the prisoners and enduring jail time in Columbus. An unannounced appearance at a socialist lecture, or a Knights district assembly meeting, concert, or benefit (such as "Dance for the Doomed"), could elicit cheers and calls for her to speak; few of her supporters ever tired of hearing her proclaim, "I will bow down to the Stars and Stripes when there is no unemployment," or "I am an anarchist! Let them strangle me if they dare!" Indeed, she showed no interest in tempering her language, instead exhorting listeners to throw bombs and dynamite to right the wrongs they suffered at the hands of the ruling class—this even in the presence of pistol-packing detectives. Meanwhile, Chicago authorities looked on warily, worried that what they considered her "bloodthirsty harangue" could trigger more deadly assaults. She was, in the words of one policeman, "a dangerous woman," especially now that adoring crowds in the East "had the effect of convincing her that she is the biggest Anarchist out of jail, and she will not hesitate to do everything in her power to convince others of this fact."[18]

For labor leaders determined to stake a claim to respectability, associating with Lucy Parsons proved problematic. In July, at the annual picnic of the conservative International Brewers and Maltsters Union in Ogden's Grove, Parsons caused a stir when she appropriated the refreshment stand for her own purposes to sell books, pamphlets, and other materials. Turning to a policeman who was menacing her, she taunted, "Mind what you're doing. There's dynamite between the leaves and you'll get blown up." She continued, "It's a pity that Bonfield and a couple hundred more of them had not been killed by the bomb." The president of the union asked her to leave, which she refused to do, saying, "I am here exercising my rights as an American citizen in free speech. If you Russians and Bohemians haven't courage to do likewise you had best go back where you came from." A row broke out between those who wanted her to stay and those who wanted her to go, with the dispute finally settled by a downpour that scattered the picnickers.[19]

On August 28, an intensely hot day, she and Tommy Morgan shared the stage at a socialists' picnic in Sheffield, Indiana, an affair that netted an estimated $2,000 for the prisoners' defense fund. When the crowd called for her, Parsons mounted the platform, and began by admitting that the strain of constant speaking had affected her health.

The chivalrous Morgan held an umbrella to shield her from the sun as she launched into a stock address, "I stand before you as an anarchist." One reporter wrote that Morgan seemed "very ill at ease during her speech," and relieved when she finished.[20]

During the late summer and early fall of 1887, Lucy showed signs of increasing desperation as she came to realize that time was running out for her husband. Albert was in a reflective mood: "Am I tired of my life? Ah, no. I am still a young man (thirty-eight years)." His upcoming death would be, he thought, "both a pleasure and an honor," though he admitted that "I worship my family and they idolize papa." Ever since the jury had rendered its decision in August the year before, the couple had held out hope that the verdict would be reversed. Judge Gary had declared on October 9 of that year that he was unwilling to overrule the jury, but the following month the Illinois Supreme Court agreed to hear the case and issued a temporary stay of execution. In March 1887, in an appeal to that court, defense lawyers argued that the evidence presented at trial was insufficient to convict the men. On September 14 the court announced that it had rejected the prisoners' appeal and set the execution date for November 11. Now the only available avenues for the prisoners were the US Supreme Court and Governor Oglesby, who had the power to issue pardons and grant amnesty. Lucy knew full well that her husband's life and the well-being of her family hinged on the governor and on the judicial system that she had so openly and often derided. Meanwhile, she ramped up her public appearances in a way that left observers confused about her motives and state of mind.[21]

At 2 p.m. on September 23, Chicago police took Lucy into custody for standing on a street corner handing out copies of a two-page letter written by Albert—the first time in her career as an agitator that the police in her home city had arrested her. She was charged with violating an ordinance that prohibited people from distributing handbills advertising their businesses or commercial services, a law clearly irrelevant in this instance. As the police prepared to lead her away, she managed to thrust the copies she had left into the hands of startled bystanders and passers-by. Albert's letter "To the American People" refuted the state's case point by point. Disingenuously, he denied that he had ever written or spoken in an inflammatory way, and once more recounted his actions on the night of May 4. He disputed the judgment of the Illinois Supreme Court and scorned the idea of a pardon or clemency: "I appeal not for mercy, but for justice!" Finally, he declared, "No, I am not guilty. I have not been proved guilty." He ended with "I know not what course others may pursue, but, as for me, give me liberty or give me death!"[22]

From jail Lucy hastily made arrangements for Lizzie Swank Holmes to care for the children, then contacted the editors of the *Arbeiter Zeitung* to bail her out for $25. Three days later she entered the courtroom, alone, for a hearing about her case. She took a seat on a bench by a window and quietly read a newspaper. Soon the matron of the jail came in and sat beside her and asked about Lulu, who had been diagnosed with a relapse of scarlet fever the week before. According to the *Chicago Mail*, Parsons had lost much of her usual fire: "Sorrow and care were graven in deep lines on her swarthy face." Allowed to address the court, she pointed out that people were always passing out circulars and handbills on the street without fear of arrest, and then made an uncharacteristic plea for sympathy: "Your honor, I am here alone, and while I wish to take no advantage of that fact, I do ask this: that you would treat me as you would have your wife treated were she in my place and you were situated as my husband is." The judge, acknowledging her "unprotected situation," pronounced her violation a "technical" one. He added, "There is not the slightest desire on my part to deal harshly with you as I know the depth of your sorrow." (One report quoted him as also saying, "I am the last man in the world to add one feather's weight to the burdens you bear.") Suspending the fine of $5, he told her she was free to go, and Parsons meekly left the courtroom.[23]

Around this time she also set about enlisting her brother-in-law in her campaign to separate Albert from his cellmates. On September 24, General William Parsons (now working for the federal customs service) gave a lengthy interview to the *New York World* from his home in Norfolk, Virginia, reminding readers that his grandfather had served as a general in the American Revolution and that his grand-uncle had lost an arm in the Battle of Bunker Hill; he was suggesting that his younger brother, though led astray by anarchists, was part of a long line of American patriots. William thought it should be noted that Albert, who had married a "talented and beautiful Mexican lady, . . . has never counseled revolution, but has prophesied it." The general kept his own name in the news by suggesting that a mysterious New Yorker had passed through Indianapolis the day before the bombing and bragged that news emanating from Chicago in the next few days would reveal what he had been carrying in his carpet-bag. William also attacked the Chicago press for knowingly suppressing the truth about the bombing.[24]

When Lucy was arrested for distributing Albert's "Appeal," she was not selling it, but giving it away. In fact, the *Tribune* had already printed a verbatim copy of it the day before. Some accounts had her welcoming the attention of police officers and even her two-hour stay in jail. As soon as she was released, she took new piles of the circulars and dropped them off at stores and saloons, and then went to see Albert, giving away more copies to prison guards and visitors. At the time, Nina van Zandt saw the arrest as a ploy, a cynical bid for publicity. Of Lucy's latest foray into the public eye, van Zandt exclaimed, "O, my God! One trouble follows another. Why can't she keep her mouth shut?"[25]

Van Zandt was not alone. On September 25, Lucy attended a meeting of the Socialistic Labor Party and tried to interrupt Tommy Morgan while he was speaking. As she stood in the hall she was surrounded by half a dozen policemen in uniform. Getting no satisfaction from Morgan—he told her that interruptions "throw me off—make me forget my line of argument"—she exited the building without having her say. Morgan was no doubt asking himself whether associating with one of the "most implacable furies of the socialistic party" truly advanced his own cause.[26]

A few days later, a telling encounter between Lucy and a *Tribune* reporter took place in the Cook County jail. Making her way past a throng of visitors, and clutching pieces of paper, Lucy approached the reporter and demanded that he look at them and see they were advertisements for a real estate firm; she had been handed them that morning as she walked down Milwaukee Avenue. She said she intended to go to police headquarters and find out if they were really interested in enforcing the ordinance that had landed her in jail the previous week. As he recorded the conversation, "the reporter hinted that unobtrusiveness would be the better policy for Mrs. Parsons at this time," but she responded angrily, declaring that all of the men would rather die than confess to a crime that they did not commit, and that "death is nobler than a long imprisonment resulting from a so-called act of mercy." To the suggestion that she would perhaps feel differently about the situation if she were soon to be hanged herself, she said indignantly, "Never. I would die, and die willingly, if I were with them or in their place." At that point, Michael Schwab's wife, Maria Ann, who was there with her children, pulled Lucy aside in an effort to end the conversation. Lucy's attempt at attention-grabbing while Governor Oglesby was considering the fate of all eight men seemed wildly inappropriate, and, according to friends and foes alike, "only served to reawaken the dread of the community."[27]

By the end of October, both Albert and Lucy seemed resigned to his fate. He admitted to a reporter that "hope and fear had almost worn themselves out, and I have become quite callous," with Lucy by his side, nodding in agreement, saying, "So have I." Albert could do little but take solace in the certainty that the laboring classes would avenge his death: "Workingmen and their friends will demand blood for blood, and they will, no doubt, have it afterward." Perhaps he felt his labors were almost complete; he was in the process of finishing his book, titled *Anarchism: Its Philosophy and Scientific Basis.* Quoting liberally from Karl Marx, he predicted the inevitable downfall of capitalism: the drive for efficiency, he said in the book, would eventually eliminate middle-class jobs, and the collapse of a consumer market would lead to "the catastrophe of production" and the demise of the system. All members of the laboring classes would find themselves pitted against each other, forced to accept starvation wages, and the most impoverished among them would not have the means they needed to survive. Indeed, according to Albert Parsons, the American worker resembled the former slave of the South: "He was free to compete with his fellow wage-worker for an opportunity to serve capital."[28]

In promoting this extended essay to reporters and jailhouse visitors, Albert went out of his way to give credit to Lucy, not only for "the idea of authorship, but for the plan of the work, and for some of its most interesting chapters." He said she had helped with much of the research: "She ransacked every labor headquarters and socialistic library in the city for facts and figures on the rise and growth of anarchy in the world. The book, therefore, is largely the work of Mrs. Lucy Parsons." Through the late spring and summer of 1887 and into the fall, Lucy had maintained a desk in an office of a local paper, the *Western Newsman*, on Third Avenue, where she had worked on the book.[29]

As the execution loomed, guards and reporters began to take careful note of the way each prisoner faced his awful fate. Reporters highlighted the plight of the wives and children who were cast into misery by the upcoming deaths of their spouses and fathers. Lulu was described to newspaper audiences as "a very bright girl," and Albert Junior as showing a "fondness for investigation and constructive talent rare in one so young"; both were said to be "of unusual intelligence." Readers were left to ponder the fate of all the "pretty children" who would soon be left fatherless.[30]

ON WEDNESDAY, NOVEMBER 2, THE COOK COUNTY SHERIFF BEGAN TO issue tickets to the execution, to be held nine days hence. The two hundred tickets were reserved for members of the jury, the reporters and editors of Chicago, and the attorneys involved in the case—none were given to family members. An Amnesty Association was aiming to present the governor with a stack of petitions no later than the ninth. General Parsons sent his own plea for his brother's life, a letter in which he claimed to have more information about the bombing, which had been perpetrated, he said, by "enemies of labor" in order to frame innocent men. Meanwhile, anticipating trouble, the authorities were making elaborate preparations for security. They sent wagonloads of arms and ammunition to the jail and posted twenty-four officers there on three rotating eight-hour shifts.[31]

On Thursday, November 3, Lucy Parsons attracted a large crowd on Clark Street as she tried to sell copies of a pamphlet titled "Was It a Fair Trial?," in the process snarling wagon traffic and attracting crowds. The police ordered her to move on, and so she walked a short way to a nearby building and stood on the steps, proceeding to sell within a couple of hours (she said) 5,000 copies at 5 cents each.

That day, Albert issued a farewell in *The Alarm*, which had been temporarily revived by Dyer Lum. Parsons urged his supporters to continue the battle against "the greed, cruelty, and abominations of the privileged class who riot and revel on the labor of their wage slaves." He refuted rumors that he had asked for clemency. Two of his cellmates, Samuel Fielden and Michael Schwab, had in fact signed such a petition. They had renounced the use of force and expressed regret if their work had caused others to believe that violence "was a proper instrument of reform." (Conventional wisdom held that Fielden had become "intoxicated with his own verbosity," an assessment that could have applied equally to Parsons.) Melville Stone, the editor of the *Chicago Daily News*, later wrote that he had responded to a request from Parsons on Sunday for a box of "good (Medium) Havana's" (cigars). Sitting on Parsons's prison cot, Stone had listened as Parsons begged him to intercede with the governor for a commutation of his sentence. Stone later recounted that Parsons had "cried out that he could never leave his children a legacy of dishonor; that at least he was not a coward," and that Stone and the other editors were "responsible for his fate." Stone cited his own duty to uphold the law, and Parsons suddenly lunged at him. A bailiff intervened, and Stone, shaken, quickly departed.[32]

On the evening of Monday, November 7, Lucy issued a statement:

My husband is dead to me, and I return home to my children to mourn for him. I spoke good-bye to him for the last time this afternoon, for I will never cross the threshold of the jail again, to be insulted and humiliated. The other women can go there and grieve before the men who turned us out this afternoon, but I will never go until I can sit at the side of my husband and talk with him without an infamous guard at my side. I want to live with the picture of my husband in a dungeon ever before my eyes. That will give me strength to bring up two revolutionists. The four men who will not belie their manhood are kept in dark dungeons because they will not sign the petition. Mr. Parsons will never sign any begging appeal. He will die, and I hope they will make a clean sweep of it and hang the whole seven. Let them hang them all, and let the men who cry for blood have all they want of it. The blood of my husband be upon them.

Although Lucy declared herself done with the effort to save Albert, others did not: the next day, the defense attorneys Captain William Black and Sigmund Zeisler, and even the jailer, appealed to the hold-outs, Parsons, Lingg, Fischer, Spies, and Engel, to petition for clemency.[33]

Black urged Parsons to petition for the sake of "his wife and babes," if not for his own sake, and believed he was a good candidate for clemency, yet Parsons refused. Parsons thought if he held out from making such a request, somehow he and the others might be saved together, since he was so obviously innocent; but in his "perverseness," in Black's words, he sealed his fate. Still, Parsons seemed to be in a good mood: "I am innocent," he said. "There is no proof connecting me with throwing the bomb. . . . I will say nothing more, and I stand by my innocence." He wrote farewell letters—one to his "Darling, Precious Little Children," telling them "how deeply, dearly your Papa loves you," and that "your Father is a self-offered Sacrifice upon the Altar of Liberty and Happiness." He urged them to "be industrious, sober and cheerful," and concluded, "Your mother! Ah! she is the grandest, noblest of women. Love, honor, and obey her."[34]

Thursday evening, the night before the scheduled hangings, Captain Black, *Labor Enquirer* editor Joseph Buchanan, and several other interested parties secured an audience with Governor Oglesby, who had decided to spare Fielden and Schwab from the hangman's noose; the two would serve life sentences at the state penitentiary at Joliet. Black argued that Parsons should be included with them, "on the ground that [he] is insane, and has been for many months, and is not responsible for his acts." A short, shocking letter written by Albert Parsons and sent via Black to Oglesby seemed to confirm this assessment; Buchanan read it aloud to the governor, but whatever chance there was for a stay of execution evaporated soon thereafter. Buchanan summarized the letter in this way: "If he [Parsons] was guilty, and must be hanged because of his presence at the Haymarket meeting, then he hoped a reprieve would be granted in his case until his wife and two children who were also at the meeting could be convicted and hanged with him." Oglesby replied, "My God, this is terrible." Parsons's claim that his children Junior and Lulu had been at Haymarket Square that night was always a frayed lifeline (because it was untrue), and now he seemed to take that claim to a bizarre, callous conclusion—if he was guilty, so, too, were his loved ones, who must also die.[35]

Why did Parsons not follow the lead of Schwab and Fielden, and confess to error in writing about dynamite as a means of resolving the sufferings of the laboring classes? First, he clearly did not throw the bomb that night at the Haymarket, and so always knew himself to be innocent of the deaths that occurred there. Second, perhaps he wanted to die, and there is evidence that some of his acquaintances—William Holmes and Dyer Lum among them—had encouraged him to aim (in the words of a reporter) "for the pearly gates by the rope route." Holmes urged Parsons not "to beg for mercy," believing his enemies had concocted a "trick" not only to kill him but disgrace him in the process by making him seem weak. Parsons reportedly asked Lum what he should do, and Lum had answered, "Die, Parsons."[36]

Finally, none of the original defendants had a realistic expectation of being set at liberty; the lives of Neebe, Schwab, and Fielden were spared, but Neebe was sentenced to fifteen years and the other two to life in prison. In all likelihood, Parsons made a terrible calculation—weighing his options—and decided that the power of his death as a rallying cry for the masses was preferable to spending the rest of his life in a tiny cell. In her introduction to his book *Anarchism*, Lucy hinted at this: ever since he had surrendered himself, she wrote, "he had never breathed a breath of pure, fresh air, never looked upon a growing sprig of grass, never beheld earth or sky; that nothing met his eye, but the frowning, bare stone walls relieved only by bolts, bars, and chains; that in his 6×8 inner tomb he was confined twenty-one hours, six days in the week, and forty hours on 'the Lord's day' from Saturday afternoon until Monday morning." Or perhaps in contemplating his future, he considered the fact that one of his greatest pleasures—declaiming in front of large numbers of people—would forever be denied him. He would never again thrill to the sound of his own voice cheered by the multitudes.[37]

On Thursday morning Lucy had again created a "scene." She arrived at the jail (despite her promise on Monday that she would never do so again), and, denied admission, "threw up her hands and fell to the floor in a dead faint." Efforts to revive her took twenty minutes, after which guards escorted her out of the building. When, that afternoon, one by one the other wives were granted a final meeting with their loved ones, Lucy was not among them. That day, Louis Lingg cheated the hangman by taking his own life, biting off the top of a dynamite cap that had been smuggled into his cell; the blast blew off part of his face, and he lingered for six hours before dying.[38]

Albert spent a restless night into Friday morning, and his mournful rendition of the Scottish ballad "Annie Laurie" before daybreak became legendary. In the song, the singer praises his lover for her brow as gentle as a snowdrift, her throat as graceful as a swan's, and her dark blue eyes: "And for bonnie Annie Laurie / I'll lay me down and die." Widely regarded at the time as a hymn to erotic self-sacrifice, the song did not seem to impress Lucy, who left it out of her accounts of Albert's last hours.

Friday morning dawned on a city girded for war. Awaiting orders, military companies were stationed at various armories, the soldiers armed with Springfield and Remington breech-loaders outfitted with bayonets. Some carried the brand new Winchester "repeating riot gun." Two Gatling guns and four Howitzers stood ready for quick deployment wherever they might be needed. Government officials issued rifles to their clerks to fend off any invasion of federal buildings by enraged "Reds." Albert Parsons complained that he had not been able to sleep because of the buzz of conversation between reporters and deputies, and, as he put it in a letter to Dyer Lum: "Caesar kept me awake till late at night with the noise (music), of hammer and saw, erecting my throne, his scaffold." He passed up the offer of a big breakfast (including alcohol) in favor of fried oysters and coffee. Taking care to dress neatly and brush his hair, he objected loudly when he was denied use of a wash basin. Beginning at 8 a.m., the Reverend Dr. H. W. Bolton of the First Methodist Church made his rounds to minister to the men, but apparently "his efforts to get Parsons to consider spiritual matters were of no avail."[39]

While Albert was fending off the insistent Dr. Bolton, Lucy and her two children, together with Lizzie and three other women kin of the condemned, were trying to gain admission to the jail to say goodbye to Albert one last time. At the Dearborn Avenue entrance they encountered a gauntlet of three hundred police officers, who, awkwardly carrying their heavy arms, were standing shoulder to shoulder to cordon off the perimeter at least two blocks from the jail. Lucy wore a black mourning dress. The children, according to an *Inter-Ocean* reporter, "were poorly dressed with dark clothes, well-worn shoes and hats; with real woolen stockings and blue scarfs around their necks, and they clung to their mother, without any apparent idea of what was going on." (This reporter mistook Lulu for a boy.) Lucy informed one officer, "I must go. I am Lucy Parsons. These are my children. We must go to jail. They must see their father." Lucy, Lizzie, and the children ran from one checkpoint to the next, trying to get in, and finally, holding a child by each hand, Lucy tried to crawl under a rope and push her way through. When she was told that she must obey the law, she exclaimed, "The law! What do I care for the law, and my husband being murdered? Shoot me, kill me if you will." To a passerby who expressed concern, Lucy screamed, "I don't want your help, nor your sympathy; I don't know who you are." The efforts of "Parsons' mulatto wife" to force her way through police lines constituted the only notable "violence" of the day.[40]

Later, Lizzie Swank Holmes would provide a heartrending account of the morning—the children, their lips blue from the cold, shaking with fear, and Lucy frantic to the point of collapse. At 9:15, the two women and two children were loaded into a patrol wagon and taken to the police station on East Chicago Avenue. In separate cells, the women were strip-searched by a matron and then booked on the charge of obstructing the streets. Lizzie wrote, "Instead of being surrounded by loving friends, [Lucy] was caged in a cell, insulted and degraded until her heart was broken." For their part, the police expressed grim satisfaction that the notorious Mrs. Parsons was nowhere near the jail at noon. But had she been there, she would have been proud of her husband for his composure during this most dreadful moment.[41]

With great ceremony, the condemned were retrieved from their cells, read the death warrant, and marched to the courtyard gallows. Along the way, Parsons said to one of the bailiffs, "I really feel sorry for Schwab and Fielden" (for refusing to embrace a noble death with the rest). Clad in white shrouds against the background of the jail's dark walls, the doomed prisoners appeared as ghostly apparitions. A Dallas reporter compared Parsons on the scaffold to a great actor in a magnificent tableau, someone who had "wrought himself to an ecstasy of self-glorification" and intended to die "in a manner to impress, if possible, on all future generations that he was a martyr." He continued: "No tragedian that has paced the stage in America ever made a more marvelous presentation of a self-chosen part, perfect in every detail. The upward turn of his eyes, his distant, far-away look, and above all, the attitude of complete resignation that every fold of the awkward shroud only seemed to make more distinct, was by far the most striking feature of the gallows picture." After the death cap had been placed over his head, Parsons demanded, in a loud, firm voice, "Will I be allowed to speak, O men of America? Let me speak, Sheriff Matson." A *New York Times* reporter said that he raised his voice, "as if beginning an emphatic speech," and cried out, "Let the voice of the people be heard, O . . . " when suddenly the trap door fell and all four bodies dangled at once. The telegraph operators who were present immediately sent the news out across the wires. A physician pronounced Parsons dead seven minutes later, at 12:04 p.m. Witnesses differed over whether he had "died hard"—from strangulation—or "easy"—from a broken neck. When they heard the door fall, soldiers on the roof of the jail threw down their weapons and clapped and cheered. The prison guards mused aloud about the boredom that lay ahead of them: "No proxy wives, no fruit-baskets, no good-looking reporters, no nothing." Front-page headlines trumpeted, "Justice Is Done."[42]

At 2:15 in the afternoon the police released Lucy, Lizzie, and the children; the two women were ordered to appear in court Saturday morning. As they left the station they were met by a reporter (at least one would remain near "the dark skinned, lustrous eyed widow of Albert R. Parsons" for the next three days), who answered in the affirmative when Lucy asked him, "Is the bloody business over?" Prodded for a reaction, she exclaimed, "My God! I can't talk to you now." But then, tears streaming down her face, she proceeded to give a lengthy account of her travails that morning, and to interrupt Lizzie, who tried to say a few words. In the boisterous crowd outside the jail, no one noticed Lucy, and already the newsboys were yelling, "Full account of execution!" and trying to shove a paper in her hands. Dispatching the children to a friend's house, the two women went directly to the undertaker a few blocks from the Parsons home on Milwaukee Avenue. There, holding Albert's certificate of death and a permit for internment, Lucy stood by the coffin as the undertaker unscrewed the lid. She bent down and carefully removed the white death cap from the corpse, and stood stony-faced as Lizzie began to weep uncontrollably.[43]

That evening, members of the local IWPA Defense Association charged with visiting the wives of all the deceased found her lying on the floor of her apartment surrounded by women friends. Rousing herself, Lucy lifted her hands and cried, "Oh papa, papa! Come back to me! Just one word from those handsome lips! They have murdered him! They have murdered my noble, generous, loving husband, who never harmed a man in his life!" Clutching his picture, she paced up and down the room, wailing.[44]

The following day, Saturday, Albert's body was delivered to the apartment, where a piece of black cloth hung on the door together with the sign "Parsons & Co., Fashionable Dressmaking." (The court case against Lucy and Lizzie scheduled for that morning had been dismissed in the absence of a prosecutor.) A distraught Lucy was there to receive the coffin, as were her children, who huddled together in a corner, crying. Outside, where a crowd had gathered, police jostled with pickpockets; all of them could hear Lucy inside, calling Albert's name as her friends sought to keep her from looking at the corpse. Meanwhile, members of the Defense Association went to the apartments of all four deceased, collecting the clothes, shrouds, and other effects of the men to prevent them from being stolen and displayed for profit: "Every little memento and relic has been carefully preserved and placed in a secure place where it will be impossible for the enterprising showman to secure a grip on this desirable material."[45]

On Sunday at noon, a huge cortege started down Milwaukee Avenue, stopping at the homes of the dead anarchists to add their bodies to the procession of an estimated 6,000 marchers. At the Parsons residence, mourners had been coming through over the past twenty hours to pay their respects. Now a great throng assembled outside the building to watch as Albert Parsons's coffin was loaded onto a wagon bearing an immense floral display that said, "From Knights of Labor Assembly No. 1307." Accompanying Lucy and the children was Joseph Buchanan.

The editor was struck by the widow's appearance: "She was not the Mrs. Parsons of old. Grief had traced its handmarks upon the comely features; long hours, days, weeks, and months of fearful suspense had been ended by an awful tragedy. With a moan scarcely human in its thrilling intensity, she fell upon the body of him whom she loved so well in life and will worship in death."[46]

Mayor John A. Roche had banned flags, speeches, and public demonstrations, but the brass bands and muffled drums played dirges. As the procession moved forward, the crowd continued to swell, with flashes of red abounding—neckties, ribbons, badges on men's coats, trimmings on women's hats. Onlookers fell silent as the hearses passed in what was a reprise of Central Labor Union parades, with German singing societies and labor unions predominating. Halting at the Wisconsin Central depot, an estimated 3,000 mourners boarded thirty-five coaches to Waldheim Cemetery, a nondenominational German burying ground located in a nearby suburb. The train had to inch its way forward because of the crush of people lining the tracks. At the cemetery, the bodies would remain in a vault for five weeks until a proper burial could take place. Tommy Morgan began his brief eulogy with Albert's last words, "Let the voice of the people be heard!" A bell tolling loudly, insistently, reminded some present of the inspiration for Albert's paper *The Alarm*.[47]

By Tuesday Lucy was back at her desk in the offices of the *Western Newsman*, editing Albert's manuscript of *Anarchism*; the first copies (which she self-published) would appear on December 10 and include the speeches the eight defendants had made to the court in October the year before, essays by Lucy and Dyer Lum on anarchy, and testimonials by William Parsons on Albert's life and by Lizzie Swank Holmes on his last hours. Lucy seemed surprisingly calm; she told a reporter that she was determined to honor the life's work of her dead husband: "It is a duty I owe to him and to the world and shall be sacredly performed. I shall give my whole time to this work for months to come. Plans for the future? I have none. I am drifting along on the river of time, knowing little and caring less where it will take me." Yet perhaps she consoled herself at the thought that, as of November 11, she, too, was enshrined in the pantheon of anarchist heroes, along with the dead, as already poems were being written to honor her: "Most bravely has thou faced the fight / And nobly battled for the right" ("To Mrs. Lucy Parsons").[48]

ON SATURDAY, DECEMBER 17, LUCY PARSONS SEEMED IN AN EXPANSIVE mood, eager to talk to a *Tribune* reporter and remark upon the calm that had pervaded the day of the executions. Bonfield and his henchmen had badly misjudged things, she contended, when "they thought we would be fools enough to dynamite some of their buildings, which a drove of slaves could rebuild in a year." The time was not right for revolution, she said. Yet among her anarchist comrades, she said cryptically, "the subject [of violence] was thoroughly discussed and a line of policy decided upon." She recalled the awful morning when the sheriff had asked Albert her address, so officers would know where his body could be deposited after his death. Sheriff Matson, she said, "knew perfectly well where I lived, and so did every policeman and detective in the city."[49]

The following afternoon, several hundred mourners boarded a specially chartered train to Waldheim Cemetery for a ceremony to mark the internment of the five bodies—those of the four who had been executed plus Lingg. It was a cold, bleak day. Atop Parsons's coffin was a large flower arrangement in the shape of a pillow that said, "Our Papa." Captain Black spoke, among others, and soon after he began, someone called out, "Make way for Mrs. Parsons!" The estimated 2,000 mourners stood back as Lucy, supported on either side by Lizzie Swank Holmes and her husband William Holmes, slowly approached the caskets positioned near the open graves. At Albert's coffin, "she gave voice to a wail which startled the crowd," according to a reporter who was present. Black stood transfixed, watching Lucy struggle to speak. Finally, he took control of the situation, saying, "Someone please take some fresh snow and rub the lady's face." Soft snowballs rubbed against her temples were apparently sufficient to revive her, and a group of friends carried her away. As the coffins were lowered into their graves, a German choral society sang "Am Grabe Unserer Freunde" (At the Grave of Our Friends). In covering the funeral, the *Tribune* announced, in a headline, "Mrs. Parsons Getting Back Some of Her Old-Time Spirit." Indeed, she was—if she had ever lost it.[50]

rays of an "all too neighboring sun," she fell into the hands and became the consort of Oliver Gathings, who now supports himself by spading up gardens and doing like ignoble service for white trash and ex-rebels, the while the despoiler of his home awaits hanging in a Chicago prison. On high days and holidays, such as the 19th of June, Oliver Gathings puts on his tony clothes and

As a freedman living in Waco, Texas, Oliver Benton, aka Oliver Gathings, claimed that a freedwoman twenty years younger than he, Lucia Carter, was his wife and the mother of his infant son. This image is from a photograph taken in September 1886, when Benton was fifty-four years old.

"Mrs. Lucy Parsons," St. Louis Globe-Democrat, September 18, 1886, 3.

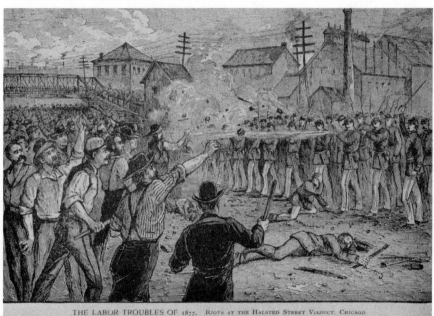

THE LABOR TROUBLES OF 1877. Riots at the Halsted Street Viaduct, Chicago

In Chicago, the Great Upheaval of 1877 pitted striking workers against militia, private security forces, federal troops, and local police. This scene, depicting the Battle of the Viaduct on July 25, evokes a state of war. The workers, armed only with rocks, bricks, and sticks, were vastly overpowered. An estimated thirty-five workers died in the week-long clashes.

Michael J. Schaak, Anarchy and Anarchists (Chicago: F. Schulte, 1889), 63.

ALBERT R. PARSONS.

Albert R. Parsons Jr. was born in September 1879. His birth certificate lists him as "Negro." Lucy Parsons included this drawing, and one of Albert's sister Lulu, in her tribute to her husband, *Life of Albert Parsons*, published in 1889.

LUCY E. PARSONS, ED., *LIFE OF ALBERT PARSONS WITH BRIEF HISTORY OF THE LABOR MOVEMENT IN AMERICA* (CHICAGO: MRS. LUCY E. PARSONS, 1889), OPP. 49.

LULU EDA PARSONS.

Lulu Eda Parsons was born in April 1881. On her birth certificate, her race is listed as "Niger." She is listed as her mother's third child, presumably an indirect reference to Lucy's first baby, Champ, who died in infancy in Waco.

PARSONS, ED., *LIFE OF ALBERT PARSONS*, OPP. 96.

Lizzie Swank's demure appearance belied her radical political ideology and fierce devotion to the plight of Chicago's needlewomen. A regular contributor to and sometime editor of *The Alarm*, she (like Lucy Parsons) nevertheless managed to avoid prosecution for the Haymarket bombing. JOSEPH A. LABADIE COLLECTION, UNIVERSITY OF MICHIGAN LIBRARY.

Born in Germany in 1850, George A. Schilling, a cooper, was a prominent Chicago labor leader. An early friend of Albert and Lucy Parsons, he remained a committed socialist and a firm believer in electoral politics while they turned to anarchy. He admired Lucy Parsons, but believed her provocative speaking style was responsible for painting all union activity with the brush of radicalism and violence. JOSEPH A. LABADIE COLLECTION, UNIVERSITY OF MICHIGAN LIBRARY.

Born in Luxembourg in 1843, Michael J. Schaak ascended the ranks of the Chicago police force after becoming a patrolman in 1869. He was promoted to lieutenant in 1879, captain in 1887, and inspector in 1896. The lead investigator for the Haymarket "riot," he was dogged and dismissive of civil liberties in his pursuit of Chicago anarchists.

THE OFFICE OF THE ARBEITER-ZEITUNG.
From a Photograph.

Chicago was well known for its vibrant radical labor press. This building at 107 Fifth Avenue (now 41 North Wells Street) housed two anarchist papers: the German-language *Arbeiter Zeitung* (Workers' Paper) as well as Albert Parsons's *Alarm*. Other labor papers published here included *Vorbote* (The Harbinger, Herald) and *Die Fackel* (The Torch). SCHAAK, ANARCHY AND ANARCHISTS, 76.

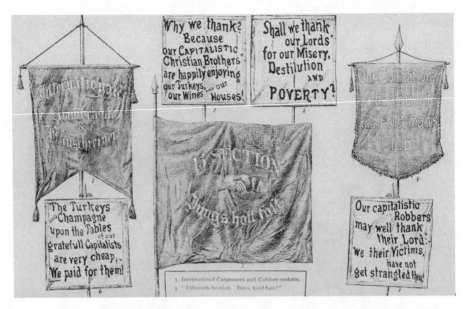

Anarchist parades were colorful affairs, with banners and floats. The talented seamstresses Lucy Parsons and Lizzie Swank probably designed and sewed these banners, several of which were displayed during the boisterous Thanksgiving demonstrations of 1884 and 1885.

SCHAAK, *ANARCHY AND ANARCHISTS*, 69.

AN ANARCHIST PROCESSION.

This portrayal of two women holding flags is no doubt a distorted rendering of the petite Lizzie Swank and her taller comrade Lucy Parsons. Swank and Parsons often appeared at the head of anarchist marches carrying the two revolutionary flags—the black one symbolized the plight of the starving poor, the red one the unity of all peoples across national boundaries.

SCHAAK, *ANARCHY AND ANARCHISTS*, 78.

ALBERT R. PARSONS.
From a Photograph.

Contemporaries often commented on Albert Parsons's dapper appearance, which ran counter to the stereotypical portrayal of the anarchist as slovenly, bewhiskered, and wild-eyed. Lucy Parsons considered this drawing to be a good likeness of her husband, and she included a variation of it in her *Life of Albert Parsons* (1889).
SCHAAK, *ANARCHY AND ANARCHISTS*, 166.

MRS. LUCY PARSONS.
From a Photograph.

Detective Michael Schaak considered Lucy Parsons a dangerous woman who, because of her gender, was unfairly absolved of accountability for her words and actions. He noted that, despite her claim of "Mexican extraction, . . . her swarthy complexion and distinctly negro features do not bear out her assertions."
SCHAAK, *ANARCHY AND ANARCHISTS*, 167.

THE HAYMARKET MEETING.—"In the Name of the People. I Command You to Disperse."

On the night of May 4, 1886, Captain John Bonfield led a contingent of police into Haymarket Square, where the anarchist Samuel Fielden was addressing a crowd. Ordered off the speaker's stand, Fielden began to protest, and an unknown person threw a bomb that landed near the entrance to Crane's Alley (to the left of the lamppost).

Schaak, *Anarchy and Anarchists*, 140.

THE HAYMARKET RIOT. The Explosion and the Conflict.

The bomb killed one police officer immediately, and later six more officers died. Sixty police and an unknown number of workers were wounded. Although this image shows workers shooting at police, the *Chicago Tribune* reported on June 27, 1886, that an internal police department investigation revealed that in the chaos "a very large number of the police were wounded by each other's revolvers," and that the police "emptied their revolvers, mainly into each other."

Schaak, *Anarchy and Anarchists*, 142.

August Brauneck, a German-born portrait photographer, took these pictures of Lucy Parsons in his New York City studio, probably in late 1886. Her fashion sense is on full display, evidenced by her elegant striped silk dress, delicate lace collar fastened with a gold pin, and hat decorated with ostrich feathers. Absent is her favorite piece of jewelry: a necklace with a charm in the shape of a gallows. Prints and Photographs Division, Library of Congress, LC-DIG-ds-10459.

Prints and Photographs Division, Library of Congress, LC-USZ62–48791.

THE GREAT TRIAL. Scene in the Criminal Court.

By modern standards, *Illinois v. August Spies et al.* was a carnivalesque affair, with the jury playing cards, the judge flirting with his female admirers, and the on-lookers restless and unruly. The trial lasted from June 21 to August 11, 1886, and featured testimony from 118 "witnesses." Schaak, *Anarchy and Anarchists*, 410.

Joseph R. Buchanan, editor of the Denver-based *Labor Enquirer*, demonstrated an ideological fluidity in his role as an advocate for organized labor in the 1880s. Buchanan's paper promoted the Knights of Labor but also served as an advocate for individual trade unions and published Albert and Lucy Parsons and other anarchists. Buchanan's steadfast support for the Haymarket defendants led to his expulsion from the Knights.

JOSEPH A. LABADIE COLLECTION, UNIVERSITY OF MICHIGAN LIBRARY.

This illustration shows "murderers' row" in the Cook County jail. The defendants are in the "cage," in the foreground; to the left of the man in the bowler hat, Albert Parsons talks with Lucy. The image is embellished with pictures of Nina van Zandt and August Spies, whom the press portrayed as star-crossed lovers. After a proxy wedding in January 1887, van Zandt referred to herself as Nina Spies and remained devoted to his memory for the rest of her life.

FRANK LESLIE'S ILLUSTRATED NEWSPAPER, OCTOBER 1, 1887.

THE EXECUTION.

Standing on the scaffold on November 11, 1887, the four remaining Haymarket defendants appear as ghostly apparitions. Left to right are August Spies, Adolph Fischer, George Engel, and Albert Parsons. Each of the condemned men spoke very briefly in turn, with Parsons's exhortation, "Let the voice of the people be heard, O . . . ," cut short by the dropping of the trap door.
SCHAAK, *ANARCHY AND ANARCHISTS*, 645.

Immediately after the executions, the condemned men became memorialized as martyrs to the cause of liberty. Louis Lingg committed suicide in his cell the day before the hangings were to take place. Albert Parsons, the only one of the five who was American-born, is placed in the center of the montage.
JOSEPH A. LABADIE COLLECTION, UNIVERSITY OF MICHIGAN LIBRARY.

Lucy Parsons was not the only radical female labor agitator to garner national attention in the late nineteenth and early twentieth centuries. Several of her contemporaries had Chicago connections. The Irish-born Mary Harris "Mother" Jones (1837–1930) moved to Chicago from Memphis after her husband and four young children died in a yellow fever epidemic. Jones disapproved of the anarchists' demonstrations and lakeside meetings, convinced they were counterproductive to labor organizing.
JOSEPH A. LABADIE COLLECTION, UNIVERSITY OF MICHIGAN LIBRARY.

IDA B. WELLS.

Born a slave in 1862, Ida B. Wells-Barnett lived in Chicago from 1893 until her death in 1931. She shared with Lucy Parsons certain life history experiences, such as early years in enslavement and a national reputation as an agitator, but apparently their paths never crossed. Wells-Barnett dedicated her life to fighting for civil rights while Parsons largely ignored the plight of the black laboring classes. PRINTS AND PHOTOGRAPHS DIVISION, LIBRARY OF CONGRESS, LC-USZ62-107756.

Born in Michigan in 1866, Voltairine de Cleyre (shown here in 1901) was a well-known writer and theorist of anarchy in her day. She favored radical individualism, in contrast to Lucy Parsons, who argued that the good society began with trade unions. In the spring of 1911, de Cleyre moved to Chicago and began to promote the cause of Mexican revolutionaries. She died the following year. JOSEPH A. LABADIE COLLECTION, UNIVERSITY OF MICHIGAN LIBRARY.

Like Mary "Mother" Jones and Voltairine de Cleyre, Emma Goldman (1869–1940) claimed the Haymarket affair radicalized her. Goldman, who visited Chicago often, considered Lucy Parsons a rival for local and national press attention. Goldman promoted the idea of "free love," whereas Parsons publicly favored conventional gender norms.
JOSEPH A. LABADIE COLLECTION, UNIVERSITY OF MICHIGAN LIBRARY.

As an icon of the labor movement and a living link to Haymarket, Lucy Parsons remained a sought-after speaker until her death. During the Great Depression, she was dismayed that many Chicago workers cast their lot with the Democratic Party and embraced the New Deal. The anarchist revolution seemed as remote as ever.
JOSEPH A. LABADIE COLLECTION, UNIVERSITY OF MICHIGAN LIBRARY.

PART 3

BLATHERKITE–
GODDESS OF
FREE SPEECH

Chapter 10

The Widow Parsons
Sets Her Course

THE COLLAPSE OF THE TRAP DOOR ON THE COOK COUNTY JAIL'S
scaffold generated depths of emotion that words can scarcely convey. The self-proclaimed "respectable classes" rejoiced, hopeful that the
pernicious doctrine of anarchism had been eradicated and its murderous preacher-practitioners silenced forever. At the other end of the political spectrum, beginning at noon on November 11, 1887, radicals of
various political persuasions vowed a new, or renewed, commitment to
the cause. Many years later, the socialist Eugene V. Debs, who still felt
overwhelmed by his sense of outrage, described the executions in terms
that would not have sounded out of place in an address by Lucy Parsons
herself: "The sordid capitalism which preys upon the life-blood of labor,
whose ethics are expressed in beastly gluttony and insatiable greed, and
whose track of conquest is strewn with the bones of countless victims,
pounced upon these men with the cruel malignity of fiends and stran-
gled them to death." The anarchist Emma Goldman, eighteen years
old in 1887, considered the deaths of the martyrs "the most decisive influence in my existence." Throughout her life, their spirits "seemed to
hover over me and give deeper meaning to the events that had inspired

my spiritual birth and growth." In Latin America, images of the four men on the gallows entered the pantheon of radical iconography. In Europe, portraits of the eight anarchists who had originally been sentenced to die adorned the wall of labor halls so that none would forget, in George Schilling's words, "the chief tragedy of the closing years of the nineteenth century."[1]

Lucy suffered deeply and in her own way. She rarely spoke about her marriage, but in 1886, before Albert's execution, she said, to a crowd in Cincinnati: "Look at me. Fourteen years ago in September I was married to Albert Parsons. Seven years after that a boy was born to us, and twenty-one months later a girl. My husband seldom spoke an unkind word and never a vulgar word, and each night when he came home the children ran into his arms, and each morning at his departure each one of us received a parting kiss. Where is that happy home now?" Still, the mantle of revered Haymarket widow did not rest lightly on her shoulders. Within six months of Albert's execution she scandalized the radical and respectable classes alike by taking a young lover, a married man. And she seemed all too eager to exploit—in a literal sense—the goodwill and sympathy extended to her by the German community in Chicago in the wake of Albert's death. She brushed off the public censure; the combined effects of her hunger for companionship, sexual and otherwise, and her need to support herself, were just too great.[2]

At the same time, she tried to stake out a new purpose for her life. She continued to speak about anarchism, but she also seemed intent on pushing the boundaries of the First Amendment, and in the process became a leading proponent of free speech—this in an age when, as she knew all too well, advocating anarchy could lead to a death sentence. Her battles with the Chicago police over what she could and could not say, and which flag she must or must not display, became legend. Indeed, the more the anarchist movement diminished in numbers and influence, the more the city's authorities—aided and abetted by the mainstream press—hounded its adherents. To carry on the fight, then, Lucy began to groom her son as a worthy namesake of his famous father. In this particular role, though, she would fail in a notably newsworthy and ultimately tragic way.

LUCY'S PERIOD OF PUBLIC MOURNING WAS BRIEF: ON DECEMBER 30, less than two weeks after the formal interment at Waldheim, she appeared in court to demand the $5,000 worth of newly bound copies of Albert's book *Anarchism* that had been seized by the police—they had been taken not because of Albert's activities, but because the printer with whom Lucy had contracted had failed to pay his rent. By January it was clear that she would have her hands full protecting her husband's legacy from the many purported friends who in her eyes would seek to despoil it. In *The Alarm* she attacked J. William Lloyd, an anarchist and author of an essay titled "Vengeance: An Open Letter to the Communist-Anarchists of Chicago." Lloyd had admitted that Albert and his comrades had done much to advance the cause, but he had warned that those gains would vanish at the first instance of violence against "innocent women and babes." In response, Lucy denounced Lloyd's apparent "quaker policy" of pacifism and chided him for his patronizing tone, saying he was "like a good mother who . . . endeavors to impress upon her naughty children the importance of her advice." As a final retort she wrote that it was a waste of her time trying to convert "one bourgeois professor."[3]

By the late 1880s, the infighting among self-proclaimed anarchists in the United States had grown bitter. Lucy identified herself as an anarchist-communist, arguing that trade unions and other small, self-governing, voluntary groups should take the place of a central government. In general, anarchist-communists supported the abolition of the state as well as the abolition of money, private property, and capitalism; in this new society, workers would own the means of production and participate in a direct form of democracy that made political parties superfluous. In contrast, Lloyd represented anarchist-individualists, extreme libertarians who were hostile toward state-sponsored institutions of any kind and for the most part indifferent toward trade unions. The views of a third group overlapped with those of socialists, who favored a strong workers' state to redistribute property; many German immigrants, including Johann Most, embraced this kind of heavy-handed anarchism. In general, anarchists rejected the ballot box, though they disagreed among themselves about the role of violence in bringing about a new society, with Most quite uniquely explicit on that score. Unlike many of her comrades, Lucy did not shrink from a close association with the reviled Most despite his call for what was essentially domestic terrorism.[4]

Around the globe, anarchists doing battle with repressive nation-states and colonial bureaucracies—in places such as Spain and the Philippines and Cuba—faced the constant threat of the firing squad. Some embraced assassination, bombings, and other forms of militant resistance as a matter of course. Citing the recent Haymarket executions, Lucy Parsons argued that her own politics amounted to a life-and-death ideology, and that violence was a necessary ingredient of the coming upheaval. Her call for revolution (crowd-pleasing to many brow-beaten workers, to be sure) was consistent to the point of rigidity.[5]

Chicago was undergoing rapid, dramatic transformations, but Lucy's speeches and writings, though prescient about the depredations of big business at the time and in decades to come, echoed old themes and ignored new realities. Between 1880 and 1890, the city doubled its population, to 1,099,850, and also doubled its area in square miles and its manufacturing capacity. The number of bookkeepers and store clerks increased twenty-fold. Almost half a million of the city's residents had been born in a foreign country, increasing numbers of them from Eastern Europe, and they constituted two-thirds of all factory workers. In the midst of widely heralded "progress," workers faced the same brutal conditions: limited housing stock that forced thousands to subsist in cramped, fetid tenements, and stagnant wages for men, women, and children, who often labored six days a week for up to sixteen hours a day. However, the growth of the white-collar labor force suggested that industrial capitalism was better able than Lucy had anticipated to absorb at least native-born white surplus labor.[6]

The collapse of the United Labor Party signaled the end of independent labor politics in Chicago. The Knights of Labor, decimated by employers' aggressive use of lockouts and private security forces, began to disintegrate. It was wracked by internal conflicts between local leaders and the head of the organization, Terence V. Powderly, and between "mixed" district assemblies and those that advocated strict autonomy among the various trades. A new, relatively conservative international group of unions for skilled craftspeople, the American Federation of Labor (AFL), benefited from the Knights' decline. Employers took advantage of a swollen, hungry labor force, replacing strikers with scabs, and skilled workers with machines or with women and children. These lords of industry exulted in the new steel mills, skyscrapers, and department stores that showcased Chicago's prosperity for a few.[7]

At the same time, the city was emerging as a giant social laboratory for groups that were determined to smooth the rough edges of industrial capitalism without overturning the system itself. These groups included clergymen, wealthy clubwomen, members of the college-educated middle class, and sociologists and political scientists employed by the new University of Chicago. The reformers compared society to a living organism, with all parts interdependent for the health and well-being of the whole. "Social" served as the universal watchword as state-socialists became respectable, reformers founded social settlements, clergy preached the Social Gospel, and supporters of unfettered "free" enterprise took up the banner of social Darwinism. In 1888, both the *Chicago Times* and the *Inter-Ocean* ran stories on the 13,000 men, women, and children toiling in the city's 800 squalid garment sweatshops. The title of the *Times* article of February 12, "Chicago's White Slaves," echoed the anarchists' denunciations of wage slavery. Parsons admitted that the piece might prove "a revelation to those who live upon the wealthy avenues," but, she added sarcastically, "My lords and ladies, I reveal to you a novelty—the human race exists!"[8]

As an articulate woman proposing solutions to the ills of society, Lucy was no lone figure on the city's political landscape. Still, within a public arena of competing ideas and legislative initiatives, she occupied a prominent niche—a revolutionary cadre of one—and fought to stay in the headlines and on the front page. Many in the white laboring classes applauded her fiery speeches as a bracing antidote to the voices of moderation and compromise that were the hallmarks of social reform. For these workers, Lucy's message of dynamite-driven resistance represented a catharsis of sorts, since she was virtually the only person bold or foolish enough to persist in speaking the Haymarket anarchists' language of force. In an effort to distinguish herself from a growing multiplicity of debaters and investigators, many of whom agreed with her basic premise about economic inequality, she began appearing at forums to which she had not been invited, emerging from the back of the hall and striding to the podium where she would hold forth, an ingenious new form of public performance.

Lucy's activities of 1888 blurred the line between agitating and money-making. In March she spoke before audiences in Boston and New York, and in December, on her first trip outside the United States, she attracted enthusiastic crowds in England and Scotland. In all these places she sold pictures of herself and copies of Albert's *Anarchism*, and her hosts took up collections for her. By this time she was also receiving regular support from the Pioneer Aid and Support Association (PASA), a Chicago group founded in December 1887. PASA, composed mostly of German immigrant women who raised money for the widows and children of the Haymarket martyrs, received liberal support, in turn, from the Central Labor Union. In the summer of 1888, she began work on a biography of Albert, and solicited subscriptions to the new volume. She also founded Labor Assembly #1, which she called the Albert R. Parsons Assembly, establishing a library and a fund to publish books, newspapers, and tracts and "to encourage and promote public speaking among our members." This group replaced Albert's Knights assembly 1307, which Powderly had recently dissolved.[9]

On June 20, 1888, she was driving around the city in a buggy decorated with banners that featured her husband's last words—"Let the voice of the people be heard!"—and a variation of August Spies's proclamation on the gallows—"My silence is more terrible than my speech." (His actual words were "The day will come when our silence will be more powerful than the voices you strangle today.") Stopped by a police officer for distributing ads for *Anarchism*, she attracted a crowd by yelling: "You blue-coated murderer, the souls of my husband and his companions will creep from their graves to haunt you, your children, and your children's children." Hauled before Chief Inspector John Bonfield, she pleaded that her son and daughter were home alone, to which he replied, "You should have thought of that before." Two days later she was back distributing handbills for the book, this time in the lobby of the elegant Grand Pacific Hotel, with Albert Junior in tow. Again people stopped to stare, "anxious to catch a glimpse of the notorious woman," in the words of the *Tribune*.[10]

In August Lucy took the children to Waukesha to visit with Daniel Hoan and his family, who had sheltered Albert during his flight. She received a warm welcome from those who remembered her husband fondly and who had come to know her son from his previous extended stay, while she was on her national speaking tour. Accompanying the Parsons family, Lizzie Swank Holmes found herself sympathetic to these simple Waukesha folk, but she believed that their dislike of capitalism was emotional and intuitive rather than the result of the necessarily difficult, extensive reading that anarchism required. For her part, Lucy Parsons resisted succumbing to any Wisconsin reverie; while there, she wrote an article for *The Alarm* reminding her readers that the Haymarket bomb had proved "that a powerful weapon could be placed in the hands of the people at small expense."[11]

In late October Parsons traveled to New York City, and on the thirtieth she set sail for London. She made the trip at the invitation of the British Social Democrats, chiefly William Morris and other well-known socialists who had vociferously denounced the Haymarket trial and pressed for the prisoners' release. The eight-day voyage on the passenger ship *Arizona* proved a delightful diversion for her, as she found herself in the company of pleasant, non-steerage strangers. The officers and staff were polite and attentive. The passengers took their meals together, and on deck they played games, drank ale, discussed socialism, and applauded Parsons's rendering of John Greenleaf Whittier's eighty-eight-line poem "The Reformer." By the middle of the journey they had come to think of themselves as a unit, all bound together by the pitching of the seas and the onslaught of seasickness, a malady that respected neither social class nor age nor gender. Free of the usual cant, her article in *The Alarm* detailing this voyage is one of the very few pieces she wrote in her life in which she admitted that she had actually enjoyed herself somewhere.[12]

Disembarking in Liverpool, Parsons traveled by train to London, marveling at the lovely English countryside. Jane Burden, the glamourous wife of William Morris, took her sightseeing to Westminster

Abbey and the Tower of London. During her stay in the city, she met the Russian prince Peter Kropotkin, a famous theorist of anarchism. In Trafalgar Square, a fog-bound Hyde Park, and other venues she regaled crowds with her claim to American authenticity: "When Columbus first came in sight of the Western continent, my father's ancestors were there to give them a native greeting. When the conquering hosts of Cortez moved into Mexico, my mother's ancestors were there to repel the invader." The Trafalgar rally of November 13 carried special meaning: it was the site of "Bloody Sunday," November 13, 1887, when, at a mass meeting protesting the Haymarket executions, the police had shot and killed three men. Now, though, memories of that clash and fears of violence had depressed the attendance at Parsons's talk. The secretary of the Social Democratic Federation assured a reporter that, although the group remained outraged over Haymarket, "we wish it to be distinctly understood, on the other hand, that as Social Democrats we are necessarily in direct opposition to anarchism."[13]

With three lectures prepared—on anarchism, the Haymarket trial, and the evils of child labor—Parsons spoke to crowds in Norwich and Ipswich and to intimate gatherings of socialists and anarchists in London. William Morris told a correspondent that "she is a curious looking woman: No signs of European blood in her, Indian with a touch of negro; but she speaks pure Yankee." *The Alarm* saw fit to republish a description offered by a London paper: "She has the full lips, the black hair, the gleaming black eyes, and the rich warm complexion that tell of the mingling of the blood. She is handsome with a strange beauty. But it is not until she speaks that the full power of her personality strikes you, for she has a perfect speaking voice. Rich, sweet, clear, and low it carries itself without any effort on her part with ten times the effect of ten times greater lung power. It is a voice mobile to every changing sentiment it expresses." Parsons considered the trip a great success, marred only by the words and deeds of a few, small-minded people: an English labor organizer named Annie Besant, who had just led a successful strike of female matchstick makers, caused a stir by condemning Parsons's "wicked and foolish advice" about the necessity of force. And then, on the return voyage, an "insolent" crew and captain went out of their way to insult her.[14]

Upon arriving back in New York City, Parsons happily acquiesced in a reporter's request for an interview, and, according to the reporter, made a startling announcement—that she was to be married to thirty-eight-year-old Eduard Bernstein, a resident of London and the editor of *The German Social Democrat*, a newspaper based there. A Jewish anarchist, the married Bernstein had been hounded out of Switzerland and now published his paper in Kentish Town. Informed of the engagement that same day, Justus Schwab, a New York City acolyte of Johann Most, denounced it as "an infernal lie," maintaining that Mrs. Parsons would never tarnish the memory of her dead husband. By the next morning Parsons was denying the whole shocking story, this "chain of unmitigated falsehoods," claiming it was "merely gotten up for sensational effect and to kill whatever little influence my return might have on our movement." She was the first to admit that "it would be a strange kind of conglomeration for me to go to London to speak at memorial meetings and return betrothed to another man." Fabricated or not, the story served as a cautionary tale about the kind of behavior the radical community deemed appropriate for Albert Parsons's widow.[15]

Lucy Parsons had told her friends that she would return to Chicago on December 17, and so that morning, George Schilling and other comrades gathered at Union Depot, planning to welcome her home. Also there were Junior and Lulu, who had been staying with separate German immigrant families during their mother's six-week absence; a Mrs. Cordts had escorted them to the station. Without notifying anyone, however, Parsons got off the train at an earlier stop and took a cab home. Later that day, Mrs. Cordts appeared at the Milwaukee Avenue apartment with the children, who were both suffering from the cold, having waited at the train station all day. Perhaps Parsons knew that a week earlier the new chief of police, George W. Hubbard, had vowed that anarchists would no longer be permitted to hold "revolutionary gatherings," including any demonstration in honor of her return; or perhaps she wanted to avoid questions about her alleged attachment to Bernstein; or perhaps she was eager to see the man who had been staying in her flat while she was abroad—twenty-eight-year-old Martin Robert Lacher, her "boarder."[16]

Born in Bavaria, Germany, in 1860, Lacher had come to the United States as a twenty-year-old and settled in St. Paul, Minnesota. In 1883, still in St. Paul, he had become a naturalized citizen and married the eighteen-year-old Helen Engelsipen, also German-born. The following year they had a daughter, Olga, and shortly thereafter they had moved to Milwaukee, where Lacher had worked as a printer for the *Evening Wisconsin*. He soon became active in socialist politics, earning the nickname "Anarchist" for his vocal support of the Haymarket defendants. He was in Chicago the day before the execution, and had been arrested "on account of his injudicious talk." In January 1888, he and his wife and daughter were living at 413 North Paulina Street, where his second child was born on the twenty-eighth of that month. That he quickly became infatuated—or obsessed—with Parsons is suggested by the fact that this daughter was named Lulu Lucy. A *Chicago Tribune* reporter described him as "an exceptionally nice-looking and intelligent young man. He has a finely shaped head, expressive brown eyes, a small black mustache, and wears rimless glasses."[17]

In the summer of 1888, Lacher left his family and moved in with Parsons. He had apparently offered to help her with the new volume she was editing, *Life of Albert R. Parsons*. Soon after Parsons returned from her trip abroad, she and Lacher began to appear in public together, and over the next two and a half years his name would frequently be linked to hers—he was probably the "black haired young man" who was described by the press in June 1889 as "usually accompany[ing] her" to anarchist meetings.[18]

Parsons had been back in Chicago for barely two weeks when she and Lacher tangled with Police Chief Hubbard. To the joy of Chicago radicals, in April 1889 Bonfield had been caught up in a corruption scandal and dismissed from the force. Hubbard, however, matched Bonfield in his animosity toward radicals. The new chief declared in late December that henceforth Parsons would be prohibited from delivering any "violent anarchistic harangue." If there were any doubts about his intentions, he made them clear: "She simply can't speak in Chicago." Within a few days, a local judge would rescind this gag order against Parsons and other labor radicals, pronouncing it a violation of free speech. In the meantime, though, Hubbard ordered the proprietor of a hall where Parsons was to appear on December 26 to refuse her entrance. That day found her and Lacher defiant, standing on a sidewalk outside the hall. She cried, "O, men of America, degenerate Yankees, is this your boasted liberty? Is this your free speech? Is this your right to assemble? O, the glorious stars and stripes!" Agitated, Lacher began to yell at the police, and he was promptly arrested for disorderly conduct. In the coming months, this scene repeated itself, with Parsons trying to address a crowd, and Lacher joining in the fray and skirmishing with police in an effort to defend her. The *Tribune* interviewed Lacher at length and found him conversant about First Amendment issues, if inclined to stretch the meaning of "speech": "The truth is that the right of free speech—if it be a positive right at all—carries with it the right of free action," he said.[19]

By 1890, the couple was socializing in public; at one point, they accompanied Lizzie and William Holmes to hear a lecture by Judge John Peter Altgeld on the injustice of incarcerating men and women who could not pay fines. It is not difficult to understand why the young German immigrant would become enamored with the beautiful and famously demonstrative Mrs. Parsons. And she had found a soul mate in the temperamental printer (the profession of her former husband), who relished a good fight with words and fists. No doubt she enjoyed his devotion and, presumably, the sexual gratification that he later said was an integral part of their relationship. Perhaps she thought of her early days in Waco, where she had never paid much mind to the sanctimonious gossips. And now, must the widow of a martyr take a vow of chastity?[20]

In mid-October, Parsons suffered another major loss in her life when eight-year-old Lulu Eda Parsons died of lymphedema (blockage of the lymph glands). It is possible that the little girl had never fully recovered from her bout with scarlet fever. Characteristically, Parsons refused to betray any sorrow in public. Delivering a lecture at the Arbeiter Bund (a German workers' group) in mid-November, she made only brief reference to her dead daughter and to any presumed heavenly reunion between Lulu and Albert: "Do you suppose they kissed each other in the beautifully described hereafter?" she asked the audience. "Bah. Don't be deceived. So-called Christians will tell you such things."

She added, "The principles of anarchy will prevail, even though it takes blood to make them supreme."[21]

A week after Lulu died, Albert Junior disappeared. Parsons looked for him herself, refusing to enlist the police in the search. After a few days, he returned home on his own; apparently, he had gone off to visit friends. He and Lulu had endured much together; because of their parents' demanding travel and speaking schedules, they had been cared for by non-family members for weeks and even months at a time. They had lived through their father's execution and witnessed their mother's romantic entanglement with another man. While Parsons was abroad in November 1888, the two children had stood together at the annual memorial ceremony at Waldheim as Schilling had read them the letter their father had written two days before his death: "O, my children, how deeply, dearly your papa loves you. We show our love by living for our loved ones. We also prove our love by dying when necessary for them." Albert Parsons's ten-year-old son and seven-year-old daughter no doubt derived little comfort from the idea that he had died for them.[22]

Around this time, Lucy Parsons began to clash with the officers of Pioneer Aid. Predictably, some comrades, especially those who were appalled at her relationship with Lacher, came to resent her insistent claims on the association. In 1890 she secured a loan from the group and with it paid off the mortgage on what a reporter called a "queer little cottage" she had built the year before in the northwest corner of the predominately German 15th Ward, at 999 Hammond Avenue (later North Troy Avenue) in the Avondale neighborhood. It was "a curious domicile" that she had designed herself: "It is unsymmetrically tall, almost perfectly square, built of pine and stands solitary in the midst of a clay waste," the reporter wrote. Even the roughhewn furniture revealed "a woman at war with society." This same reporter, who visited her there in December 1889, met Junior, whom he described as "a manly, healthy and apparently intelligent boy."[23]

In the summer of 1890, Louis Zeller, a member of the Central Labor Union, initiated an effort to withhold PASA funds from Parsons. The Central Labor Union taxed its members for her support, and some of them had grown weary of what they considered Parsons's disingenuous complaints about straitened circumstances. At a meeting where she was accused of uttering half-truths and prevarications, she became so angry that she seized a book and tried to hit Zeller over the head with it; she would have used a chair for the same ends had someone not restrained her. Lacher, who happened to be the treasurer of PASA, was called to account for abandoning his wife and daughters for Parsons. He replied, "I do not want to conceal that my domestic relations are unhappy. My wife and I have separated, but I have supported her all the time. There is nothing out of the way in Mrs. Parsons keeping a boarder." He believed Zeller and Schilling had a vendetta against him and Parsons.[24]

In September, the CLU enumerated several charges against Parsons: She had raised money for herself in Europe and New York all the while neglecting to inform supporters in those places that she was receiving assistance in Chicago. She had insisted on stipends for two children even after Lulu's death (PASA had paid for Lulu's funeral). She had "a couple of houses and lots in this city," and presumably made a decent living from renting these out, as well as from accepting lecture fees and the proceeds from sales of publications. She had failed to repay the construction loan for her cottage on Hammond Avenue. She kept a "boarder, Mr. Lacher, who has a sickly wife and two children, who are certain to be neglected by the absence of the husband and father, for nobody can serve two masters at once." In response to Parsons's supporters, who felt it "was the sacred duty of the association" to keep her on the payroll in perpetuity, her critics charged that "her conduct is not such as to meet the approval of her acquaintances." Within a few months, her request from the association for $300 in cash to offset expenses incurred in the publication of *Life of Albert R. Parsons* met with another round of protests from a group of benefactors. PASA leaders called her machinations "eine erste Klasse Schwindel" (a first-class swindle). The *Tribune* wrote about a "Row Among the Reds."[25]

Parsons's personal life with Lacher had attracted notice and censure. At the same time, she betrayed no doubts about thrusting her children into the public spotlight. She considered Junior "the picture of his father," her dead husband's heir apparent in the struggle against capitalism, saying, "Let the children take up the work where the fathers left off." She told reporters that she was raising her son to avenge the injustice visited upon his father, a comment that prompted some angry editorializing about her determination that he become (in the words of the *Tribune*) "a kind of human blood hound whose sole purpose in life shall be to spill the blood of his fellow beings." Apparently she had decided soon after Albert's death that, positioned carefully next to their grief-stricken mother at certain events, the children could provide a compelling *tableau vivant*. In New York, before Lulu's death, she had provoked the ire of Johann Most, who had refused to appear with Parsons on stage when she had announced that she was planning to bring her son and daughter along "for dramatic effect"; he said he would not be part of her "baby show."[26]

Increasingly, Parsons pressed her son into helping her sell tracts and his father's writings. Still, she confounded her critics with her domestic life in her "humble home." In late December 1888, she welcomed a reporter, who described the scene—a picture of Albert on an easel, a Christmas tree, and the children's toys strewn about the floor. Noting that the "babies" had just gone off to school, Parsons proceeded to give her stock speech, prompting the headline writer to title the piece, "Lucy Wanted Blood." She presented herself as a weary, widowed mother, at the same time declaring that "her life would be devoted to agitation, organization, and revolution, the latter of which was sure to come." Responding to questions from another reporter, this time with Junior present, she told of running into Judge Joseph Gary on the sidewalk a few days earlier and berating him: "You bloody old murderer, if I had a knife I'd stab you where you stand, you miserable old villain." For the reporter, she then pulled out a red scarf and put it around Junior's collar, saying, "He is my brave little anarchist," while "affectionately hugging the little fellow."[27]

Perhaps for Albert Junior all of this seemed too much; one morning in the middle of April 1891, instead of going off to school as usual, he disappeared again. This time Parsons contacted the police for help. Six weeks later, the thirteen-year-old was finally located in Waukesha, presumably with the Hoans, though why no one there contacted Parsons to tell her that he was safe is a mystery. Perhaps he missed his sister and went off to grieve, or craved the attention of the Hoans and the peace of Waukesha, or resented his mother's efforts to offer him up as his father's successor.[28]

Or Albert Junior might have been reacting to an escalation of tensions between Parsons and her lover. In early July, she swore out a warrant for Lacher's arrest, charging him with "malicious trespass," and the police took him into custody on July 15. By this time the couple's relationship had devolved into mutual, bitter recrimination. Apparently Parsons had given an "entertainment" at her house and, when one of her invited guests met with Lacher's disfavor, they had quarreled, and he had hit her in the face. She had fought back, flinging a flatiron at him. On the sixteenth she told a judge that she had locked Lacher out of the house, only to have him return with an axe, which he had used to smash in the front door and reduce much of her furniture to splinters.[29]

In his defense Lacher said that it was he who had written most of *Life of Albert R. Parsons*, and that he had also paid many of Parsons's bills while the two were living together. The furniture that he chopped to pieces was his, he said. He told the court that "for the past three years this woman and I have lived together as man and wife. During that time I learned to love her devotedly, notwithstanding that I was cognizant of the fact that she was continually intimate with other men. It was at her continued solicitations that I abandoned my wife and two children, and when my wife threatened to have her arrested I myself bribed her with a folding bed to drop the case. Our intimacy continued up till two weeks ago." As proof that they cared deeply for each other, he showed the judge a pin in his possession, a miniature gallows and noose, "a love token" that she had given him. According to a reporter present, Lacher added that he had recently lost his job, "and that Mrs. Parsons had seen fit to transfer her favors to some one better able to pay for them." Parsons was standing nearby in the courtroom and listening; enraged, she shook her parasol at him and cried, "If you say that again I'll kill you." The judge fined Lacher $25 and court costs; but the drama would continue.[30]

The year of her fortieth birthday, Lucy Parsons was bereft of her husband and daughter, rid of a lover, and apparently estranged from her son. Her iconic status as Haymarket widow had suffered among even some former allies from her tempestuous affair with Lacher and her suspect claims to financial assistance. Yet the attention paid her by adoring crowds, solicitous reporters, resentful comrades, and paranoid police and politicians gave her life purpose and meaning.

IN EARLY DECEMBER 1888, WILLIAM HOLMES, LIZZIE SWANK HOLMES'S husband, addressed several hundred socialists at Waverly Hall on Lake Street. He felt compelled to answer a pointed question posed by the *Chicago Tribune*: During Thanksgiving week, the churches had fed the poor with turkey and soup, but what had the anarchists done? Holmes fumed, "We have done nothing to degrade the poor by making them recipients of charity," and furthermore, "We are rousing that spirit of discontent that that is bound to bring its fruitage; above all we are arousing that feeling of independence characteristic of our forefathers."[31]

What were anarchists actually doing for the poor? It was not a new question, but one that took on more resonance in an age of social reform. Lucy Parsons dismissed charity as "only hush money to hide the blushes of the labor robbers." When she declaimed upon the "Gospel of Discontent," she seemed to be ridiculing the pervasive "Social Gospel" movement, which called upon religious-minded, well-to-do folks to address human suffering in a tangible way.[32]

The reformer Jane Addams called the 1890s the "decade of discussion," and indeed, all of Chicago seemed to be debating the proper roles of different entities—city and state government, employers, labor unions, intellectuals, politicians, the clergy, and clubwomen—in the grand project of reform. Though Addams came to represent the spirit of the Progressive Era in turn-of-the-century America generally, in fact her ideas about social change were very much the product of Chicago's ferment. Addams saw herself and other people of goodwill as being wedged between two dangerous, opposing forces—arrogant industrialists, on the one hand, and the impoverished, angry laboring classes, on the other; both groups were similarly unreasonable in that they promoted "propaganda as over against constructive social effort." The reformer's task, Addams said, was to find a middle way that would ease the everyday suffering of the poor while allowing the wealthy the pleasure of their profits. Addams's social settlement, Hull House, was, in her words, "quite as much under the suspicion of one side as the other." To a street heckler doubtful of her motives, she later wrote, "I quickly replied that while I did not intend to be subsidized by millionaires, neither did I propose to be bullied by workingmen, and that I should state my honest opinion without consulting either of them." Still, neither the railroad-car magnate George Pullman nor Lucy Parsons could abide Addams's well-meaning ways.[33]

Late 1880s Chicago was a showcase for women leaders determined to deploy moral suasion and secure passage of municipal or state legislation to counter a coldhearted capitalism. In June 1888, Elizabeth Morgan, wife of socialist leader Tommy Morgan, helped to found the AFL-affiliated Ladies Federal Labor Union (LFLU) no. 2703, a group that included women in a variety of crafts, including candy-making, as well as typists and clerks. The LFLU and the Chicago Trade and Labor Association (by 1888 part of the AFL) appointed Elizabeth to head a commission charged with investigating the sweatshop system and its spawn, the "sweater [boss], a human parasite." Morgan visited workshops throughout the city, documenting the miserable lives of men, women, and children who toiled for pennies a day in windowless attics, cellars, and sheds for six and a half days a week. Released in September 1891 and titled "The New Slavery," her report highlighted the malnourished, sleep-deprived children who ate and slept in tenements surrounded by garbage and horse manure, and the workrooms overwhelmed with the stench of human excrement. In such close, filthy conditions, diseases such as tuberculosis and typhoid spread quickly.[34]

The report prompted passage of a new factory-inspection law by the Illinois legislature that limited the hours for women in manufacturing to eight a day and established a factory inspector with a staff of twelve. Not surprisingly, the sweaters resisted the new law, and careworn parents continued to order their children to work. A dozen inspectors could not possibly inspect the many hundreds of small shops tucked away in the city's vast neighborhoods. However, the Factory Act did reveal a larger impulse among the middle-class women and men of the city, who, it seemed, were willing to mediate between rapacious employers, on the one hand, and vulnerable workers, on the other.[35]

Albert Parsons would have appreciated the faith of the Progressives in the compilation of statistics related to social, economic, and demographic trends, and Lucy Parsons must have felt some satisfaction now that both reformers and newspaper editors were rendering the plight of sewing women as a form of slavery. Yet Lucy Parsons was neither a labor organizer nor a social reformer. A prominent actor in Chicago's "decade of propaganda," she could expound on history, literature, and political theory, and she specialized in rousing the indignation of the laboring classes. Yet unlike many of her debating partners (real or imagined), Parsons resisted describing in much detail the new social order she envisioned in a future, anarchistic world. In early 1891, a *New York World* reporter, partly tongue-in-cheek, tried to pin her down on controversial issues of the day. Striking in her all-black dress adorned with only a "blood red badge," and her gold necklace with the gallows charm, she said she believed that the laboring classes "should rise and overthrow aristocracy by means of dynamite."

> The wealth of this country should be equally distributed, she thinks. If one man through shrewdness should then amass more wealth than his neighbor, this surplus should be taken away from him. Every man should carry arms and have the right of self-defence. Shops and means of transit should be free. There would be no need of elections, police or a standing army to keep a handful of Indians in subjection. Give the Indians all the land they want, there is plenty of it. If they kill you let your friends kill them. Every man should bring his products to an immense clearinghouse in each city or town, and every family to receive an equal portion.

What to do with criminals? All of them "are more or less insane," their misdeeds in most cases the result of greed for money. The mansions of the labor barons? "We will let them stand as monuments of shame for the elements to decay." Coast and harbor defenses? No need for them: "We hope to conquer the world. This country is not our only field of conquest." Free postage stamps and mail delivery; free beer, newspapers, and public schools. And her Chinese policy? "I really cannot say, said Mrs. Parsons after a moment's meditation. These small details must be arranged afterwards."[36]

In addition to continuing her hectic speaking schedule, Parsons remained a prolific writer and editor. In 1889 she published *Life of Albert R. Parsons, with Brief History of the Labor Movement in America*, a 255-page book that sold for $1.50 a copy. The volume included George Schilling's lengthy testimonial for Albert in the form of a history of the Chicago labor movement; Albert's autobiography as originally published in *Knights of Labor*; his letters to *The Alarm* and to Lucy recounting his agitation trips throughout the Midwest; accounts of the Haymarket trial; newspaper articles; reminiscences by Captain William Black (the attorney), Lizzie Swank Holmes, William Holmes, and others; and drawings of Albert, Lucy, and the children. (Lucy's picture prompted a lively conversation in Waco in April 1889, when someone sent a copy of the book to the town newspaper, the *Examiner*. A leading Waco businessman, the insurance and real estate agent Captain John E. Elgin, took the book to a local polling place on April 2 and passed it around to the "election crowd." Several of Lucy's former employers recognized her, as did Oliver Benton, who confirmed it was his "truant wife," saying, "Lucy was a good girl if she was smart and was too fond of fine clo's[;] dat was her failing.")[37]

From 1890 to 1892, Lucy Parsons edited *Freedom: A Revolutionary Anarchist-Communist Monthly*, described as "the only English organ in America advocating those principles for which our martyrs died and which we live to spread." For her purposes, this publication superseded the second iteration of *The Alarm*, which had folded in February 1889, several months after its editor, Dyer Lum, had moved to New York City. As ever, in *Freedom* Lucy proved an eclectic writer, her essays and editorials including a learned survey of the history of communism from the pre-Christian era, as well as a sly explanation of "The Part Dynamite Plays": in modern discourse, she said, "it is a mere trick on the part of capitalists to be always associating anarchists with dynamite." Publishing the paper proved to be problematic, since apparently Martin Lacher was involved in it, at least through the summer of 1891. That autumn, after their falling out, Parsons used the editor's column to charge him with embezzling from a local Arbeiter Bund. She also claimed that in collecting money for *Freedom* subscriptions, he issued "a guarantee that the comrade with whom he had trouble [that is, herself] should have nothing to do with the paper." She warned of his "treachery" and his attempts to destroy the paper and injure the movement because of "personal spite." By this time he had moved with his wife and two daughters to Denver, where he became active in socialist politics. *Freedom* ceased publication in August 1892.[38]

Parsons's speaking schedule continued to be robust. She bolstered the flagging spirits of Jewish cloak-makers. She lectured on what she considered the misguided (though, among socialists, wildly popular) new novel by Edward Bellamy, *Looking Backward*, which promoted the state socialism she despised. She spoke on the merits of compulsory education. As always, she relished a good debate, at one point taking on a sparring partner who suggested that John D. Rockefeller's Standard Oil was an exemplar of anarchism in its contempt for the law; she countered that, to the contrary, anarchism promoted liberty, Standard Oil only slavery.[39]

This new phase of Parsons's career took place within a city where elites were loudly and insistently urging the police to crack down on the remnant of anarchists, "Law or no Law." When he took office, Chief Hubbard announced that it would be "folly" for the city to tolerate "revolutionary gatherings," and that he would no longer allow anarchists to meet on the lakefront or at Market Square. However, his main strategy consisted in forcing hall proprietors to refuse to rent out spaces to radicals; failing that, he sent in uniformed and plainclothes police to intimidate the speakers and their audiences. Like his predecessors, Hubbard had to choose between tolerating the free expression of Parsons's unsettling ideas or arresting her and drawing even more attention to them.[40]

The same dilemma bedeviled police chiefs in other cities Parsons visited—for example, in November 1890, in Newark, New Jersey, where she was scheduled to speak on the third anniversary of the executions. At the last minute she found herself locked out of a hall. The local police had made it clear that they intended to target "the anarchistic element" and "crush it out." Loudly protesting, she was arrested for "attempted riot" and jailed; that, plus subsequent developments, including a bail hearing and an appearance before a judge, kept her in the local newspapers, inspiring mass protests for several days in the greater New York area.[41]

Back in Chicago, a strong law-enforcement presence at meetings unnerved some labor leaders, who at times blamed Lucy Parsons for the scrutiny accorded the most innocuous of gatherings. The prospect of dozens of officers hovering over a picnic or rally could demoralize those who favored speechifying over confrontation; one Pioneer Aid fundraiser attracted one hundred policemen, half in uniform, half in plain clothes. (Captain Michael Schaak, taking note of Parsons's per-sistent calls for workers to "buy yourselves good Winchester rifles," ob-served that her appeals to violence had "made herself obnoxious to the more peaceable and conservative Socialists.") In June 1891, the commit-tee to raise money for a monument to the Haymarket martyrs refused to let her speak. Some supporters of PASA had predicted as much, be-lieving that her money-grab within that organization had discouraged donors from contributing to the proposed statue. The following year during the annual May Day celebration, the Coal Unloaders bowed out of the parade because of what they called "too much red in the line"—including Parsons, who, together with Junior, seized the occasion to sell stacks of copies of *Freedom*.[42]

Tommy Morgan came to dread Parsons's attempts to hijack so-cialist meetings. Once she stood to talk, it was difficult to get her to sit down, especially in gatherings where a vocal segment of the audi-ence venerated her as a secular saint. A reporter for the *Inter-Ocean* de-scribed the beginning of a routine meeting of socialists at Waverly Hall, when Parsons "and about a dozen fellow anarchists filed in to the rear of the hall." The mere sight of the intruder rattled Morgan and the oth-ers: "Apprehensive and knowing glances were exchanged by the leading socialists," the reporter recounted. More often, however, Parsons en-tered the hall quietly and sat in the back, only to rise dramatically from her seat later in the proceedings, march to the front, and mount the podium, to the delight of the crowd. At one meeting of two hundred persons, Morgan was decrying the use of physical force, claiming that it "indicates a low degree of civilization" and undermines the morality of social reform, when, according to a reporter, "at this juncture Mrs. Lucy Parsons, haughty and arrogant, strutted down the center aisle to a seat in front of the platform." Morgan paused, "and a deafening and prolonged cheer went up from the crowd." For a while Parsons listened, becoming more and more agitated, but finally she interrupted subse-quent speakers, agreeing wholeheartedly that the rallying cry among the Haymarket martyrs had always been "Prepare to use force."[43]

Despite the angst of leaders like Morgan, among the admirers of her heated rhetoric Parsons rarely failed to disappoint: "Before we can have peace in a society like ours, rivers of blood will have to run," she would say. She condemned the ballot and vowed to see the heads of capitalists impaled on spikes. She taunted her enemies: "When the great revolution does come we will shake the upper classes like jelly." And she defended the use of dynamite: "In years to come, those in America will bless the hand that threw the bomb in Haymarket square."[44]

At times Parsons also gave her explicit approval of assassination. In the summer of 1892, at his Homestead steel plant near Pittsburgh, Andrew Carnegie locked out members of a union, the Amalgamated Association of Iron and Steel Workers, in an effort to destroy it. His manager, Henry Clay Frick, ordered three hundred members of Pinkerton's security forces to break the picket lines thrown up by the strikers. Alexander Berkman, a twenty-two-year-old Russian immigrant, anarchist, and self-professed follower of Johann Most, traveled from New York to Homestead, where (according to a plan he had devised with his lover Emma Goldman) he confronted Frick in his office and shot and stabbed him. Frick survived the attack, and Berkman spent fourteen years in prison for his "propaganda of the deed." In the August 1892 issue of *Freedom*, Lucy Parsons titled an article "A Just Blow at a Tyrant," and wrote, of the botched assassination, "We have only the greatest admiration for men like Berkman." Yet she failed to anticipate how similar anarchists' attacks and assassinations in France and Spain between 1892 and 1894 could reverberate in Chicago and affect her own prospects as provocateur.[45]

By the early 1890s, Parsons had successfully defied attempts to silence her completely, but she was still fighting a wider war for the free expression of radical views. Both the mayor and the chief of police, emboldened by the unconditional support of leading industrialists, felt justified in not only banning the red flag from workers' meetings and parades, but also insisting that the American flag be flown. Parsons framed such efforts as the violations of the First Amendment that they were, and, in addition to issuing the familiar calls for revolution, focused her speeches on the constitutional right to peaceful assembly. Later, she would trace the beginnings of her career as a free-speech proponent from these Chicago battles over flags and words.[46]

The ban on the red flag prompted a cat-and-mouse game that the police could not hope to win, even though Mayor John Roche declared,

"I will not tolerate this red flag business." In 1891, for the annual Haymarket commemoration, hundreds braved a cold, drizzling rain at Waldheim Cemetery; they left their red flags at home, but brought red floral arrangements and displayed red streamers. At a meeting in Turner Hall the evening of November 12, Hubbard and his officers burst in and stormed the stage, demanding that an American flag be displayed. According to a reporter present, the chief's order unleashed pandemonium: "Hiss after hiss and yell after yell frantically rose until the audience seemed a thousand demons instead of human beings." Parsons exclaimed, "Hang the murderers of my husband!" and then declared, "That flag is an infamous lie." She proceeded to refine her indictment: "Every star in that flag is but the concentrated tear drop of outraged American womanhood." The police arrested twenty-three people that night. Hall proprietors began telling anarchists that they must not display any red flags, banners, or bunting, producing some "severely plain" backdrops for meetings, even on momentous occasions, such as the Haymarket commemoration of 1892.[47]

IN RECOGNITION OF HER SINGULAR ROLE IN CHICAGO'S POLITICAL discourse in general—and her constant talk of dynamite, in particular— Parsons earned epithets from the press that implicitly linked her to the massive destruction wrought by the great fire two decades before. This dusky devotee of dynamite engaged in "verbal pyrotechnics"; her speeches were "fiery," "inflammatory," "incendiary." A "fire-eating," "red-mouthed" anarchist, she served up doctrine "red hot." Certainly she did her best to avoid the taint of middle-class social reform: "I don't want to be respectable," she declared at one meeting. "I want to be wholly disreputable and die so, and so do we all, I hope." The thunderous applause that greeted these particular comments served as a rebuke to all those at various points on the political spectrum who had tried to discredit, undermine, or dismiss her.[48]

George Schilling, for one, took this rebuke personally. He had contributed to the Life of Albert R. Parsons a respectful, even reverent, appreciation of Albert's work. In his piece Schilling acknowledged that they were "living in an age of universal unrest," and he couched his critique of the Chicago political economy in terms that Lucy Parsons could applaud: "The justice of grinding little children's bones and blood and life into gold in our modern bastiles [sic]of labor, so that a few might riot in midnight orgies, is being questioned by some." Yet he could not now refrain from writing directly to Lucy Parsons and scolding her for keeping the police and the politicians in a constant state of war against the workers through her rhetoric. Acknowledging that she possessed "more than ordinary intellectual power," he nevertheless believed that her unrelenting calls for violence had been a "wasted force as far as any permanent results for good are concerned." Indeed, in her determination to "terrorize the public mind and threaten the stability of society with violence," he wrote, she accomplished little more than allowing the police to justify harsh measures against labor leaders and strikers. Schilling thought she should temper her language in an effort to appeal to a broader American constituency: "Those seeking economic progress must shape their conduct in accordance with the traditions and environment of the country in which they live."[49]

By urging Parsons to modify her *conduct* (and not just her words), Schilling was perhaps betraying the deep disappointment that he must have felt over her scandalous affair with Martin Lacher, behavior that he and many others believed defiled the memory of her husband and compromised all radicals' claim to the moral high ground. He ended by reminding her of the fate of the five men who lay entombed at Waldheim Cemetery, including her husband of beloved memory: "They worshipped at the shrine of force; wrote it and preached it; until finally they were overpowered by their own Gods and slain in their own temple."[50]

Whether or not Parsons read Schilling's letter, she failed to heed it. Even now, a new, drastic economic downturn in Chicago and throughout the country was evoking the dire conditions that had inspired her to write "Tramps," her first, but far from last, paean to dynamite.

❧ Chapter 11 ❧

Variety in Life, and Its Critics

I F LUCY PARSONS SEEMED TO LIVE IN THE PAST, FOR MUCH OF HER life she believed that, from the vantage point of the laboring classes, at least, the present did not seem all that different from recent history. In fact, at times she remained defiantly oblivious to or dismissive of the great historical forces sweeping over the city of Chicago and the United States, forces that were prompting new strategies for addressing economic inequality and social injustice. The economic and political dislocations of the 1890s and the early twentieth century gave rise to rural and urban reformers who believed that *more* local, state, and national government was the answer to the chronic disaster of industrial America. Now ideas promoting state socialism, though diametrically at odds with Parsons's anarchism, gained not just radical but also mainstream, moderate cachet.

Parsons's overall orientation toward small cooperative groups, such as trade unions, served to estrange her from socialists and even from a substantial number of anarchists. In addition, at least two other issues exacerbated her disagreements with radicals of various persuasions. In the 1890s, a new generation of anarchists was injecting the issue of human sexuality into political discourse, a development she found repugnant. At the same time, small numbers of terrorists at home and

233

abroad were engaging in assassination and murder, crimes she denounced with disingenuous indignation. Some adjustments were called for: gradually she retreated from her public approval of violence against the established order, preferring a relatively tame life of writing and speaking. She hoped to avoid what was becoming the increasingly likely alternative—not just a night in the Cook County jail, but a years-long stint in prison.

These crosscurrents of change and continuity were on full display in Parsons's activities during the summer of 1893. That August, at the beginning of what would become a five-year depression, she was back at the lakefront, holding forth during daylong mass meetings of the jobless: "By force we were robbed by the people who coin your sweat into Gatling guns to kill you," she declared, "and by force must they be dispossessed." The economic "panic" that began earlier that year marked the beginning of the nation's deepest depression to date; soon hundreds of banks would close their doors and thousands of businesses would fail. In major US cities, as many as four out of ten workers found themselves unemployed. For Parsons, the crisis of the early 1890s evoked the unrest of two decades earlier, when she and her husband had arrived in Chicago and begun their lifelong careers of agitation. Now, she wrote, "How long can this condition of affairs last? How much longer must the schoolhouse be robbed that the robbers' factory may be filled with the fair roses that bloom at the firesides of poverty and fade in these hells?" Parsons saw in the careworn faces of her listeners the eternal verities of capitalist depredations—the bloody clashes between wage slaves and government militia backed by employers' private security forces, the wretched living and working conditions of the poor. The country seemed caught in an endless cycle of boom for the Marshall Fields and the George Pullmans and bust for the laboring classes. How much longer, indeed?[1]

Proving that she still possessed the power to provoke, that summer Parsons reprised the raw anger of "To Tramps," promising listeners (and newspaper readers) that "men with that unsatiated gnawing at their vitals can be made to understand the tenets of anarchy. . . . I say to hell with the gang of thieves, robbers, murderers, destroyers of our homes." Chicago authorities as well as editors around the country derided her "lunacy"; she was a "she devil" bent on painting "lurid pictures of famine and want" calculated to incite "murder and other forms of lawlessness." The *Chicago Tribune* urged the police to restrain her as they would "an enraged tigress."[2]

The wounds wrought by the Haymarket bombing still festered for many. On June 25 in Waldheim Cemetery, several thousand people watched as fifteen-year-old Albert Junior pulled a string on a red curtain and unveiled a monument to the martyrs. His part in the program offered a fitting piece of symmetry to Memorial Day in 1889, when the son of the fallen Major Mathias Degan played a similar role in commemorating the policemen who had died as a result of that fateful night of May 4, 1886. Both monuments became objects of scorn from their foes—in Haymarket Square, the statue of a policeman, arm raised as if in a gesture of peace and goodwill; in Waldheim Cemetery, a hooded, bronze figure of justice standing atop a base inscribed with (again, a variation of) the last words of August Spies: "The day will come when our silence will be more powerful than the voices you are throttling today."[3]

And then, the day after the Haymarket statue dedication, to the great surprise of everyone, Governor John Peter Altgeld pardoned Oscar Neebe, Samuel Fielden, and Michael Schwab. In ordering that they be released from prison, Altgeld (who had taken office only six months earlier) affirmed the critique of the trial offered by the convicted men—that Cook County officials had packed the jury with men who had prejudged the case, that the prosecutor had never linked the defendants to the bomb-thrower, and that Judge Gary had been too biased to preside over a fair proceeding. Parsons published the full text of Altgeld's pardon under the title "His Masterly Review of the Haymarket Riot."[4]

In an ironic twist, the release of the three men signaled the end of their association with Albert Parsons's widow. Thereafter, they ostentatiously boycotted her speeches and repudiated anarchism, which would forever be associated in the public mind with domestic terrorism. Interviewed by a reporter the year after he gained his freedom, Neebe responded to a question about Lucy Parsons by saying that he had not seen her recently, "and I don't want to see her either." His comrades agreed with him: "They do not like to talk of her at all, but it is understood that there is general dissatisfaction with her personal conduct." By this time rumors were circulating that Johann Most and Lucy Parsons enjoyed a close relationship that went well beyond their shared devotion to anarchist ideology. Her feud with the Pioneer Aid and Support Association over money, combined with what was perceived as her unfaithfulness to Albert's memory due to her affairs with Lacher and possibly Most, diminished her in the sight of some former comrades.[5]

Parsons's old circle was receding from her life. Dyer Lum committed suicide in April 1893. Lizzie Swank Holmes and her husband, William, had moved to Colorado, but not before Lizzie had joined the middle-class New Century Club and rehabilitated her reputation as a pioneering reformer and advocate of sewing women. Tommy Morgan, George Schilling, and other Chicago labor leaders were pursuing the kind of moderate, ballot-driven socialism that Parsons deplored. Governor Altgeld appointed Schilling secretary of the Illinois Board of Labor Statistics, signaling the growing respectability of some socialist leaders within the state's political establishment.[6]

Around this time there appeared a new cohort of radical editors, labor organizers, and orators, men and women toward whom Lucy Parsons felt great ambivalence. In Chicago in June 1893, Eugene V. Debs founded the American Railway Union, an industrial union of railroad employees. Debs, a thirty-eight-year-old native of Indiana, had been a longtime member of the Brotherhood of Locomotive Firemen, more a fraternal order than a labor union. The following year, the bitter strike of Pullman railroad-car workers just outside Chicago would spread throughout the nation and claim the lives of thirty-four men (the US 7th Cavalry suppressed the strikers); Debs defied an injunction and went to jail. The Russian Jewish immigrant Emma Goldman, who first met Lucy Parsons in Philadelphia in 1887, was rapidly gaining notoriety for her advocacy of sexual freedom; she began to make periodic stops in Chicago under the sponsorship of the journal *Free Society*, which praised "variety" in love. Honoré Jaxon was a newcomer on the Chicago scene. Well educated, he had been born in 1861, in Toronto. Jaxon claimed (falsely) to be a Métis Indian, and he reveled in his role as one of the despised and persecuted. He became known as "the father of labor slugging" for his efforts during a carpenters' strike in 1886, when he organized squads of workers into an "invading army" to strong-arm reluctant employees into joining the strike. Meanwhile, Chicago's German immigrant community was becoming more assimilated, and Parsons was instead finding a new receptive audience in Russian Jewish garment workers, who appreciated her anticlericalism and her steady focus on unionization.[7]

Throughout the 1890s, true to her principles, Parsons remained warily on the sidelines of Progressive reform. She had no monopoly on the litany of execrations unleashed upon arrogant police and robber barons; but she bristled at radical Christians, socialists, and Progressive reformers, who in turn routinely lambasted anarchism as an inherently violent ideology. And though she maintained an active schedule of writing and public speaking, she found no intellectual home among the Progressives or in anarchist circles, the latter riven by deep divisions over the meaning of virtually anything and everything, whether the *attentat* (a burst of violence that would ignite a revolution), labor unions, or the act of sexual intercourse.

IN THE LAST DECADE OF THE NINETEENTH CENTURY, CHICAGO'S population continued to grow rapidly, adding 700,000 in the course of the decade, for a total of 1,698,575 in 1900. The city was now world-famous as a commercial crossroads between East and West, notable for its new, fireproofed, metal-framed skyscrapers and for its prosperity. (An anarchist dictionary defined "prosperity" as "a condition of affairs said to exist in the U.S., and which manifests itself chiefly in strikes, riots, business depression and financial flurries.") Meanwhile, people had discovered new ways to spend their money and time. The so-called retail wars of the decade allowed the big department stores, such as Marshall Field and Carson Pirie Scott, to build upon the ruins of their smaller, bankrupt competitors. Clustered on and around State Street, these giant stores beckoned to buyers with revolving doors, colorful window displays, and tastefully arranged merchandise on low-lying shelves. In the middle of the shopping district could be found Kinetoscope parlors and penny arcades that gave viewers glimpses of startling scenes, such as exotic animals on the run. Baseball games drew crowds of spectators, as did boxing and wrestling matches.[8]

Most thrilling of all were the new amusement parks, affordable even for the working poor, where the universal appeal of rides and "freak shows" broke down social hierarchies (except those that subordinated African Americans). White men and women, boys and girls, rich and poor rubbed shoulders in line and on rides. Insular ethnic entertainments—the Sunday-afternoon picnics in Ogden's Grove, the political meetings in Turner Hall, the family gatherings in private homes—now seemed old-fashioned compared to attractions that lured people out of their neighborhoods. For many Chicagoans, commercialized leisure beckoned in the form of a grand, fantastical democracy, with all people sharing in the pleasures of watching spectacles and buying brand-name goods. For skeptics on the left, such amusements amounted merely to unwelcome distractions, where spending money superseded waging class warfare.[9]

However, this emerging consumer culture could not forestall larger economic developments with international reverberations—a crash in wheat prices, the overproduction of goods, and the overbuilding of railroads. The ensuing nationwide depression, compounded by decades of hardship among ordinary families, gave rise to the defining political movement of the 1890s—the People's, or Populist, Party, which aimed to unite hard-pressed farmers with the urban laboring classes. The Populists favored popular referenda, government ownership of railroads, and relief for debtors, offering an alternative to the Republican and Democratic parties, which both seemed to be in thrall to industrial and landed interests. Some Illinois socialists initially found the new group promising. Lucy Parsons was among the few women delegates to Chicago's local Populist convention held in late July 1892 (after the national meeting in Omaha earlier that month), and she attended at least one subsequent meeting. However, she believed that the Populists' proposed reforms, such as the currency-expanding coinage of silver, would only serve to prop up the capitalist system and forestall the revolution, and her disdain for political parties of any kind meant that her flirtation with the Populists would be brief and half-hearted. At the same time, conservative commentators compared some of the Populist women firebrands to Parsons, dismissing Mary Ellen Lease, who was famous for her call to farmers to "raise less corn and more hell," as "principally of the Lucy Parsons style." Soon most Chicago socialists too would abandon the Populists, whom they associated with farmers and other groups outside the boundaries of the urban proletariat.[10]

Chicago was no longer the place Albert Parsons had first visited when he had marveled at the exhibits in the Exposition Hall two decades before. The city was much larger, and its achievements much grander. Between May 1 and October 30, 1893, the city hosted a World's Columbian Exposition, meant to showcase its complete and dynamic recovery from the Great Fire of 1871. Situated on the shores of Lake Michigan, the fair sprawled over seven hundred acres and featured a total of two hundred buildings, fourteen of them magnificent structures (though of flimsy wood construction) in the Beaux Arts style, all painted a glistening white. Avid city boosters applauded the exposition as a rebuttal to critics from both the radical Right and the radical Left, foreign and domestic, and groups in between. The British author Rudyard Kipling had visited the city in the summer of 1889, and after describing the "collection of miserables" who lived there, declared, of the "grotesque ferocity" of Chicago, "Having seen it, I urgently desire never to see it again." He unfavorably compared the place, with its waterways "black as ink, and filled with untold abominations," to far-off sinkholes: its ignorant inhabitants were "money-mad," he wrote, "and its air is dirt."[11]

Reformers contrasted Chicago's claim to hard-earned greatness with its shameful sweatshops and tenements. In "The New Slavery," Elizabeth Morgan asked "liberty-loving and patriotic Americans" whether they wanted visitors from around the world to see evidence that "the 'sweater' is king" over subjects toiling in hundreds of squalid dens scattered throughout the "Garden City of the Great West." The British journalist William T. Stead timed his scathing indictment of the Chicago establishment to coincide with the exposition. In his book *If Christ Came to Chicago!* he lambasted the city's famously corrupt politicians; the churches "at ease in Zion," ignoring the poor; the lawless police; and the smug businessmen who lorded over it all.[12]

The fair attracted an estimated 27 million visitors from the United States and abroad and boasted exhibit halls sponsored by forty-six foreign governments. Newness and innovation were the watchwords:

in technology—phosphorescent lamps, the forerunner of the zipper, and a moving walkway along the Lake Michigan shoreline; in commercial products—Quaker Oats and Juicy Fruit gum; and in the science of racism—"civilized" Americans juxtaposed to "savage" dark-skinned peoples. Not surprisingly, the fair was a flashpoint for controversy; the clergy and middle-class arbiters of morality feared that keeping it open on Sundays (the only day working-class families could attend) would degrade the Sabbath and attract "an element which is a constant menace to law and order, and even to human life."[13]

The so-called White City lived up to its name in a literal sense. Organizers intentionally left African Americans out of the planning, excluded black male applicants from the fair's elite police corps, and banned black patrons from the fairgrounds except for "Colored People's Day," August 25—"Darkies Day at the Fair." Attendees on that day were given free watermelon. Exhibits sponsored by the various US states portrayed black workers as servants and menials. The fair's practices mirrored the exclusion of blacks from many Chicago theaters and amusements. More broadly, though, the White City promoted the idea that African Americans belonged to a "race" inherently inferior to whites.[14]

The exposition provided the intellectual rationale for the constraints under which Chicago's blacks residents lived and labored every day. Within this expanding city, most were forced to "loiter around the edges of industry," in the words of a black activist and public intellectual at the time, Kelly Miller. The women served as domestics, the men as unskilled laborers who were periodically enlisted as strikebreakers whenever white teamsters, stockyard workers, wagon and carriage makers, and coal miners walked off the job. Prominent white Chicago reformers, including the proprietors of Hull House, remained indifferent to the plight of blacks, or went public with their bigotry: Frances Willard, founder of the Women's Christian Temperance Union, approved the lynching of southern black men as a means to ensure "the safety of woman, of childhood, of the home." Socialists remained preoccupied with factory and craft workers; Tommy Morgan showed interest in blacks only when they discussed joining a third party—which they did periodically, the Republicans and Democrats having failed them completely. Debs excluded blacks from the founding American

Railway Union convention and tolerated a discriminatory division of labor favored by white workers. His decision contributed to the failure of the Pullman strike in 1894, when black men served as scabs. For her part, Lucy Parsons made a single, passing reference to the problem of lynching in the South in an issue of *Freedom*, but ignored the plight of black wage slaves. Her views were in keeping with the attitudes of those radicals in whose circles she moved.[15]

Although Chicago's black community represented less than 2 percent of the city's population, by the 1890s it boasted a vibrant, if tiny, middle class of physicians, lawyers, and editors; its own newspaper, the weekly *Conservator* (edited by a lawyer, Ferdinand Lee Barnett); four churches; small businesses, such as saloons and barbershops; and a number of charitable, fraternal, and mutual-aid societies. Outspoken leaders pressed for legislation to end lynching and disfranchisement in the South and institutional bias in the North. Women activists took the lead in these efforts. Alarmed at the mean-spiritedness animating the World's Columbian Exposition, Fannie Barrier Williams, the wife of Barnett's law partner, told the exposition's Board of Lady Managers, "We ask to be known and recognized for what we are worth. If it be the high purpose of these deliberations to lessen the resistance to woman's progress, you cannot fail to be interested in our struggles against the many oppositions that harass us."[16]

Lucy Parsons had no affinity for the high-minded protests of Barrier Williams, a national leader in the black women's club movement and a proponent of the politics of respectability and "uplift." Yet it is intriguing to speculate about the way Parsons might have reacted to another black woman of Chicago, newcomer Ida B. Wells, who in 1895 married the *Conservator*'s Barnett. Born in Memphis in 1862, Wells-Barnett had taught school and edited that city's black paper *Free Speech and Headlight*. In 1889, whites lynched three of her friends, grocers who had competed with a white store in town. She condemned the atrocity in no uncertain terms, indicting not only the killers and the Memphis authorities but also the larger white South for its complicity in state-sponsored terrorism. In response, while she was away from the city, a white mob burned her office. She never returned to Memphis. Recognized as the nation's most fearless anti-lynching agitator, she arrived in Chicago in the spring of 1893, fresh from a speaking tour in England. She quickly began to raise funds to publish a pamphlet, "The Reasons Why the Colored American Is Not in the World's Columbian Exposition." Wells-Barnett wrote two of its four essays, including one on "Lynch Law," consisting of graphic written and visual accounts of actual murders. As in her other writings, *Southern Horrors: Lynch Law in All Its Phases* (1892), *A Red Record* (1895), and *Mob Rule in New Orleans* (1900), Wells-Barnett blamed "the better class of citizens" in the South for tolerating lynching, and she exposed the myth of the black rapist as a mere pretext for the mutilation, hanging, and burning alive of black men.[17]

Wells-Barnett resembled Parsons in certain striking respects. Born a slave, she, too, attained only a basic common education but proved to be a gifted writer, newspaper editor, and speaker who was sought after by sympathetic audiences in the United States and Europe. She urged black households to keep loaded rifles in their homes and to use them if necessary. Observers contrasted her ladylike demeanor with her bold forays into taboo subjects, such as sadistic torture and the political use of threats or false claims of sexual relations between black men and white women. However, even some who admired her courage considered her writings and lectures to be reckless and self-defeating, and certain to offend potential supporters. She and Parsons both opposed the United States' new imperialist ventures in the 1890s, with Wells-Barnett making explicit links between the oppression of blacks at home and the exploitation of dark-skinned peoples abroad. Yet it is doubtful that Parsons and Wells-Barnett ever met, and neither referred to the other in her writings.[18]

At the end of August 1893, the World's Columbian Exposition organizers convened what they called a Congress on Labor. The meeting took place against a backdrop of workers' daily demonstrations at the lakefront; on August 21, 400 unemployed packinghouse workers chanting "We want work" had fought with police. Speakers at the labor conference included not only Samuel Gompers, Terence V. Powderly, Eugene V. Debs, and Henry George, but also Jane Addams, Mary Ellen Lease, Frederick Douglass, and Booker T. Washington. On August 30, delegates responded to the tumult out-of-doors and adjourned to the lakefront, where Debs and Morgan mounted wagons to address a crowd of 25,000. Social reformers and conservative labor leaders acknowledged the plight of the masses, but they were moving toward strategies for change—such as government intervention, and conservative unions—that took them in the opposite direction from where Lucy Parsons and her comrades were heading.[19]

THE FEW BELEAGUERED CHICAGO ANARCHISTS MIGHT HAVE considered Lucy Parsons's absence from the Congress of Labor to be a major lapse on the part of the conveners, but only the most naïve observers would have expected her to receive such official sanction. The police were still looking for discreet ways to silence her—ways that would not cause alarming headlines about angry protests to be splashed across the front pages of the city's newspapers. Gone were the days when undercover agents and mainstream journalists sought a cozy, mutually beneficial relationship with the anarchists. Authorities now feared that attention from the press could give the mistaken impression that anarchism as a movement was gaining ground in the city. Increasingly common were meetings where Parsons would begin to speak, only to have a police officer, or in some cases the chief himself, step forward, lay hands on her, and warn her "to mention no names and to preserve order" (as at Turner Hall in November 1895). In some instances an officer actually pulled her off the stage as she struggled to resist; she would call out "Liberty is dead in Chicago."[20]

Parsons, however, remained a favorite at mass meetings among unemployed and striking workers, fundraisers for radical newspapers, and assemblies of diehard anarchists. She maintained her reputation as Chicago's "leading anarchistress" and an agitator of "intemperate gall." On April 27, 1894, she addressed the members of (Jacob) Coxey's Army, a protest started by an Ohio businessman of the same name to demand public works jobs for the poor. Together with Lizzie Swank Holmes, she joined the Women's Commonweal Society. This female auxiliary was supposed to offer good cheer to the army's 1,028 members streaming in from all over the Midwest, a new and rather demure role for the unpredictable Mrs. Parsons. On April 28, the men clamored for her to speak, but march organizers stopped her, fearing that she would discredit the movement if her listeners did not comport themselves in an orderly way. Nevertheless, one day she spontaneously joined the program of speakers and told the army "that they were belched up from the hearts of the people . . . and they deserved the good things of the earth." The rumor that Parsons was the mysterious veiled lady who traveled with the army proved to be unfounded, but it did nothing to dispel her mystique in the mainstream press as an anarchist femme fatale.[21]

Almost every November 11, Parsons addressed the annual Haymarket observance, although from 1895 onward Waldheim Cemetery refused to allow mourners to gather there, forcing them to regroup in Turner Hall or Greif's Hall. She objected to the call for the Pioneer Aid and Support Association to disinter the corpse of her husband and the others and relocate them to a more hospitable burial ground, arguing that the thousands of dollars such a move would cost might be better spent elsewhere. The editors of the *Arbeiter Zeitung* refused to publish her objections to the plan, suspecting that she feared that her own stipend would be reduced if funds were earmarked to move the bodies.[22]

Some years on November 11 she observed the day in Milwaukee, on at least two occasions (in 1893 and 1895) in the company of Johann Most. In Chicago in 1896, a police captain interrupted her speech in Turner Hall, just as she was denouncing "You hideous murderers!" and refused to let her continue, prompting an "uproar" and a near-riot among the crowd. The Reverend Graham Taylor, a Presbyterian minister who founded the Chicago Commons settlement house in 1894, later vividly remembered the event. Describing his first impressions of Lucy Parsons, he wrote: "Her appearance on the platform was impressive. Tall, well built and poised, self-possessed and commanding attention by her serious manner and resonant voice, she began to speak thus: 'I am the widow of Albert R. Parsons and the mother of his son. I charge the police and the court with murdering my husband. I live to bring up his son to take up the work which was stricken from his father's hands.'" At that point the police officer mounted the stage, "touched her lightly," and arrested her for disorderly conduct.[23]

The politics of the commemoration were on display each year with the choice of speakers. Parsons attended but did not speak in 1893, when the ceremony honored the freed prisoners Neebe, Fielden, and Schwab, and she did not appear at all in 1899. The featured speaker that year was someone whom Parsons might have immediately recognized as a rival— the thirty-three-year-old Philadelphia anarchist Voltairine de Cleyre. Named for the French philosopher, de Cleyre had grown up in a poor household in Michigan. Of her formative years in a Catholic convent, she later said: "It had been like the Valley of the Shadow of Death, and there are white scars on my soul, where ignorance and superstition burnt me with their hell fire in those stifling days." De Cleyre wrote and spoke extensively, especially on what she considered the baneful influence of organized religion on the individual's freedom of sexual expression.[24]

During these years Chicago anarchists hardly constituted a movement, but they did seek a wider audience, and they basked in the attention flowing from periodic visits of well-known activists based elsewhere, including de Cleyre, Emma Goldman, and one of anarchy's best-known theoreticians, Peter Kropotkin. Parsons also belonged to a wider radical community forged in the pages of papers published around the country. She read *Lucifer the Lightbearer* (edited in 1883–1907 by Moses Harman), *Demonstrator* (1903–1904, various editors), *Firebrand* (1895–1897, Henry Addis), and *Free Society* (1897–1904, Abe Isaak), among others. She found no ideological home in Benjamin Tucker's Boston paper *Liberty* (1881–1908), with its focus on radical individualism as the basis of a new society, in opposition to her emphasis on trade unions. Writing for another Boston anarchist paper, *Rebel: A Monthly Journal Devoted to the Exposition of Anarchist Communism*, in 1895, she sought to contextualize the anxieties of the age, bringing Marx into conversation with the "frontier thesis" that historian Frederick Jackson Turner first explained at the 1893 Chicago exposition. Now that the East Coast cities were coming to resemble the crowded factory towns of England, it would not be long before "the billows of discontent will roll up from the masses, the ruling class will attempt to drive them back in a sea of blood, but the pages of history show how futile has ever been this attempt, when those billows were along the lines of evolution."[25]

IN THE LATE 1890S PARSONS RECOILED FROM WHAT SHE CONSIDERED a shocking new trend in anarchist ideology—radical libertarianism in the form of sexual freedom for men and women, called "varietism" in sexual relations. *Lucifer* ran essays with titles such as "Nudity" ("Why should nudity be considered immodest?"), and *Firebrand* discussed "Sex Ethics" (against "false modesty") and "The Sexual Organs" (men and women should succumb to each other's "magnetism"). Parsons lost little time in distancing herself in print from the idea that "it is not greater restriction that is needed in sexual relations, but greater freedom," as one writer in the *Firebrand* put it. The September 27, 1896, issue of the paper published a letter she wrote to the editor under the title "Objections to Variety." Parsons ridiculed the idea of free sex as wishful thinking among people past reproductive age; but she also expressed apprehension about how such a "damnable doctrine" might corrupt younger people and ultimately poison the parent-child relationship, since presumably the mother could never be sure of the identity of the father of her offspring. To Parsons, "family life, child life" were the "sweetest words." She held that women's subordinate status stemmed not from a sexual double-standard that denied them "variety" in life, but from their dependence on men that made them perpetual drudges at home.[26]

Parsons wrote that women would never freely choose "variety" in sex: "We love the names of father, home and children too well for that." If "varietism" had anything to do with anarchism, she said, "then I am not an Anarchist." In subsequent issues, writers chided her for allowing "old prejudices and time-worn theories to overpower her," when what was needed was "a candid and scientific discussion of the question she has essayed to denounce." By September 1897, the articles in response to her letter, plus other explicit writings, had attracted the attention of Portland, Oregon, authorities, where *Firebrand* was published, and they shut down the newspaper and jailed three of its editors—A. J. Pope, Abe Isaak, and Henry Addis—under the provisions of the 1873 Comstock Act, which prohibited the use of the United States Postal Service for transmitting obscene material.[27]

The way that Parsons upheld the traditional double sexual standard in public was, of course, at odds with the way she lived her life in private, including the affair with Martin Lacher, at least; but here, when it came to matters of sex, as with blackness, she protested too much. The false narrative she offered of herself as a Mexican Indian maiden mirrored the false narrative she presented of the respectable widow with morals beyond reproach. Parsons seemed to believe that certain sorts of suspect behavior, such as sexual promiscuity, along with her birth as a slave, would likely discredit her in the eyes of her supporters, while other kinds of behavior, such as her shocking language in the service of anarchy, would invariably please them. At any rate, she was convinced that neither the circumstances of her birth nor her personal life-choices had any relevance to her broader political message. Thus she would pick and choose among ways of being in the world, always calculating, at times dissembling: just being Lucy Parsons must have been exhausting.

Other women in her circle chose differently. While Parsons fell back on Victorian platitudes extolling family life, Lizzie Swank Holmes grappled in the open with complicated issues of female sexuality and independence. In 1893, Moses Harman's free-love paper *Lucifer* serialized Swank Holmes's novel *Hagar Lyndon*, which portrayed a young woman struggling to maintain her integrity in the midst of a disapproving world. The novel includes several elements that appear to be at least semiautobiographical: Hagar has two children but yearns for the carefree days of her youth. She leaves her hot-tempered husband and works as a seamstress, eventually choosing to become a single mother; but even in the big city she faces stern disapproval from neighbors and acquaintances. She throws herself into organizing impoverished sewing women, only to have them resent her meddlesome ways. To save her son from disgrace, she finally agrees to marry a friend, who offers her the refuge of respectability as well as a measure of freedom. Thus Hagar compromises her principles against marriage to live in a world that seemingly has no room for a woman truly free.[28]

Lucy Parsons eschewed that kind of public soul-searching, but it was not often that she endured the scorn of other anarchists, who now took her to task for her narrow-mindedness, citing her defense of "slavery"—in this case the "bondage" that was monogamy. As if that were not insult enough, she also probably resented the emerging fame of the most famous free-love proponent, the anarchist Emma Goldman, who made Chicago a regular stop on her tours around the country. Goldman expressed little faith in labor unions—indeed, one of her favorite themes was "the cancer of trade unionism and the corruption of its leaders." Instead, she stressed the destructive effects of laws that promoted marriage and punished adultery in an effort to regulate the sex lives of men and women. Although both anarchists were prone to fiery pronouncements, Parsons and Goldman preached different gospels to the faithful.[29]

Much to Parsons's aggravation, the popular press in Chicago and around the country often yoked her to Goldman—both were called "red-mouthed anarchists"—although the two women were not shy about acknowledging their differences. In October 1897, Goldman arrived in Chicago to raise money for the defense of the three jailed *Firebrand* editors, finding a dirty, smoky city overwhelmed by the stench of slaughterhouses and full of "tattered creatures, crippled, gaunt faces." She observed, "Chicago is undoubtedly London on a reduced scale; in no other city in America does gray misery stare you so glaringly in the face as here." She spoke to a large group at a fundraiser on October 13, and later expressed dismay about the event:

> The success of the meeting was unfortunately weakened by Lucy Parsons who, instead of condemning the unjustified, vile arrest of the three comrades in Portland and the ever increasing censorship by Comstock and associates, took a stand against the editor of the *Firebrand*, H. Addis, because he tolerated articles about free love in the columns of the *Firebrand*. Apart from the fact that anarchism not only teaches freedom in economic and political areas, but also in social and sexual life, L. Parsons has the least cause to object to treatises on free love. . . . I spoke after Parsons and had a hard time changing the unpleasant mood that her remarks elicited.

Goldman considered Parsons a hypocrite who followed free-love principles in her own life, but spoke openly only of her desire for conventional respectability. More generally, Goldman would become convinced that Parsons's fame depended wholly on her widow-martyrdom, rather than on any original contributions she made to the cause of anarchism. In spreading this view, Goldman failed to appreciate Parsons's courage as an orator-agitator and as a source of inspiration to a segment of the laboring classes.[30]

Goldman and Parsons had appeared together on a Chicago stage several months earlier, in June, when they were among the delegates to the founding convention of the Social Democracy of America (SDA), a group launched by Eugene Debs. Emerging from prison after the Pullman strike a committed socialist, Debs favored a cooperative commonwealth that hearkened back to agitation in the 1870s and 1880s. Lucy Parsons admired Debs's commitment to industrial unionism, and, for a while, together with Honoré Jaxon, she played a leadership role in the SDA, serving on its board of directors. She also headed its Branch 2. Yet within a matter of weeks Debs sought to censor her and the branch. On September 10, 1897, police had killed nineteen striking miners in Pennsylvania, prompting Branch 2 to issue a statement in which its leaders "not only denounced the Hazleton shooting as a well-planned murder, but endorsed the eye for an eye and tooth for a tooth policy of killing millionaires in retaliation and of burning the homes of the rich." Debs quickly suspended the charter of the branch, declaring, "We believe in the ballot, not in bullets." By this time authorities were condemning the SDA as a plot instigated by "Herr Most, Mrs. Lucy Parsons and others of that ilk"—in other words, it was treason under the guise of free speech. Debs had hoped that his faith in political action would inoculate him from criticism, but his association with what the press called "the anarchist negress" and her "bloodthirsty followers" threatened to cripple his efforts. Speaking to a rowdy meeting of Branch 2 members, Parsons had denounced Debs—"there is not a fool in all the world with a bigger heart and a smaller brain"—and the "toads" who were his followers. In feuding with Goldman and Debs, Parsons set herself apart from the most prominent anarchist and the most prominent socialist of that generation.[31]

AT THE END OF THE NINETEENTH CENTURY, REPORTERS BEGAN TO take note of Parsons's relative inactivity, what they called her "fretful silence," as defined by her absence from the columns of the daily newspaper. Meanwhile, her life had settled into a largely predictable routine. She still lived with her son in the same two-and-a-half-story frame dwelling in Avondale (the street name and number would change to 1777 North Troy Street). She enjoyed tending her front-yard flower garden. For income she depended on her stipend from Pioneer Aid, the proceeds from *Life of Albert R. Parsons*, and the boarders who occupied part of the house. She also made small sums teaching anarchist Sunday school and selling eggs and chickens. In April 1898, she went on a speaking tour of the East Coast, addressing audiences in Philadelphia, New York City, and Boston.[32]

Around this time she became a peddler, traveling around her neighborhood selling tea, coffee, soap, and spices from a horse-drawn wagon. She thus joined several thousand other Chicagoans who took up this livelihood because of its low capitalization costs (she did not need to keep her wares hot like the pieman or cold like the iceman), the flexibility it offered in terms of working hours, and the sociability inherent in going door-to-door among neighbors. The 15th Ward was still home to sturdy German immigrant householders, mainly small entrepreneurs and skilled craftsmen and women. Although it is hard to reconcile the image of the plodding peddler of teas with the famous labor agitator, Parsons needed to make money, and she could probably count on the patronage of those who knew her best.[33]

Perhaps mistakenly believing that the legendary Mrs. Parsons had entered into genteel retirement, reporters would come to her door periodically and ask for an interview. On a Friday in December 1894, M. I. Dexter found her at home; it was her day off from peddling. Once he assured her he was not a bill collector, she received him, dressed (he wrote) in "blood-red garments," her long, dark hair straight, "comely for one in whose veins flows a considerable infusion of negro blood, and of much more than average intelligence." "Altogether she presents a striking appearance," he wrote, more taken with her looks than with her views.[34]

Parsons continued to suffer her share of personal crises, some of her own making. In February 1895, she took a nasty fall, hurting her arm, and employed a neighbor, a Mrs. Witherspoon, to help her around the house. Later that month Parsons sued the woman's husband, John Witherspoon, for breaking down her front door. He explained to the judge that "Mrs. Parsons was trying to pour socialistic teachings into the mind" of his wife, but the court did not consider this a sufficient defense, and fined him $25. And then early one morning in August 1896,

Parsons left a gas stove on while she went to the basement, and came back upstairs to find the house engulfed in flames. Lost were mementos of Haymarket, including the easy chair that Albert had used in jail, and one of the toy boats he carved, as well as part of her extensive library, painstakingly assembled over many years. Her son managed to escape, as did her boarders—John McIntosh and his mother, and Charles M. Secondo, a thirty-six-year-old Swiss-born marble-cutter. She tried to sell the hundreds of copies of *Life of Albert R. Parsons* damaged by smoke and water for 30 cents each, a literal fire sale.[35]

Parsons had spent her East Coast tour of 1898 denouncing the atrocities of the Spanish toward the Cuban people as well as the US imperialist ventures that she believed had been conducted under the pretext of ending those atrocities. Anarchists around the world played a prominent role in the anticolonial struggles of this period, although Parsons seems not to have engaged in her writings with these freedom fighters. In July 1899, however, the US-Spanish-Cuban-Filipino War assumed a personal dimension for her. On the blistering hot day of the sixteenth, she was standing on a State Street sidewalk, calling upon young men to shun military service. The United States was seeking to crush Filipino rebels, the heirs of freedom movements everywhere, including the American Revolution of 1776: "Every stripe of the American flag has become a whip for the monopolist to thrash your backs with. Every star in that flag represents the distilled tears of the children who work out their lives in the factories." American troops would only do the bidding of American millionaires bent on subjugating the Filipino people.[36]

Parsons had placed an ad in the paper the night before announcing this sidewalk address, and so a large and expectant, if sweat-drenched, crowd gathered to hear her. Regardless of their reaction, her argument, directed to young men—suggesting that they "refuse to go to those far-off islands for the purpose of riveting the chains of a new slavery on the limbs of the Filipinos"—failed to resonate with her own son. Now twenty-one, Albert Junior was a high school graduate and employed as a clerk. Ignoring his mother's agitation against the deployment of young male "fighting machines" to serve abroad, he announced that he intended to enlist in one of the new regiments and ship off to the Philippines. The news precipitated a physical altercation between the two of them, and on July 21 Lucy Parsons took her son to court, claiming he tried to stab her with a knife. A week later, she switched venues, moving the case from Cook County's criminal court to the county insane court. At a hearing she made the startling charge that Albert Junior was "mentally unsound." In response to the judge's queries, according to a reporter, the youth answered "in a calm, well-balanced intelligent manner," and then accused his mother of wanting to be rid of him so she could get hold of his property. Several of Albert's friends told the judge they saw no signs of mental instability. Nevertheless, the judge pronounced him insane and ordered him sent to the Elgin Asylum, where he would spend the rest of his life in misery.[37]

It is impossible to account fully for what appears to be Parsons's act of gratuitous cruelty toward her son (not to mention the willingness of the judge to comply with her spiteful wishes). Certainly Junior's decision to join the army represented a dramatic repudiation of his own mother, and she was not one to suffer public humiliation in silence. It is possible that she genuinely feared that he posed a physical threat to her; perhaps the losses he had suffered in life had made him an angry, resentful young man. Certainly, Albert was not the dutiful son she had wanted; by this time he had turned to spiritualism, signaling he would not be following in his father's footsteps. He might have considered his mother's extramarital sexual activity unforgivably disrespectful toward the memory of his father. And he had run away before. Whether Parsons intended to teach her son a (temporary) lesson, or truly wanted him out of her life altogether, and whether she saw Elgin as the better alternative compared to the Cook County jail or the state prison in Joliet, cannot be known; regardless, mental institutions such as this one had a well-deserved reputation for the physical and emotional abuse of their inmates.[38]

On June 5, 1900, a federal census-taker recorded that Lucy Parsons was living in her mortgaged Troy Street house and that her business was "coffee." She gave her birthdate as 1854 and reported that she and her father had been born in Texas, her mother in Mexico. Living with her since at least 1896 was Charles M. Secondo, the Swiss-born marble-cutter. Accurate or not, rumors persisted about Lucy Parsons's proclivity for young immigrant men—her long-term "boarders."[39]

Parsons was forty-nine years old, and more than a quarter century removed from Waco. She might have left behind small-town Texas, never to think of it again, but the citizens of Waco still reminisced about the Parsonses. In 1896, speaking to a reporter for *The American Magazine of Civics*, the president of Baylor University, the Reverend Rufus C. Burleson, talked about Albert Parsons and took the opportunity to muse upon the evils of drink. Burleson said that Parsons had become "a victim of the saloon, left college, lost caste, and joined his fortunes with the corrupt elements in local politics, and sunk so low that even white scalawags turned against him. An unusually intelligent mulatto woman, until then a respectable married woman, became infatuated with him, and the pair fled together to Chicago, where the subsequent record of both is well known." It is doubtful that Albert Parsons ever overindulged in alcohol; indeed, he always showed remarkable self-discipline in his roles as editor and orator. Yet the portrait of the upstanding-young-man-gone-wrong offered a narrative that absolved Baylor (if not the good citizens of Waco, who licensed the saloon) of any responsibility for his later waywardness.[40]

Perhaps other Wacoites also pondered the fate of Lucy and Albert Parsons, wondering what might have been had she not fallen in love with the ambitious young Republican. Lucy's former owner, T. J. Taliaferro, had died in 1886. Oliver Benton had married a woman named Della when she was just seventeen—about the same age as Lucy when he had first met her—and he would turn sixty-five in 1900. Living at home with Oliver and Della were eight children ranging in age from seven to twenty-five, with Effie, thirteen, and Mary, twelve, in school, a testament to Oliver's reliability as a breadwinner and his abiding faith in schooling for girls. For all Lucy Parsons's insistent evocations of those sweetest of words, "family life, child life," she had chosen to sever, irrevocably, her connections to her son, Albert; her mother, Charlotte; her stepfather, Charlie; and Oliver Benton.[41]

IN THE FIRST MONTHS OF THE NEW CENTURY, LUCY PARSONS SEEMED unmoored. The police feared her, and social reformers regarded her with curiosity touched with pity. The immigrant laboring classes honored her as the widow of a Haymarket martyr, but their leaders marginalized her and tried to keep her off the platform at their meetings. She remained at war with the local anarchist press. In 1897, the anarchist periodical *Free Society* (the successor to the defunct *Firebrand*) moved to Chicago; its editors, the Russian Mennonites Abe Isaak and his wife, Maria, and their son, Abe Junior, published pieces by well-known radicals, including Goldman, de Cleyre, Charlotte Perkins Gilman, Joseph Labadie, and Jay Fox, a blacksmith and member of Debs's American Railway Union who had been wounded at the Haymarket when he was sixteen. As for Lucy Parsons, she no longer had an outlet in the form of a periodical that she controlled.

Still, Parsons remained one of Chicago's best-known radicals. In October 1900, she seemed pleased to talk to a reporter, and he returned the favor by writing that she was "the dominating figure in the anarchist circles of Chicago." The story ran in several newspapers with the headline, "An Anarchist Queen: Lucy Parsons, the Head of the Chicago Reds." Like many of his profession before him, the reporter was struck by her appearance: "Her face is brown, oval, and well shaped, although her ears are rather badly turned." He wrote that Parsons had been born "on the brown barrens of a Texas ranch" of a Creek mother and a "pure Mexican father." Relatively little space in the piece was given over to her ideas, which in any case received lighthearted treatment: "Her creed is education, agitation, evolution, with an occasional revolution thrown in to make things lively." In subsequent months Parsons would be featured in other articles on "Noted Women Anarchists." The *Cleveland Leader* ran a story suggesting that her career "goes far to justify a theory lately pronounced, namely, that anarchy is most virulent in races of African and Oriental admixture." Anarchism's appeal for Albert Parsons could be found most clearly in his marriage to a woman who "claims Mexican descent, but is unmistakenly a mulatto." According to this new pseudo-scientific racism, Lucy was a radical because it came to her "naturally," via her genes.[42]

Over the next few years, dramatic developments at home and abroad convinced Chicago's authorities that Parsons still represented a real threat to national and local security. Robert Pinkerton, the brother of Allan Pinkerton and now the head of the eponymous private security force, recommended that the United States establish "an anarchist colony, a place where every person who wants anarchy can have it"—preferably on some island in the Philippines. There, Parsons, Goldman, and Most might rant and rave, but they would be forced to support themselves by tilling the soil as peasants of old.[43]

The authorities' renewed apprehension over Parsons and other radicals stemmed from instances of political violence abroad, fears of crime and other sources of disorder in Chicago, and the growing—to some observers insidious—respectability of socialists in the United States. US journalists' accounts of the assassination of King Umberto I in Italy by an anarchist in July 1900 often mentioned Parsons as either a possible influence on the killer or one of his backers, connections she did not seek to discourage. In early August, at a boisterous meeting called to express approval of the recent "removal" of the Italian king, Parsons announced to the press that she was helping to plan a conference of like-minded radicals in Paris the following month (if it took place, she did not attend). On August 5, she was on her way to a daytime meeting to discuss "the Execution of the King of Italy" when she found the door to the hall locked. Seeking shade from the sun on the steps of a nearby building, she was taken aback when several police officers rushed her. One seized her by the arm and ordered her to move along, which she refused to do. He charged her (and four others) with disorderly conduct, obstructing the street, distributing incendiary literature, and resisting arrest. In dispersing the crowd that had gathered, forty-five policemen beat and wounded twenty-five protesters. They hesitated to detain Parsons, but her "defiant manner" left them no choice. She was subsequently fined $50, which she refused to pay, and the newly formed Chicago Free Speech League offered to defend her. Gradually, violent events abroad were putting Parsons on the defensive; anarchy, she now maintained, stemmed not from the desire to create chaos, but from the need to recapture "the democracy of 70 years ago."[44]

When Parsons predicted that the assassination in Italy would spark "a renaissance of anarchy," she did little to calm the nerves of anxious Chicagoans, who saw mayhem everywhere. In the city, peaceful demonstrations by striking workers often turned bloody, thanks to the brutal tactics of police and private security forces. An 1890s uptick in violent crime (especially domestic abuse, murder, and armed robbery) reflected not only a growing population in the city but also the proliferation of street gangs and chronic underemployment among young men. Armed now with service revolvers and not just batons, and instructed to "shoot to kill," police on the beat shot innocent bystanders as well as suspected criminals. As a result, the police homicide rate increased fivefold between 1870 and 1920, and Chicago became the most violent city in the nation. Muckraker journalist Lincoln Steffens summed up Chicago this way: "First in violence, deepest in dirt; loud, lawless, unlovely, ill-smelling, irreverent, new; an overgrown gawk of a village, the 'tough' among cities, a spectacle for the nations."[45]

So disgusted were middle-class reformers at the rot that lay at the heart of the city's political economy that they were willing to listen to almost anyone who had a plan to restore democracy and take government out of the hands of what Steffens called "the enemies of the republic." In April 1901, the anarchist Kropotkin visited Chicago as a guest of Jane Addams, and received a respectful hearing at, among other places, the Hull House–based Chicago Arts and Crafts Society, the High School Teachers Club, the Twentieth Century Club, the Industrial Art League, and the University of Illinois. Lucy Parsons believed that Kropotkin would surely enhance the credibility of local anarchists among the do-gooding, chattering classes who were seeking a way out of pervasive municipal corruption. On April 18, the prince and Parsons, who had met twelve years earlier in London, reunited at Hull House. She proposed starting a school of "elementary studies in anarchy" and naming it after him, but he declined the honor.[46]

Addressing a large audience at Central Music Hall on the evening of April 21, Kropotkin spoke at length about the Haymarket martyrs— presiding over the event, attorney Clarence Darrow had noted that at least Russia exiled its anarchists, while America hanged them. The prince made a point to acknowledge the presence of Parsons, who was seated on the platform next to him. Of her dead husband and his comrades, he said, "Their names are not forgotten in Europe, nor in any place where the fight is being carried on in the cause for which they bravely died." At the same time, Kropotkin disavowed the use of violence, which, he said, is "not characteristic of anarchists or the Anarchist party." He told his listeners that true anarchists accepted "the principle that no man nor no society has the right to take another man's life."[47]

On September 6 of that year, in Buffalo, New York, an attack on President William McKinley by a self-proclaimed anarchist led to renewed scrutiny of Parsons. McKinley died nine days later. Parsons was under a cloud of suspicion in any case because the editors of *Free Society*, the Isaaks, had moved to Chicago earlier that year. Going out of their way to applaud the killing of King Umberto, they tainted everyone who was a *Free Society* subscriber or personal acquaintance, including Parsons. When questioned about the attack on McKinley, she condemned it, averring that the assassin, Leon Czolgosz, was "undeniably a lunatic," despite his claim at the time: "I am an anarchist. I did my duty." She told a reporter, "No person of sound intellect would assail the head of this republic." When the president dies, she noted, his place is immediately filled by his successor. Lest the interviewer think that she had mellowed, she added, "The trusts and those persons who control the necessaries of life are the ones against whom the energies of all classes must be focused." Moreover, she said, "anarchism is crankism nowadays," with ignorant, violent characters eager to wrap themselves in its mantle.[48]

After the McKinley assassination, Chicago authorities immediately rounded up a number of anarchists as accessories to the crime, including the Isaak family and Emma Goldman, who described the assassin as a man with the "beautiful soul of a child and the energy of a giant." Johann Most and Carl Nold, a Detroit anarchist whom Parsons knew, were imprisoned for their alleged encouragement of the deed. McKinley's death stoked fears of anarchy nationwide. Chicago's Jane Addams automatically linked the assassination to anarchism and the fear it inspired: "It is impossible to overstate the public excitement of the moment and the unfathomable sense of horror with which the community regarded an attack upon the chief executive of the nation as a crime against government itself which compels an instinctive recoil from all law-abiding citizens."[49]

Even within this charged political atmosphere, on occasion Parsons did penetrate the walls of Chicago's major middle-class reform institutions. She spoke before the Friendship Liberal League, the Chicago

Philosophical Society, and the New Century Club. In January 1902, the Community Club of the Chicago Commons settlement house invited her to appear on the same stage with a Protestant minister, the Reverend Jenkin Lloyd Jones, and a resident of the Commons, Raymond Robinson, to discuss anarchy.[50]

This appearance proved a challenge for both Parsons and her hosts. The head of the Commons, Graham Taylor, had heard her speak on November 11, 1896, and had been impressed by her dignified bearing then, but he expressed second thoughts once the invitation from the Commons had been tendered: "I offered no objection to the proposal, which I knew would be regarded as a supreme test of the freedom of the floor," he said. Still, before her talk,

> I suggested to her it might be an opportunity to disappoint her enemies by the calmness of her manner and the reasonableness of her speech, of which she was reputed to be incapable. Reminding her that she was not likely to be interrupted and silenced by arrest at such a privately conducted meeting, as she had been hitherto on public occasions, I expressed a hope that she could and would frankly and freely state the underlying motive which justified, to herself at least, her attitude toward the social order. The suspicioning look of one who was hunted faded from her face as she replied; "You will not be disappointed in having spoken kindly to me."

During the presentations, she sat quietly as Robinson pointedly referred to her and said, "Progress does not come through noise and shrieks, and you cannot explode yourself into liberty." She then delivered a prepared paper on the events and ideas that had radicalized her.[51]

Taylor summarized the talk this way: "Sympathetic with the poor, indignant at the harsh treatment of the unemployed, especially the foreign born when attempting public demonstrations to call attention to their plight, she traced her gradually increasing convictions until she became convinced that nothing short of the end of the existing capitalistic industrial order would bring either justice or peace." These comments must have struck him and other leading Chicago reformers as neither particularly novel nor very threatening. It was her demeanor as much as the substance of her talk that astonished her listeners: "Then, calmly as unexpectedly, and with a reserve that was as dramatic as it was surprising to me and everyone else in the crowded room, she took her seat." To shouts for her to continue, she replied, simply, "I have finished."[52]

Parsons's Commons speech represented no turning point in her life either in style or substance. She continued to parry with the Isaaks and other Chicago anarchists over the fate of their paper *Free Society*, which stressed sexual freedom and variety in life of all kinds ("We eat not one food, but many foods; health depends on judiciously varying our diet"). She tried to revive her publishing career by issuing a new edition of *Life of Albert R. Parsons*, telling potential buyers, "Friends, I am compelled to solicit your subscriptions in advance, because I am personally without means." The 1903 edition featured an introduction by Clarence Darrow, who had become a noted labor lawyer and anti-imperialist; the October 1887 speeches of the convicted men; a testimonial from William H. Parsons; additional writings from Albert; and Governor Altgeld's pardon. She replaced a drawing of herself with what she believed was a more flattering photograph—a three-quarter-length view showing her in a form-fitting striped dress. Left out of this edition were pictures of her children as well as the Pittsburgh Manifesto of the International Working People's Association, which called for violent revolution.[53]

Through the 1890s and into the new century, Parsons wrote for several anarchist papers, but she avoided a new Chicago publication, *International Socialist Review* (*ISR*), founded in 1900 by Charles H. Kerr, the son of abolitionists. The *ISR*, a passionate advocate of the laboring classes, featured exposés and editorials with which Parsons no doubt agreed. Kerr's company would go on to publish many works related to radical thought and action, including the history of Haymarket. However, Parsons began to lump socialists and reformers together, and even to include some anarchists in her critique, lamenting, to an audience at the Chicago Philosophical Society in 1903, that the current push for social change was "not revolutionary, but consisted of kid-glove anarchists and philosophers, who had, so to say, killed the revolutionary spirit." For their part, "the revolutionary anarchists had crawled into their holes since 1887," and the younger generation had been duped into debating extraneous issues such as sex.[54]

Parsons defined her own brand of anarchism in a speech she delivered around 1905 (probably to a well-educated, middle-class audience), and later distributed and sold in pamphlet form at 10 cents a copy. She began by reiterating her opposition to partisan politics: men running for office, she suggested, always engaged in bait-and-switch tactics, on the stump appealing for the support of the laboring classes, and then, once elected, serving the interests of the wealthy. In office, Republicans and Democrats alike pursued dictatorial policies limiting the freedom of all Americans. Anarchism, or the absence of government, was the safeguard of liberty: "Anarchism is the usher of science—the master of ceremonies of all forms of truth. It would remove all barriers between the human being and natural development." Government relied on force, which was responsible for "nearly all the misery, poverty, crime, and confusion existing in society." Capitalism was bound to collapse under its own weight as production became ever more efficient and increasing numbers of workers found themselves jobless. Hope lay in education and action. "Passivity while slavery is stealing over us is a crime," and individuals had the responsibility to study and become "self-thinking" in the process. A violent revolution (if not the *attentat* to spark it) was inevitable because the powerful would not cede their power voluntarily.[55]

Since nature had existed before government, anarchism represented a pure existence uncorrupted by "thrones and scaffolds, mitres and guns." People were naturally generous and eager to improve themselves and their families, and they gravitated toward voluntary associations, such as those organized around specific trades. Parsons hesitated to outline in any detail the ideal society because "the best thought of today may become the useless vagary of tomorrow, and to crystallize it into a creed is to make it unwieldy." Still, she predicted that a plethora of self-regulating bodies would rely on the goodwill of their members and not the coercive powers of a state: "Every man will stand on an equal footing with his brother in the race of life, and neither chains of economic thralldom nor menial drags of superstition shall handicap the one to the advantage of the other."[56]

People must free themselves from the shackles of money and labor for more noble aims: "Some higher incentive must, and will, supersede the greed for gold." All people had "instinctive social inclinations," as revealed in everyday family life: within a household, the members provided for themselves out of love, and protected and cared for the weakest among them. Indeed, the guiding emotion of fellow-feeling would unleash the potential of all humankind: "The Earth is so bountiful, so generous; man's brain is so active; his hands so restless, that wealth will spring like magic, ready for the use of the world's inhabitants. We will become as much ashamed to quarrel over its possession as we are now to squabble over the food spread before us on a loaded table." Parsons ended with an exhortation befitting the times, as the American Federation of Labor continued to hawk its insipid reformism, despite the "manifestations of discontent now looming upon every side": "I say to the wage class: Think clearly and act quickly, or you are lost. Strike not for a few more cents an hour, because the price of living will be raised faster still, but strike for all you earn, be content with nothing less." It was no wonder that, of the countless lectures she gave, Parsons chose to reprint and sell this one, a succinct, forthright statement of her views. Copies were still available years later, and one ended up in the files of the Federal Bureau of Investigation (founded in 1908), the only one of Parsons's works so recognized.[57]

Parsons could hardly have anticipated that the year 1905 would mark a new beginning for anti-capitalist activists, not only in the United States, but also abroad, where a real revolution was already taking hold. As the dramatic events began to unfold, she would find renewed purpose and embrace yet another generation of friends and foes.

❦ Chapter 12 ❧

Tending the Sacred
Flame of Haymarket

I N THE FIRST YEARS OF THE TWENTIETH CENTURY, LUCY PARSONS was in danger of being rendered superfluous—relegated to a ceremonial role at annual Haymarket commemorations. For many Chicagoans, she had become an enduring, if increasingly irrelevant, presence on the political scene. Although she might still excite—and incite—crowds of white laboring men, she had little to say about the brutal turf wars among various labor unions, and in her writings she focused more on national and international issues than on working conditions in her own city. She continued to delight in tormenting the local police; but it was during this time that she found a new mission in life—keeping alive the memory of her husband, relentless in her denunciation of the miscarriage of justice that was the Haymarket trial. Lessons from the past could help to inform organizing strategies for the present, she argued. In promoting this message, she sought out new audiences and new customers for her books on the West Coast, an effort that revitalized her. And she retained staying power among ordinary working men and women who saw her as a symbol of ongoing resistance to bosses, capitalists, and the state.

In seeking to revive memories of Haymarket and at the same time agitate for a new approach to labor organizing, Parsons found a vehicle in the Industrial Workers of the World (IWW), founded in Chicago in 1905. Members of the group, including socialists, anarchists, and other labor radicals—Wobblies, as they were sometimes called—aimed to position themselves in opposition to the conservative, exclusionary, craft-based American Federation of Labor. Coming together in Brand's Hall on June 27 was an eclectic, ideologically diverse lot aiming to form "one big union" that would inspire the masses and destroy capitalism. The preamble of the IWW's constitution featured the uncompromising rhetoric favored by the anarchists: "The working class and the employing class have nothing in common. There can be no peace so long as hunger and want are found among millions of the working people and the few, who make up the employing class, have all the good things of life. Between these two classes a struggle must go on until the workers of the world organize as a class, take possession of the means of production, abolish the wage system, and live in harmony with the Earth."[1]

Yet from the very beginning, the IWW amounted to an imperfect vehicle for Parsons's message. She remained a solo activist-entrepreneur, unwilling to bow to the demands of the group over her own interests in selling her husband's writings, starting her own newspaper, and advancing her name as principled contrarian. Her role in the founding of the IWW was an inauspicious one: it was not a triumphant resurgence of her career, but rather a troubling encounter with men who regarded her as more icon than leader. Eugene Debs was one of the founders of the group, and other native-born socialists like him predominated. On the first day of the proceedings, two of the twelve women in attendance, Lucy Parsons (now age fifty-four) and the venerable Mary "Mother" Jones (sixty-eight), sat on the platform flanking William D. "Big Bill" Haywood (thirty-six), secretary of the Western Federation of Miners (WFM) and chair of the convention. It was Haywood who famously remarked, "Fellow workers, this is the Continental Congress of the working class"—a comment interpreted by some anarchists, at least, as evoking the American Revolution and legitimizing the violent overthrow of the current government. Later, chroniclers of the event would describe Parsons's role primarily as that of an "honored guest," a kind of "platform decoration" providing "dramatic visual continuity" between past and present.[2]

Predictably, Parsons chafed at this dismissive view of her role. On the afternoon of June 28 she made an angry speech protesting the rule that only official delegates representing specific labor organizations could vote during the proceedings. Such a rule, she charged, stifled the free exchange of ideas and encouraged power-plays based on the number of votes that delegates "carry around in their pockets." For herself, she wanted the official status of delegate, though not the ballot that came with it. Always principled in her opposition to voting anytime, anywhere, for any person or cause, Parsons now decried "the force of numbers," the notion that ultimately "Might makes Right." As an informal "individual delegate," she spoke on behalf of factory children, weary mothers, and even "that great mass of outraged humanity," the prostitutes of Chicago. Sarcastically, she noted, "Had I simply come here to represent myself, I might as well have remained at home and not taken up the time of your deliberative body." Her inferior status seemed to mock the core principle of the new organization, for supposedly "we are here as one brotherhood and one sisterhood," and not as men and women invested with varying degrees of electoral privilege.[3]

The following day, responding to an invitation to address the convention, Parsons seemed mollified, but began her speech with false humility: "I tell you that I stand before you and feel much like a pigmy before intellectual giants." She went on to lecture her listeners on the "solid work" that lay before them, arrayed as they all were against a common enemy fortified with money and legislative power, with guns and the hangman's noose at the ready. She warned against making the IWW a creature of the ballot box and urged the new group to leave "no room for politics at all." The vote had never freed a single man from the wage system, nor had it prevented man from tyrannizing woman, "the slave of a slave." The general strike was labor's most formidable weapon: if the landless would only seize the land, and the toilers their tools, "then there is no army large enough to overcome you, for you yourself constitute the army."[4]

Calling for unity in the midst of "such differences as nationality, religion, [and] politics," Parsons urged the delegates to rally under the banner of "revolutionary socialism," and reminded them of that fateful day eighteen years ago, when, just two blocks away, courageous men had met their death. After the executions, the doubters had crowed, "Anarchy is dead, and these miscreants have been put out of the way." Pausing, Parsons noted slyly, "Oh friends, I am sorry that I even had to use that word, 'anarchy,' just now in your presence, which was not in my mind at the outset." She must have enjoyed the sight of the socialists squirming in their seats.[5]

Parsons took note of the turmoil now engulfing Russia. An attack on peaceful protesters at the St. Petersburg imperial palace six months earlier, on "Bloody Sunday," January 22, had unleashed a torrent of strikes and demonstrations, which had been countered by brutal repression. She alluded to a headline on the front page of the June 27 issue of the *Chicago Tribune*—"Red Flag Raised All Over Russia"—as peasant revolts and urban insurrections shook the continent from Poland to the Caucasus. She saw the crimson banner as "the greatest terror to the capitalist class throughout the world—the emblem that has been the terror of all tyrants through all the ages." Just as the czar and his murderous minions, the Cossacks, were awed by the sight of the flag, so, too, were the cruel robber barons of America, who understood that "the red current that flows through the veins of all humanity is identical, that the ideas of all humanity are identical."[6]

At the same time, Parsons made only oblique reference to the upheaval taking place that day on the streets of Chicago. Indeed, while she was extolling the latent power of the laboring classes, a "Great Labor War" was raging there outside Brand's Hall. In December 1904, nineteen cloth-cutters had struck against the Montgomery Ward department store for its use of nonunion subcontractors. Before long, the city was reeling from sympathy strikes, not only among other garment workers, but also, by early April, among the teamsters and the various unions of the building trades. Merchants belonging to the Employers' Association hastily formed an Employers' Teaming Association, which began to bring in hundreds of black strikebreakers from St. Louis and other points south. Pitched battles broke out between union sluggers and strikebreakers, between strikers and the police, and between blacks and whites. On April 29, the police fought hundreds of strikers, bringing business to a halt; a week later, a riot erupted involving 5,000 people. On May 21, two people were killed and twelve injured as a result of clashes between black scabs and white strikers. By midsummer, 21 people lay dead and 416 had been wounded.[7]

Several street demonstrations took place throughout the night of June 26, the eve of the first day of the IWW convention. By this time, leaked grand jury testimony implicated merchants and strike leaders alike in systematic bribe-taking; at the convention, Debs would denounce the heads of both the AFL and the International Brotherhood of Teamsters (IBT, a union formed two years before), calling them "misleaders of the working class." Yet in her speech Parsons mentioned the ongoing strife only in passing, when she blandly suggested that the strike might have been successful had women banded together to boycott State Street stores in solidarity with the workers. She also scolded women consumers for oppressing their toiling sisters "when we go down to the department store and look around so cheap." As for the revolutionary potential of Chicago's laboring classes, she had nothing specific to say.[8]

From a great distance, Parsons could see in the Russian revolutionaries a purity of motive that was absent in her own working-class neighbors. Certainly, to a degree, Chicago's labor conflicts lacked moral clarity. (Around this time the journalist Hutchins Hapgood searched in vain for a "typical" worker in Chicago, "the place where labor is most riotous, most expressive," but he found that diverse, "vigorous personalities" and "the richness of human material" made generalizations about labor impossible.) Within the wagoners' retail, construction, and service industries, craft-union labor leaders and small-business employers were in the process of developing systems of self-governance enforced with threats, fists, and guns. These trade systems remained apart from the large companies that dominated meatpacking, steel, retail sales, and banking—businesses for which Chicago's corporate elite was world-famous. The craft economy depended on clusters of laborers, some skilled, some not, who provided fuel, food, and shelter to the city's swelling population (it had grown by more than 800,000 in the last decade and a half). Within this subeconomy, union leaders colluded with small businessmen and bribed public officials to enforce territorial

imperatives—neighborhood boundaries fixed by one group or another—that remained outside the reach of lawmakers and reformers.[9]

This state of affairs contradicted Parsons's narrative of a monumental clash between good worker and evil employer. During a 1902
teamsters' strike, members of that union attacked meatpackers trying
to make deliveries. Restaurants and commercial laundries were firing
black workers and hiring white women, and even the tentatively egal-
itarian Culinary Alliance was forcing black members from its ranks.
Slaughterhouse workers contended with deskilling, not only as a result
of new machinery, but also because bosses reduced their jobs to many
small tasks and replaced skilled butchers (the "aristocrats" of their
craft) with unskilled immigrants. Unrest in the spring of 1905 seemed
a grim reprise of the stockyard and packinghouse workers' actions the
summer before, when employers imported 2,000 black scabs, and then
fired them after the defeat of the strike. Had Parsons faced up to facts
such as these, she would not have expressed bafflement that the "ordinary, everyday wealth producers" remained dispirited and passive even
"as the aggressions of capital become more and more acute." Despite
the city's many violent strikes, she saw no sign of a radicalized working
class, no sign that anarchism was gaining broad-based favor.[10]

Not surprisingly, given the political heterogeneity of its supporters,
the IWW soon dissolved into factionalism and infighting. Delegates
to the founding convention disagreed about whether or not the new
organization should endorse sabotage in the form of machine breaking,
working slowly, or supporting guerrilla tactics over strikes. Debs and
Jones opposed the IWW's stance against partisan politicking, Debs because he hoped the group would become an arm of the Socialist Party,
Jones because she believed that two million AFL members represented
a formidable potential voting bloc, which, if weaned off retrograde leaders, might add to the Wobblies' clout. In Detroit, IWW members disapproved of what they considered their Chicago counterparts' fixation
on free speech. And though the founders agreed that organizing all
industrial workers would help to bring about the revolution, the effi-
cacy of the AFL remained in question—were craft unions obsolete, or
were they useful tools for the eventual dismantling of capitalism? These
ongoing disputes, combined with Chicago's chaotic labor scene, meant

that the "one big union" would not make much headway in the city of its birth.[11]

Nevertheless, Lucy Parsons quickly began to build on the excitement generated by the IWW among radicals of various persuasions; the new group offered up possibilities for her as editor, speaker, and purveyor of radical literature. On September 3, she launched *The Liberator*, a new publication named for the abolitionist paper edited by William Lloyd Garrison. The masthead of the weekly stated that it was "Issued under the label of the IWW" (though not as an official organ of the group) and "devoted to revolutionary propaganda along lines of anarchist thought." Readers were assured that the new union was a product of "industrial evolution[;] hence it is bound to succeed." Subscribers paid $1 a year, and single copies sold for 2 cents each. Parsons, the sole editor, worked out of an office at 466 Van Buren Street.[12]

This latest publishing venture represented an exhilarating challenge for Parsons. She controlled the content of each issue, and wrote many of the articles herself, demonstrating her reach and erudition. "Everyday Reflections" served up exhortations: "Workingmen, the landlords and bosses generally trust you to provide the army and the police to protect their right to plunder you. Let their 'trust' be in vain." Her series "Labor's Long Struggle with Capitalism" began with Greek and Roman slavery and progressed through feudalism and the dawn of industry up to the present day, with trade unions gradually passing into the mists of history. She included poetry and recycled speeches and writings by herself and her late husband. She also published material by the famous anarchist C. L. James; Andrew (Al) Klemencic, a tailor who had worked as a labor organizer in Hawaii; and Albert Ryan of the Western Federation of Miners. Issues of *The Liberator* carried ads for her books, the sales of which served as the bedrock of her livelihood— *Life of Albert R. Parsons* (available clothbound for $1.25, in half-morocco for $1.75), *Altgeld's Pardon of the Anarchists*, and *Famous Speeches*, reproducing speeches of the Haymarket martyrs. The special issue of November 11, 1905, took the form of a commemorative pamphlet ($2 for one hundred copies, $1.50 for fifty).[13]

In the April 1906 *Liberator*, Parsons offered a succinct endorsement of a free press: "The press is the medium through which we exchange

ideas, keep abreast of the times, take gauge of battle and see how far
the class conflict has progressed. It is by the press we educate the public
mind and link the people of most distant parts together in bonds of
fraternity and comradeship. We can keep track of the work and accom-
plishments of our comrades in no other way, except by the medium of
paper." It was as an editor, as well as both writer and speaker, that Parsons earned distinction as a consistent fighter on the free-speech front-
lines and found a way to associate herself with, and at the same time
remain outside, the IWW, whose leaders saw her as merely decorative.[14]

The *Liberator* Group, a small band of devoted followers of the paper
who raised money for it, also provided the kind of community that had
been sorely lacking in Parsons's life for several years. Reminiscent of the
old days, the group met fortnightly and heard lectures (some in Yid-
dish); it also sponsored picnics, debates, and evening concerts. In what
was perhaps an effort to compete with more modern entertainment
fare, the group held an Easter "Necktie Party" in the spring of 1906. In
the March 11, 1906, issue of the paper, wedged between the fourteenth
installment of "Labor's Long Struggle with Capital" (on the Great Railroad Strike of 1877) and Albert Parsons's speech to the court of October 9, 1887, was a notice, "More about the Necktie Party":

Girls, don't bring a small tie
like you buy in the stores, but a
large one to match your apron,
and so you can make a
BEAUTIFUL, LARGE
BOW
When you tie it on the gentle-
man's neck, and he will look just lovely!

The evening included an auction and a "grand necktie march" followed by
a "Necktie quadrille." The fundraiser sought to appeal to the flirtatious
inclinations of the younger set, who were increasingly drawn to dimly
lighted dance halls that were home to the risqué tango and shimmy.[15]

The effort to sustain *The Liberator* was an ongoing struggle. Initially
Parsons had faced opposition over her decision to start the paper and

publish it in Chicago. Jay Fox, whom Parsons knew as a frequent writer for *Free Society*, was an aspiring editor himself. He wanted to launch the paper in the anarchist commune of Home, Washington, where production costs for such a weekly would be much lower than in Chicago. Apparently he also felt that Parsons's *Liberator* was geared more toward immigrants (mainly Russian Jews), and that it focused too narrowly on labor conflict. He believed that the paper needed a strong native-born contingent to manage it—what he called an "American committee." (Parsons was quick to remind her readers that Fox himself had been born in Ireland.) She would later accuse him of stealing money from *Liberator* fundraisers, and of dissuading her readers from supporting the paper in favor of his own *Demonstrator*. As usual, though, she seemed to relish the feud, which spawned indignant articles, editorials, and letters to the editor lamenting what she called "the split," caused by "the dirty work of genuine political rascals." Though she promised that in the paper "personalities will be rigidly excluded; we are working for the good of humanity at large," her own personality was certainly an integral part of the content.[16]

Parsons found the paper useful when she wanted to defend herself from her critics across the ideological spectrum. In October, she attended a dance sponsored by *The Liberator* and Arbeiter Ring (a Russian workingmen's circle) for Jews "who had recently participated in ghetto riots" against the czar in the old country. The event, held on Yom Kippur, the Jewish holy day of fasting and atonement, had the apparent purpose of riling the Orthodox, for it featured a lavish spread of ice cream, pickles, cake, and cream puffs. A police contingent appeared in the hall just as Parsons rose to speak; they claimed that the affair had been billed as a dance (advertised in *The Liberator* in English and Hebrew as the "Grand Yom Kippur Concert and Ball"), and that Parsons had failed to secure permission to turn it into a political rally. She backed down, but proceeded to sell copies of the paper to the merry-makers. Afterward, a reporter from the *Daily Inter-Ocean* ridiculed Parsons in an article with the headline "Anarchists Have Degenerated into Eaters of Ice Cream Puffs Instead of Drinkers of Blood and Throwers of Bombs." In the October 15 issue, a regular writer for *The Liberator*, "Rex" (probably Parsons herself) denounced the mainstream press as "liars and lickspittles," and reminded readers that she was "a woman who has borne more sorrow and troubles for the good of humanity than these scurrilous little writers ever heard of."[17]

The Liberator's pages contained little mention of Chicago's recent labor strife, but did follow the unrest in Russia ("Russia to Be Free" read one optimistic headline on October 29). It lauded the uprisings, which were, it said, winning the workers grudging respect from the czar and "other rich loafers." In contrast, in America, home-grown "aristocrats" had nothing but contempt for "the whimpering lot of whipped curs who sneak back buttonless [i.e., because they had been forbidden by their bosses to wear their union buttons] and beg for work"—a not-so-veiled reference to Chicago workers' capitulation in the wake of recently lost strikes.[18]

And, somewhat belatedly, a decade after the demise of the Populists, Parsons began to write about farmers' rights to land and machinery, and their need to market their crops without the encumbrance of predatory middlemen. Apparently rural folk were only now "awakening" to their true interests. Or perhaps Parsons was moved by the recent book written by *International Socialist Review* editor Algie Simons, *The American Farmer* (1902); in it Simons observed that American family farmers (some over-mortgaged, the rest landless) were more akin to an industrial proletariat than Marx had realized. He argued convincingly that American farmers did not fit the traditional category of the "hereditary peasant, generally ignorant and reactionary, and looking to the ruling class for all new ideas even concerning his own industry." At the same time, *The Liberator* ignored the struggles of African Americans, North or South, with the exception of an account of a recent meeting of a black civil rights group, the Georgia Equal Rights Association, in the April 1, 1906, issue. Not an article—or a paragraph, for that matter—covered the distressed Chicago black laboring classes, which were rapidly losing their jobs to immigrants and to white women, and widely reviled among whites for the strike-breaking activities of a desperate few.[19]

Parsons was no different from her anarchist comrades in consistently turning a blind eye toward black workers. Nevertheless, she proved a prescient observer of certain critical elements of the American political economy. In the pages of *The Liberator*, she continued to warn about the erosion of the middle class in the face of technological innovation. She decried the profit-making imperatives that made so many workplaces sites of soul-deadening boredom, repetition, and physical danger. In the new consumer economy, "everything now has a price": but in the future, "when labor is no longer for sale, society will produce free men and women who will think free, act free, and be free." She exposed the corrupting influence of corporate money on politics, and charged that authorities used prisons as a means of controlling their critics. She lamented the vulnerability of the elderly, "worn-out working people" reduced to penury after a long life of honest toil. She railed against the employers who one day professed horror at workers defending themselves and the next day paid thugs to beat strikers nigh unto death. She exposed the hypocritical arrogance of reformers who chided the working man for spending 5 cents for a beer on a Saturday afternoon. She excoriated a system that placed property rights over human rights. Even her Victorian-inflected defense of children—for example, comparing the little brother and sister on their way to a sweatshop with the vulgar, lavish wedding of a daughter of John Jacob Astor—had a universal, timeless quality. Still, she paid obeisance to gender conventions when she went on about woman's "highest aim and ambition"—to find a husband, because "she wants a quiet place she can call home, a haven where she and he can sometimes retire from the storms of the world and be at rest."[20]

The Liberator avoided discussion of "sexual varietism," though Parsons did discuss the problem of woman's persistent dependence on man, which she considered a throwback to ancient times, when physical strength determined one's place in the world. She also penned a series titled "Famous Women of History" that included Florence Nightingale, Jenny Lind, and Louise Michel, among others. She alluded to birth control in a piece titled "The Woman Question Again," which dealt with the tragic end of one Mary Markham of Kewanee, Illinois. Markham had killed her seven children, all under eleven years old, and then killed herself: "Poor, burden-bearing, poverty stricken, care worn, child-bearing to excess, Mary Markham, you are gone! . . . but you were a victim of our false society which makes it a crime to impart information that would have made your young life a mother's joy with a few healthy children to caress you, but instead, you saw from day to day, a helpless burden of poverty and despair."²¹

Four months into the publication of *The Liberator*, Parsons was reporting that the paper, which cost $50 a week to produce, was in dire straits, and that subscribers should send her postage stamps as an economy measure. Announcing she would be going east to drum up subscriptions, she blamed *The Liberator*'s troubles on "a small clique of so-called Anarchists [who] did everything to prevent the paper from coming out" by traveling around the country to discourage radicals from subscribing or contributing (no doubt a reference to Fox and his allies). She predicted "the little 'bunch' of soreheads will soon be left alone to nurse their own little boils."²²

In the spring of 1906, Parsons set out on an "agitation tour" of the East. New York City anarchists had started a *Liberator* group, and she hoped to lecture and sell subscriptions and copies of her books. In offering an account of her trip, she once again proved herself a gifted writer of travelogues. She enjoyed the long train ride, speeding along at fifty miles per hour through the open countryside, eavesdropping on conversations of the other passengers (no doubt embellished in the telling), and contemplating the resources buried in the earth: "It was the Lehigh Valley that proved most interesting to us . . . the heart of the great anthracite coal region. Think of it, beneath those frowning hills nature stored up her forests, floods, and sunbeams; then by her eruptions she covered them deep down, far out of sight, until long ages should elapse, when her children could delve for them and bring them to the surface for light and cheer and comfort. But man, because of his stupidity, is not utilizing these free gifts to all for all." Arriving in New York City, she was struck by the sad faces of hungry children on the Lower East Side. There, while on a "'slumming' expedition," she found "thousands of human beings living in heaps, piled upon one another, packed like sardines in tenement houses, poor, ignorant and dejected, helplessness and despair deep furrowed upon their blank faces." She described the early evening, when "the tall factories belch forth their quota of human beings" who must find their way to their "stuffy little rooms" and fall into a fitful slumber to prepare themselves for yet another day of misery. She recounted being set upon by gang members, who made off with her handbag and $20: "New York, nevertheless, is a great and wonderful city."[23]

On April 1, Parsons addressed a memorial service at New York's Grand Central Palace for Johann Most, who had died on March 17. The crowded hall was awash in color, with red banners, hats, and badges set against the blue uniforms of the dozens of police present, and she delivered a characteristically stirring speech to the overflow audience. The *New York Times* titled its story "Woman Anarchist Calls Our Flag a Sham," a reference to her mention of the Stars and Stripes as a mere rag for luring immigrants, "a brazen lie." She had called the officers standing near her "vile hirelings of the capitalistic spirit personified in a club and a few brass buttons." She ended, however, on an optimistic note, saying that "there never has been a time when there was so much unrest in the world, and from this unrest will be born the sturdy child of liberty."[24]

The Liberator could not survive without money, nor could it survive without Parsons. Soon after she returned from the East, she set off on another trip, this one to Cleveland and Cincinnati. At that point she was forced to abandon the paper for good. She thought that anarchism was "too far away from the mental level of the masses; hence they have not been attached to us." Many "young, inexperienced people" lacked the mental discipline to pursue "the realization of the anarchistic ideal." Meanwhile, Emma Goldman, in April, had announced the first issue of her own paper, *Mother Earth*; the publication, which included reviews, criticism, poetry, fiction, and cartoons, reflected its editor's view that art was a critical weapon in the arsenal of class struggle. Compared to *The Liberator*, *Mother Earth* was more creative, more in tune with modern literary trends, and more appealing to a wide range of radicals—cultural as well as political—and not just anarchists. By this time Parsons had become disillusioned with the inaction of the IWW, writing, in one of the last issues of *The Liberator*, that the group, with its official organ, *Industrial Worker*, proposing "no line of action," appeared "to be floundering around like a ship lost at sea without a rudder."[25]

With *The Liberator* no longer publishing and the IWW no longer holding her interest, Parsons now began to agitate on behalf of a series of labor leaders whose persecution or death at the hands of mobs or judicial authorities made Haymarket's legacy still meaningful and in-structive. In December 1905, three members of the Western Federation of Miners were accused of murdering the former governor of Idaho, Frank Steunenberg, by planting a bomb at the entrance to his home. Grilled for three days by the police, WFM member Harry Orchard claimed that Charles Moyer, the president of the WFM; Bill Haywood, the group's secretary; and George A. Pettibone, a labor activist, had hired him to kill more than two dozen mining bosses throughout the West. Rather than go through the extradition process, in February Idaho officials enlisted a Pinkerton agent to engineer the kidnapping of the three accused men, who were in Denver at the time, and spirit them to Boise to stand trial. Their defense quickly became a cause célèbre among the white laboring classes.[26]

On February 17, 1907, Lucy Parsons helped to lead a tumultuous protest demonstration sponsored by the Chicago Federation of Labor (CFL); later that day, though, CFL leaders signaled their disapproval as they listened to her "anarchistic doctrine, served hot," in the words of the *Tribune*. In March the year before, she had written about the WFM defendants in an article for *The Liberator* called "The Proposed Slaugh-ter." She had drawn parallels between their treatment and that of the Haymarket martyrs—the pursuit by the police, charges of a mysterious conspiracy, the lack of evidence tying the accused to the crime, per-jured testimony, the ensuing hysteria among the general public, which was kept "in breathless expectancy." In the sensationalistic warning of the current Idaho governor—"a conspiracy that is going to shock civi-lization"—she heard distinct echoes of the hyperbolic police chief John Bonfield, Detective Michael J. Schaak, and State's Attorney Julius S. Grinnell. In May and June, Parsons again took to the podium at mass meetings, but she clashed with organizers who counseled "moderation and education." The display of red flags and banners proclaiming "To hell with the Constitution" embarrassed the Women's Trade Union League, the CFL, and other sponsoring groups.[27]

After hearing an eleven-hour summation by lead defense attor-ney Clarence Darrow, on July 29 a jury acquitted Haywood and the other two defendants, prompting a celebration in Chicago on August 1. Darrow had focused on the defendants' advocacy of miners, urging a not-guilty verdict regardless of the evidence because "I know their cause is just." At least some saw the trial's outcome as a sign that Americans were becoming increasingly receptive to radical ideals and more skeptical of state-power overreach. Parsons proposed starting a national defense fund for labor leaders who might face crushing legal fees in the future. A few days later, she wrote an article for Fox's *Demonstrator* comparing the Haywood and Haymarket trials. She claimed that although "the Pinkerton plague is still at large in society," the recent acquittal of the men signaled a new era: "For the first time in American history the working class was united and stood shoulder to shoulder. They became 'class conscious' in recognizing the fact that it was not Haywood the mineowners were really after, but the labor organization he represented."[28]

Despite these hopeful signs, Parsons feared that anarchism had dissolved into a collection of individuals without a movement: "The anarchist cause has lacked concentration of effort, and a vivifying force to lend energy and direction toward a common aim." She therefore conceived her newfound life's work as highlighting every case of "judicial" or mob murder, and every trial of a major labor leader, as the kind of injustice that Haymarket had anticipated. She introduced *Life of Albert R. Parsons, Famous Speeches*, and *Anarchism* to a new generation of activists and would-be revolutionaries. She drew lessons about the need for direct action, and the danger in letting enemies "put their own interpretation upon our ideas," as she saw more and more people "turning from the past to the future." Younger activists hailed her as an honored forebear. Years later, Elizabeth Gurley Flynn recalled meeting Parsons for the first time at the 1907 IWW convention in Chicago: "I was thrilled to meet Mrs. Lucy Parsons. . . . I remember Mrs. Parsons speaking warmly to the young people, warning us of the seriousness of the struggles ahead that could lead to jail and death before victory was won. For years she traveled from city to city, knocking on the doors of local unions and telling the story of the Chicago trial. Her husband had said: 'Clear our names!' and she now made this her mission."[29]

Gradually, tending the sacred flame of Haymarket became a full-time preoccupation—and occupation—for Lucy Parsons. By this time, Albert Parsons had reached legendary status among anarchists, who called him "a pioneer in the American revolutionary labor movement and the first Anarchist-Communist agitator in America in the English language." Lucy took it upon herself to correct anyone who had the temerity to lecture on "Lessons of the Haymarket Episode" (as one Terence Carlin did before the Chicago Social Science League) without also preaching "active resistance." She disputed the label "Haymarket Riot," reminding her listeners that "there was no riot at the Haymarket except a police riot." She also defended her late husband in response to the fictional accounts of the Haymarket events that began to claim the public's attention. In 1909, the Chicago-born journalist and novelist Frank Harris published a novel titled *The Bomb*, which made Louis Lingg the hero and Rudolph Schnaubelt the bomb-thrower. The book portrays Albert as a gifted orator and an honorable comrade, but also as "a little florid," noting "it's the shallow water [that] has the lace foam on it." August Spies was "far better read than Parsons and a clearer thinker." Lucy Parsons was incensed by the book; she thought "it was a lie from cover to cover," and she also ridiculed Emma Goldman's endorsement of the novel as of "more importance to the anarchist movement than the monument in Waldheim Cemetery." Goldman later admitted that Parsons's ire was to some extent justified, since "Harris had not kept to the actual facts, and also because Albert emerged from the pages of the book a rather colourless person."[30]

In the process of guarding the memory of her husband against those who would sully it, Parsons set herself apart from Goldman, her chief rival for publicity and resources. In May 1906, Goldman and Alexander Berkman, who had recently been released from prison, set up housekeeping together in Chicago. Goldman used *Mother Earth* to needle American-born anarchists, whom she considered too attached to parlor-room theory while Russian Jews were carrying the weight of transforming the workplace. Yet Goldman herself made a comfortable living by traveling around the country and speaking, as she charged substantial admission fees for her lectures on modern drama (and later Russian literature). In her speeches and in *Mother Earth* she spoke directly to reformers and the intelligentsia, rather than to the unlettered working classes, and saw no need to apologize for doing so. Voltairine de Cleyre disapproved of Goldman's financial acumen, telling Berkman,

"To lecture for money for comrades I neither could nor would; to lecture to the general public on topics they would pay for I am not 'business woman' enough to undertake." In 1910, de Cleyre despaired that radicalism had become a "kid glove thing," appealing to well-heeled clubwomen. In contrast, Parsons stuck mainly to trade union and IWW venues, eking out a living selling her publications.[31]

A steep economic downturn in November 1907 sent tens of thousands of unemployed men and women into the Chicago streets, and Lucy Parsons noted the predictable consequences: "The free coffee wagons and soup kitchens are in full operation, and cheap lodging houses are filled to suffocation." The city's established relief organizations, including the Bureau of Charities, could not keep up with the demand. Once again Parsons prepared to take her place at the head of marches and at the front of halls filled with those who were out of work or worried they soon would be. Yet now Goldman and her entourage seemed bent on dominating the scene and crowding Parsons off center-stage, if not the entire stage.[32]

On the evening of January 17, 1908, five hundred people who had gathered in Brand's Hall for a meeting hissed at the mention of President Theodore Roosevelt and loudly demanded the overthrow of the US government. Mother Jones was there, calling the presence of uniformed police in the hall an "insult to honest workingmen." Presiding over the meeting was Dr. Ben Reitman, an eccentric twenty-nine-year-old physician who dressed like a hobo; a gifted self-promoter, he had transformed communing with the dispossessed into a fashionable pastime. (He and Goldman would soon become lovers.) Reitman tried to ignore Parsons's attempt to speak, but the repeated cries of "Mrs. Parsons! Mrs. Parsons!" forced him to relent. She mounted the stage, and, according to a reporter, "offered to lead an army to city hall next Thursday afternoon"; the demonstration would mark the third anniversary of St. Petersburg's "Bloody Sunday" and force the city's authorities to address the crisis of poor relief. She told the restless crowd that "she was ready to die on the scaffold as her husband had done if it would further the cause of human liberty." The meeting resolved "to unite to overthrow the capitalist system." Then Reitman stepped up and told Parsons, "I am sorry to refuse the lady, but this is strictly a men's meeting and we don't want women speakers." He called for a motion to adjourn, but Parsons stood up once again, this time reminding him that she represented the many women who were out of work.[33]

The chief of police, George Shippy, was determined to prevent the "Bloody Sunday" march from taking place; he did not worry that the socialists would cause trouble—*they* only *talked* about revolution—but he feared that the anarchists, led by Parsons, might incite a riot. Shippy, warning that a renewed "Red peril" was menacing Chicago, claimed that "the Reds" were mimicking workers' angry cries in the days before the Haymarket bombing. Lucy Parsons, he told reporters, had proved a chief instigator of the present disorder: "Never in the history of Chicago have anarchists and other enemies of law and order been more dangerous than at present." He defended efforts to prevent radicals from speaking and boasted that the city's current undercover "anarchist [or Red] squad" included ten veterans who had served the night of the Haymarket riot. (One of them, called to quell disorder at a mass meeting, exclaimed, "There's Lucy Parsons. . . . I haven't seen her for fifteen years, and she doesn't look a day older.")[34]

On March 2, a twenty-year-old Russian immigrant, Lazarus Averbuch, made his way to Shippy's home and, under circumstances that remain unclear, stabbed the chief and shot and wounded his son Harry, who had come to his father's rescue. Shippy then mortally wounded Averbuch. Described as an acolyte of Emma Goldman, "Queen of the Reds," Averbuch had reportedly become enraged when he had learned that Shippy had ordered the hall's proprietors to deny Goldman a place to speak.[35]

The Averbuch attack on Shippy sent reporters rushing to Lucy Parsons's home for her comments. Playing upon the fears of the police and the general public, she stated, menacingly, that "steadily the anarchist spirit has been growing." She boasted that Chicago had forty such groups—which clearly was not the case—and that a number of University of Chicago professors were joining with sweatshop workers to advance the anarchist cause. Reporters speculated that the boardinghouse she operated was actually a school for anarchy. In her home, while standing in the kitchen cooking dinner, presumably she was instructing the young Jewish men living there in the principles of social disorder. As usual, Parsons gladly accepted credit for what the police claimed she was doing—presiding over a vast cabal of anarchists in Chicago and beyond.[36]

Goldman managed to evade the prohibition on her speaking when she accepted an invitation from the Anthropological Society to appear on March 15, and Parsons was present to hear her and Ben Reitman lecture on "The Use of Vaccination and Anti-Toxin." Despite the heavy police presence, the event proceeded without incident. The Shippy shooting, and Goldman's defiance in the face of efforts to silence her, prompted President Roosevelt to deliver a special message to Congress in April declaring that while the country must be free, "it must also be safe." He added, "If the anarchist cares nothing for human life, then the government should not be particular about his," and called for laws that would outlaw anarchists and deport them. Still, the Anthropological Society and other groups regularly invited socialist academics and Progressive reformers, as well as anarchists like Goldman, to speak: critiques of capitalism were a la mode. In November 1908, Eugene Debs ran for president on the socialist ticket and received more than 400,000 votes.[37]

Parsons was happy to claim credit as Chicago's leading anarchist in the coverage of Averbuch's attack on Shippy, but she wanted nothing to do with Averbuch specifically and began to distance herself from him, just as she had distanced herself from Leon Czolgosz, President McKinley's assassin, seven years before. Indeed, her readers and listeners would not have been able to tell from her writings and speeches that, beginning in 1899, political assassination and dynamite explosions had become the favorite strategies of disaffected groups and individuals. And these strategies would remain popular for two decades thereafter. In 1899 in Idaho, the Western Federation of Miners had used 4,000 pounds of dynamite to blow up a huge piece of mining equipment, retaliating against an employer who refused to raise wages or recognize the union. Strikers in a number of cities dynamited the machinery they operated (such as streetcars), or structures that nonunion labor had built (dams, bridges). The brothers James and John McNamara confessed to the October 1910 bombing of the *Los Angeles Times* building, a blast that killed twenty-two workmen; they were not anarchists, but members of the AFL-affiliated International Association of Bridge and

Structural Iron Workers. Between 1906 and 1911, the same union dynamited one hundred worksites financed by antiunion employers.[38]

On the East Coast, a new cadre of anarchists, mainly Italian immigrants under the leadership of Luigi Galleani, pursued Johann Most's
propaganda-by-deed strategy, openly advocating spontaneous insurrec-
tion. In his paper *Cronaca Sovversiva* ("Subversive Chronicle," published
from 1903 to 1918), Galleani refused to offer his vision of the good society; the future would reveal itself after the revolution, he said. The
Galleanist terrorists seemed to constitute a tangible upwelling of *The
Alarm*'s rhetorical threats two decades before, but Lucy Parsons was
now retreating, haltingly, from her own earlier bluster.[39]

Beginning in the spring of 1909 and continuing for another nine
years, she spent less time in Chicago and more time on the West
Coast and in the Northwest. The repressive conditions in her home
city meant that she could not even distribute handbills there without
facing arrest—as she tried in October 1908 to publicize an upcoming
meeting to raise money for the estimated 15,000 children who went to
school hungry every day. Too, the Chicago-based IWW continued to
disappoint her, its leadership verging on the desultory. Ralph Chaplin,
a fearless Wobbly agitator in his own right and a gifted poet, artist,
and songwriter, believed that even the newest hero of the Left had become too self-involved to accomplish anything, writing, years later, "Bill
Haywood was swivel-chair king of an almost uninhabited revolutionary domain"—presumably, Haywood was content to hold forth in his
Chicago office, unwilling to venture into the fray of IWW-led strikes
around the country. The titular head of the IWW, Vincent Saint John,
had arrived in Chicago in 1907, but as long as he held that post—until
1915—he dismissed Lucy Parsons and her ilk as "anarchist freaks." And
Emma Goldman's frequent appearances in lecture halls throughout the
city, combined with *Mother Earth*'s promotion of free love, birth control, and au courant literary sensibilities, seemed to distract the public
from Parsons and her unwavering message of class struggle.[40]

It was no wonder then that Parsons was drawn to the IWW's
bloody free-speech campaigns in the West. In an effort to organize migratory laborers, the Wobblies targeted local prohibitions on radicals'
outdoor meetings. These efforts began in September 1909 in Missoula,

Montana, and then in Spokane, Washington, later that year, lasting through 1916 in a total of twenty-six cities. Parsons appreciated the organizers' emphasis on declaiming freely from sidewalk soapboxes and park benches. The protests had a strong performative component: in concerted acts of civil disobedience, activists encouraged their listeners to resist arrest and pack the jails. Jury trials became show trials and in many cases elicited sympathy from middle-class Americans and not just the laboring classes, with activists testifying to the beatings they suffered at the hands of police and prison guards. In Spokane, jailers used brutal, life-threatening tactics, including switching prisoners from the sweatbox to a frigid room, in an effort to discourage other protesters from trying to get arrested. "But still they came," Chaplin later noted. "Never, since the early Christian martyrs, were men more fanatically willing to sacrifice for a cause they believed in." Here was exemplary evidence of the "direct action" necessary to organize harvest-time wage hands, lumberjacks, miners, and marine transport workers. As transients, these men were ineligible to vote in any case. "To hell with politics!" was their motto. One of the original "jawsmiths," Lucy Parsons approved.[41]

However, at least during her initial visits to the Northwest, Parsons did not partake of any of the city-specific free-speech campaigns. Working adjacent to the Wobblies rather than within the group, she sought to capitalize on the enthusiasm they generated for radical ideas by selling more copies of her books—in the spring of 1909, and then again in the spring of 1910, in the fall of 1913, and for most of 1914. Indeed, with the exception of her visit to Los Angeles in 1910, she missed the months-long free-speech brawls in other places—Spokane, Missoula, and Denver—though she made stops in all those cities in quieter times. She boasted of selling many thousands of copies of *Famous Speeches* and *Life of Albert R. Parsons*, great pieces of "propaganda literature" that, she believed, "when circulated among organized labor are bound to bear fruit."[42]

By the time Parsons began her western tours she was well known not only as a Haymarket widow but also as the editor of the short-lived *Liberator* and a frequent contributor to *Firebrand*, *Agitator*, and *Demonstrator*, all of which ran ads for her books and featured the anniversary of

Haymarket prominently every November. When seeking lodging and speaking venues, she drew upon a dense network of comrades as hosts, primarily men who were agents and writers for these papers, members of anarchist groups, and owners of bookstores. (This last group included Cassius V. Cook and his wife, Sadie, of Vancouver; Cassius had served as a bail bondsman for Goldman when she was arrested in 1909 in San Francisco, where he was active in the city's Libertarian League and Free Speech League.) Parsons must have been pleased by the attentiveness of local reporters, such as the one in Seattle who wrote, "Mrs. Parsons is still a fine-looking woman, despite her years and what she has gone through." Even editors of the *Intermountain Catholic*, published in Salt Lake City, accorded her a respectful hearing, though her lecture in that city "pleads for the abolition of marriage and the Catholic church."[43]

Parsons's two-month trip in the spring of 1909 took her to Kansas City, Seattle, Butte, Denver, Los Angeles, San Francisco, Vancouver, and Salt Lake City. She focused on AFL unions, describing the topic as a "new field" for her—"that of conservative organized labor, and indeed it is a field from which an Anarchist speaker is nearly always excluded." She took pleasure in traveling as much as speaking, providing, for example, a vivid description of the Rocky Mountains that she saw from her train, which, "like a giant serpent, winds its way in and out among the cliffs that tower three thousand feet above"; its whistles echoed through the canyons more shrilly than the roars of a "deep-lunged" giant in a fairy tale. She also visited with the writer Jack London and his wife at their home in Glen Ellen, California, where she spent a lovely few days in their tiny guest house—"No paint, no varnish, no veneering for covering up dirt of any kind, but just a sweet, clean cottage. I fear I shall never sleep so soundly or dream such pleasant dreams again!" The fifty-nine-year-old traveler arrived home in Chicago feeling "worn out" but pleased with herself.[44]

Upon her return, Parsons soon learned of the renewed police crackdown on radicals in her hometown, and so, during the summer and fall of 1909, she conducted a virtual one-person free-speech campaign. She believed she could find a way around the new prohibitions by presenting herself as "the apostle of a new religion," one of her own devising. In the process she would expose the double standard that allowed foot

soldiers of the Salvation Army free access to city parks and street cor-
ners while radicals were routinely harassed. Denied a speaking permit
by the acting police chief, Herman Schuettler (present at Haymarket,
and an early member of the Chicago anti-anarchist Red Squad), she
decided to go forth mockingly clutching a Bible: "Religions seem to be
the style, and I do not see why I should not start one. I have some decided opinions on the matter of religion and I do not think the police
have any right to interfere with me so long as I am not infringing on the
rights of others." On August 29, the police arrested her while she was
speaking in Washington Square Park (nicknamed Bughouse), across
from the Newberry Library. According to one account, "Mrs. Parsons
was considered the real brains of the Anarchist gang, and the police
take no chances with her." In trying to elude the authorities, her ingenuity knew no bounds—but rarely worked for long.[45]

In 1910 she spent April, May, and most of June visiting Los Angeles,
Vancouver, Anaconda (Montana), and Salt Lake City. The following
year she made at least two trips to New York City, appearing with Haywood and pitching her appeal specifically to the "young bloods" among
the radicals she met. She still had the ability to inspire, as she did on a
final visit to Philadelphia, when she impressed a little girl named Emma
Gilbert, named after Goldman (little Emma's brother, Voltaire, was
named after de Cleyre). In an interview, Gilbert later said: "My first
recollection of a black person was Lucy Parsons, who came through
Philadelphia several times to lecture and would stay with us at the Radical Library, where we lived, at 424 Pine Street." Parsons also traveled
to Milwaukee in the company of her friend Carl Nold from Detroit,
who noted, to a correspondent, "If a white [man] is in her company in
public, he is naturally subjected to the gawking of the public, but of
course I made nothing of it, and we merrily drank."[46]

It is possible that Parsons was out of town in mid-May 1911, when
Voltairine de Cleyre came to Chicago and met with a number of comrades to found the Chicago Mexican Liberal Defense League. For several years a small group of American radicals had followed events in
Mexico, where an uprising against the dictator Porfirio Díaz had led
to brutal reprisals against his critics, some of whom had fled to the
United States. Working out of Los Angeles, they published a bilingual

(Spanish and English) newspaper, *Regeneración*, and formed a "junta" on behalf of the Partido Liberal Mexicano (PLM—Mexican Liberal Party), which had been founded in 1905. In 1911, four of these junta leaders, including Cipriano Ricardo Flores Magón and his brother Enrique Flores Magón, were serving twenty-one-month sentences in the McNeil Island penitentiary on Puget Sound in Washington State on charges of conspiracy. (They would be in and out of jail for years.) De Cleyre's group rejected the conventional wisdom that only the urban proletariat could spark a revolution, writing, "The longer we studied developments, the clearer it became that this was a social phenomenon offering the greatest field for genuine anarchist propaganda that has ever been presented on this continent." By seizing the lands of the elites (with the approval of the PLM), Mexico's peasants were engaging in the kind of "direct expropriation" that anarchists had been advocating for years. De Cleyre urged uncompromising support for *Regeneración*, and, alluding to Goldman, shamed those who would "squander their money in cafes while they discuss 'Chanticleer'" and preferred to live in "clouds of theory." Now that the opportunity for action presented itself, de Cleyre said, "we are so theory-rotted that we are hopeless to face it." In Chicago, she had a staunch ally in Ralph Chaplin, who had spent two years, 1907 to 1909, in Mexico. *Regeneración*'s records in 1911 and 1912 listed both Parsons and de Cleyre as subscribers.[47]

Parsons would later write and speak in more detail about the Mexican revolutionaries, but for now she could not help but notice the loss of several comrades. De Cleyre's work on behalf of the PLM rebels was one of her last radical acts. Always in poor health, she died of meningitis on June 20, 1912, at the age of forty-six, and was buried near Albert Parsons and his comrades in Waldheim Cemetery. A few months later, Tommy Morgan, Parsons's former friend and recent nemesis, was killed in a train wreck en route to California, where he had planned to retire. General William H. Parsons, Albert's brother, had also passed from the scene, dying at the home of his son, in Chicago, in October 1907. Parsons was losing touch with Lizzie Swank Holmes and her husband, William, who for a while lived in Colorado, not far from where pardoned Haymarket defendant Sam Fielden was leading a reclusive life on a modest ranch.[48]

In April 1912, a group of Chicago IWW members went public with their charge that the organization consistently denigrated traditional craft unions, including those affiliated with the AFL. They argued that the IWW should concentrate on cultivating radical factions within those unions, factions that would serve as revolutionary vanguards and gradually lead toward "direct action" and away from the timid policies espoused by the parent body. Perhaps because of her recent travels, where she had received a warm welcome from trade unionists on the West Coast, Parsons embraced this idea, and not only lent her name, but also her living room, to the founding of a new group that sought to pursue this goal—the Syndicalist League of North America (SLNA). Others present at that initial meeting were *Agitator* editor Jay Fox (who had recently relocated from Washington State); William Z. Foster and his wife, Esther Abramowitz, who were boarding in Parsons's home at the time; the Norwegian-born Samuel Hammersmark, who had been radicalized by Haymarket when he was a teenager; and the activist Earl Browder, based in Kansas City. Foster, born in Massachusetts in 1881, had joined the IWW in 1909, when he took part in the free-speech struggle in Spokane. He would soon become one of Chicago's most effective union organizers.[49]

With the approval of Fox, the Chicago syndicalists took over *The Agitator* and renamed it *The Syndicalist*. In the first issue, published on New Year's Day in 1913, Fox outlined the aims of the new organization with a series of negative statements, a less than promising beginning, to be sure: The SLNA, he wrote, was not a party, not a union, and not a "body of theorists." It had "no new fangled ideas to propagate." It did not urge workers to quit their jobs or join a new party or union, nor did it seek to "take them into new fields of effort, where they were unacquainted." It would not confuse them with the idea "that they could be a member of the IWW and the AFL at the same time." It was, in essence, a "modern" approach to labor organizing, requiring only that the workers appreciate their own power to "bore from within" and transform traditional craft unions into agents of anti-capitalist theory and action. The SLNA rejected arbitration but promoted sabotage, the "means whereby our working class enemies, the scabs, who support the capitalist system, as well as the capitalists themselves, can be defeated."

In sum, "the workers must realize that the 'brotherhood of man' of capitalism is a sham, and that the only way they will ever better their condition is by open warfare with their masters."[50]

The Syndicalist maintained strong ties with and ran articles by the
English-language editor of *Regeneración*, William C. Owen, a Los Angeles anarchist. Included in the pages of the SLNA paper were sporadic
dispatches from the few other syndicalist leagues around the country
along with reports on strikes with revolutionary potential. Yet in Chicago, pitched battles between and within unions held little promise for
a new society; in the buildings trades, for example, the plumbers and
the steamfitters vied for power with one another, rather than with the
bosses, and relied on slugging and drive-by shootings (the "death car")
to maintain dominance.[51]

The Syndicalist paid special attention to developments from abroad,
highlighting strategies there that American workers were exhorted to
emulate. Foster had toured Europe in 1910 and 1911, and he made the
time-honored mistake of believing that lessons learned there were easily transferable to the United States. In a lengthy pamphlet he wrote
with Earl C. Ford, Foster drew upon the General Confederation of
France as a model, denouncing America's "barren" socialists and hailing the "militant minority, organized and conscious of its strength" in
France as a transformative force in labor relations. As for the nature
of the struggle, he wrote that "every forward pace humanity has taken
has been gained at the cost of untold suffering and loss of life, and the
accomplishment of the revolution will probably be no exception." Foster
would soon change the name of the SLNA to the International Trade
Union Educational League, and become an officer in the Chicago local
of the Brotherhood of Railway Carmen.[52]

The high-water mark of political Progressivism came in November,
with the election of Democratic candidate Woodrow Wilson. Wilson
defeated the incumbent, William Howard Taft, and former president
Theodore Roosevelt, who was now running on the Progressive Party
ticket. Debs ran again as well and won 900,000 votes. As usual, Lucy
Parsons remained aloof from mainstream politics; indeed, not even
the IWW or the SLNA could hold her attention or allegiance, even
as she remained close to some of their leading members. Both groups

illustrated a common characteristic of US radicalism—the seemingly endless splintering, reconfiguring, and renaming of organizations.

Instead of involving herself in the internecine fighting, Parsons continued on her own path. In Cleveland in February 1913 she lectured on "Syndicalism, Sabotage, and Direct Action," and "Dynamite Conspiracies of the Capitalist Class." The *Plain Dealer* printed what it claimed were excerpts from her speech; if rendered accurately, her comments indicated that authorities in that city were much more tolerant of her provocations than those in Chicago. Explaining syndicalism as a form of "French trade unionism," she urged her listeners to disrupt production at its source: "If this cannot be done by peaceful methods, use force, tear machines apart, destroy property, and force capitalists to listen to the demands of their employees." She reportedly ended by saying, "An anarchist is a man with a bomb in each hand and a knife between his teeth."[53]

By April, she was back in Los Angeles, and on Sunday the eighteenth she was arrested for selling copies of the *Famous Speeches* without a license (the book would soon appear in its seventh edition). She was in town to speak at the local Labor Temple on "Direct Action, as Exhibited in Mexico and Throughout the Labor Movement." Her arrest attracted attention because, once she was in the police station, a matron made her take off all her clothes, even though she was charged with only a misdemeanor. According to the *Industrial Worker*, when she refused to remove a ring, "two burly policemen pounced upon her and forcibly removed it from her finger." *Regeneración* also covered the story, outraged that "Mrs. Parsons—naturally a woman most conservative in statements"—had to spend a night in jail, while various other purveyors of literature were allowed to sell their wares on streets throughout the city. It was not the last time that Parsons was roughly treated by the police. However, this incident marked the first time that the name George Markstall was linked to Parsons in newspaper articles. He had been arrested with her, and they were both arraigned and confined to the city jail overnight.[54]

The son of German immigrants, Markstall was born in Altoona, Pennsylvania, in 1871. He had led a nomadic life, spending most of his years before 1913 in Omaha (where he worked as a steamfitter), but also taking up residence briefly in Waukesha, Wisconsin, as well as Kansas

City. (The possible Waukesha connection is intriguing; Parsons might have met Markstall during her visit there, or perhaps through mutual acquaintances who lived there.) In 1910 he was staying in an Omaha boardinghouse as a single lodger and working as a day laborer. He had been active in Socialist Party politics in Omaha and Kansas City, running for the local school board in the former, and the city council in the latter. He might have gravitated toward the West Coast and the free-speech fights there, or Parsons might have met him on her recent speaking tour. In any case, they apparently arrived together in Los Angeles in April, and they would remain inseparable for the rest of their lives. Markstall's companionship did not tempt Parsons to return to housekeeping in Chicago, however; she continued to travel widely, to do battle with the police wherever she went, and to tend the flickering flame of Haymarket.[55]

The Wobblies' first decade prompted Parsons to hold out hope that itinerant laborers, no less than factory workers, might be mobilized and brought into the anarchists' fold, ready and willing to join the still-elusive revolution. Though she remained supportive of the IWW, Parsons nevertheless remained untethered from it, preferring to make a living from the Haymarket legacy, as interest in Albert's trial waxed with each new instance of labor-related strife. Like most radicals, though, she could not foresee the fierce backlash soon to come.

❧ Chapter 13 ❧

Wars at Home and Abroad

FROM 1913 TO 1915, LUCY PARSONS WOULD BE BACK IN THE NEWS, reprising her fin de siècle street fights with the police. In the midst of state-sponsored repression brought on by a confluence of crises— global war and the Russian and Mexican Revolutions, and, at home, mass migrations, wartime dissent, and labor strife—she seethed at scenes and situations that were all too familiar to her: peaceful rallies of workers disrupted by nightstick-wielding police, the speakers rounded up and jailed. These years represented a coda of sorts to her career as a fearless provocateur dodging police and vexing reformers. Somehow she managed to avoid more than a few hours of incarceration herself, but she witnessed firsthand the persecution of union leaders and the evisceration of the IWW.

If the upheavals and crackdowns of the 1910s effectively brought to a halt Parsons's decades-long role as a menace to the established order, they also posed a distinct challenge to her own political ideol- ogy, which had remained remarkably—stubbornly—consistent for many years. The intense radical activity leading up to and during the war years prompted her and other anarchists to believe that the world was aflame with far-reaching revolutions, that capitalism was dying. Yet in the United States, heavy-handed authorities were hollowing out civil liberties in a way that only seemed to confirm the insistent warnings of Parsons and others about the inherent tyranny of government. Her long-held view that capitalism had run its course crashed headlong into an expanding national state intent on flexing its muscle at home as well as abroad.

Parsons was in her element when, in mid-July 1913, a bitter strike at a local fruit cannery roiled downtown Portland, Oregon. On Tuesday, July 15, IWW speakers mounted a wooden soapbox one after another to condemn the Oregon Packing Company and urge support for the women and children workers who were protesting starvation wages and filthy working conditions. An IWW organizer, Tom Burns, called for the red flag of anarchy to fly over the city, prompting the police to arrest not only him but also each of the nine speakers who followed him in turn on the box. The next evening, under police orders to curtail their meeting at 10 p.m., the strikers gathered at three different locations, where they listened to more speakers who were willing to risk jail time. One of them was Lucy Parsons, who positioned herself on a wooden stool at Sixth and Washington Streets and began to speak at 9:50. In response, a police captain maneuvered his car through the crowd, driving straight toward Parsons; she continued to talk, managing to leap onto the curb (in a long dress no less) just before the car crashed into the box and smashed it to bits. She escaped the captain's grasp and ran to another strikers' meeting on Main Street, where she resumed her speech and charged the police with trying to run her over. A month later, Parsons was still taunting the police, such as the one officer, who, in the words of a reporter, his face "white with rage or fear, one could not tell," pulled her off a soapbox.[1]

By this time, the strikers had won a few of their demands but lost their jobs. The protest had started on Friday, June 27, when some of the workers had walked out of the factory. Employed only in the summertime, and often cheated out of their full pay, girls as young as twelve or thirteen and women as old as sixty were making 40 cents for a workday that lasted as long as nineteen hours at the height of the season. Working elbow-deep in decayed fruit, they suffered from swollen arms and hands; members of an investigative commission called the unsanitary conditions "very deplorable." The strikers demanded a minimum weekly wage of $9 and a maximum workday of nine hours. A strike committee fed as many as two hundred girls lunch every day, and nightly speakers sought to keep their morale high. Nevertheless, the strike ultimately collapsed when the packers agreed to a wage of $1 a day, $6 a week, and fired all of those who had walked off the job.[2]

The Portland cannery strike had all the hallmarks of an IWW organizing drive, including an impressive cast of women agitators, mass spectacle, and a vicious response from authorities in the form of clubbings and jailings. Rudolph Schwab, son of Haymarket defendant Michael Schwab, and Rudolph's wife, Mary Rantz Schwab, were there, working as Socialist Labor Party organizers. Rudolph labeled the three newspapers in town "mental prostitutes" and warned that "the iron fist of the Employers Association has crushed out the law of the state of Oregon." "Girl pickets" marched from 6:30 a.m. to 8 p.m. under the supervision of Rantz Schwab and Dr. Marie Equi, a forty-one-year-old physician and lesbian who cut an eye-catching figure in her man's suit. Rantz Schwab, after being arrested three times and bailed out each time, persisted in addressing the strikers. Equi tried to intervene and prevent a police officer from manhandling a pregnant woman, and jabbed an officer with a hatpin when he attempted to arrest *her*. The striking workers marched through downtown Portland under the banner of a cannery apron stretched across two poles; another banner read, "Forty cents a day makes prostitutes." When police forbade picketing, the girls marched to the plant and stood outside, three rows deep, their arms folded in silent protest. The picketers brandished steel pipes, the legs of a speakers' stand recently dismantled.[3]

Parsons left Portland in the wake of the failed cannery strike, and on September 13 arrived in Seattle, where another free-speech campaign was underway. There protesters faced the wrath of superior court judge John E. Humphries, who seemed bent on accommodating the Wobbly strategy of filling the jails to capacity with defiant speakers. At a dramatic court hearing on October 2, Humphries sentenced twelve men and six women to jail for ignoring his injunction against street-speaking. Included in the group were the attorney for the local Free Speech Defense League and a mother with her little boy and baby. When the judge said he did not want to send the baby to jail, the woman responded sharply, "Never mind. The baby is as guilty as I am." During this hearing, the judge saw fit to lecture the packed courtroom on "the evil of street speaking," invoking the name of Albert R. Parsons, hanged because he "was guilty of murder through incitement to riot." According to a reporter, at those words, "an elderly woman dressed in black, standing on a chair in the rear of the courtroom, cried, 'That is untrue. He was an innocent man. I am Parsons's widow.' To which the judge shot back: 'Widow or no widow, you had better keep quiet or you'll find yourself in the county jail.'"[4]

On November 12, Parsons spoke on "The Judicial Murder of 1887" in Tacoma, Washington. Later that month immigration authorities refused to allow her to board a steamer bound for Vancouver, where she was scheduled to deliver a lecture arranged by bookstore owner Cassius V. Cook. She remained on the West Coast for another year, however, spending January through April in San Francisco, then moving on to Washington and Montana, and back to Washington. With its large numbers of migratory workers in agriculture, mining, food packing, and lumbering, the West and Northwest offered fertile ground for labor organizing— and for speechifying and book selling: "I am pretty well known out here now," Parsons told Cook in a letter. In January 1914 she took a leading role in protests against the San Francisco Co-Operative Employment Bureau, which was notorious for its fraudulent practices. On the twenty-first, she was charged with rioting, after a street meeting ended in window-smashing. One headline read "Imitates Husband's Work."[5]

In early 1915, Parsons took the fight back to Chicago. For seven years, Hull House had sponsored weekly meetings of the jobless on Sunday afternoons in its Bowen Hall. Parsons appeared at the meeting of January 3, a cold, windy day, and tried in vain to get the assembled throng to leave the hall and march into the streets. Two weeks later, a large group once again crammed into the settlement house. Ralph Chaplin was there, and he described the men as "representative of Chicago's unemployed; Slavic and Latin laborers, wintering migratories and white-collared 'stiffs,' still proud and dreading the plunge into the yawning depths beneath them." Mingling among the crowd were "the red, beefy faces of the 'gum-shoe' thugs, watching the jobless crowd with cat-like care, and waiting uneasily for the signal to spring the plot that was to cover them with 'glory'—the plot that was to punish men for the crime of being hungry."[6]

The crowd listened glumly to a series of speakers, the most radical of whom, according to Chaplin, was Lucy Parsons, though even her comments were relatively mild. She said, "The only property working men possess is their own bodies, and they should guard and protect these bodies as jealously as the master class guards and protects their possessions. . . . As long as the capitalists can throw their cast-off rags and a few crusts of bread at the working class in the name of 'Charity,' just so long will they have an easy and cheap solution for the unemployed." Chaplin expressed his disappointment: "Mrs. Parsons was, as a rule, both frightening and beautiful in her intense earnestness. But at Bowen Hall she proved to be anything but a firebrand."[7]

More compelling as a speaker that afternoon was a young Jewish immigrant, a Russian-born baker named Aron Baron, a veteran of the 1905 uprising in his homeland who had been arrested in Russia during the events of that year and exiled two years later. Baron exclaimed to the group, "I am a baker, and I am expected to starve because I cannot get work baking the bread you people need and cannot buy!" His wife, Fanny, led a group called the Russian Revolutionary Chorus in song. (The following winter, Aron Baron and Parsons would work together in a new Chicago group founded by Russian Jewish anarchists, the Free Society Group, and serve as coeditors of a revived *Alarm*, which lasted only a few issues, from December 1915 to February 1916.) Noted Chaplin, "As a whole the speaking was far from fiery, and the audience was anything but boisterous."[8]

Despite the relative tame speeches, the meeting then voted to take their grievances outside, displaying banners that read "Hunger" and "Give Us this Day our Daily Bread" in white letters against a black background. Honoré Jaxon, who provided an account of the event for the London-based anarchist paper *Freedom*, singled out Parsons "as the heroine of this latest episode," which, he thought, had the potential to lift the Chicago anarchists out of their recent doldrums. Parsons and the others had barely begun to march through the streets when they were set upon by plainclothes police swinging billy clubs and by uniformed officers firing shots over their heads. Before long, thirty mounted police appeared—Chaplin called them Cossacks—scattering the crowd. Jaxon described the group's "clever Indian tactics of dissolving at each police barrier, 'leaking through' amid the crowds of spectators, and reforming automatically on the farther side," with a determined few avoiding capture and marching "an astonishing number of city blocks." The next day, the papers lied: one headline read, "I.W.W.'s Start Riot at Meeting in Hull House. Led by Widow of Haymarket Anarchist, Smash Windows and Maul Cops."⁹

Parsons was among the six women and fifteen men arrested during the incident. Mary H. Wilmarth, a wealthy widow who had supported Chicago waitresses in their recent strike, bailed Parsons and others out of jail soon after they were arrested. The arrest of the Reverend Irwin St. John Tucker, the twenty-nine-year-old editor of *The Christian Socialist*, represented a departure from the usual roundup of labor leaders and anarchists. At a hearing on January 18, the defendants (many of them wearing bandages to bind up their wounds) asked for a jury trial. Sophonisba Breckinridge, a Hull House settlement worker, disputed newspaper accounts that Parsons had urged the men to go out and break windows, explaining that she had merely distinguished labor from other commodities—hardly an incendiary statement. Still, Detective Schuettler claimed, "I know Lucy Parsons' record and I know what she says when she makes a speech." He needed no eyewitness to tell him otherwise. Jane Addams spoke out against the arrests, saying that the only crime of those who had been sent to jail was parading without a permit. She also defended Parsons as an advocate for the long-term unemployed, a group often ignored by labor organizers. Local papers ran a photograph of Parsons behind bars wearing a floral-trimmed hat with a brim. With the urging of Addams and other prominent reformers, authorities dismissed the charges against all the accused.¹⁰

Two weeks later, on January 31, Parsons was determined to lead another parade, this time through a wintry mix of rain and sleet. Addams disapproved: the marchers had already won "a splendid victory" two weeks before, she said, and, considering the bad weather and lack of a permit, they should not press their luck. Nevertheless, with Parsons at the forefront, the procession got underway. Leaving nothing to chance, the "Cossacks" watched and listened warily as she exhorted her listeners. "If you want jobs," she said, according to one reporter, "then make the warehouses of the rich so insecure that through fear they will give you work." Parsons continued to speak out, exasperated by the timid socialists and the no-show IWW. The anarchists resolved, "From now on we will take such steps as we deem necessary to alleviate our conditions, whether or not such actions are considered legal or illegal. Necessity knows no law."[11]

In 1915, Parsons was keenly aware of the lack of organized resistance, apart from a handful of militant trade unions, that might challenge city elites in a swaggering way via street theater. Indeed, radicalism now encompassed new, not altogether welcome, meanings. Popular perceptions of anarchism had shifted, with poets and writers claiming the label and embracing individualistic or "Bohemian" impulses that challenged the stultifying moral codes of the respectable middle classes. These new anarchists replaced shock-talk about abject wage slaves with shock-talk about long-standing sexual taboos, using rhetoric (and action) certain to offend churchgoers. At the same time, Progressives were co-opting elements of the socialist program related to public ownership of utilities and regulation of the workplace, ameliorating conditions in a way that seemed to make the overthrow of government not only unnecessary but also counterproductive. Few could deny that Jane Addams's April 1915 testimony before Illinois state legislators describing the effects of punishingly long hours on the health and well-being of garment workers was more effective in ushering in an eight-hour day than Lucy Parsons's impassioned speeches (accompanied by the inevitable street skirmishes with police), though the two women were making the same point.[12]

The IWW had drained some trade unions of their radical members, leaving those groups more conservative and focused exclusively on bread-and-butter issues. William Z. Foster threw himself into the heavy work of union organizing, but his theory-minded comrades did not; too many of them, he thought, were retreating into lofty discussions of Plato and Nietzsche, and "bellyaching about the stupidity of the masses assuming an air of intellectual 'hauteur.'" He and other syndicalists began to adopt a more measured tone about the possibilities of radical change: "Impractical dreamers," he wrote, must recognize that "our ideas are not immediately recognizable; we do not hesitate to admit it. But they will become so through the energy exerted by more who understand them." By the end of 1914, the Syndicalist League of North America was defunct.[13]

Lucy Parsons absorbed these changes directly. In Chicago, to more and more workers, Labor Day was a day of rest, not protest; they preferred to spend precious free time picnicking rather than listening to orators call for the liberation of the laboring classes. On her speaking tours, Parsons at times now found herself hosted by artists rather than members of the proletariat. She spoke under the auspices of groups that attracted middle-class reformers and university professors, including the Modern Thought League of Chicago, the Spokane Economic Club, the Tacoma Social Science League, and the San Francisco Materialistic Association. She remained alienated from the Chicago IWW, which was headed by the anarchist-averse Vincent Saint John.[14]

More generally, by this time Wobbly free-speech campaigners were wondering where their short-term victories would lead them. Did the repeal of municipal anti-street-speaking ordinances offer salvation to the underemployed lumberjack or the exhausted cannery girl? Despite the spectacular strikes of textile workers in Lawrence, Massachusetts, in 1912, and of silk workers in Paterson, New Jersey, in 1913—which both garnered intense publicity and enlisted the energies of thousands of workers and high-profile organizers, such as Elizabeth Gurley Flynn and Bill Haywood—the Wobblies, even in those two cities, could point to few long-term gains for the working class.

Meanwhile, Parsons had to make a living for herself, and that meant not only selling books and pamphlets and charging for lectures (she kept a strict accounting) but also staying out of jail. Indeed, whether out of fatigue (in 1915 she was sixty-four years old), or devotion to her lover George Markstall, who had settled in with her in the house on North Troy Street, or eagerness to avoid the discomforts of incarceration, she maintained a remarkably low profile through turbulent times that upended the very foundations of her world.

AFTER THE OUTBREAK OF WAR IN EUROPE IN JULY 1914, MANY Americans seemed content to let the great empires reconfigure or destroy themselves without aid or interference from the United States. In 1915, Jane Addams became active in the Woman's Peace Party; she and other Progressives and anti-imperialists favored a peaceful resolution of the conflict, fearing that the war would only divert resources away from domestic problems and enrich arms makers and other suppliers of military materiel. Socialists went further, arguing that virtually all of the combatants were both exploiting the indigenous populations of Africa and Asia and oppressing their own citizens, who were now being forcibly enlisted to serve as cogs in a modern war machine. Anarchists saw the state as ultimately culpable, for without its administrative apparatus, global conflicts would not exist: in September 1915, Lucy Parsons asked, "Could wars ever be carried on were it not for that institutionalized credulity which manifests in reliance upon 'The State'?" She took aim at "German scientific Socialism"—that is, state-sponsored socialism—which, she said, had once seemed "so promising" but now was offering up the rationale for war, helping "their imperial master lay a war levy of a billion marks or more for the prosecution of a war on workers of other countries."[15]

In January 1917, Parsons lectured on "War as a Great Equalizer" at Chicago's Economic Forum; but for the most part she limited her speaking and writing in these years to Haymarket commemorations, the plight of modern-day labor martyrs, and a non-suffragist brand of "woman's advancement," eschewing comment on either the war abroad or its impact at home. She did, however, continue to place ads for her edited books in such publications as *Songs of the Workers: On the Road, in the Jungles and in the Shops* (1910), a collection of Wobbly favorites; *Mother Earth* (1909–1912); and *The Public: An International Journal of Fundamental Democracy* (1916).[16]

Although the United States did not enter World War I until April 6, 1917, the battles in Europe nevertheless had an immediate impact on Chicago. The city's large German and Irish communities felt a historical affinity for the Central Powers, including Germany, Austria-Hungry, Turkey, and Bulgaria, in opposition to the Entente—Britain, France, and Russia. Republican mayor William Thompson, boasting that he led "the sixth largest German city in the world," urged the United States to remain neutral, hoping to retain the support of two vital ethnic constituencies. This stance became untenable after a German submarine torpedoed the British passenger ship *Lusitania* in May 1915, an attack that took the lives of 1,198 people, including 124 Americans. Faced with increasing hostility, German Americans downplayed their cultural roots—changing the name of the Germania Club, for example, to the Lincoln Club. As foreign immigration to the United States slowed, Chicago's *Deutschtum*—Germany-away-from-home—could not replenish itself with newcomers, and radical labor politics held little appeal for the second generation. A once-proud, vibrant community, Parsons's longtime home, became a casualty of a wartime fear of all names and words German.[17]

At the same time, a severe labor shortage forced employers to look to new sources of workers. For decades, Chicago industrialists had welcomed large numbers of Eastern Europeans willing to toil for pitiable wages in factories and meatpacking plants. Bosses preferred to hire non-English-speaking immigrants rather than open up the workplace to southern native-born Americans identified as "black." From an employer's point of view, the ideal workplace consisted of whites separated from each other by language, religion, and ethnic loyalties, and cowed by the possibility that scabs-in-waiting would take their jobs if they went out on strike. Now, however, key sectors of the Chicago labor market opened up jobs to southern blacks for the first time. Rather than endure a white-supremacist reign of terror any longer, thousands of black men, women, and children voted with their feet and boarded trains all over the Mississippi Valley, arriving at Chicago's Twelfth Street Station eager to begin a new life. One of them, a young man named Richard Wright, from Jackson, Mississippi, spoke for many when he wrote that he had "a hazy notion that life could be lived with dignity, that the personalities of others should not be violated, that men should be able to confront other men without fear or shame, and that if men were lucky in their being on earth they might win some redeeming meaning for their having struggled and suffered here beneath the stars." Between 1910 and 1920, the city's black population increased from 44,103 (2 percent of the total) to 109,458 (4.1 percent). Migrants entered previously all-white workplaces in packinghouses, stockyards, farm machinery plants, steel mills, and foundries. They also registered to vote for the first time. If Lucy Parsons, an avid reader of the local Chicago press, perused the new black paper *The Defender*, she might have appreciated these developments and readjusted her idea of the industrial proletariat.[18]

Life in Chicago was hardly the paradise that some migrants expected—or that *The Defender* promised. Hemmed in by predatory real estate practices on the city's South Side, black Southerners found crowded, overpriced lodgings in the midst of Chicago's red-light district, and had no choice but to take the worst jobs that employers had to offer—the kill floor of the packinghouse, the stifling foundry in the steel mill. Many of their white coworkers regarded them with suspicion, and unions persisted in their exclusionary policies. Ragen's Colts, an Irish American street gang on the South Side that became a Democratic political organization and athletic club, deliberately stoked white resentment against blacks. (The group's motto, "Hit Me and You Hit 2,000," gave potent meaning to the term "worker solidarity.") Yet the southern refugees continued to arrive—for the steady work, or the chance to see a White Sox game, or to sit at the front of the bus. Wrote one black woman to her sister back home: "I am quite busy. I work in Swifts packing Co. in the sausage department. My daughter and I work for the same company—We get $1.50 a day and we pack so many sausages we dont have much time to play but it is a matter of a dollar with me and I feel that God made the path and I am walking therein."[19]

By 1920, almost three out of every ten black men in Chicago were employed in factory work, up from virtually none ten years earlier. Nevertheless, many of the radical periodicals that Parsons read portrayed black people as lazy, ignorant creatures, scabbing when they were working at all. Some of her acquaintances—Dyer Lum and Jack London, for example—were unapologetic bigots. (In a letter to de Cleyre, Lum expressed satisfaction upon hearing that a southern mob had burned a black man at the stake: "I would have carried the wood myself if I had been there!" Torture served a larger purpose, he thought: "Burning him made the flesh of every nigger brute in the South to creep.") Such opinions would have clearly discomfited Parsons—but at the same time, she would have adamantly rejected *The Defender*'s defense of black strikebreakers, the view that "unions cannot expect to close the working door in his [the black person's] face in peaceful times and expect his co-operation in troublesome times." She no doubt dismissed the eagerness with which black men and (after 1920) black women began to vote; indeed, compared to eligible white voters, they registered in disproportionately large numbers, and some of them, including Ida B. Wells-Barnett, were rewarded by Mayor Thompson with political patronage jobs.[20]

Another black paper, *The Broad Ax*, carried a May 15, 1915, notice of a recent meeting of the African American Alpha Suffrage Club, formed by Wells-Barnett, at which "plans were completed for an entertainment at which Mrs. Lucy Parsons, whose husband lost his life in the Haymarket riot, will be the chief speaker." Yet no evidence exists that Parsons ever delivered the speech. By this time, Wells-Barnett had fallen from favor among the city's black women's clubs. For years she had suffered humiliation at the hands of the white women of the city and the nation. In 1913, an Illinois delegation to a Washington, DC, suffragist parade dithered and debated over allowing her to march with them, preferring that she stay with the other black women in the march. She refused: "I shall not march with the colored women. Either I go with you or not at all. I am not taking this stand because I personally wish for recognition. I am doing it for the future benefit of my whole race." Later, although the white suffragists had denied her the privilege, she slipped unobtrusively into the ranks of the white delegates anyway. Yet, as Chicago's black population swelled, and institutions created by the old-timers were supplanted by new groups, such as the National Urban League, Wells-Barnett lost her leadership status. She also lost her patronage job as a probation officer. The white head of the NAACP from 1917 to 1932, Mary White Ovington, with whom Wells-Barnett frequently disagreed over the group's less-than-confrontational tactics, remarked at one point that the black woman was "perhaps not fitted to accept the restraint of organization"—a rebuke that could also have been leveled at Parsons.[21]

Parsons ignored the stirrings of black activism nationwide and in her city, instead continuing to find in revolutions elsewhere the promise that was eluding workers in the United States. The story of Haymarket had resonated with oppressed peoples around the world. The Cuban freedom fighter José Martí, for example, wrote a series of articles on the bombing and trial in 1888 for the Buenos Aires paper *La Nación*. In 1913, Parsons began raising money for the defense of Mexicans-in-exile who had been charged with trying to return to their native country to support the revolution, and for the beleaguered Magón brothers, who were still editing *Regeneración* in Los Angeles. The brothers reached out to the American radical community, vowing to the readers of *Mother Earth*, "We tell you: Lead us in solidarity and we will bury the capitalist system in Mexico." Enrique Flores Magón boasted of the revolution-aries' indigenous roots, which he believed made him and his comrades less corrupt than anarchists elsewhere: "Thanks to our tribal traditions; thanks to our being mostly Indians and, therefore, close-to-Nature ag-ricultural people; thanks to our being illiterate and, hence, unspoiled by the so-called education of the capitalist class, our national or race soul and mind are apt to assimilate modern ideas."[22]

Emissaries from the Mexican revolutionaries found a receptive audience in Chicago's Free Society Group, which sponsored a weekly speakers' forum. However, not all American radicals were convinced that peasants' "tribal traditions" could ignite a true class-based revolt, and socialists were uneasy with the rebels' embrace of anarchism. Par-sons herself ignored the question of whether or not rural peasants might form the vanguard of a workers' revolution. Speaking to audi-ences in Chicago and elsewhere, she nevertheless claimed to be a na-tive of Mexico and also a native speaker of Spanish. She focused on the Magón brothers' struggle to sustain *Regeneración*, assailing the raid on their offices and the recurrent jailings of the men.[23]

For his part, Enrique Flores Magón drew lessons from Haymar-ket in a direct way. In the fall of 1916, he wrote a piece called "My First Impressions" for the paper, and it was translated into English and pub-lished in *Mother Earth* in November. He recalled as a little boy hearing of the execution of "our comrades Parsons, Fischer, Engel and Spies"; yet at the time, "under the bloody tyrant Porfirio Diaz' regime, it was so common to learn of men being shot, hanged or who had otherwise vanished from the face of the earth, that the news of the tragedy, read by my father to my mother, did not attract my attention except the fact that it happened in the United States." Later, when his father read an

account of a Haymarket memorial meeting to him, Magón wrote, "I
listened intently and wondered how the bodies of the hanged men must
have looked, dangling from the ropes fastened to the branches of a tall
and leafy oak, as men are hanged in Mexico." Even now in his mind's
eye he could see them ascend the gallows "with manly poise, serene,
smiling, conscious of the end, but conscious also of the immortality of
their Ideals for which they were made to die. I thought of the human
herd, humbly placing their necks in their daily yoke in factories and
sweat-shops instead of rising in rebellious protest against the murder of
their comrades."[24]

Parsons had no opportunity to learn firsthand of the Russian Revolution of 1917, but that did not prevent her from extolling the presumed
virtues of the new regime. Like other anarchists, she hailed the fall
of the Russian czar, Nicholas II, on November 7, 1917, as the culmination of radical trade unionism: the first working-class nation-state
emerged as a beacon to people everywhere—in Gurley Flynn's words,
"Everything that we of the left-wing movement heard from there [Rus-
sia] through the press fired us with enthusiasm." Comrades in Chicago
bade farewell to the Russian dissidents Aron and Fanny Baron, who
now returned to their homeland to, in Ralph Chaplin's words, finish
the process of "industrial freedom established along lines mapped out
in the 'One Big Union' chart." He added, "As good Wobblies, we promised to back the Russian revolution to the limit." Presumably, the Bolsheviks' bloody suppression of their political opponents, evidenced, for
example, in genocidal pogroms against Jews, amounted to a temporary
measure necessary to secure the success of the fragile new Soviet Republic. In late 1917, Russia withdrew from the war with Germany, and
the Bolsheviks turned to defeating enemies at home.[25]

By this time, the IWW had left little doubt about where it stood
on American involvement in the war. In August 1914, at its convention
in Chicago, the delegates had declared that "while the army of the unemployed is growing by legions, the Masters of Bread are preparing to
ship the murderous hordes of Europe the foodstuff that the workers
have produced, and this with the connivance of the United States Government which has under way plans to subsidize ships for that purpose." A resolution urged the masses to raid granaries and storehouses

and "help yourselves" rather than waste time protesting at city hall or the state capitol: "Where food is being shipped, confiscate it, if you have the power." Chaplin listened and later expressed his misgivings: "To me that declaration fell into the category of the 'Call to Arms' that found its way into the *Arbeiter Zeitung* just prior to the Haymarket bomb incident in 1886."[26]

In 1912 and 1913 the IWW had sponsored a number of spectacular strikes in the East and South, labor actions that brought together workers from many different nationalities in the face of wage cuts, speed-ups, and the introduction of labor-saving machinery. Beginning in the spring of 1917, however, as the United States prepared to officially enter the war, the group tried a new tack—organizing industries essential to the war effort, such as lumber, copper, and oil, and encouraging workers in those industries to walk off the job and halt production in the process. That summer, thousands of miners in Bisbee, Arizona, and Butte, Montana, faced the wrath of local authorities. In Butte, six men dragged the IWW organizer Frank Little from his boardinghouse room, beat him, and hanged him from a railroad trestle. Despite lynch mobs and other extreme measures of repression—1,200 Bisbee miners were forced into stifling boxcars and deported to the New Mexico desert—the Wobblies were beginning to wed their denunciations of the war effort in general and the military draft in particular with real results in the forests and mines. In a related effort in Chicago, William Foster capitalized on the heightened wartime demand for meat to convince rival stockyard unions to come together in a Stockyards Labor Council. Subsequent arbitration resulted in an eight-hour day and a five-day workweek, but those gains evaporated in 1919, and the unions were still denied recognition. In 1917, IWW membership stood at an all-time high—an estimated 150,000.[27]

The response of governors, mayors, and local sheriffs was swift and furious. In an effort to obliterate the IWW, these officials conducted mass trials and imprisoned many of its members and supporters, viciously suppressing even the most innocuous forms of protest against the war. Authorities trained their sights on dissenters generally, and individuals across the political spectrum were caught up in the dragnet, with even the upstanding reformer Jane Addams labeled a "dangerous

Red." Still, neither the Progressive movement nor the Socialist Party felt the full wrath of the US Justice Department or its state and local allies the way the Wobblies did. This latest iteration of a "Red Scare" amounted to a renewal of the repression with which Lucy Parsons had contended for more than two decades, but she now remained conspicuous for her silence.[28]

Beginning on September 5, 1917, and continuing sporadically thereafter, federal and local officials nationwide raided and ransacked IWW halls and arrested IWW members, claiming that the organization was beginning to hamper the war effort in material ways. The June 1917 Espionage Act and the May 1918 Sedition Act provided legal cover for the silencing and punishing of dissenters. The Sedition Act mandated harsh prison sentences and crushing fines for any persons "disposed to utter, print, write or publish any disloyal, profane, scurrilous or abusive language about the form of the government of the United States." A number of states passed criminal syndicalism laws, vague statutes used as a pretext for breaking up radical groups and jailing their members. On September 28, 1917, a grand jury convened in Chicago—the international headquarters of the IWW—and indicted 166 Wobblies on a total of 10,000 charges. Two months later, 116 of those defendants stood trial, and 101 of them were convicted. During the months they languished in the Cook County jail awaiting arraignment, many of the defendants, including Ralph Chaplin and Bill Haywood, found themselves in the same cells that had been occupied by Albert Parsons and his comrades three decades before, the wooden beams of the gallows still visible at the far end of the cellblock. Haywood wrote, "Their words seemed to reverberate throughout the prison. Their silence spoke an undying tongue."[29]

These prosecutions represented the country's most egregious assault on civil liberties since the founding of the republic, abrogating constitutional rights to freedom of speech and assembly, and the vast majority of citizens remained mute, apathetic, or cowed. Antiwar speakers faced arrest and conviction for criticizing the war, informing young men of their rights as draftees, denouncing war profiteers, expressing optimism about the Bolshevik Revolution, displaying a red flag, or writing for a socialist or anarchist publication. Gurley Flynn noted that "'Thou shalt not kill' became subversive doctrine, sending even religious conscientious objectors to prison." By 1918, papers such as *Regeneración* and *Mother Earth* were either shut down or banned from the mails.[30]

Many people whom Parsons knew well, or organizers she had encountered on her trips around the country, now faced long prison terms—Ricardo and Enrique Magón, Ralph Chaplin, Bill Haywood, Vincent Saint John, Eugene Debs, and Elizabeth Gurley Flynn. Cassius V. Cook, who had recently arrived in Chicago to head the League of Humanity, a new civil liberties group, was arrested and charged with conspiracy to obstruct the draft. Debs had declared, "I would rather a thousand times be a free soul in jail than be a coward or a sycophant on the streets. . . . Our hearts are with the Bolsheviki of Russia." Sitting in jail, he once again ran for president and in 1920 polled a million votes, even though the federal government had stripped him of his citizenship. Marie Equi joined the IWW after the Portland cannery strike and participated in militant antiwar marches. Arrested and convicted under the Sedition Act for speaking out against US involvement in the conflict and denouncing those industrialists who profited from it, she was sentenced to San Quentin. The prosecutor in her case had warned the jury that "the red flag is floating over Russia, Germany, and a great part of Europe. *Unless you put this woman in jail*, I tell you it will float over the world!" After an eight-day trial in July 1917, Emma Goldman and Alexander Berkman were convicted of obstructing the draft. The two of them, both "alien anarchists," along with hundreds of others, were deported to Russia the following year.[31]

As this fresh wave of hysteria washed over the country, Parsons chose to focus not on the plight of her friends and acquaintances, but on national cases of individual labor organizers who had been killed by mobs, wrongly accused of violent crimes, or incarcerated for their radical writings—Joe Hill, executed November 15, 1915, for murder; Frank Little, lynched in Butte; Thomas Mooney, convicted of a bombing at a 1916 San Francisco Preparedness Day parade and imprisoned for twenty-two years before he was pardoned. Parsons had refrained from defending the McNamara brothers in the *Los Angeles Times* case. They had no connection to anarchists, though the paper's publisher called them "anarchic scum."[32]

During these years, Parsons's writings were sparse. She did support a short-lived paper—this one, *The Social War*, edited in Chicago by Hippolyte Havel, lasted only a few months, from May to November 1917. According to the first issue, "We want a state of society where the individual, freed from every fetter, having only to fight against natural difficulties, may be able to move at ease, associate according to his needs and affinities, breaking the association whenever it fetters him, or when it shall have accomplished the work for which it was formed, and to re-make other groups, to satisfy fresh needs, and to attain new ends." The paper folded after its editor was called to appear before a Chicago grand jury in September.[33]

On November 11, 1918—the thirty-first anniversary of the Haymarket executions—the Allies signed an armistice with Germany and ended the Great War. Nevertheless, the year 1919 saw the continuation of civil unrest in the United States, with Chicago its epicenter: a toxic mix of labor conflict, racial tensions, and persecution of labor radicals would ensure that the city would have no peace. Strikes engulfed US Steel, Armour and Swift, and International Harvester, part of a general wave of labor actions claiming the energies of four million workers nationwide throughout the early 1920s.

The traumatic events that spanned the twelve months of 1919 paved the way for the ultraconservative politics of the 1920s, as many Americans conflated labor strife and other forms of social conflict with domestic terrorism. Parsons caught a brief glimmer of white working-class consciousness in early 1919 only to see that light quickly extinguished. In January and February, a Seattle shipyard workers' walkout sparked a general strike among employees in a wide range of workplaces throughout the country. Around this time, 3,700 inmates at Leavenworth, many of them her friends, engaged in a massive protest against the lack of food, and the poor quality of what there was of it. In late April a series of booby-trap bombs were sent to politicians, judges, and other prominent Americans, including US Attorney General A. Mitchell Palmer and oil baron John D. Rockefeller. That month, Lucy Parsons announced in *Regeneración*, which was revived after the war, that she intended to begin a speaking tour in the East to defend the jailed Magón brothers and to explain the Mexican Revolution "from the other [i.e.,

Mexican] side." She wrote, "As I read Spanish, I can show what has been accomplished within Mexico, I think."[34]

June brought more domestic terrorist attacks, with eight bombs planted in eight cities, this time larger than the ones used in April, and Palmer targeted again. These bombings were carried out by followers of Luigi Galleani, who was determined to advance Johann Most's "propaganda by deed" with mass murder. The Galleanists told victims of the June 2 bombs: "War, class war, and you were the first to wage it under the cover of the powerful institutions you call order, in the darkness of your laws. There will have to be bloodshed; we will not dodge; there will have to be murder: we will kill, because it is necessary; there will have to be destruction; we will destroy to rid the world of your tyrannical institutions."[35]

On June 5, Chicago police arrested Parsons's lover George Markstall, charging him with making comments that were overheard on a streetcar threatening the life of President Woodrow Wilson. Markstall reportedly exclaimed, "The anarchists will soon run this country. The American people can't stop us." He also called Wilson a "grafter" and said he wished he were "out of the way," ill-timed remarks, coming so soon after the June 2 bombings. Markstall was placed under $10,000 bond, packed off to a psychiatric hospital for observation, and released soon thereafter. The *Tribune* identified him as Parsons's second husband.[36]

On July 27, the sweltering heat sent thousands of Chicagoans to the lakeside. Not far from shore, a black youth named Eugene Williams held on to a railroad tie and drifted perilously close to a segregated beach, provoking a white man to throw a rock at him; Williams drowned. His death and the refusal of police to arrest his assailant led to thirteen days of fighting that left twenty-three blacks and fifteen whites dead and more than five hundred injured. The attacks on black people exposed the social fault lines of Chicago, where whites, regardless of age, religion, or ethnicity, could cheer for the Ku Klux Klan and the "holiness of its exploits."[37]

Three years after the riot, an investigative panel, the Chicago Commission on Race Relations, conducted an in-depth study of the working and living conditions among migrants from the South. Lucy Parsons's theories and writings, derived mostly from European communists and anarchists, seemed wholly divorced from the awful reality faced by black Chicagoans. Between 1917 and 1921, whites set off nearly sixty bombs, which caused thousands of dollars' worth of damage to homes owned by black people and killed two of them, all in an effort to keep black families from moving into white neighborhoods. A handbill distributed by a group of white homeowners screamed, "Shall we sacrifice our property for a third of its value and run like rats from a burning ship, or shall we put up a united front and keep Hyde Park desirable for ourselves?" For radicals who continued to insist that the liberation of the white laboring classes would eradicate prejudice based on skin color, Chicago offered abundant evidence to the contrary.[38]

On August 15, 1919, Albert Parsons Junior died of tuberculosis at Northern Illinois Hospital for the Insane (the Elgin Asylum). He had lived in the asylum for twenty years and fifteen days. Apparently, his father's nephew—General William Parsons's son Edgar—lived in Chicago during this time and received periodic reports from the hospital about Albert Junior's condition. William Parsons's children told Carolyn Ashbaugh, a biographer of Lucy Parsons, that the guards and other inmates had routinely abused him, presumably because of the activities of his notorious mother, and that "he was put in confinement and in constraints, and he repeatedly fought with guards and other patients." On August 18, George Markstall accompanied the body to a local cemetery, where it was cremated. Lucy kept his ashes in her home. She had outlived not only her husband and all her children but also (probably unbeknownst to her) Oliver Benton, who had died in Waco in 1916.[39]

In early September 1919, a group of radicals met in Chicago and founded the Communist Party of the United States of America (CPUSA). William Z. Foster had spent the summer organizing steelworkers, a move that caused their employers to turn to large numbers of Mexican and African American strikebreakers. Around this time, in Centralia, Washington, members of the local American Legion attacked the IWW Hall, whose members had been organizing the region's lumber workers, leaving six dead. Wesley Everest, a Wobbly who was arrested for his part in the melee, was seized from the jail and murdered, another martyr whom Parsons would compare to her husband.

On December 21, when the *Buford* sailed from New York City, among the 249 deportees aboard were Emma Goldman and Alexander Berkman. Luigi Galleani had been sent back to Italy in June.

As the turbulent year of 1919 came to an end and a new decade dawned, George and Lucy were living together on North Troy Street. Boarding with them were a boilermaker and his wife and four children. George was working as a machinist, but Lucy, now sixty-eight years old, had no occupation, perhaps as a result of her failing eyesight. For more than four decades she had proved herself a resilient champion of the dispossessed, grabbing headlines and impressing even younger comrades with her fearlessness. Yet never again would she have access to the kind of boisterous public stage she'd had in the Hull House hunger demonstrations. The 1920s would usher in a new chapter in her life, with her sphere of influence now considerably diminished by her advanced age and by the uniquely reactionary nature of the times.

PART 4

THE FALLING
CURTAIN OF MYSTERY

❦ Chapter 14 ❧

Facts and Fine-Spun Theories

O N WARM-WEATHER DAYS, DENIZENS OF CHICAGO'S LOW-RENT district—called Hobohemia—congregated in leafy Washington Square Park, a vibrant, city-block-sized marketplace of sales pitches and unconventional ideas, where speakers held forth from five scattered soapboxes. Not far west of the mansions lining Lake Shore Drive, the park lived up to its popular name, Bughouse Square—"bughouse" was slang for insane asylum—and attracted political idealists, the artistic avant-garde, runaways, and drifters. In the 1920s, some Bughouse regulars knew Lucy Parsons only as a frail, somewhat eccentric orator among many others of the type; in her long, old-fashioned dress and floppy flowered hat, she looked like an interloper from a bygone era. Yet her voice was still strong, and her name still reverberated among many Hobohemians. A small boy named Louis Terkel who lived near the square was struck by her appearance—"poorly dressed, but genteel," he later recalled—and by her "fiery" speeches. He vividly remembered his amazement at seeing one man, an "old, battered Wobbly," reverently drop a whole dollar into the hat Parsons passed around after one speech. Parsons was in straitened circumstances—George Markstall was often out of work—and so to support herself she spoke frequently in the square. She also kept selling her pamphlets and books, which she carried around in tattered shopping bags.[1]

Now well into her seventies, Lucy Parsons continued to agitate against what she considered Haymarket-like injustices—the incarceration of the Italian anarchists Nicola Sacco and Bartolomeo Vanzetti, who had been accused of murder and armed robbery in Massachusetts, and of the Chicago-born militant socialist Tom Mooney, who was accused of a bombing in San Francisco in 1916. By the mid-1920s, Parsons had joined a new group of comrades in the International Labor Defense (ILD), which, founded in 1925 by Chicago communists, served as the American section of the Soviet Union's International Red Aid network. Its aim was to provide lawyers and arouse public outrage on behalf of jailed leftists. Headed jointly by William Z. Foster and former Wobbly James P. Cannon (until the two had a falling-out in 1928), the ILD never seemed to lack for causes, given the persistently high level of repression against radicals of all stripes during the postwar period. Parsons later explained that she became active in the organization "because I wanted to do a little something to help defend the victims of capitalism who got into trouble, and not always be talking, talking and doing nothing." Yet increasingly, accounts of her speeches appeared not on the front pages of the mainstream press, as they once had, but in nostalgic features, such as "From the *Tribune's* Columns," recounting her exploits ten or twenty-five years before.[2]

In the popular imagination, 1920s Chicago was the era of the Dreamland Ballroom, where a pert, bob-haired flapper, cigarette in one hand and glass of bootlegged gin in the other, swayed to the seductive lyrics of "My daddy rocks me in a steady jelly roll / My daddy rocks me and he never lets go." Yet the reality was less glamourous: The end of the war had ushered in a recession that threw many black people out of work and left many whites chronically underemployed. The drop in demand for labor wiped out the wartime gains made by unions representing the steel, meatpacking, and farm-machinery industries. A continual influx of blacks and Mexicans to Chicago kept wages low and the number of scabs in reserve high. (Perhaps it was not a coincidence that, as Chicago's Mexican immigrant community grew, in her public speeches, at least, Parsons failed to mention her previously oft-repeated claim that she was of indigenous and Spanish descent.) Chicago's largest firms created in-house unions and instituted the trappings of welfare capitalism, as if company baseball teams could compensate for long hours, poor pay, and hazardous working conditions. Finley Peter Dunne, writing as the sharp-eyed Irish immigrant Mr. Dooley, described the employer's ideal company union: "No strikes, no rules, no contracts, no scales, hardly any wages, an' dam' few members." And as unions declined, the ranks of a revived Ku Klux Klan swelled; Chicago proved fertile territory for the Klan's antiblack, antiforeign, anti-Semitic, and anti-Catholic diatribes, and the city was home to 50,000 members of the hate group out of a total of 2 million nationwide.[3]

Lucy Parsons had once lived in a dusty horse-and-buggy Texas cow-town; now, in the 1920s, Chicago's State Street was clogged with automobiles. She and the city had grown up together, and over the decades she watched as the place added hundreds of thousands of people, while Gilded Age inequities persisted despite dramatic structural changes in the economy. And certainly the emergence of a new iteration of the KKK indicated that the more the pace of technological innovation accelerated, the more likely it became that a significant portion of the white laboring classes would seek refuge in a narrow tribalism.

The city still reeked of offal emanating from the stockyards even as it was growing out and up at a rapid rate—its 2.7 million residents in 1920 would mushroom to 3.3 million a decade later. Skyscrapers in the art-deco, neo-Gothic, Beaux Arts, and Prairie styles sprang up on Michigan Avenue and its environs; the magnificent new 605-foot-tall limestone Board of Trade Building on West Jackson Avenue was embellished with stone carvings of crops, and topped off by Ceres, the Roman goddess of grain, on its copper pyramid roof. Yet in the midst of all the new construction and the expanding economy, many Chicagoans continued to live in tight-knit neighborhoods bounded by their workplaces, houses of worship, and cultural and charitable organizations. As always, Democratic and Republican politicians paid only lip service to the laboring classes, denouncing all radicals as foreign and inherently un-American. The object of their ire included the dwindling number of anarchists and Wobblies, which had been weakened almost to extinction by state-sponsored persecution, as well as the members of a new group that had been founded in Chicago in 1919, the Communist Party, acolytes of Russia's revolutionary Bolsheviks. Despite these radicals' thin ranks, as Mother Jones noted, the members of *any* group trying to "turn the world upside down" were dismissed as "Reds."[4]

Parsons saw stubborn continuities even as a powerful new political economy in the form of mobster capitalism was taking hold in the city. In 1923, the gangster Al Capone moved into the Lexington Hotel at East Twenty-Second Street and South Michigan Avenue and began his murderous reign over bootlegging, prostitution, and gambling in the city. Capone operated as the quintessential predatory capitalist; at the same time, his modus operandi departed from that of the anarchists' stereotypical villain: his seat of power was not the workshop or the factory, but the bookie joint, the brothel, the speakeasy, the police station, and the district courthouse. His method of enforcement was not the club-wielding cop or private-security thug, but the loyalist with a Thompson submachine gun, aka the "Chicago typewriter." By 1929 he was making $6 million a week. The political system was corrupt and violent; the "pineapple primary" of 1928 was named for the hand grenades that rival groups of Republicans lobbed at each other.[5]

With their brutal sense of territorial imperative, keen organizational skills, and hypermasculine demeanor, the Prohibition-era gangsters seemed to Chicago elites to resemble nothing so much as leaders of Parsons's beloved trade unions: Did not union leaders and mobsters both extort distributors in an effort to fix prices and fatten their profits at the expense of consumers? Indeed, many politicians and businessmen began to see workers' organizations as inherently criminal enterprises, and, with the backing of local courts, to treat them as such. In 1927, local judges and members of the Employers' Association were using the term "racketeers" to describe not only bootleggers but also organized barbers, dry cleaners, and truckers. Labor unions in general felt the full weight of "anti-corruption" courts and prosecutors.[6]

Meanwhile, Chicagoans gradually began to create new kinds of communities among themselves, proclaiming themselves "fans" of certain movie actors, radio and nightclub singers, and professional athletic teams. They listened to political debates, comedy, and music on the radio station WGN (sponsored by the *Chicago Tribune*—"the world's greatest newspaper")—including new musical forms, such as jazz, rag-time, and the blues, which had been brought north by Louis Armstrong and other southern black migrants. Moviegoers flocked to the immense Uptown Theater, a 25,000-square-foot "picture palace" in the Spanish Renaissance style with a 34-piece orchestra, a staff of 130, and seats for 4,400 patrons. On the silver screen Hollywood glorified gangster shootouts with the cops.[7]

The ideal of a wageless economy, a cooperative commonwealth, had long since receded. The masses had turned out to be consumers, not rev-olutionaries. Now people worked to make money, not just to feed their families, but also to buy new radios, phonographs, telephones, and tick-ets to movie theaters and amusement parks. As the sociologists Robert and Helen Lynd observed in 1925, "more and more of the activities of living [were] strained through the bars of the dollar sign." These new consumer communities forged social bonds that at times competed with those among workers on the job, in the union hall, or on the picket line.[8]

Despite her involvement in the International Labor Defense, Par-sons regretted her own increasingly constricted world of action and thought. She wrote to her old friends Cassius and Sadie Cook (they were by this time divorced, he living in Los Angeles, she in Chicago) lamenting that "the dreams of us dreamers, are, after all, but dreams; iridesent [sic] dreams!" Chicago possessed a vibrant cultural scene, but to Parsons the city seemed pinched, parochial, ungenerous: "The great, rushing, restless, headless mob, called 'the public,' or the people, care nothing, absolutely nothing for the pleadings and philosophizing of the radical who wishes to change the economic conditions," Parsons wrote her friends. "There is careless indifference, a supreme contempt for all progressive ideas that is simply amazing!" She advised them, "Lay a solid foundation for your *personal* comfort when the shadows of life's journey are slanting toward the setting sun."[9]

Politically, Parsons found herself caught between her anarchist principles and the communists' headline-grabbing activism. By this time, the center of American anarchism had shifted from the Germans and the Russian Jews of Chicago to the Italians of Boston and New York. Younger Chicago anarchists honored Parsons's effort to keep alive the Haymarket legacy, but some, such as Irving Abrams (a member of the Pioneer Aid and Support Association), considered her a dupe of the communists because of her new association with the ILD. The communists, in turn, labeled her a purveyor of hopelessly outdated ideas favoring anarcho-syndicalism. (The term, which came into use in the 1920s, was a new label for Parsons's long-held belief that trade unions were the vehicles of revolutionary change—the overthrow of the wage system and capitalism.) In Chicago, the Communist Party of the United States of America (CPUSA) underwent bitter factional fights, splintering in the process. The IWW seemed to recover from the government repression of World War I only to cannibalize itself in its own disputes over ideology and decentralized leadership over the next two years. For yet another period of her life, Lucy Parsons found herself with no natural political home.[10]

AFTER WORLD WAR I, PARSONS MADE FEWER OUT-OF-TOWN TRIPS. She apparently visited Bartolomeo Vanzetti in prison in Charlestown, Massachusetts, in 1923 (a trip paid for by the men's defense committee), and on occasion she represented the ILD at official events. Still, increasingly, she traveled outside Chicago under the cloak of anonymity, in contrast to her speaking tours of old, when the mainstream press had covered her obsessively. Now she generally confined her perambulations to Chicago's Water Tower neighborhood, defined by the landmark 1869 North Michigan Avenue structure that survived the Great Fire of 1871, and to the West Side of the city. Living in her longtime home in the "Old World ghetto" of North Troy Street, she would take a streetcar for the four-and-a-half-mile ride to Bughouse Square on Walton and the Dil Pickle Club tucked away in Tooker Alley. On the West Side was Turner Hall, at Twelfth and Halsted, Wobbly headquarters at 1001 West Madison, the ILD offices at 23 South Lincoln Street, and Ben Reitman's Hobo College in a basement at Washington and Desplaines, where university professors debated politics with the homeless and the unemployed.[11]

It was a well-trod sidewalk that took Parsons around the block from Bughouse Square to the Dil Pickle, Chicago's lively public-forum-*cum*-coffeehouse operated by the estranged husband of Elizabeth

Gurley Flynn, Jack Jones. (The couple had married in 1908, separated in 1910, and divorced in 1920.) An unprepossessing entrance led into a converted barn furnished with chairs and benches, a lectern, a sandwich and coffee bar, and a stage. In the evenings, speakers expounded on a range of topics, from birth control and homosexuality to vegetarianism and Hinduism. There, patrons could hear Gordon Owens of the African Blood Brotherhood speak on black nationalism (the absence of a color line was an unusual feature for even the most daring free-speech forum); Harry "Kill Christ" Wilson on atheism; and Dorothy Day on Catholic socialism. Poetry as a form of political advocacy found expression in the works of Ralph Chaplin and journalist Carl Sandburg, who were regulars at both IWW headquarters and the Pickle. Sandburg described his ambitions: "I had high hopes the new poetry one way or another would be able to get at the real stuff of American life, slipping its fingers into the steel meshes and copper coils of it under the streets and over the houses and people and factories and groceries."[12]

Although Lucy Parsons made appearances at the Pickle during its heyday, from 1917 to 1926 or so, she was not a regular, nor did she see the raucous place as a particularly congenial space. A number of her old acquaintances, including George Schilling and August Spies's wife-by-proxy, Nina van Zandt, frequented the club, and she empathized with the prostitutes, alcoholics, and hoboes who gathered there (the "tramps" of her 1884 manifesto), but many of the patrons shared neither her class consciousness nor her voracious reading habits. She probably agreed, at least in theory, with the premise that a panhandler, con artist, or roughneck had just as much to say about the meaning of life as a Northwestern University sociologist—in fact, the Pickle was "looking for bums who talked like professors," according to one patron—but, as someone who had always aspired to a higher level of respectability, she was likely offended by the profusion of self-proclaimed "cranks" and misfits. The sign outside the club warned: "Step high, stoop low, and leave your dignity outside."[13]

Moreover, with their dilettantish ways, members of the "Near North Side intelligentsia" probably struck her as silly and self-indulgent. No doubt she also objected to the Pickle's performative culture—its motto was "Heckling Is a Fine Art and Intelligence Sandbags the

Cliché-Klingers," and Parsons always hated interruptions from the audience. Yet there were moments to savor: a game requiring players to talk about a topic for three minutes one night featured the Irish-born former-Wobbly-turned-communist Jim Larkin on the necktie: "There are all kinds of neckties. There is the bow, the four-in-hand, the Ascot, the striped, the plaid, the polka dot. . . . But the greatest tie a man ever wore, was the tie in the rope around his neck when he went to the scaffold for freedom."[14]

Parsons appeared at least once at the Dil Pickle with Martha ("Red Martha") Biegler, a tall, imposing woman who had graduated from Indiana University with a major in philosophy. In 1919, the fifty-five-year-old "Field Marshal" Biegler enlisted Parsons as a speaker on the topic "Women Are the Slaves of Men's Suppression, Oppression, and Depression." The program had been announced in a local labor paper as intending to "prove the majority of men are low-grade morons." Frank O. Beck, an ordained Methodist preacher and chronicler of Hobohemia, probably had Parsons in mind when he wrote that Biegler's acquaintances "included almost all of the manifold varieties of female crackpots of the city's underworld."[15]

Such language suggests how Parsons had become something of a cultural artifact, an object of curiosity among Chicago's middle classes. Frank Beck and Ben Reitman sponsored what they called Fellowship of Reconciliation tours, which catered to the city's reformers and intellectuals and to college students who saw encounters with the city's "exotics" as a form of high-minded entertainment. Bringing well-to-do whites in conversation with sexologists, black activists, labor radicals, and diverse clergy, the all-day bus tours cost 50 cents a person and alighted at stops around the city, with short lectures punctuating the day. A story in the Northwestern University student newspaper chronicled a trip to "Little Hell" (a reference to a Sicilian-immigrant neighborhood at the time) that included a visit to the Dil Pickle, where Lucy Parsons "described vividly some of the revolutionary leaders she has known." (The headline read "Atheists, Free Lovers, Hoboes Discourse on World Ills.") Later, Beck would write that Parsons, at his behest, had often recounted her life's journey to small groups of college students. Her lectures on Haymarket, the IWW, the history of anarchism, and other aspects of her background—including her early years as Lucy Diaz, born in El Paso, Texas—earned her a little cash and kept her in the public eye, but definitely not in the political vanguard where she had once been.[16]

THE EARLY 1920S CAUSED PARSONS TO DESPAIR, AND WITH GOOD reason. Many of her old Wobbly comrades had emerged from prison broken in health and spirit, ready to give up the fight and the IWW. Ralph Chaplin was the exception: in his memoir, *Wobbly*, he recounted in graphic detail the ordeals that he and other alleged "conspirators" had faced at the hands of sadistic guards and prison wardens—including being handcuffed to the bars of their cells, beaten mercilessly, thrown into isolation for months at a time, and starved nigh unto death. Richard Flores Magón, in the cell next to his, had a heart attack and died in the absence of timely medical care. The physical and emotional torture exacted a lasting toll: "We had to harden ourselves in order to avoid cracking up," Chaplin wrote. "I have seen strong men broken and weak men hounded to madness." Nevertheless, when President Warren G. Harding commuted his sentence in 1923, Chaplin immediately returned to work for the IWW, now in San Francisco as an editor of *Industrial Worker*, bent on exposing unions that were under the sway of dictatorial strongmen.[17]

Other Wobblies, including Jay Fox, Sam Hammersmark, and Elizabeth Gurley Flynn, embraced the Communist Party as a harbinger of a worldwide revolution. Some former anarchists turned to Christianity, or sought out a reclusive life. Honoré Jaxon moved to the Bronx, where he built a dwelling out of pieces of wood and corrugated tin, and dabbled in real estate. Nina van Zandt ran a Chicago boardinghouse, where she took in stray cats and dogs. Her speech, dress, and movements became increasingly erratic, distressing those who remembered her as the glamorous society girl in love with the handsome, doomed anarchist.

With communists in the ascendancy and anarchists of the old school in a state of dissolution, Parsons found herself in the middle of debates over the meaning of the new Soviet Union. Such debates divided formerly like-minded individuals, tearing apart radical newspaper staffs, communes, and alternative schools all over the country. Exiled to Russia, Emma Goldman had quickly become disillusioned with the Soviet Union's totalitarian tactics in suppressing dissent. In an interview with a *Chicago Tribune* reporter, she declared that "Bolshevism is rotten"; the Soviet people, she said, were "entirely subject to the whims of a bureaucracy which excuses its tyranny on the ground. It all is done for the welfare of the workers." Goldman wrote to Eugene Debs in 1926 that Soviet Russia was but "a delusion and snare. That in its stead there is a machine which has a stranglehold on the Russian masses and which is undermining the true revolutionary elements as represented by the socialist and anarchist wings in the country." Bill Haywood, in contrast, remained a staunch supporter of the Bolsheviks, and he was disgusted that Goldman would withdraw her support for them. He had fled to Russia while out on bail in April 1921, leaving his comrades back home with the immense task of paying his $61,000 bond. He took Goldman to task, at one point invoking Lucy Parsons, who, he claimed, rightly or wrongly, "severely criticizes Emma Goldman because she sold herself to the capitalist press of the United States. She characterizes the Goldman articles as a rehash of the supercilious vapourings of capitalist reporters."[18]

Parsons defended the Bolsheviks through the 1920s, although later she would admit that the news out of Russia in those years was too spotty to allow for reasoned judgments to be made about the emerging soviets. She rationalized the bloody suppression of rebellious sailors in the port city of Kronstadt in 1921 by arguing that the revolution must be secured at all costs, and that by taking up arms against the new government, the sailors were by definition reactionary enemies of the state. The fact that the Bolsheviks used military force—well, there was "nothing new about it." She almost certainly did not learn about the fate of her comrades Aron and Fanny Baron, with whom she had marched in the 1915 hunger demonstration. Full of hope, in 1917 the couple had returned to Kiev, where Aron was elected as a delegate to the Soviet of Workers' Deputies. Soon both he and Fannie began to denounce the Bolsheviks as agents of totalitarianism, and together the couple launched a new anarchist paper. Feared by Communist Party leaders, Fannie was executed for terrorism in 1921. Over the next sixteen years Aron Baron was in and out of Soviet prisons and concentration camps. He remained steadfast through hunger strikes, exile, and hard labor, never renouncing his conviction that the party had betrayed the ideals of the revolution. He was executed in 1937.[19]

Parsons remained alert to the possibilities of introducing a new generation to Haymarket, and finding fresh markets for her books. In the spring of 1922, she reacted indignantly to the recent publication of *Daily News* editor Melville Stone's book *Fifty Years a Journalist*. In the book and in magazine articles, Stone claimed that venerated Chicago socialist George Schilling, among others, had regularly informed him of "the progress of 'the impending revolution.'" Parsons's defense of Schilling rested on the fact that he had never been "a part of the revolutionary anarchist groups," as Stone alleged. Parsons did, however, confirm that Stone had offered a "substantial monetary consideration" if Albert would surrender to him and not the court in June 1886. (Albert's attorney, Captain Black, had declined the offer.) This spat over Stone's book offered Parsons an opportunity to send letters to the editors of several newspapers and remind readers about the history of Haymarket.[20]

In March 1926, Parsons wrote to Eugene Debs to congratulate him on his decision not to beg for the restoration of his citizenship after his release from prison in 1921. She saluted him as "Grand Old Rebel!" and reminded him that her husband, too, had refused to prostrate himself before a judge for a pardon. Furthermore, she noted, if Debs saw fit to cite her works in his own writings, he should note that *Life of Albert R. Parsons* was available for $3.25, and a copy of *Speeches* could be had for $1.25. Debs died in October of that year, his health compromised by long years of incarceration. In an elegy for the famous socialist, Sandburg wrote, "Over in Valhalla, if Valhalla is not demolished, rebuilt, renamed, he [Debs] speaks at ease with Garrison, John Brown, Albert Parsons, Spartacus."[21]

Parsons lost a number of other comrades during the 1920s, including those with direct links to Haymarket and the IWW. Bill Haywood died alone and embittered in a Moscow hotel room in 1928. His ashes were divided between the Kremlin Wall and Waldheim Cemetery. Lizzie Swank Holmes died in Denver in 1926, and her husband, William, died two years later. Mother Jones rallied striking Chicago dressmakers in 1924; it would be her last visit to the city before her death in 1930. Gone by the late 1920s were virtually all the other principals of the Haymarket trial, including Samuel Fielden, who died in 1921, the last remaining defendant, and the only one not to be buried at Waldheim; Judge Joseph Gary; the twelve jurors; all the lawyers except for Sigmund Zeisler; the seven justices of the Illinois Supreme Court; and the nine justices of the US Supreme Court.

Parsons's personal losses, combined with the fractious relations among radicals in the city and beyond, left her bereft of an ideological community. By simultaneously maintaining ties with the communist International Labor Defense and its bitter rivals, the Free Society Group and the IWW (which had its own Workers' Defense League), she managed to alienate at least some members of all these groups. At the same time, she had to deal with young labor radicals, mostly men, who were determined to start over and remake the world. Some—no doubt those whom she considered ill-informed—found her sharp-tongued, quick to ridicule them and to belittle their ideas. She refused to mellow with age.[22]

One of these young men was Sam Dolgoff, a house painter. Born in Russia in 1902, he moved to the United States as a child, and in the early 1920s became a Wobbly and a popular Bughouse soapboxer. He met Parsons at a Free Society Group when she congratulated him on a paper he delivered, "Is Anarcho-Syndicalism Possible?" (His answer was not only yes, but yes, it was inevitable.) Though Dolgoff was dismayed when she became what he called a "Communist sympathizer," he took it upon himself to respond to charges leveled by his comrades that she was a "turncoat." He believed, instead, that "she was very naïve." Moreover, "she was not able to grasp the distinction between anarchism and bolshevism and other ideologies. For her, anyone against capitalism was ipso facto a revolutionist and she saw no reason why all of them should not bury the hatchet and get together." And then came the most cutting comment: "Besides, she was most susceptible to flattery, which the communists applied in large doses."[23]

Dolgoff was probably referring to the blandisher James P. Cannon, secretary of the ILD from 1925 to 1928. Cannon had joined the Wobblies in 1911 at the age of twenty-one and, under the tutelage of

Haywood, had set about organizing workers in his native Kansas and the greater Midwest. When he read *Speeches* in 1917, the story of the Haymarket martyrs made a lasting impression on him. He joined the communists and, after a brief visit to the new Soviet Union, moved to Chicago, where William Z. Foster introduced him to Parsons. Cannon seemed to have a genuine appreciation for the legendary Mrs. Parsons, and he was eager to use her name and still considerable oratorical abilities to advance the ILD. In seeking to win her favor, he made sure that the ILD sold her books and gave her the proceeds.[24]

Parsons was drawn to the ILD for a number of reasons. Ever since she had embarked on her defense-fund tour of the country through the fall of 1886 and the spring of 1887, she had argued for the creation of a permanent organization that could pay the legal fees of jailed leftists. She had known Foster for many years. Perhaps she paid close attention to the early defense efforts of Sacco and Vanzetti, which seemed to prove the deficiencies of anarchism as a means of coordinating legal strategy. Italian anarchist defense committee members on the East Coast remained true to their principles, rejecting effective organization and snubbing potential middle-class allies in the effort to save the accused men.[25]

Parsons found the Sacco and Vanzetti case a worthy claim on her money and energies because of the trial's familiar themes of prejudiced judge and packed jury, which created real doubts about the defendants' responsibility for the murder of which they were convicted. Subsumed under that popular narrative, however, was the fact that both men had professed devotion to the militant, bomb-throwing Galleanists. And it is possible that, to avenge their arrests, one of their compatriots was responsible for the Wall Street explosion on September 16, 1920, that killed thirty-eight people—not the lords of finance, but messengers, clerks, and bookkeepers. Vanzetti was pleased with her visit, remarking in the fall of 1923 that of all the people in the world, he had wished to meet Eugene Debs and Lucy Parsons, and his wish had come true. Despite the worldwide outcry over the unfair trial that Sacco and Vanzetti received, the two were put to death in 1927. Cannon sought to make the relevance of Haymarket explicit, writing, "America shows its real face to the world and the mask of democracy is thrown aside."[26]

That year Parsons joined the ILD executive committee, which included the writer Upton Sinclair as well as Elizabeth Gurley Flynn, Clarence Darrow, and Ralph Chaplin, among others. At the November annual meeting in New York City (which also marked the fortieth anniversary of Haymarket), she was the guest of honor, accepting accolades from the 286 delegates representing thirty countries. The following year she lectured in support of the ILD in Milwaukee and Cleveland, where activists cheered her, a living link to history, and in 1930 she made an appearance in Detroit, home to an ILD branch that was named for her.[27]

Although Parsons worked with the ILD, she eschewed any broader participation in Chicago's Communist Party. In July 1929, she wrote a piece for the ILD's monthly *Equal Justice*—the renamed *Labor Defender*—focusing on a textile workers' strike in Gastonia, North Carolina. Communists helped to lead the strike, but Parsons confined her observations to a warning that an upcoming trial of its leaders might rely on twelve openly prejudiced jurors: if so, she wrote, "the electric chair looms in the not far distance!" As was now customary, her purview remained limited to Haymarket and the state's efforts to frame innocent men and women, rather than extending to the injustices that had prompted the workers to strike to begin with.[28]

Still, for Parsons, aspects of the party's activities in the 1920s must have recalled the 1880s, a time of mass demonstrations and surefire certainty that lessons from abroad would speed the revolution at home. Sponsoring concerts, picnics, and other social events to build solidarity and raise money for the *Daily Worker*, the party evoked the efforts of the German immigrant anarchists to support *The Alarm* years before. And, much like the anarchists of the late nineteenth century, the communists ultimately fell victim to infighting and factional disputes; as one Chicago Communist Party member put it, no doubt referring, at least in part, to the split between Foster and Cannon, the "political differences hardened into personal antagonisms. . . . The factionalism was incapacitating the Party, and we were unable to resolve it ourselves."[29]

Nevertheless, Chicago communists were notable for their willingness to break from the tradition of socialists, anarchists, Democrats, and Republicans and began to address black civil rights. In 1915, the head of the Soviet Communist Party, Vladimir Lenin, declared

southern black sharecroppers to be a modern vanguard of the proletariat, and later the Communist International (Comintern) argued
that black Americans were deserving of their own "nation-within-a-
nation" status. Chicago party members launched concerted organizing
efforts on the city's South Side. They hoped to tap into the deep well
of discontent among the black men and women who lived there and
help them win real power, in contrast to what they considered to be the
window-dressing offered by established local organizations, such as the
National Urban League and the NAACP.

The ghetto, hailed as a "Black Metropolis," boasted large black-
owned businesses, such as Robert Abbott's *Defender* and Jesse Binga's
bank, as well as a flowering of the arts akin to the Harlem renaissance
during the same decade. Community leaders, so-called New Negroes,
expressed a relentless optimism for the future if only residents would
patronize their neighbors' stores and professional services in the area,
which was, in the words of writer Dempsey J. Travis, "100 percent black
after sundown when the white landlords and merchants closed their
offices and shops and went home to the suburbs."[30]

Such boosterism, however, could not overcome the effects of the
recession on Chicago's black population. Throughout the 1920s, at a
time when black musicians, painters, and writers were experimenting
and innovating, black workers were suffering from high unemployment
and chronic layoffs. Investigators from the Women's Bureau of the US
Department of Labor documented the health risks and occupational
hazards borne by black women who worked at washing the fat off slabs
of meat, packing sausages, and stacking boxes. These workers were
forced to stand all day to do their jobs, and the toilets made available
to them were dirty and unventilated. In the early evening, workers returned home to dark, cramped rooms where the commotion emanating
from next-door speakeasies and brothels made it difficult to get a good
night's sleep.[31]

Not all white communists believed it necessary to reach out to
blacks. The views of Karl Marx (which Parsons had spent much of her
life promoting) held that black people constituted a subset of workers and not a unique, historically aggrieved group in their own right.
Furthermore, in the 1920s, the Communist Party in Chicago persisted

in elevating dogmatism over pragmatism (and common sense), alternately refusing to reach out to the black community and reaching out in a way that was hamstrung by ideology: the party attacked A. Philip Randolph and his new all-black union of 12,000 members, the Brotherhood of Sleeping Car Porters, on the grounds that it was insufficiently radical and hence harmful to the well-being of the working class as a whole. White party leaders disapproved of all forms of profit-making, seemingly oblivious to the fact that successful black businesses were the pride of the South Side. The charge that government workers were puppets of capitalist masters found little traction among blacks in a city where almost a third of all postal carriers were black, the highest rate in the nation, and where southern migrants saw the ballot as a precious, hard-won right. To entertain and instruct South Side residents, communist groups staged Russian plays with Russian actors speaking Russian. The party founded a workers' group, the American Negro Labor Congress (ANLC), in 1925, only to see it founder from doctrinal squabbling within a couple of years. Some members argued that even anti-lynching campaigns were an unnecessary distraction from the class struggle.[32]

At the same time, a host of other groups competed aggressively for black membership and dollars—among them the NAACP and the Urban League, which both focused on opening up "white" jobs to blacks; and the black nationalist Universal Negro Improvement Association and African Blood Brotherhood, attempts to offer an alternative to the communists' ANLC. In the eyes of William Foster and other whites, black-led groups, including churches, were little more than bourgeois collaborators, and all black people remained a "problem." Parsons, however, was not a part of these discussions, in keeping with her lifelong effort to distance herself from black struggles.

On May 1, 1930, Chicago communists led an estimated 25,000 marchers through the West Side, an event advertised via 200,000 leaflets distributed throughout the city in the weeks before. The procession, which was escorted by a squad of police on motorcycles, featured marchers singing Russian folk songs and carrying red banners. At the end of the route, the march culminated with an address by Lucy Parsons to a mass meeting in Ashland Auditorium. At the beginning of her speech, Parsons expressed the fear that her voice was not strong enough to carry through the vast hall—not because of her advanced age, but because of the poor acoustics, she assured the crowd—and then took the audience back to 1886, when thousands of men, women, and children walked off the job and told the bosses, "I will be damned if I go back to work under such conditions."[33]

Parsons said she had lived long enough to know that each generation of radicals left its own mark on history, and she believed that the communists would "go on and on, and will not pass away like the other organizations, because I think they have the substantiality." Nevertheless, she must have startled her hosts when she declared, "I am an anarchist: I have no apology to make to a single man, woman, or child, because I am an anarchist, because anarchism carries the very germ of liberty in its womb." She took heart from the size of the audience, people willing to "drop their work in times like this, when work is so scarce, to come out in the mid-week [Thursday] and defy the capitalist classes, and come out in the sunlight." Holding aloft a scarlet cloth, she recited a poem: "The workers' flag is deepest red / It shrouded oft our martyred dead." In the near future, she predicted, women would not have to sell their bodies for a morsel to eat, able-bodied men would not lack for work, children would not have to toil in a factory. She ended by extolling her dead husband and his comrades for their noble and enduring contributions to the class struggle. And if anyone wanted to learn more, they could purchase copies of her edition of their speeches, available right there in the hall that day.[34]

The stock market crash of October 1929 plunged Chicago and the rest of the country into a deep economic depression. Because of its factory base and shaky municipal finances, the city immediately registered the dire effects of bank closures and the lack of available credit. The few unions in the city were either too weak to act, or too corrupt to care. Within a few months, unemployment was approaching a third of the working-age population—with fully half of all black workers and manual laborers unable to find jobs. Religious and private charities were overwhelmed by the needs of destitute families. Between 1930 and 1940, the city's population of 3,376,438 would grow by only 20,000, a sure sign that the local economy had ground to a virtual halt.

When the federal census-taker came calling in the spring of 1930, Parsons offered a narrative of her life: She reported that she was the proprietor of a boardinghouse and had two lodgers: the sixty-six-year-old marble-cutter Charles Condo (Secondo), who had boarded with her since 1896; and George Markstall, who reported his occupation as drill press operator. She said she was sixty-five years old (in fact she was seventy-nine), and she estimated the value of her frame house at $6,000 (about $83,000 in today's money). Her anarchist colleague Irving Abrams, who remained active in the Pioneer Aid and Support Association, later claimed that Parsons and Markstall had married in 1927, but it is doubtful that the antigovernment couple formalized their union in any way. No marriage certificate is on file in the Cook County offices.

Lucy Parsons had lived and worked through several devastating economic downturns. (In 1931, the *Cleveland Plain Dealer* reminded its readers that periodic high rates of unemployment among the laboring classes were to be expected, quoting from a speech that Parsons had delivered in Chicago in August 1893.) She was accustomed, too, to the relentless self-promotion of elites even in the midst of widespread suffering. Sixty years after her husband toured the Inter-State Industrial Exposition during the recession of 1873, and forty years after the World's Columbian Exposition was staged amid the depression of 1893, Chicago sponsored the Century of Progress Exposition, with the motto "Science Finds, Industry Applies, Man Conforms." For Parsons, the six-month spectacle meant only the possibility of a reunion with a few "Old Timers," as fellow radicals traveled to Chicago to take in the event.[35]

During the depression, Parsons was deeply disappointed that so many Chicago workers enthusiastically supported the Democratic Party and the federal initiatives of the Franklin D. Roosevelt administration. Beginning soon after his inauguration in January 1933 and continuing through 1938, Roosevelt ushered through Congress a series of legislative initiatives designed to smooth the rough edges of industrial capitalism—unemployment compensation, minimum wages and maximum hours, and Social Security, as well as public jobs programs and temporary cash aid. Prohibition was repealed, and the courts gradually reversed the restrictions on free speech that had been the hallmark of the World War I era. Yet neither radicalism nor repression ended. The

Congress of Industrial Organizations (CIO), which included unions in mining, car manufacturing, steel, and meatpacking, was birthed in bloody strikes in Chicago, Detroit, and elsewhere. On Memorial Day Sunday in 1937, striking Chicago steelworkers picnicking with their families were attacked by the police; in what became known as the Memorial Day massacre, ten people were killed (most of them shot in the back) and at least one hundred wounded. Louis Terkel—later better known by his nickname, Studs—observed sardonically, "Baskets of fried chicken, pierogi, potato salad and cole slaw were the picknickers' weapons in a full-fire zone." The next day, the *Tribune's* front-page headline read, "Police Repulse Mob Attack."[36]

Many years before, Parsons might have seen in such an outrage the dawning of a revolution in the form of a new burst of organizing on behalf of the aggressive, militant CIO. Now, however, she expressed profound disillusionment with craft unions, such as the carpenters and milk-wagon drivers, trade groups run by hierarchical, rule-laden bureaucracies. Moreover, despite attacks from both the Left and the Right over the years, the two-party system remained intact; seeking to capture the center, the Democrats had never truly delivered for the laboring classes. And so she lauded the communists for what they were doing to move the country forward: "They are very good propagandists; they stir things up," she said, referring to the neighborhood Unemployed Councils, citywide mass protests, and militant union-organizing drives. During the first five years of the Great Depression, the party would lead or take part in more than 2,000 demonstrations. Intrepid CIO organizers, and especially the women, acknowledged their debt to Parsons's long history of labor agitation. Vera Buch Weisbord (a socialist-turned-communist, and organizer of textile and maritime workers) and others found themselves star-struck in her presence, honored to grasp her hand. To them, Parsons always seemed taller than she really was because they were accustomed to seeing her on a raised platform looking down upon their upturned, eager faces.[37]

Parsons continued to support the ILD and to represent it in public. In March 1932, she appeared at a mass protest meeting with two other women whose male kin had endured persecution at the hands of the so-called justice system—Mary Mooney, eighty-four, the mother

of jailed labor leader Tom Mooney, and Viola Montgomery, mother of
Olen Montgomery, one of the young Scottsboro men who were falsely
accused of raping two white women on a train the year before. Viola
Montgomery had undertaken a nationwide speaking tour to publicize
the plight of not only her son and the other eight young men but also
black women of the rural South. Appealing to mothers everywhere, she
wrote, "I tell the world that I am a working woman and an unhappy
one because I all ways [sic] worked and I could not have nothing that
I wanted nice to eat or wear." A remarkable photograph published by
the *Tribune* on March 19, 1932, shows Parsons standing between Montgomery and Mooney at the Waldheim memorial, perhaps the only time
in her life that she joined forces—even for an evening—with another
African American woman speaker-activist.[38]

Throughout the 1930s, Parsons stuck to her anarchistic principles;
she believed that the New Deal and its agent the Democratic Party
would prove not only inadequate to the task of crushing the capitalistic
system but absolutely destructive of radical possibilities. The Roosevelt
administration's policies amounted to a "wind that has blown the radical movement to Hell!" she declared. The initial flurry of legislation
meant that "despotism is on horseback riding at high speed." Anarchists in general were appalled that support for a strong federal government had gained radical cachet, and, even more distressing, that their
own opposition to an emerging welfare state now put them in the same
political camp as the abhorrent business-minded Republicans. Many
workers maintained a faith in capitalism—or perhaps, more accurately,
the *idea* of capitalism—and looked to the Democrats and large industrial unions to tinker with the system in ways that mitigated the un-
certainty of old age and periodic unemployment. The new CIO would
seem to resemble the IWW, but, according to anarchists, it merely bolstered industrial capitalism; and its duplicitous leader, John L. Lewis of
the United Mine Workers, was all too eager to toady to the Democrats.
Most of the much-heralded social-welfare legislation applied only to
employees in large plants; deprived of basic worker protections were all
seasonal, agricultural, domestic-service, and part-time laborers.[39]

By 1934, both the Communist Party and the ILD were allying with
liberal reform groups, noncommunist unions, and even the Democrats

in a reformist turn called the Popular Front. The party also took to embracing the Founding Fathers; presumably Benjamin Franklin, like Lenin, was an idealist and "tactically flexible." CP leaders expressed general support for many New Deal initiatives. In Chicago, party members engaged in grassroots organizing on the South Side, where fully 90 percent of the black population was impoverished. Here was a modern dystopian cooperative commonwealth with an informal, wageless economy. In researching their book *Black Metropolis*, sociologists St. Clair Drake and Horace R. Cayton found that "a girl might 'do the hair' of a neighbor in return for permission to use her pots and pans. Another woman might trade some bread for a glass of milk. There was seldom any money to lend or borrow, but the bartering of services and utensils was general." Local black groups sponsored "Don't Buy Where You Can't Work" campaigns, and neighbors threw rent parties—where party guests paid admission to raise funds for someone's rent—to forestall foreclosure.[40]

Subsisting on a functionary's wage of $5 a week, Steve Nelson and other white communists working on the South Side soon learned that ordinary people had no interest in the fine points of communist dogma, but did need help in applying for government aid and paying for groceries. He noted, "We couldn't just give speeches about the downfall of capitalism, and we couldn't lead from a distance. We had to be with the people." Likewise, Vera Buch Weisbord applauded incremental gains, but termed her own activism on behalf of the party "the long wait." The New York politician Adam Clayton Powell Jr. acknowledged the tentative, contingent appeal of the communists for ordinary black men and women: "The Negro neither fears the communist nor leans over backwards in admiration. The communist is the same to him as a Holy Roller, Republican, or Elk. He is just another human being to be judged individually on one basis—is he fighting for full and complete opportunity for black people?"[41]

Interviewed by the *Daily Worker* in April 1934, Parsons (described as "this grey-haired woman") drew parallels between the communists' Popular Front and the "united front" that had brought together unions of all kinds on the first of May in 1886. Now, forty-eight years later, she was the honorary chair of the Chicago May Day parade. A living symbol of the class struggle, she was happy to recall the events leading up to Haymarket: "This woman, sitting in her rocking chair, her chin cupped in her hand, is an inspiration to every worker," wrote the *Daily Worker*. "She is herself part of the revolutionary tradition of the Chicago working class, a tradition that survives and is carried on by the Communist Party, a tradition that will smash through every effort of the Social-fascists to divide and confuse the workers."[42]

Interviews like this one prompted Parsons to look back to the heady days of her past and contemplate her own mortality. She recalled old comrades and wondered who among them had "checked out for the undiscovered country." She donated Albert's notes of his trial, together with the scrapbooks with clippings from her first national speaking tour, to the University of Wisconsin. She wrote to George Schilling, addressing him as "Dear Old Friend," asking if he thought human nature tended toward love or hate. She assured friends that she was not a member of the CP but continued to work with its members, "as they are the *only* bunch who are making a vigorous protest against the present horrible conditions!" Her failing eyesight left her despondent, barely able to read or write.[43]

Meanwhile, Parsons and her small circle of friends continued to "get together in our little groups, talk to each other and go home." In a reflective mood, she mourned the fact that "anarchism has not produced any organizing ability in the present generation, only a few little, loose struggling groups scattered over this vast country" that met intermittently and then dissolved until the next gathering. Such sporadic activity hardly constituted a "movement," she admitted. At the same time, she blamed herself and her comrades, who, for the past half-century, had been skilled "at showing the shortcomings of others," but totally unable to achieve tangible gains. Ultimately, "this busy, practical world cares nothing for fine-spun theories; they want facts and[,] too, they want a few examples shown." In short, she concluded, "anarchism is a dead issue in American life today."[44]

Nevertheless, as always, Parsons was able to muster enough energy for some score-settling. She had read Emma Goldman's 993-page autobiography, *Living My Life*, soon after it came out in 1931, and considered it worthless for revolutionists eager to discover a way forward. In a letter to Carl Nold, she wrote, "This great big busy world cares but little about Emma Goldman's scraps with the cops 25 years ago, at least not enough to pay $7.50 good dollars to learn it, at least this is my Judgement, I may be mistaken." However, she saved her harshest words for what she called the "sex stuff," an affront to the "thoughtful element." "Just why she [Goldman] should have thought it interesting or instructive, or educating to list 15 of her 'lovers' is beyond me to understand," she wrote Nold. "Certainly it is a poor specimen of a woman who can't get a number of you men to accommodate her Sexually." Parsons considered Goldman's graphic account of her love affair with Reitman to be "Simply disgusting!" to any readers but those of a "debasted [sic] and depraved mind."[45]

For her part, the exiled Goldman cited Parsons as an example of a radical undone by her own moral weakness. She recalled the Martin Lacher scandal three decades before, when Parsons "dragged a man she had been living with into court over a few pieces of furniture." Such was human frailty: "It's in people; the movement or lack of it has nothing to do with such things." She also indicted Parsons for her inconstancy in "go[ing] with every gang proclaiming itself revolutionary, the IWW [and] now the communists. Not to speak of her horrible treatment of [Albert R.] Parsons' son, whom she drove into the army and then had him put in a lunatic asylum."[46]

Parsons's social life now consisted of mostly modest pleasures. She entertained friends who passed through Chicago; in 1931, on his way home from California, Nold stayed with her, later reporting that she "kissed me heartily and served me wine." Two years later she hosted him for more than a week; she was, he said, "well and happy." Her house was sparsely furnished, but contained hundreds of volumes of European and American literature, including poetry, history, novels, and political theory. Pictures of her children as well as the urns containing their ashes were prominently displayed. She tended chickens and listened to the radio.[47]

She especially enjoyed going to dinner at the North Mohawk Street home of Eugene Jasinski and his mother, who were both active radical labor organizers. The three would sit in the backyard surrounded by grapevines and lilac bushes, with shade from the apple, catalpa, and balsam trees, and Parsons would sing songs and recite classical poetry.

Markstall (Parsons called him "Marks"), a short, quiet man, would sometimes accompany her, but he said little, preferring to read a book or write while the others talked. Usually expansive while recounting her turbulent life, she avoided mention of Lulu and Junior, and demurred when asked about them directly. Those who knew her well urged her to move somewhere so that someone could take care of her and make sure she had enough food in the house. The Chicago socialist *Call* began to commend her to their readers as an appropriate object of charity at Christmastime. She was receiving a small government pension for the blind, but she preferred her independence and her little house full of books. She did rely on party members to fetch her and drive her to parades and meetings, often in the company of Nina van Zandt.[48]

Parsons's writings and infrequent speaking engagements now took on added poignancy. In September 1934, she welcomed delegates to the Second U.S. Congress Against War and Fascism to Chicago; they were sponsored by the New York–based Communist Party of the USA. On April 12, 1936, she spoke at van Zandt's memorial service, a huge event featuring a long car procession that traveled through Haymarket Square and on to Waldheim Cemetery. Not long before, the IWW had honored van Zandt at a meeting in Wobbly Hall. Ralph Chaplin described the scene: "Lucy Parsons was led to the platform to speak a few words. Mrs. Parsons was blind; Nina [van Zandt] Spies, almost in rags and wearing men's shoes, made a pathetic effort at public reconciliation with her ancient rival." Since Haymarket, the two had attended meetings together but never appeared together on the same speaking platform. At the memorial service, Parsons, who was the featured speaker, recounted a conversation with van Zandt when on one Haymarket anniversary they had found themselves together laying flowers on the graves at Waldheim Cemetery: "'When I croak, will you speak at my funeral?' 'Yes, replied Nina, 'unless I go first. In that case you must speak at mine.'" Parsons gave a sad goodbye: "You and I, Comrade Nina, have passed these 50 years together. Now the great curtain of mystery, death, has fallen and you are beyond. It is only a matter of days or months or hours before I must render my account with nature. If there be another world we will join hands and march on together, but I know nothing about that. Comrade Nina, fare thee well."[49]

Yet such sentimentality was uncharacteristic of Parsons, and perhaps in the end wholly disingenuous. Parsons was horrified to learn later that van Zandt had left her entire estate of $3,000 to care for stray animals, and not to further the cause of freedom. In a letter to a friend, Parsons railed about the former society girl, claiming she disgraced the name of August Spies—"he who died for the cause of the working class, he who flayed the rich exploiters during his lifetime." She was certain that Spies himself never considered the marriage valid, citing his habit of referring to Nina as "Nina van Zandt" and never as his wife. Parsons confessed that she had only spoken at the service because people assumed they were rivals, and she feared that if she turned down the invitation, "I would be accused of being 'jealous.'" Now she thought she had wasted her time.[50]

Fifty years to the day after that fateful rally in Haymarket Square, Parsons was again featured in a May Day parade, this one on a rainy Friday, with 4,000 to 5,000 people processing through the Loop, holding aloft red banners and singing the *Internationale*. Joining in the parade was Studs Terkel, who had recently graduated from the University of Chicago Law School. Now on his way to becoming an activist-writer, he spoke to the crowd from a wagon, as Albert and the others had done a half-century before. The event received some surprising publicity in the *Chicago Defender*, with the headline "Labor to Honor Race Woman Widowed by Haymarket Riot"—the first and only time the paper acknowledged that Parsons was of African descent. In the article, Lucy Parsons was identified as "a member of the Race."[51]

The following year the procession was similar, what the *Tribune* called "radical labor's annual May Day parade." Local communists and socialists cooperated in planning the event at an earlier meeting, where Parsons spoke after being introduced by the head of Albert's old Typographical Union No. 16. During the parade on May 1, the marchers passed by, scarlet banners flying, singing, "Arise you prisoners of starvation!" One disillusioned communist watched from the sidelines, his anguish revealing the party's failures and foretelling its ultimate demise. Richard Wright had moved to Chicago from Mississippi in 1927, and found work in the post office. An aspiring writer, he at first resisted the entreaties of communists to contribute to the *Masses* and *Left Front*:

"'I don't want to be organized,' I said." Still, because he thought party recruiters "conceived of people in too abstract a manner," he decided to join: "I would tell Communists how common people felt, and I would tell common people of the self-sacrifice of Communists who strove for unity among them." His comrades welcomed him—"We write articles about Negroes, but we never see any Negroes. We need your stuff," one admitted.[52]

Wright found party members to be "fervent, democratic, restless, eager, self-sacrificing." Yet before long, even his fellow black comrades were expressing suspicions based on his dress—"my shined shoes, my clean shirt, and the tie I had worn," and his manner of speech—"He talks like a book," one sneered. Wright persisted in his own work with youths ages eight to twenty-five at the South Side Boys' Club, recording their "word-rhythms and reactions." Suspected of an "anti-leadership attitude," he was labeled a "traitor." By the time of the 1937 May Day parade, he had renounced his own stories "in which I had assigned a role of honor and glory to the Communist Party. . . . For I knew in my heart that I should never be able to write that way again, should never be able to feel with that simple sharpness about life, should never again express such passionate hope, should never again make so total a commitment of faith." He would go on to a distinguished career as a writer, exploring the disastrous consequences of the idea of "race" for all Americans, stories beyond the limited purview of many white radicals. Wright's political sensibilities, and also his dark skin color, made it impossible for him to ignore the depredations of racists, even as Parsons's light skin color and persistently Europe-centric views had allowed her to do just that.[53]

On the fiftieth anniversary of the Haymarket executions, the Free Society Group and the Pioneer Aid and Support Association organized a commemorative ceremony held in Ashland Auditorium. The Communist Party refused to contribute. Sam Dolgoff, who had been absent from Chicago for several years, remembered Parsons's speech that day, a day the communist *Daily Worker* called her "yearly Gethsemane": "Lucy stepped out on the platform, bent with age, almost totally blind—but still defiant, still hurtling curses at the powers-that-be, still calling for the overthrow of capitalism. We exchanged greetings, and

I was almost overcome with emotion when she remembered me." She was, he wrote, "the indomitable, fearless rebel."[54]

In an article for the IWW's *One Big Union Monthly* around this time, Parsons felt called upon to disabuse the general public of the notion that the Haymarket defendants were bomb-throwers. (Sam Dolgoff spoke to the widespread negative associations with anarchists when he wrote, "The crackpots, fadists and theorists have always given anarchism a bad name.") She recounted Albert's composure on the gallows and her thwarted wish that the children could see him one last time. She ended the piece, "Oh, Misery, I have drunk thy cup of sorrow to its dregs but I am still a rebel."[55]

It was around this time, according to Alexander Trachtenberg, that Lucy Parsons joined the Communist Party. Trachtenberg was the "cultural commissioner" of the CPUSA and head of International Publishers, which in 1937 published Alan Calmer's book *Labor Agitator: The Story of Albert R. Parsons*, to which Parsons had contributed a brief introduction. Trachtenberg's claim is doubtful, however. Even at her advanced age, Parsons was still in possession of her faculties, and by this time she must have well understood that the kind of anarchist-communism she had championed bore no resemblance to Stalin's communism. In CPUSA articles about her there was no mention that she was a member; certainly the party would have been glad to claim her as one of their own had she joined.[56]

At an outdoor rally on the bitterly cold day of February 22, 1941, Parsons delivered her last recorded address. She spoke to a thousand strikers—members of the Farm Equipment Workers Union, which was affiliated with the CIO—at the International Harvester's McCormick works, the location where workers had been killed during the May 3 demonstration leading up to Haymarket in 1886. Later that spring, to celebrate their victory, union members had Parsons ride on their float in the annual May Day parade, "a beautiful tribute to her past," in the words of Elizabeth Gurley Flynn.[57]

In December 1941, the United States again went to war, and this conflict, too, would be followed by a Red Scare reminiscent of the state-sponsored repression in the wake of World War I. During the

1950s Lucy Parsons's name would be invoked by those who sought to cast aspersions on the ILD and all its members as "un-American."[58]

Parsons, however, was not present to defend herself or her cause. On March 7, 1942, the woodstove in her frame house caught fire, and Lucy Parsons, age ninety-one, died in the conflagration; she had suffered burns over 25 percent of her body. Firefighters found her corpse in the kitchen. Markstall, who had been out shopping for groceries and arrived to see the building in flames, rushed in to try to save her, but he, too, was overcome by the smoke and fire, and he died in the hospital the next day.

Epilogue

THE RUINS OF THE HOUSE ON NORTH TROY WERE STILL smoldering when the many legacies of the enigmatic Lucy Parsons began to take shape. A neighbor named Estelle Golenda on Cortland Street provided details for the death certificate: that Lucy Ella Parsons Markstall, a woman "about 83" years of age, had been born in 1859, in Buffalo Creek, Texas, to parents who were natives of Mexico, Pedro Diez and Maries Gonzalez.[1]

Early on the morning of the day after the fire, police officers and FBI agents, poking through the dwelling's charred remains, prevented anyone else from getting near the house. At some point, what was left of Parsons's personal library (before the fire, as many as 3,000 books) vanished from the premises. Many years later a British art and antiques dealer put a volume with an estimated value of £250 to £300 up for sale—a signed copy of William Morris's book *The Signs of Change: Seven Lectures* inscribed "To Lucy E. Parsons, from William Morris, Nov. 15th 1888," and bearing Library of Congress and FBI ink stamps. The Red Squad and federal agents had apparently hauled the library away to become part of the city's collection of confiscated radical reading materials, and then either sold the books or otherwise disposed of them, perhaps sending them to the Library of Congress.[2]

On March 12, three hundred people attended a double memorial service for Parsons and Markstall held in a funeral home at 3946 Milwaukee Avenue. As Parsons had requested, Ben Reitman presided; she must have been grateful to the faux hobo for the cash she was able to earn from his Fellowship of Reconciliation tours, and for his willingness to drive her out to Waldheim Cemetery every once in a while. During the service, Reitman referred to Parsons as "the last of the dinosaurs, that brave group of Chicago Anarchists." It is true that she represented the first generation of Chicago anarchists; however, she would have objected to this inelegant turn of phrase. A mourner sang one of her favorite songs, "Joe Hill," about the Wobbly who had been framed for murder and executed by firing squad in 1915: "I dreamed I saw Joe Hill last night / Alive as you and me / Says I, 'But Joe, you're ten years dead' / 'I never died,' says he / 'I never died,' says he." Some wondered why the choice was not "Annie Laurie," the song Albert sang his last night on Earth, but those who knew her swore that "Joe Hill" was her favorite.[3]

On the very day he presided at her funeral, Reitman wrote to the *Chicago Daily News* and pronounced her the "Dark Lady" of anarchism, and as distinctly subordinate to the two whom he considered the greatest women of the movement—Voltairine de Cleyre and Emma Goldman. It is unclear on what basis Reitman was judging Parsons, though she was certainly not an iconic cultural figure like Goldman, or an anarchist theoretician like de Cleyre. Reitman did believe, however, that while "Lucy Parsons was not a great woman," she "did have great ideas to which she was faithful all her life." His remarks perhaps reveal Parsons's isolation and estrangement from certain members of subsequent generations of radicals, though Reitman himself was no champion of the laboring classes. Lucy Parsons's ashes, together with those of Markstall and her son, Albert Junior (they had been retrieved from a small urn in the wreckage of her house), were buried under a marker near the Haymarket Monument at Waldheim Cemetery.[4]

Most mainstream publications provided perfunctory notices of her death and burial, but some others were more revealing of editors' views of the person the *Daily News* called "Dark Lucy." The chief editorial writer for that paper, Charles H. Dennis, recounted the night of May 4, 1886, and repeated the myth that Lulu and Albert Junior had sat next to Lucy on the wagon at Haymarket Square. Most of his recollections (he had been on the staff of the paper since 1882) focused on Parsons's relationship with Nina van Zandt; he portrayed the two women as competing for the public's attention after Haymarket. He opined of Parsons that "until recently she was the sibyl of extreme radical movements in this country. Her Mexican blood was discernible in her pigmented features." Her obituary in the *Illinois State Journal*, based in Springfield, read, in part, "Lucy Parsons, participant in one of the world's most sensational peacetime dramas, ended her career at 83 years with a theatrical exit—she was burned to death in the little home in which she had lived in Chicago many, many years," as if she had scripted her own gruesome death for maximum newsworthiness. This paper, like others, either consciously or unconsciously, invoked Parsons's famously fiery persona, though such associations might be considered in poor taste, considering the way she had died: "She wrote well but spoiled her efforts by too strong a use of inflammatory abuse."[5]

The radical press was more respectful, but it painted a distorted picture of Parsons that has proved enduring. The New York socialist *Call* devoted two-thirds of her obituary to Albert Parsons, apparently considering her long, active life ancillary to his career. The communist *Daily Worker* made the patently false claim that she "was proud of her Mexican and Negro ancestry." Writing in the same publication, Elizabeth Gurley Flynn offered a bit of unfounded speculation: "What a great satisfaction to her it must have been to realize the number of splendid young women, many of her color, who are enrolled in [the CIO] today."[6]

In probate court, as she had in life, Parsons caused controversy. Her estate consisted of two fire-insurance policies totaling $2,500; $500 in personal property (including "one old gold wedding ring," valued at $3); and a balance of $45.93 in a bank account she and Markstall shared. Since she died with no known next of kin, the court appointed an attorney named Bernard W. Mages to administer her estate. He dispersed funds to settle the hospital bill for Markstall and the rest of the Markstall estate ($500) to demolish what was left of the house and to pay miscellaneous other expenses associated with claims adjustment and legal paperwork. Mages also hired two men to appraise her library (presumably at an off-site location) as well as an undertaker. This last expense, of $470.13, charged by the Sademan and Finfrock funeral directors, caught Mages's attention, and to his credit he hired another lawyer to challenge that exorbitant amount, which included $225 for a casket (over $3,000 in today's dollars); $31.50 for a robe and underwear; and $75 for embalming. These preparations for burial might have made sense and pleased the ever fashion-conscious Lucy Parsons had there been an open-casket service and then burial, but instead the undertaker cremated the body, for $30. Mages managed to get the total charge reduced to $270. What was left after these disbursements (about $450) went to the Pioneer Aid and Support Association for the maintenance of the martyrs' graves at Waldheim.[7]

OVER THE NEXT THREE-QUARTERS OF A CENTURY, ANARCHIST, socialist, communist, liberal-reformer, Hispanic, Indian, and African American activists and scholars would claim Lucy Parsons as one of their own. She was heralded as a "Chicana socialist labor organizer," her name rendered in the Spanish way, Lucia González de Parsons, and as "the first Black woman to play a prominent role in the American Left." Much scholarly debate has ensued over how to define her, a task made more difficult not only by her reinvention of her ethnicity but also by her pragmatic approach to radical political theory. From the 1880s on she embraced core principles—that voting was counterproductive to revolutionary action; that trade unions were the building blocks of a new order; that the laboring classes must seize the material means to protect themselves from capitalists and their minions, including police; and that freedom of assembly and speech were integral in the fight for a good society. Yet she was never an ideologue, and she always confounded the labels of "socialist" and "anarchist."[8]

In May 2004, the Park District Board of the City of Chicago approved the "Lucy Ella Gonzales Parsons" pocket park on Belmont Avenue between North Keating and North Kilpatrick, about a mile west of the site of her former home on North Troy. (During her lifetime she used the middle name Eldine more than Ella.) Some Chicagoans were appalled that the city would honor a professed advocate of dynamite; others sought to memorialize the anarchist, socialist, communist, anticommunist, or suffragist that she was (or was not) as an inspiration to subsequent struggles; and still others expressed skepticism that she would want any type of governmental entity to honor her in any way. Truly, Parsons Park is a park for all seasons of radical sensibilities.[9]

LUCY PARSONS PROMOTED ANARCHY BY WRITING AND SPEAKING about it; she declared herself an anarchist. But did she live as an anarchist?[10]

For her, the anarchic ideal offered a road map that led up from and out of the dark pit of wage slavery and into the bright light of voluntary associations of like-minded, generous people. Her particular brand of anarchy amounted to a literal call to arms among the laboring classes— men, women, and children at risk from predatory police and private security thugs no less than from the soul-crushing might of industrial capitalism. She and Albert thought in terms of grand economic forces, the relentless march of history, and he, especially, had a penchant for quantitative data that reduced workers to so many factors in a scientific equation. Yet if their sweeping message was life-and-death grim, their day-to-day existence certainly was not. As a mixed-race married couple, they showed considerable courage in the face of widespread disapproval among whites, a testament to the love they had for each other. Together and alone they shared pleasurable times with their children and comrades, partaking of the music, dancing, picnicking, and general conviviality that were the hallmarks of the German American community in Chicago. Lucy Parsons knew the exhilaration that flowed from defiance to authority—the protest march that blocked the flow of downtown traffic, the disrupted meeting that caused consternation among its leaders, the editorial that shocked the respectable classes. Perhaps most indelible are the images of her dodging the police, running from one street corner to the next, barging her way into a lecture hall, sprinting past a barricade. For Lucy Parsons, those were moments of joy and deep satisfaction.

At the same time, mostly on account of her circumstances, she never achieved a kind of anarchic life that was both more playful and more profound. This kind of life presupposes freedom from material deprivation, to be sure, but also freedom from stifling social conventions, and from the everyday tyranny of mean-spirited bosses and abusive parents and partners. It suggests a kind of liberation that would have allowed her to speak openly and honestly of her enslavement as a youth and of her free-spirited sexuality. Instead, she remained bound by the prejudices of the overwhelming majority of white Americans, including the Chicagoans and others who stared at her on the street and cruelly labeled her and her children "niggers." Among the many ironies and contradictions of her life, perhaps the greatest was her own fractured existence, a bifurcated way of being in a world that forced her to deny, or suppress, her childhood as a slave and her adulthood as a sexual being even as she became an infamous radical.

Parsons gave little public expression to that collection of memories, resentments, and regrets that derived from her enslaved past and her love affairs, which remained hidden to all but herself. Nevertheless, her private self constantly intruded on her public life. She no doubt assumed that the absence of a Mexican American community in Chicago would allow her to "pass" as a Latina, albeit one who did not speak Spanish. She did not anticipate that Wacoites would point out that the young freedwoman they once knew and the famous Chicago anarchist were one and the same. In a similar vein, Emma Goldman and others called attention to her hypocritical bid for conventional (sexual) respectability. Because of these various efforts to "expose" her, Parsons had to conduct a perennial rearguard action in order to bolster her claim that her only real identity was as a champion of the laboring classes, the wife and then widow of Albert Parsons. Looking forward to a time when wages did not exist, "when labor is no longer for sale," a time when "society will produce free men and women who will think free, act free, and be free," she tacitly acknowledged the strictures under which she, too, lived and labored.[11]

ONE OF THE MOST STRIKING FEATURES OF PARSONS'S ACTIVISM WAS her self-proclaimed love of informed debate and disquisition, on the one hand, and her unswerving invocation of the virtues of explosive devices, on the other. At some point, surely she understood that dynamite has no politics. Through her association with Johann Most, and through her own writings, calculated to send fear into the hearts of the capitalist class, she exhibited not only a callous disregard for human life, but also a willful thoughtlessness about the consequences of what she advocated. Certainly, subsequent attacks on American soil by terrorists, whether on the Left or the Right; whether foreign-born or native; whether the Weather Underground, the Ku Klux Klan, Al Qaeda, or the Tsarnaev brothers, have resulted not only in the loss of innocent lives, but also in furious backlashes against civil liberties.[12]

The notion that, by asserting the blessings of dynamite, Lucy and Albert and their comrades hoped merely to issue a stern threat to elites hardly serves to exculpate the anarchists. In their own time, the Parsonses insisted on being taken seriously, and articles in *The Alarm* went so far as to suggest that the deaths of members of the laboring classes constituted an acceptable form of collateral damage in the service of the class struggle. Later, defenders of the pair would take Albert's lead and suggest that his roles as loving husband and father absolved him of any charges that his motives had been tainted or his actions criminal: hence the recurring image of Lucy Parsons and Junior and Lulu sitting on the wagon together the night of the Haymarket bombing. Yet that image was based on myth, and the fact is that both she and Albert, strenuously and unapologetically, had repeatedly called for the use of violence against capitalists and government officials.

If all Americans who work for a just society can be judged by a single, dominant standard, it is the degree to which they confronted (and confront) the hard facts about the legacy of slavery. Though the Chicago anarchists hailed John Brown as their hero, they evinced little concern for the vast majority of blacks, a group deemed either unexceptional within, or totally outside, the bounds of the proletariat as defined by Karl Marx. These white radicals shared an active hostility toward the black men and women who took the jobs of striking white workers. Moreover, Lucy Parsons and her comrades denigrated the black freedom struggle as most Chicago South Siders perceived it—the right to vote and the opportunity to advance within the workplace, to swim at a lakefront beach on a hot summer day, to send their children to decent schools, and someday to buy a modest house to call their own. That these aspirations were identical to those of the white laboring classes (and, with the exception of the right to vote, to the Parsonses' own aspirations, for that matter) only heightens the tragedy of white anarchists, socialists, and communists: these were men and women who claimed for themselves the mantle of radical change, but whose own prejudices served to replicate the unequal society against which they professed to be fighting.

Still, Parsons and her fellow radicals were correct in highlighting the unbridled aggression of local, state, and federal armed forces in attacking strikers, workers attending peaceful meetings, and speakers exercising their constitutional rights. In turn-of-the-century Chicago, anarchists were forced to defend themselves, just as the Black Panthers of the 1960s would later be forced to do, an effort that elites saw as a license for police officers to kill indiscriminately, both in the 1890s and in the 1960s. The Chicago Police Department's Subversive Activities Unit ("Red Squad") conducted unlawful surveillance of political dissenters until 1974, when it destroyed thousands of records related to radical individuals and organizations. Well underway during Lucy Parsons's time, rogue policing fed off enforced residential segregation and the immiseration of much of the black population, and police-initiated violence ruined untold numbers of lives well into the twenty-first century. In her active, noisy resistance to restrictions on free speech and assembly, Lucy Parsons bequeathed a usable legacy to Americans today. For this reason, were she alive today, Parsons would no doubt laud the Chicago-based transparency nonprofit named in her honor. Lucy Parsons Labs declares that its mission is "to engage our community in a horizontal manner while organizing around digital rights issues, supporting free and open source projects and seeking the free flow of information globally"—information related, for example, to police expenditures and to illegal police activities such as surveillance, abuse, and cover-ups.[13]

In the end, there are few lives that are not a bundle of contradictions and shortcomings—saying one thing and doing another, abandoning deeply held principles in the midst of temptation or anger, turning a blind eye to conditions that do not fit one's stubborn view of the world. Born a slave, Lucy Parsons lived a singularly eventful life that spanned more than nine decades, a life full of remarkable achievements in her roles as orator, editor, and writer, as well as a life full of unrequited longings and suppressed desires. Her early years on a Virginia slave plantation and later in Waco no doubt shaped her outlook in ways she never admitted to family or friends, or perhaps even to herself, influences impossible to know today. Although the considerable body of her commentary, both written and spoken, yields little about her inner struggles, her power to inform and fascinate is enduring, and her story, in all its complexity, remains a powerful one for its useful legacies no less than its cautionary lessons.

Acknowledgments

MANY INDIVIDUALS CONTRIBUTED TO THIS BOOK WHILE I WAS researching, writing, and revising it, and I am grateful to each and every one of them for their expertise and generosity.

At the outset I would like to highlight the work of Carolyn Ashbaugh, who early appreciated and wrote about Lucy Parsons as a significant labor agitator, editor, and orator in American history. In 1976, Ashbaugh published the first full-length biography of Parsons, titled *Lucy Parsons: An American Revolutionary*, and soon after publication donated her notes as well as newspaper clippings, correspondence, and audio recordings to the Newberry Library in Chicago. The Carolyn Ashbaugh Collection ensures that future scholars will continue to benefit from her research. The collection includes not only documents but also taped interviews with some of the men and women who knew Parsons later in her life.

I relied on reference librarians and archivists who located and duplicated a wide range of materials for me. In my quest for the Texas marriage records of Lucy and Albert Parsons, I am indebted to Christy Costlow, Travis County archivist; Marion Loftin, deputy clerk, Cherokee County, Texas; Kerry McGuire, researcher, McLennan County Archives; and especially Rick Toms, Travis County Clerk's Office. I am also grateful to Tony Black, appraisal archivist, Archives and Information Services Division, Texas State Library and Archives Commission. At the Perry-Castañeda Library (PCL) of the University of Texas (UT) at Austin, the librarian Paul S. Rascoe in Government Documents,

Maps and Electronic Information Services helped me find elusive government documents. The interlibrary loan staff was efficient and resourceful in tracking down essential books, articles, and pamphlets in libraries all over the country. Thanks, too, to the PCL circulation and microfilm staffs. At the Dolph Briscoe Center for American History, Brenda Gunn, director for research and collections, and Margaret Schlankey, head of reference services, assisted me on a number of fronts as the project progressed.

Eric Frazier in the Rare Books and Special Collections Division at the Library of Congress provided guidance as I navigated through the Paul Avrich Collection, a treasure trove of materials related to the history of anarchy and anarchists. In Chicago, Carolyn Sanders, Cook County Clerk's Office, and Bureau of Vital Records–Genealogy, helped me locate birth certificates for Albert Junior and Lulu. Special thanks to Julie Herrada, curator, Joseph A. Labadie Collection, and Kate Hutchens, reader services coordinator, Special Collections Library, University of Michigan; Lee Grady, reference archivist, Library Archives Division, and Jonathan Nelson, collection development archivist, Wisconsin Historical Society; Christine Colburn, reader services manager, and Barbara Gilbert, Reading Room coordinator, Special Collections Research Center, University of Chicago Library; Sean Sutcliffe, Waco Public Library; Cheryl Schnirring, curator of manuscripts, Abraham Lincoln Presidential Library, Springfield, Illinois; Alison Hinderliter, manuscript and archives librarian, and Martha Briggs, Lloyd Lewis Curator of Modern Manuscripts, Newberry Library, Chicago; and Peggy Glowacki, special collections librarian, University of Illinois at Chicago, Special Collections, Richard J. Daley Library, Chicago. Dr. Rob Heinrich took time from writing his own book to assist me in collecting materials in the Boston area. I would also like to acknowledge the special skills of Dr. Matthew Bunn, German translator, and of Suloni Robertson and Bethany Wong, University of Texas Liberal Arts Technology Services image scanners. I relied on a number of efficient graduate research assistants, including Deirdre Lannon Albrecht, Juan Carlos De Orellana, Nick Roland, and Henry Wiencek.

I appreciated the enthusiasm and encouragement that I received from the very first audiences for this work, both of them close to home—those at the University of Texas at Austin Gender Symposium, and those at the President's Luncheon of the 2015 Annual Meeting of the Texas State Historical Association.

Throughout this project, many friends and colleagues took an interest in it and provided both support and resources relevant to the project. I thank Michael Parrish of Baylor University and my UT colleagues Emilio Zamora and George Forgie. I would also like to single out Mark Jacob, the *Chicago Tribune*'s metro editor, who possesses an unparalleled level of knowledge about Chicago and its geography, neighborhoods, and history. Mark not only provided me with a detailed critique of an early draft but also shared documents and other materials that he had found as a result of his own research on Lucy and Albert Parsons. This book is much better for Mark's interest in it and help with it.

Steve Hahn, Jim Sidbury, and Michael Willrich gave me extensive comments and prompted me to reconsider how I rendered both the details and the larger meanings of Parsons's story. For their deep knowledge of Texas history, I am grateful to Carl Moneyhon and Randolph "Mike" Campbell. Don E. Carleton and Joe William Trotter read the manuscript and gave me positive feedback. Kali Gross urged me to consider the various traumas that Lucy Parsons must have suffered as a young enslaved woman and to factor those traumas into a discussion of her subsequent way of being in the world. Vicki Ruiz helped me to think about why and how Parsons decided to present herself as a woman of indigenous and Hispanic descent.

The History Department at the University of Texas at Austin is a particularly supportive and collegial place to work. I would like to acknowledge my faculty colleagues, who make going into the office each day a pleasure. The History Department staff has contributed to this book in direct and indirect ways; together, these women and men make the job of chairing such a large, busy, and productive department an enjoyable one. Special thanks, for their professionalism, patience, and good humor, to Laura Flack, Art Flores, Courtney Meador, Jackie Llado, Martha Gonzalez, Jerry Larson, Nichole Powell, Marilyn Lehman, Judy Hogan, Kelli Weaver, Nancy Sutherland, Tom Griffith, and Jason Gentry.

My good friends Ellen Fitzpatrick, Karin Lifter, Robin Feuer Miller, Nina Tumarkin, and Sandy Baum have sustained me through this project as through others in years past. I appreciated Sandy's hospitality in Chicago, not far from where Lucy Parsons used to declaim from a soapbox in Bughouse Square.

My agent Geri Thoma read a complete early draft of the manuscript and offered excellent comments, to the benefit of all those who read subsequent versions. At Basic Books, editorial assistant Alia Massoud and project editor Stephanie Summerhays cheerfully and expertly kept me on track throughout the production process. Brian Distelberg proved a skillful commentator on Parsons's story, and I am grateful for his timely interventions in the manuscript. Katherine Streckfus did an outstanding job of copy-editing, and I appreciate all of her hard work and meticulous attention to detail. My editor Lara Heimert, publisher at Basic Books, reacted enthusiastically to my first mention of Lucy Parsons as the subject of a potential biography—a leap of faith perhaps, considering that many people today have never heard of the so-called goddess of anarchy, or know of her only as Albert Parsons's widow.

I would like to thank the extended Jones and Abramson families for providing me with a warm community of unconditional love. I regret that Albert and Sylvia Jones and Albert and Rose Abramson are no longer with us to share the many life-cycle celebrations that give us all so much pleasure. Sarah Jones Abramson and Steven John Halloran and Anna Jones Abramson and Erica Doudna have followed my progress on this biography with great interest, and Amelia Esther Abramson Halloran and Henry Albert Abramson Halloran have offered delightful distraction throughout the process. My husband of thirty-seven years, Jeffrey Abramson, has listened patiently to my too-frequent ruminations on the idea of race and the parameters of anarchy; in more ways than he knows, he helped me see this book through to the end. Together we spent memorable days in Chicago, the city that Lucy Parsons knew so well, following in her footsteps from place to place.

Finally, it gives me great pleasure to dedicate this book to Steve and Henry Halloran, father and son, two wonderful guys.

Abbreviations in Notes

Aberdeen WN	*Aberdeen (SD) Weekly News*
Abilene TCN	*Abilene (TX) Taylor County News*
AG	*Arkansas Gazette*, Little Rock
AHR	*American Historical Review*
ALH	*American Literary History*
ALPLM	Abraham Lincoln Presidential Library and Museum, Springfield, Illinois
Alton ET	*Alton (IL) Evening Telegraph*
AQ	*American Quarterly*
ARP	Albert Richard Parsons
ARP Papers	Albert R. Parsons Papers, 1876–1893 (MSS 15A, Microfilm 523), Library Archives Division, Wisconsin Historical Society, Madison
Atchison DG	*Atchison (KS) Daily Globe*
Austin WS	*Austin Weekly Statesman*
AZ	*Arbeiter Zeitung*
Bismarck DT	*Bismarck (ND) Daily Tribune*
BRFAL	Bureau of Refugees, Freedmen, and Abandoned Lands (Record Group 105), National Archives and Records Administration, Washington, DC
Brownsville DH	*Brownsville (TX) Daily Herald*
Centralia E and T	*Centralia (WI) Enterprise and Tribune*
Charleston N and C	*Charleston (SC) News and Courier*
Chicago DB	*Chicago Day Book*
Chicago DN	*Chicago Daily News*
Chicago MN	*Chicago Morning News*

CHS, HADC	Chicago Historical Society, Haymarket Affair Digital Collection
Cincinnati CT	Cincinnati Commercial Tribune
Cincinnati EP	Cincinnati Evening Post
Cincinnati TS	Cincinnati Times-Star
Cleveland DH	Cleveland Daily Herald
Cleveland LH	Cleveland Leader and Herald
Cleveland PD	Cleveland Plain Dealer
Columbus DE	Columbus (OH) Daily Enquirer
CT	Chicago Tribune
CWH	Civil War History
Dallas DH	Dallas Daily Herald
Dallas MN	Dallas Morning News
Dallas WH	Dallas Weekly Herald
DBCAH	Earl Vandale Collection, Dolph Briscoe Center for American History, Austin, Texas
Decatur HD	Decatur (IL) Herald Despatch
Denver EP	Denver Evening Post
Denver RMN	Rocky Mountain News (Denver)
Detroit ALL	Advance and Labor Leaf
Detroit FP	Detroit Free Press
DI-O	Chicago Daily Inter-Ocean
DISR	Daily Illinois State Register (Springfield)
DN	Evanston (IL) Daily Northwestern
DW	Daily Worker
El Paso DH	El Paso Daily Herald
Evansville C and P	Evansville (IN) Courier and Press
FMC	Federal Manuscript Census (available online at Ancestry.com)
Fort Worth DG	Fort Worth Daily Gazette
Galveston DN	Galveston Daily News
Houston WT	Houston Weekly Telegraph
HW	Harper's Weekly
IC	Intermountain Catholic
ILWCH	International Labor and Working-Class History
ISJ	Illinois State Journal
ISR	International Socialist Review
IW	Industrial Worker
JAAH	Journal of African American History
JAC	Journal of American Culture

JAH	*Journal of American History*
JIH	*Journal of Illinois History*
JISHS	*Journal of the Illinois State Historical Society*
JNH	*Journal of Negro History*
JPE	*Journal of Political Economy*
JSH	*Journal of Social History*
JUH	*Journal of Urban History*
Juneau DR-M	*Juneau (AK) Daily Record-Miner*
KL	*Knights of Labor* (Chicago)
LE	*Labor Enquirer* (Denver)
LMS	Lizzie May Swank
LP	Lucy Parsons
ME	*Mother Earth*
Milwaukee DJ	*Milwaukee (WI) Daily Journal*
Milwaukee DS	*Milwaukee (WI) Daily Sentinel*
Milwaukee YN	*Milwaukee (WI) Yenowine's News*
MLR	*Monthly Labor Review*
MQ	*Midwest Quarterly*
MQR	*Mennonite Quarterly Review*
NA	National Archives and Records Administration, Washington, DC
NAR	*North American Review*
New Orleans T-P	*New Orleans Times-Picayune*
New York CA	*New York Commercial Advertiser*
New York DP	*New York Daily People*
New York DT	*New York Daily Tribune*
New York EW	*New York Evening World*
NYT	*New York Times*
OBUM	*One Big Union Monthly*
OH	*Ohio History*
OHQ	*Oregon Historical Quarterly*
Omaha DB	*Omaha (NE) Daily Bee*
Omaha MWH	*Omaha (NE) Morning World Herald*
Pittsburgh GE	*Pittsburgh Grassroots Examiner*
RA	*Radical America*
RG	Record Group, National Archives and Records Administration, Washington, DC
Rockford DR	*Rockford (IL) Daily Register*
Rockford R-R	*Rockford (IL) Register-Republican*
Sacramento R-U	*Sacramento (CA) Record-Union*

St. Paul DG	*St. Paul (MN) Daily Globe*
SHQ	*Southwestern Historical Quarterly*
SSH	*Social Science History*
St. Louis G-D	*St. Louis Globe-Democrat*
TA	Chicago Trade Assembly
Tacoma DN	*Tacoma (WA) Daily News*
Topeka SJ	*Topeka (KS) State Journal*
TSLA	Texas State Library and Archives, Austin, Texas
Waco DE	*Waco Daily Examiner*
Waco EN	*Waco Evening News*
Waco TH	*Waco Times Herald*
Wilkes-Barre TL	*Wilkes-Barre (PA) Times Leader*
WP	*Washington Post*
WST	*Wyoming State Tribune,* Cheyenne

Notes

INTRODUCTION

1. "I am not a candidate": *Cincinnati TS*, October 13, 1886.

2. Steve Fraser, *The Age of Acquiescence: The Life and Death of American Resistance to Organized Wealth and Power* (Boston: Little, Brown, 2015).

CHAPTER 1: WIDE-OPEN WACO

1. *St. Louis G-D*, September 18, 1886, 3. This newspaper article is the Rosetta Stone of Lucy Parsons's early life. Information that can be verified independently includes the name of her mother and her and her mother's owner, the name of her mother's husband and his place of work, and details about Oliver Benton aka Oliver Gathings.

2. "shooting around . . . a little fun": Dorothy Waties Renick, "This Place We Call Home: A Serial History of Waco and McLennan County," *Waco TH*, May 4, 1924, 2; William H. Curry, *A History of Early Waco with Allusions to Six Shooter Junction* (Waco: Library Binding Company, 1968), 32, 129–131; "actresses": John Sleeper and J. C. Hutchins, compilers, *Waco and McLennan County, Texas, Containing a City Directory of Waco, Historical Sketches of the City and County* . . . (Waco: Dayton Kelley, 1876; reprint, Texian Press, 1966).

3. McLennan County District Court Minutes, vol. F, 1869–1871, microfilm reel 984506, and vol. B, 1863–1871, reel 984503, Baylor University, Waco, Texas; Bureau of Refugees, Freedmen, and Abandoned Lands, Records of the Assistant Commissioner for the State of Texas, M821, reel 32, Record of Criminal Offenses Committed in the State of Texas, vols. 1–3, Case #1574, Record Group 105, National Archives and Records Administration, Washington, DC (either M821 or M822, reel number, BRFAL, RG 105, NA, hereafter).

4. Anne Bailey, *Between the Enemy and Texas: Parsons's Texas Cavalry in the Civil War* (Fort Worth: Texas Christian University Press, 1989), 5–6; "on the range": Lucy E. Parsons, ed., *Life of Albert R. Parsons with Brief History of the Labor Movement in America* (Chicago: Mrs. Lucy E. Parsons, 1889), 1–7. See also Gary Goodman, "Albert R. Parsons in Texas: The Origins of a Radical Agitator," typescript in the Paul Avrich Collection, Library of Congress, Washington, DC. Albert's birthdate of 1845 is the one given by his father when he was interviewed by a Montgomery census-taker in 1850. Albert routinely claimed that he was born in 1848.

5. Bailey, *Between the Enemy and Texas*, 7; "so hot for secession": Renick, "This Place We Call Home," 2. For the broadside advertising Parsons's book (which was apparently never written, or at least never published), see Earl Vandale Collection, Dolph Briscoe Center for American History, Austin, Texas (DBCAH hereafter).

6. William D. Carrigan, *The Making of a Lynching Culture: Violence and Vigilantism in Central Texas, 1836–1916* (Urbana: University of Illinois Press, 2006), 95.

7. Ellis Bailey, *A History of Hill County, Texas, 1838–1965* (Waco: Texian Press, 1966), 40–41; Gathings genealogy: Margaret Reid, "Re: James Jackson Gathings, Jr., Hill Co. TX," Genealogy.com, April 8, 2000, http://genforum .genealogy.com/gathings/messages/4.html; David Minor, "Gathings, James J.," Handbook of Texas Online, Texas State Historical Association, n.d., www .tshaonline.org/handbook/online/articles/fga44.

8. Walter L. Buenger, "Secession Convention," Handbook of Texas Online, Texas State Historical Association, n.d., www.tshaonline.org/handbook -search-results?arfarf=secession%20convention; Clayton E. Jewett, *Texas in the Confederacy: An Experiment in Nation-Building* (Columbia: University of Missouri Press, 2002).

9. Tony E. Duty, "The Home Front—McLennan County in the Civil War," *Texana* 12 (1974): 197–199; William H. Parsons, *Condensed History of Parsons' Texas Cavalry Brigade, 1861–1865* (Corsicana, TX, 1903); Bailey, *Between the Enemy and Texas*, 8–14.

10. "frontier boy": Parsons, ed., *Life*, 7; 1860 Federal Manuscript Census, Texas, Galveston County, Galveston (FMC with date and place hereafter), available online at Ancestry.com; Maury Darst, "Galveston News," Handbook of Texas Online, Texas State Historical Association, n.d., www.tshaonline .org/handbook/online/articles/eeg03.

11. "These were stirring . . . Wild Bill": Parsons, ed., *Life*, 8; Bailey, *Between the Enemy and Texas*, 4–5; Anne Bailey, ed., *In the Saddle with the Texans: Day-to-Day with Parsons's Cavalry Brigade, 1862–1865* (Buffalo Gap, TX: State House Press, 2003), 186–191. Albert Parsons gave his age as eighteen when he enlisted

in 1861, but he was sixteen. His early military record is available online at Fold 3, www.fold3.com/image/12959966 (Co. B, 11, Spaight's Battalion Texas Vols [Sabine Pass]; Capt. I. R. Burch's Art'y Co., Likens' Batt'n Texas Vols [enlisted November 8, 1861, for 12 months, paid December 1862]). See also Compiled Service Records of Confederate Soldiers Who Served in Organizations from the State of Texas, ID 586957, M323 War Department Collection of Confederate Records, Record Group 109, National Archives and Records Administration, Washington, DC.

12. "freedom war": George P. Rawick, ed., *The American Slave: A Composite Autobiography* (Federal Writers Project Slave Narratives), Texas Narratives, vol. 16, pt. 2, 1; pt. 4, 195; Supplement Series 2, Texas Narratives, 507; "folks everywhere": Texas Narratives, vol. 16, pt. 1, 305.

13. "who have not *settled*": Ira Berlin, Thavolia Glymph, Joseph P. Reidy, and Leslie Rowland, eds., *Freedom: A Documentary History of Emancipation, 1861–1867*, Series 1, vol. 1, *The Destruction of Slavery* (Cambridge: Cambridge University Press, 1986), 774, 188, 676, 681, 780–781, 773–774; Dale Baum, "Slaves Taken to Texas for Safekeeping During the Civil War," in Charles D. Grear, ed., *The Fate of Texas: The Civil War and the Lone Star State* (Fayetteville: University of Arkansas Press, 2008), 83–104. Unless otherwise noted, emphasis is reproduced from the original.

14. "Cause nobody": *American Slave*, Texas Narratives, vol. 16, pt. 3, 142; *American Slave*, Supplement Series 2, Texas Narratives, 480; Dale Baum, *The Shattering of Texas Unionism: Politics in the Lone Star State During the Civil War* (Baton Rouge: Louisiana State University Press, 1998), x, 211, 235; "so long and so far": Roy P. Basler, ed., *The Collected Works of Abraham Lincoln*, vol. 7 (New Brunswick, NJ: Rutgers University Press, 1953), 4. See also *NYT*, December 23, 1863, 10. I am indebted to George Forgie for these citations.

15. Leon Litwack, *Been in the Storm So Long: The Aftermath of Slavery* (New York: Vintage, 1980), 32–34; *American Slave*, Supplement Series 2, Texas Narratives, 179–180, 481; *American Slave*, Texas Narrratives, vol. 16, pt. 3, 79; pt. 4, 219.

16. "from sun to sun": *American Slave*, Texas Narratives, vol. 16, pt. 4, 219; W. R. Poage, *McLennan County Before 1980* (Waco: Texian Press, 1981), 113–115.

17. Baum, "Slaves Taken," 85–86, 89; Duty, "Home Front," 216–217.

18. Stephen Lynn King, *History and Biographical Sketches of the 46th Tennessee Infantry, CSA* (Bowling Green, KY: S. I. King, 1992); Edwin H. Rennolds, *A History of the Henry Co., Commands Which Served in the C. S. Army* (Jacksonville, FL: Sun Publishing, 1904), 182–185, 195. For Taliaferro's military record, see National Archive Catalogue ID 586957, Compiled Service Records of Confederate General and Staff Officers and Nonregimental Enlisted Men, M331,

RG 109, NA, available online on Fold3.com. For evidence of Taliaferro's land purchases in McLennan County, see McLennan County, Texas, Archives, Tax Rolls, 1878–1905, Assessment Roll of Property in McLennan County, Owned by Residents Rendered for Taxation by Owners or Agents Thereof, for the Year 1883, p. 26. Taliaferro owned 200 acres valued at $2,000; another 96 acres worth $288 was entered in his wife's name. See Tax Office, McLennan County, http://co.mclennan.tx.us/DocumentCenter/Home/View/275.

19. "comely": *St. Louis G-D*, September 18, 1886, 3; Herbert Gutman, *The Black Family in Slavery and Freedom, 1750–1925* (New York: Vintage, 1977), 75–76; 1870 FMC, Waco.

20. Tennessee State Marriages, 1760–2002, Ancestry.com; Rebecca A. Kosary, "'To Punish and Humiliate the Entire Community': White Violence Perpetrated Against African-American Women in Texas, 1865–1868," and James M. Smallwood, "When the Klan Rode: Terrorism in Reconstruction Texas," in Kenneth W. Howell, ed., *Still the Arena of Civil War: Violence and Turmoil in Reconstruction Texas, 1865–1874* (Denton: University of North Texas Press, 2012), 327–353, 215; Carrigan, *Making of a Lynching Culture*, Appendix A; Barry A. Crouch, *The Freedmen's Bureau and Black Texans* (Austin: University of Texas Press, 1992); "Letter of the Secretary of War (Texas)," *Executive Documents of the Senate of the United States*, no. 6, 39th Cong, 2nd sess., 1866–1867 (Washington, DC: US Government Printing Office, 1867), 142–144; Cases 77–89, M821, reel 32, BRFAL, RG 105, NA (reported by Philip Howard).

21. "drum-head": Report of William H. Sinclair, Galveston, December 23, 1866, M821, reel 8, BRFAL, RG 105, NA; René Hayden, Anthony E. Kaye, Kate Masur, Steven F. Miller, Susan E. O'Donovan, Leslie S. Rowland, and Stephen A. West, eds., *Freedom: A Documentary History of Emancipation, 1861–1867*, Series 3, vol. 2, *Land and Labor, 1866–1867* (Chapel Hill: University of North Carolina Press), 178–184.

22. "lofty spirit": Brevet Major General C. C. Andrews quoted in *Report of the Joint Committee on Reconstruction* (39th Cong., 1st sess., 1865–1866) (Washington, DC: US Government Printing Office, 1866), 125; Carrigan, *Making of a Lynching Culture*, 116, 123, 96, 124–125, 138–139, 142; Kosary, "To Punish," in Howell, ed., *Still the Arena of Civil War*, 338.

23. Barry A. Crouch, "'To Enslave the Rising Generation': The Freedmen's Bureau and the Texas Black Code," in Paul A. Cimbala and Randall Miller, eds., *The Freedmen's Bureau in Reconstruction: A Reconsideration* (New York: Fordham University Press, 1999), 261–287.

24. "traded a good mule . . . reaped the harvest": Parsons, ed., *Life*, 8; *Dallas MN*, July 20, 1897; "Catalogue of the Trustees, Officers and Students of Baylor University (Male Department) (Waco Registrar's Office, 1866). Parsons is

listed under the "preparatory class" for 1866–1867. For a history of Waco Lodge 92 of the Freemasons, see www.wacomasonic.org/about-us. See also Carolyn Ashbaugh to Mrs. Lucie Price, Chicago, December 14, 1973, Lucie Clift Price Papers, 1838–1938, DBCAH. Carolyn Ashbaugh is the author of *Lucy Parsons: American Revolutionary* (Chicago: Haymarket Books, 2013 [1976]).

25. "To the same old persecuting": Andrew J. Evans quoted in Carl J. Moneyhon, "'Texas Out-Radicals My Radicalism': Roots of Radical Republicanism in Reconstruction Texas," in David O'Donald Cullen and Kyle G. Wilkison, eds., *The Texas Left: The Radical Roots of Lone Star Liberalism* (College Station: Texas A&M University Press, 2010), 21; "the reconstruction measures . . . go into politics": Parsons, ed., *Life*, 9. On Germans in Texas politics during this period, see Walter Kamphoefner, "New Perspectives on Texas Germans and the Confederacy," in Grear, ed., *Fate of Texas*, 105–120.

26. Terry G. Jordan, "Germans," Handbook of Texas Online, Texas State Historical Association, n.d., www.tshaonline.org/handbook/online/articles /png02; Rudolph L. Biesele, "German Attitude Toward the Civil War," Handbook of Texas Online, Texas State Historical Association, n.d., www.tsha online.org/handbook/online/articles/png01; Walter L. Buenger, *Secession and the Union in Texas* (Austin: University of Texas Press, 1984); Nicholas K. Roland, "'Our Worst Enemies Are in Our Midst': Violence in the Texas Hill Country, 1845–1881," PhD diss., University of Texas at Austin, 2017.

27. *St. Louis G-D*, September 18, 1886, 3; Texas Marriages, 1817–1965, Ancestry.com.

28. "all his cash": *St. Louis G-D*, September 18, 1886, 3.

29. "The colored are well united": D. F. Davis to E. M. Wheelock, Waco, 1866, M822, reel 11, BRFAL, RG 105, NA; correspondence of James D. Scarlett from Waco in the spring of 1869, Letters Received, M822, reel 8, BRFAL, RG 105, NA. See also Alwyn Barr, "Early Organizing and the Search for Equality: African American Conventions in Late Nineteenth-Century Texas," in Debra A. Reid, ed., *Seeking Inalienable Rights: Texans and Their Quests for Justice* (College Station: Texas A&M University Press, 2009), 1–16; James Smallwood, *Time of Hope, Time of Despair: Black Texans During Reconstruction* (Port Washington, NY: Kennikat Press, 1981).

30. "Until the present generation": Sub-Assistant Commissioner's or Agent's Monthly Report, M822, reel 11, BRFAL, RG 105, NA.

31. "sort of a custom": *St. Louis G-D*, September 19, 1886, 6; Charles Haughn to Lt. E. Morse, Waco, September 30, 1868, Records of the Superintendent of Education for the State of Texas, Letters Received, M822, reel 6, BRFAL, RG 105, NA; "young bloods . . . shape": Martha Downs quoted in *Waco EN*, April 3, 1889, 4: "black hair": Horace Stuart Cummings, *Dartmouth College Sketches of*

the Class of 1862 (Washington, DC: Rothrock, 1884), 50–51; Carrigan, *Making of a Lynching Culture*, 100.

32. Barry A. Crouch, *Dance of Freedom: Texas African Americans During Reconstruction* (Austin: University of Texas Press, 2007); "The life": Gregg Cantrell, "Racial Violence and Reconstruction Politics in Texas, 1867–1868," *SHQ* 93 (January 1990): 346; Carrigan, *Making of a Lynching Culture*, 116, 123.

33. "love of display": James J. Emerson to William G. Kirkman, Waco, July 14, 1867, Letters Received, M821, reel 5, BRFAL, RG 105, NA; Robert Crudup to Judge Evans, July 28, 1868, Box 401-862, folder 862-13, Reconstruction Records of the Texas Adjutant General's Department, Texas State Library and Archives, Austin, Texas (Reconstruction Records, TSLA, hereafter); Randolph B. Campbell, "Reconstruction in McLennan County, Texas, 1865–1876," *Prologue* 27 (Spring 1995): 17–35.

34. See, for example, the report David F. Davis submitted for April 30, 1866, "Report of School for Freedmen," M822, reel 11, BRFAL, RG 105, NA; *Executive Documents*, 147; "what I have": Davis's April 1866 Monthly Report, M822, reel 11, BRFAL, RG 105, NA; "he was proud": *Columbus DE*, September 17, 1886, 5.

35. "hug fast . . . old ideas": Davis quoted in Campbell, "Reconstruction," 26; Cummings, *Dartmouth College Sketches*, 7.

36. "Mr. Davis": Charles Haughn to Lt. E. Morse, Waco, September 30, 1868, Letters Received, M822, reel 6, BRFAL, RG 105, NA.

37. William M. Sleeper and Allan D. Sanford, *Waco Bar and Incidents of Waco History* (Waco: Hill Printing, 1941), 129–130.

38. "My political career . . . associates": Parsons, ed., *Life*, 9; "multitude of ignorant": ibid., 216; "incessant talker": *Dallas MN*, May 7, 1886, 1.

39. Duty, "Home Front," 222; Parsons, ed., *Life*, 217–218; "A violent agitator": *Waco Day*, May 6, 1886; "he was always on hand": *Galveston DN*, May 15, 1886.

40. "Africanization": Baum, *Shattering of Texas Unionism*, 174; "all at once": quoted in Jack Noe, "Representative Men: The Post-Civil War Political Struggle over Texas's Commissioners to the 1876 Centennial Exhibition," *SHQ* 120 (October 2016): 166; "many old army friends": W. H. Parsons to Editor, *San Antonio Express*, October 7, 1869, and "the Republican Party": N. Patten to Newcomb, Patten's Mills, August 18, 1869, both in Box 2F105, General Correspondence Folder, 1869, James P. Newcomb Sr., Papers, 1833–1911, DBCAH; "Negro subordination . . . subserved": Broadside for "Negro Slavery, Its Present, Past and Future," Vandale Collection, DBCAH.

41. Parsons, ed., *Life*, 216.

42. Ibid., 216–217.

43. *Houston WT*, March 11, 1869, 1.

44. Ibid.

45. Parsons, ed., *Life*, 9.

46. *Journal of the Reconstruction Convention, Which Met at Austin, Texas,* June 1, 1868 (Austin: Tracy, Siemering, 1870); *San Saba (TX) News,* September 3, 1893; "no rebel officers": David F. Davis to Gov. Davis, Waco, March 22, 1870, Papers of Governor Edmund. J. Davis, TSLA (Davis Papers, TSLA, hereafter).

47. Carl H. Moneyhon, *Republicanism in Reconstruction Texas* (Austin: University of Texas Press, 1980), 138; Alwyn Barr, "Black Legislators of Reconstruction Texas," *CWH* 32 (December 1986): 340–352.

Chapter 2: Republican Heyday

1. "cheaper Goods": *Waco DE,* October 6, 1875, 1; *St. Louis G-D,* September 18, 1886, 3.

2. "scourged": *St. Louis G-D,* September 18, 1886; 1870 FMC, Waco. See also "The Negro's Romance: Poor Old Oliver Gathings and His Pretty Mulatto Wife Whom Albert Parsons Stole Away," *Columbus DE,* September 17, 1886, 5.

3. 1870 FMC, Waco.

4. Ibid.; "most intense": *Report of the Joint Committee on Reconstruction, at the First Sess., 39th Cong.* (Washington, DC: US Government Printing Office, 1866), 37; Dorothy Waties Renick, "This Place We Call Home: A Serial History of Waco and McLennan County," *Waco TH,* May 4, 1924, 2.

5. Carl H. Moneyhon, *Republicanism in Reconstruction Texas* (Austin: University of Texas Press, 1980).

6. Alwyn Barr, "African American Conventions in Late Nineteenth-Century Texas," in Debra A. Reid, ed., *Seeking Inalienable Rights: Texans and Their Quests for Justice* (College Station: Texas A&M University Press, 2009), 2–3; General Correspondence Folder, August-September 1870, in Newcomb Papers, DBCAH.

7. "enemies . . . Republicans": Box 2014/110-7, Folder 93, Davis Papers, TSLA; "being an Ex Rebel . . . laborers are few": ARP to Newcomb, Austin, September 9, 1870, Box 2F105, General Correspondence Folder, August-September 1870, Newcomb Papers, DBCAH.

8. "we suffered": Petition of November 8, 1870, in Box 2F105, General Correspondence Folder, October-November 1870, Newcomb Papers, DBCAH; "the Parsons faction": Flint quoted in Randolph B. Campbell, *Grass-Roots Reconstruction in Texas, 1865–1880* (Baton Rouge: Louisiana State University Press, 1997), 183; "too vain": ARP to Newcomb, Waco, May 1, 1871, Box 2F105, General Correspondence Folder, April-May 1870, Newcomb Papers, DBCAH; *San Saba (TX) News,* September 23, 1892. See also the petition of September 27, 1870, sent from Waco to Davis (signed by ARP and three others, including Shep Mullins) in Box 2014/110-17, folder 211, Davis Papers, TSLA.

9. *Senate Journal of the 12th Legislature of the State of Texas* (Austin: J. G. Tracy, 1871), 19.

10. "for the purpose": ibid., 159–160, 28, 32.

11. Ibid., 47, 369, 428, 404.

12. "black mail": ibid., 316. See also 519.

13. H.P.M.N. Gammel, *The Laws of Texas, 1822–1897*, vol. 6, *General Laws of the Twelfth Legislature of the State of Texas, Called Session, April 26–August 15, 1870*, 1266, 1253, 1608–1609.

14. "a set of men": *The [Austin] Reformer*, September 23, 1871, 2; "Report of the Special Joint Committee of the Thirteenth Legislature for Investigation into the Official Conduct and Accounts of the Superintendent of Public Instruction and of His Subordinates (Austin: John Cardwell, 1873), 144.

15. Davis to Col. A. R. Parsons, September 29, 1871, Box 2014/110-31, Letter Press Books, July 10, 1871–November 11, 1872, Davis Papers, TSLA. For the Romeo Hill quotations, see the correspondence from Romeo Hill to Joseph Welch for May 25, 1869, May 29, 1869, August 2, 1869, and May 31, 1870, in M822, reel 6, BRFAL, NA.

16. "not an 'ornamental' . . . whites": Lucy E. Parsons, ed., *Life of Albert R. Parsons with Brief History of the Labor Movement in America* (Chicago: Mrs. Lucy E. Parsons, 1889), 218; William D. Carrigan, *The Making of a Lynching Culture: Violence and Vigilantism in Central Texas, 1836–1916* (Urbana: University of Illinois Press, 2006), 101–102; James M. Smallwood, "When the Klan Rode: Terrorism in Reconstruction Texas," in Kenneth W. Howell, ed., *Still the Arena of Civil War: Violence and Turmoil in Reconstruction Texas, 1865–1874* (Denton: University of North Texas Press, 2012), 214–242; *Waco Day*, November 1, 1887; *Joint Committee on Reconstruction*, xix.

17. Campbell, *Grass-Roots Reconstruction*, 23.

18. "Stop the Madman!": Tony E. Duty, "The Home Front—McLennan County in the Civil War," *Texana* 12 (1974): 224–231. See also Robert M. Kisselburgh, "Enforcers or Conspirators: Texas District Court Judges' Impact on Lawlessness During Reconstruction," master's thesis, Texas A&M University, 2004.

19. Marriage Records A, December 26, 1870–March 24, 1878, Marriage Certificate Registry, Office of the County Clerk, McLennan County, Texas. Information on Ancestry.com indicates that the marriage took place in Cherokee County, Texas. See also Charles F. Robinson II, "Legislated Love in the Lone Star State: Texas and Miscegenation," *SHQ* 108 (July 2004): 65–87; *Galveston DN*, September 26, 1887. The text of the *Honey v. Clark* decision can be found at E. M. Wheelock, *Reports of Cases Argued and Decided in the Supreme Court of the State of Texas*, vol. 37 (Houston: E. H. Cushing, 1874), 686–709.

20. *San Antonio Express*, August 22, 1873; *Dallas DH*, August 22, 1873, 2; Anne Bailey, *Between the Enemy and Texas: Parsons's Texas Cavalry in the Civil War* (Fort Worth: Texas Christian University Press, 1989), 206; Moneyhon, *Republicanism*, 190; "as infernal": quoted in Donaly Brice, "Finding a Solution to Reconstruction Violence: The Texas State Police," in Howell, ed., *Still the Arena of Civil War*, 203; W. C. Nunn, *Texas Under the Carpetbaggers* (Austin: University of Texas Press, 1962), 259–260; Jack Noe, "Representative Men: The Post–Civil War Political Struggle over Texas's Commissioners to the 1876 Centennial Exhibition," *SHQ* 120 (October 2016): 162–187.

21. *Cincinnati CT*, September 20, 1873; *NYT*, September 23, 1873; Dale Baum, *The Shattering of Texas Unionism: Politics in the Lone Star State During the Civil War* (Baton Rouge: Louisiana State University Press, 1998), 239. The *Texas Farmer and Stock Raiser* (Austin) published its first and only issue in November 1873.

22. "precious cargo . . . hospitalities": *Dallas WH*, September 27, 1873; *CT*, September 25, 1873, 1. On Chicago during this period, see William Cronon, *Nature's Metropolis: Chicago and the Great West* (New York: W. W. Norton, 1992).

23. "the largest and best": *NYT*, September 27, 1873, 5; *CT*, September 25, 1873, 1; ibid., September 26, 1873, 2.

24. *NYT*, September 23, 1873, 4, 5; ibid., September 24, 1873, 1; ibid., September 27, 1873, 5; *CT*, September 21, 1873, 2; ibid., September 26, 1873, 8; ibid., September 25, 1873, 5; W. R. Poage, *McLennan County Before 1980* (Waco: Texian Press, 1981), 114.

25. Moneyhon, *Republicanism*, 190–192.

CHAPTER 3: A LOCAL WAR

1. "Black Marias": Perry R. Duis, *Challenging Chicago: Coping with Everyday Life, 1837–1920* (Urbana: University of Illinois Press, 2006), 27; Carolyn Ashbaugh, *Lucy Parsons: American Revolutionary* (Chicago: Haymarket Books, 2013 [1976]), 17.

2. "It consists . . . politicians": *CT*, December 23, 1873, 1; ibid., 4; ibid., September 10, 1872, 2; *Chicago Times*, December 21, 1873, 3; Karen Sawislak, *Smoldering City: Chicagoans and the Great Fire, 1871–1874* (Chicago: University of Chicago Press, 1995), 265–267; James Green, *Death in the Haymarket: A Story of Chicago, the First Labor Movement and the Bombing That Divided Gilded Age America* (New York: Anchor Books, 2007), 47–49; John B. Jentz and Richard Schneirov, *Chicago in the Age of Capital: Class, Politics and Democracy During the Civil War and Reconstruction* (Urbana: University of Illinois Press, 2012), 155–167.

3. *CT*, December 23, 1873, 1; Sawislak, *Smoldering*, 269.

4. "I found": Lucy E. Parsons, ed., *Life of Albert R. Parsons with Brief History of the Labor Movement in America* (Chicago: Mrs. Lucy E. Parsons, 1889), 10.

5. "I decided": ibid., 10; Bessie Louise Pierce, *A History of Chicago*, vol. 3, *The Rise of a Modern City, 1871–1893* (Chicago: University of Chicago Press, 1957), 21. I am grateful to Nick Roland for suggesting possible links between Chicago and Austin, and between German immigrants and Albert Parsons. See John Morris, "Chicago's Forgotten Turner Halls: Turnverein Vorwaerts," Chicago Patterns, April 4, 2016, http://chicagopatterns.com /chicagos-forgotten-turner-halls-vorwaerts-turnverein.

6. Sawislak, *Smoldering*, 114–115; *KL*, November 6, 1886; David Roediger, "Albert Parsons—The Anarchist as Trade Unionist," in David Roediger and Franklin Rosemont, eds., *Haymarket Scrapbook* (Chicago: Charles H. Kerr, 1986), 31–33.

7. Christiane Harzig, "Chicago's German North Side, 1880–1900: The Structure of a Gilded Age Ethnic Neighborhood," in Hartmut Keil and John B. Jentz, eds., *German Workers in Industrial Chicago, 1850–1910: A Comparative Perspective* (DeKalb: Northern Illinois University Press, 1983), 127–144.

8. William Cronon, *Nature's Metropolis: Chicago and the Great West* (New York: W. W. Norton, 1992); Sawislak, *Smoldering*, 163, 4; Pierce, *History of Chicago*, 58–61, 146–147, 171, 176.

9. "the poor": Mary Field Parton, ed., *The Autobiography of Mother Jones* (Chicago: Charles H. Kerr, 1925), 2.

10. Edith Abbott, *The Tenements of Chicago: 1908–1935* (Chicago: University of Chicago Press), 25; *Report of the Board of Health of the City of Chicago, for the Years 1870–73* (Chicago: Bulletin Printing Company, 1874), 13, 65, 136, 139; Pierce, *History of Chicago*, 53–54, 240; "Great Rebuilding": Sawislak, *Smoldering*, 163, 190, 204, 206; Donald L. Miller, *City of the Century: The Epic of Chicago and the Making of America* (New York: Simon and Schuster, 1996), 113, 193.

11. Pierce, *History of Chicago*, 123; Hartmut Keil and John B. Jentz, eds., *German Workers in Chicago: A Documentary History of Working-Class Culture from 1850 to World War I* (Urbana: University of Illinois Press, 1998), 71–72, 80, 109, 111; "self-dependence": *CT*, December 23, 1873, 4.

12. "army": *Socialist* [Chicago], July 26, 1879, 2.

13. "There is a silver lining": *CT*, October 1, 1873, 4; David Montgomery, *Beyond Equality: Labor and the Radical Republicans, 1862–1872* (Urbana: University of Illinois Press, 1981), 15, 183, 433, 434, 439.

14. Sawislak, *Smoldering*, 12, 261.

15. "baser elements . . . manner": *Address and Reports of the Citizens' Association of Chicago, 1874–1876* (Chicago: Hazlett and Reed, 1877), 4–6; Sawislak, *Smoldering*, 12, 152, 261; Richard Schneirov, "Chicago's Great Upheaval of 1877: Class Polarization and Democratic Politics," in David O. Stowell, ed., *The*

Great Strikes of 1877 (Urbana: University of Illinois Press, 2008), 79; Jentz and Schneirov, *Chicago*, 179–186.

16. "You have but to combine": *CT*, February 2, 1874, 4.

17. Charles Nordhoff, *The Communistic Societies of the United States: From Personal Visit and Observation* (New York: Harper and Brothers, 1875); John Merriman, *Massacre: The Life and Death of the Paris Commune* (New York: Basic Books, 2014).

18. *CT*, September 10, 1872, 2; Paul Avrich, *The Haymarket Tragedy* (Princeton, NJ: Princeton University Press, 1984).

19. *CT*, January 4, 1872, 4; ibid., December 26, 1872, 6; ibid., April 18, 1880, 18; Pierce, *History of Chicago*, 48, 237; St. Clair Drake, *Black Metropolis: A Study of Negro Life in a Northern City* (New York: Harcourt, Brace, and World, 1970), 50.

20. James Dorsey, *Up South: Blacks in Chicago's Suburbs, 1719–1983* (Lima, OH: Wyndham Hall Press, 1986), 25–32; Margaret Garb, *Freedom's Ballot: African American Political Struggles in Chicago from Abolition to the Great Migration* (Chicago: University of Chicago Press, 2014).

21. "ladies' man": Green, *Death in the Haymarket*, 62; Michael J. Schaak, *Anarchy and Anarchists: A History of the Red Terror, and the Social Revolution in America and Europe, Communism, Socialism, and Nihilism in Doctrine and Deed, the Chicago Haymarket Conspiracy and the Detection and Trial of the Conspirators* (Chicago: F. Schulte, 1889), 160; William Scharnau, "Thomas J. Morgan and the United Labor Party of Chicago," *JISHS* 66 (Spring 1973): 41–47.

22. "wholesale hunger": Parsons, ed., *Life*, xvi.

23. *DI-O*, June 17, 1875, 3; "keeps a house . . . dealt with": ibid., July 27, 1876, 8.

24. "difficulty in getting": Van Patten quoted in Howard H. Quint, *The Forging of American Socialism: Origins of the Modern Movement* (Columbia: University of South Carolina Press, 1953), 19; "practically the only": Parsons, ed., *Life*, xv.

25. "We hold": Keil and Jentz, eds., *German Workers in Chicago*, 360–362.

26. Avrich, *Haymarket Tragedy*, 22, 40; Pierce, *History of Chicago*, 244; *CT*, April 28, 1878, 3; ibid., August 1, 1879, 3.

27. "pretext for many": Schaak, *Anarchy and Anarchists*, 45; "at large": ibid., 59; *CT*, January 1, 1877, 4; Mari Jo Buhle, *Women and American Socialism, 1870–1920* (Urbana: University of Illinois Press, 1983), 6–8, 14; Paul Buhle, "German Socialists and the Roots of American Working-Class Radicalism," in Keil and Jentz, eds., *German Workers in Industrial Chicago*, 224–235.

28. "there is no help . . . employees": *CT*, July 26, 1877, 4; John P. Lloyd, "Labor's Rebellion: Albert Parsons, Joseph Medill, and the Legacy of the Civil War in the Strike of 1877 in Chicago," *JIH* 10 (Autumn 2007): 166–190; Michael Bellesiles, *1877: America's Year of Living Violently* (New York: New Press, 2010);

CT, June 30, 1877, 4; *NYT,* July 23, 1877, 5; *CT,* July 23, 1877, 3; Schneirov, "Chicago's Great Upheaval," 76–104.

29. "We want work . . . to that end": *CT,* July 22, 1877, 8; Jentz and Schneirov, *Chicago,* 194–213.

30. *CT,* July 23, 1877, 3.

31. "Grand Army . . . hang them": *CT,* July 24, 1877, 5; ibid., July 25, 1877, 7; Avrich, *Haymarket Tragedy,* 30; Schneirov, "Chicago's Great Upheaval," 84.

32. "discharged . . . street": Parsons, ed., *Life,* 11–13; *CT,* July 25, 1877, 7.

33. "to be near . . . threatened to strike": Parsons, ed., *Life,* 13–14; *CT,* July 24, 1877, 5; ibid., July 25, 1877, 7; "originating . . . conspirator": *DI-O,* August 3, 1877, 3.

34. Schaak, *Anarchy and Anarchists,* 59; Schneirov, "Chicago's Great Upheaval," 94.

35. "unsexed . . . Amazons": *DI-O,* July 27, 1877, 1; "Chicago's workers": Keil and Jentz, eds., *German Workers in Chicago,* 231; see also ibid., 161–162, 231–232.

36. "The city was alive": *DI-O,* July 27, 1877, 1; *NYT,* July 31, 1877, 5; "seat of local war": ibid., July 28, 1877, 1; Richard Schneirov, *Labor and Urban Politics: Class Conflict and the Origins of Modern Liberalism in Chicago, 1864–1897* (Urbana: University of Illinois Press, 1998), 69–76.

37. "Judge Lynch": quoted in Avrich, *Haymarket Tragedy,* 18; Pierce, *History of Chicago,* 250–252; Ashbaugh, *Lucy Parsons,* 20; "this formidable army": *NYT,* July 27, 1877, 1; "tramp army . . . rebellion": Bellesiles, *1877,* 116–120, 167; *NYT,* July 28, 1877, 1.

38. *Address and Reports of the Citizens Association of Chicago,* 44, 89; "had entered . . . overwork": *CT,* October 7, 1877, 3; Sam Mitrani, *The Rise of the Chicago Police Department: Class and Conflict, 1850–1894* (Urbana: University of Illinois Press, 2013), 131–132.

39. "My enemies": *KL,* October 23, 1886; "*Partners in business*": Medill quoted in Lloyd, "Labor's Rebellion," 172.

40. "the First": *Alarm,* June 27, 1885; "was the tocsin": Samuel Gompers, *Seventy Years of Life and Labour: An Autobiography* (New York: E. P. Dutton, 1925), 46; Nick Salvatore, *Eugene V. Debs: Citizen and Socialist* (Urbana: University of Illinois Press, 1982), 36–37.

41. "it was during the great . . . discontent": Lucy Parsons, "The Principles of Anarchism," c. 1905–1910, in Gail Ahrens, ed., *Lucy Parsons: Freedom, Equality and Solidarity. Writings and Speeches, 1878–1937* (Chicago: Charles H. Kerr, 2004), 29.

CHAPTER 4: FAREWELL TO THE BALLOT BOX

1. "[I] sold suits": *Illinois v. August Spies et al.,* testimony of ARP, vol. N, 138, Chicago Historical Society, Haymarket Affair Digital Collection (hereinafter

CHS, HADC); "No audience": Lizzie Holmes quoted in Lucy E. Parsons, ed., *Life of Albert R. Parsons with Brief History of the Labor Movement in America* (Chicago: Mrs. Lucy E. Parsons, 1889), 191. The Joseph Labadie Collection at the University of Michigan Special Collections Library in Ann Arbor includes the text of a "calling card" for "Parsons & Co., Manufacturers of Ladies and Children's Clothing, Factory 306 Mohawk St., Chicago," call no. SVF, title "Anarchism—Parsons, Lucy," "Inglis, Agnes—Anarchism."

2. "a martyr": *CT*, October 7, 1877, 3; Michael J. Schaak, *Anarchy and Anarchists: A History of the Red Terror, and the Social Revolution in America and Europe, Communism, Socialism, and Nihilism in Doctrine and Deed, the Chicago Haymarket Conspiracy and the Detection and Trial of the Conspirators* (Chicago: F. Schulte, 1889), 66; "greed": Allan Pinkerton, *Strikers, Communists, Tramps, and Detectives* (New York: Arno Press, 1969 [1878]), 265; "viciousness . . . punishment": ibid., 388.

3. *Socialist*, November 23, 1878, 8; ibid., December 14, 1878, 8; ibid., July 19, 1879, 8.

4. *CT*, April 7, 1878, 8; "Go to the polls": Schaak, *Anarchy and Anarchists*, 67; Richard Schneirov, *Labor and Urban Politics: Class Conflict and the Origins of Modern Liberalism in Chicago, 1864–1897* (Urbana: University of Illinois Press, 1998), 86.

5. "had no difficulty": *CT*, April 6, 1878, 7; "Force, as represented": ibid., April 26, 1878, 7; "We intend to carry": ibid.; "What Communism": ibid., April 28, 1878, 4; ibid., June 17, 1878, 5.

6. *DI-O*, August 5, 1878, 8.

7. "swarthy": quoted in Bruce Nelson, *Beyond the Martyrs: A Social History of Chicago's Anarchists, 1870–1900* (New Brunswick, NJ: Rutgers University Press, 1988), 60; *LE*, March 1, 1884; *Socialist*, March 15, 1878, 8; Mari Jo Buhle, *Women and American Socialism, 1870–1920* (Urbana: University of Illinois Press, 1983), 19, 22.

8. Rima Lunin Schultz and Adele Hast, eds., *Women Building Chicago, 1790–1990: A Biographical Dictionary* (Bloomington: Indiana University Press, 2001), 842–843, 762, 608; Meredith Tax, *The Rising of Women: Feminist Solidarity and Class Conflict, 1880–1917* (Urbana: University of Illinois Press, 2001), 40–48; Edward T. James, Janet Wilson James, and Paul Boyer, eds., *Notable American Women: A Biographical Dictionary* (Cambridge, MA: Harvard University Press, 1971), 187–188; David R. Roediger and Philip S. Foner, *Our Own Time: A History of American Labor and the Working Day* (New York: Verso, 1989), 166; "Work of the Sex," *Chicago Times*, September 2, 1894.

9. "From her meek": *CT*, August 7, 1886, 2; *Chicago Times*, September 2, 1894; Dorothy Richardson, "Trades-Unions in Petticoats," *Leslie's Monthly Magazine* 77 (March 1904): 489–500.

10. Biographical information from FMC, Marriage and Birth Records, Military Records, on Ancestry.com and Wikitree, www.wikitree.com/wiki/Hunt-7409 and www.wikitree.com/wiki/Hunt-8007.

11. *Lucifer the Light-Bearer*, May 28, 1898; *Cleveland DH*, December 22, 1862; *New York Herald*, December 6, 1857. Biographical information based on Erin Dwyer, "From the Pen of a Kicker: The Life and Circle of Lizzie Swank Holmes," master's thesis, Tufts University, 2006.

12. Wendy Hayden, *Evolutionary Rhetoric: Sex, Science and Free Love in Nineteenth-Century Feminism* (Carbondale: Southern Illinois University Press, 2013), 47–49; Gina Misiroglu, ed., *American Countercultures: An Encyclopedia of Nonconformists, Alternative Lifestyles, and Radical Ideas in U.S. History* (New York: Routledge, 2008), 75.

13. Blaine McKinley, "Free Love and Domesticity: Lizzie M. Holmes, *Hagar Lyndon* (1893) and the Anarchist-Feminist Imagination," *JAC* 13 (Spring 1990): 55–62.

14. "can frill": *DI-O*, December 11, 1875, 6; Lizzie Swank Holmes, "Women Workers of Chicago," *American Federationist* 12 (August 1905): 509; Tax, *Rising*, 45–46; Carolyn Ashbaugh, *Lucy Parsons: American Revolutionary* (Chicago: Haymarket Books, 2013 [1976]), 50.

15. "Can Women . . . virtuous": *DI-O*, September 2, 1878, 8; *CT*, July 28, 1879, 7; *Socialist*, March 15, 1878, 3.

16. "prohibition": *Socialist*, June 21, 1879, 1; "their rightful": ibid., August 16, 1879, 2.

17. Buhle, *Women*, 16–17.

18. *CT*, June 17, 1878, 5; Buhle, *Women*, 16–17.

19. "harmony of employer . . . earned it": *Socialist*, December 7, 1878, 2; "But alas": ibid., January 25, 1879, 5.

20. "Hints to Young Housekeepers . . . aristocracy": *Socialist*, February 1, 1879, 3; "Hear, ye who love": ibid., February 15, 1879, 6.

21. *CT*, September 29, 1878, 8.

22. Illinois, Cook County Birth Certificates, 1878–1922 (available on Ancestry.com); Ashbaugh, *Lucy Parsons*, 269n.9. A copy of the birth certificate was obtained from the Cook County (Illinois) Clerk, Bureau of Vital Records, Genealogy Office, Chicago, Illinois.

23. Parsons, ed., *Life*, 18–19; "Causes of General Depression in Labor and Business. Chinese Immigration. Investigation by a Select Committee of the House of Representatives . . . Testimony taken at Chicago, San Francisco, and Other Cities" [December 10, 1879] (Washington, DC: US Government Printing Office, 1879), 192–200; *DI-O*, October 27, 1879, 3; *Journal of United Labor* 1 (May 15, 1880), 3.

24. "communistic proclivities": *DI-O*, August 5, 1878; ibid., July 2, 1879, 6; *CT*, January 31, 1879, 8; "secret": ibid., July 29, 1878, 8.

25. "who are invited . . . Union is strength": *CT*, November 10, 1879, 8; "feasibility" *DI-O*, April 12, 1880, 3; "the slaves of Chicago . . . slavery": *CT*, April 12, 1880, 8; "They preferred": Swank Holmes, "Women Workers," 509; "A great deal": *LE*, August 18, 1884.

26. Schneirov, *Labor and Urban Politics*, 86, 94; "those lordly": *Socialist*, September 14, 1878, 2.

27. "stinking lard": *Socialist*, May 10, 1879, 4; "The Chinese . . . must go": ibid., May 24, 1879, 1.

28. Nelson, *Beyond the Martyrs*, 67–68; Parsons, ed., *Life*, 16; "My experience": ibid., 28; "that every law": ibid., 18, xx–xxi; Ashbaugh, *Lucy Parsons*, 18.

29. "doggedly": Parsons, ed., *Life*, 16; John B. Jentz and Richard Schneirov, *Chicago in the Age of Capital: Class, Politics and Democracy During the Civil War and Reconstruction* (Urbana: University of Illinois Press, 2012), 213.

30. Schneirov, *Labor and Urban Politics*, 89–91.

31. *Socialist*, December 7, 1878, 1; *Truth*, November 17, 1883, 1.

32. "a new . . . value of life": *Socialist*, July 12, 1879, 1; "gory-red banner": *DI-O*, July 5, 1879, 7; Roediger and Foner, *Our Own Time*, 138.

33. "Experience has taught": Philip Van Patten to George A. Schilling, Detroit, August 2, 1880, Box 1, Folder 1, George A. Schilling Papers, Abraham Lincoln Presidential Library and Museum, Springfield, Illinois (Schilling Papers hereafter).

34. Nelson, *Beyond the Martyrs*, 68, 80; "We all feel": Morgan quoted in Ashbaugh, *Lucy Parsons*, 40; John R. Commons, David J. Saposs, Helen L. Sumner, E. B. Mittelman, H. E. Hoagland, John B. Andrews, and Selig Perlman, eds., *History of Labour in the United States*, vol. 2 (New York: Augustus M. Kelley, 1966 [1921–1935]), 289–290; Schneirov, *Labor and Urban Politics*, 86.

35. "The Communist": *CT*, August 1, 1879, 3; "the blood": *Socialist*, March 22, 1879, 3; "The Reds": ibid., March 23, 1879, 7; Schaak, *Anarchy and Anarchists*, 67–68; Buhle, *Women*, 16–17.

36. "to avoid": Van Patten quoted in Christine Heiss, "German Radicals in Industrial America: The *Lehr-und-Wehr Verein* in Gilded Age Chicago," in Hartmut Keil and John B. Jentz, eds., *German Workers in Industrial Chicago, 1850–1910: A Comparative Perspective* (DeKalb: Northern Illinois University Press, 1983), 216; ibid., 206–223; "the International": testimony of John F. Waldo, vol. M, 169, CHS, HADC.

37. "A. R. Parsons has suffered": *AZ*, November 1, 1880. See translations on "Foreign Language Press Survey," Newberry Library Online, http://flps .newberry.org/#filters/keyword/arbeiter%20zeitung?page=1.

38. "Chicago Commune . . . mob": *DI-O*, August 30, 1880, 1.

39. *AZ*, August 3, 1880.

40. Christiane Harzig, "Chicago's German North Side, 1880–1900: The Structure of a Gilded Age Ethnic Neighborhood," in Keil and Jentz, eds., *German Workers in Industrial Chicago*.

41. *KL*, October 8, 1887, 13.

42. "a thorough lady": ibid.; "a long period": Parsons, ed., *Life*, 193; James Green, *Death in the Haymarket: A Story of Chicago, the First Labor Movement and the Bombing That Divided Gilded Age America* (New York: Anchor Books, 2007), 54.

43. Carolyn Ashbaugh to Mrs. Price, Chicago, November 15, 1973, Price Papers, DBCAH; Ashbaugh, *Lucy Parsons*, 41, 269n.15.

44. *Journal of United Labor* 2 (April 1882), 217; *Report on Condition of Woman and Child Labor Wage-Earners in the United States*, vol. 10, *History of Women in Trade Unions*, 61st Cong., 2nd sess., Doc. 645 (Washington, DC: US Government Printing Office, 1911), 127, 129; Joanne J. Meyerowitz, *Women Adrift: Independent Wage Earners in Chicago, 1880-1930* (Chicago: University of Chicago Press, 1991), 28–29; Tax, *Rising*, 49; Ashbaugh, *Lucy Parsons*, 49.

45. "grand demonstration": *DI-O*, August 22, 1881, 8; "The Cannstatt Festival Immense Crowd at Ogden's Grove," *Illinois Staats Zeitung*, September 1, 1879, at Foreign Language Press Survey, http://flps.newberry.org /article/5418474_8_0067; Ashbaugh, *Lucy Parsons*, 43; Paul Avrich, *The Haymarket Tragedy* (Princeton, NJ: Princeton University Press, 1984), 59; Schneirov, *Labor and Urban Politics*, 85–86; Hartmut Jentz and John B. Keil, eds., *German Workers in Chicago: A Documentary History of Working-Class Culture from 1850 to World War I* (Urbana: University of Illinois Press, 1998), 11, 204, 210–212.

46. "anarchists . . . fish": Philip Van Patten, "Socialism and the Anarchists," *Bulletin of the Social Labor Movement* (December/January 1881): 3.

47. Albert Parsons, *Anarchism: Its Philosophy and Scientific Bases as Defined by Some of Its Apostles* (Chicago: Mrs. A. R. Parsons, 1887), 93; "We are called": *Alarm*, April 18, 1885.

48. Beverly Gage, *The Day Wall Street Exploded: A Story of America in Its First Age of Terrorism* (New York: Oxford University Press, 2009), 41–50; Frederic Trautmann, *The Voice of Terror: A Biography of Johann Most* (Westport, CT: Greenwood Press, 1980); Michael R. Johnson, "Albert R. Parsons: An American Architect of Syndicalism," *MQ* (Winter 1968): 195–206.

49. Avrich, *Haymarket Tragedy*, 74–75, 83; Green, *Death in the Haymarket*, 93; Nelson, *Beyond the Martyrs*, 86–87, 88, 91, 98, 101; Commons et al., *History of Labour*, 99.

50. "Autobiography of Samuel Fielden," Anarchy Archives, http://dwardmac
.pitzer.edu/Anarchist_Archives/haymarket/Fielden.html.

51. Trautmann, *Voice*, 219; David Roediger and Franklin Rosemont, eds.,
Haymarket Scrapbook (Chicago: Charles H. Kerr, 1986), 14.

52. "the embryonic groups": Parsons, *Anarchism*, 110; "so exceedingly": Parsons, ed., *Life*, xxi.

53. Parsons, ed., *Life*, 19–22; *Truth*, November 17, 1883, 1; "Dynamite: Plain":
ibid., April 21, 1883, 3; "Dynamite Will": ibid., June 23, 1883, 3.

54. "inevitable": Parsons, *Anarchism*, 52; Parsons, ed., *Life*, xv; Keil and Jentz,
eds., *German Workers in Chicago*, 250–251; "a scientific subject": *Socialist*, May
24, 1879, 1.

55. *LE*, March 1, 1884; "extravagance": ibid., June 7, 1884; "agents": ibid., May
3, 1884.

56. Keil and Jentz, eds., *German Workers in Chicago*, 105–115; *LE*, March 1,
1884.

57. "Mrs. A. R. Parsons . . . wage-workers' cause": *CT*, April 4, 1884, 7; "blood
and thunder": ibid., May 21, 1884, 3.

58. Commons et al., *History of Labour*, 360; Keil and Jentz, eds., *German
Workers in Chicago*, 258–259; "agitation trips": Parsons, ed., *Life*, 190; "to be
forewarned": ibid., 126–128.

Chapter 5: A False Alarm?

1. William Salisbury, *The Career of a Journalist* (New York: B. W. Dodge,
1908), 110; *Chicago DN*, March 13, 1886.

2. "Pinkerton Army": *Alarm*, October 17, 1885; "I say": testimony of Andrew
C. Johnson, vol. J, 398, CHS, HADC.

3. "bathed in a sea": *Alarm*, May 2, 1885; *CT*, April 29, 1885, 2.

4. "A new board": *CT*, April 29, 1885; "buy a Colt's": Michael J. Schaak, *Anarchy and Anarchists: A History of the Red Terror, and the Social Revolution in
America and Europe, Communism, Socialism, and Nihilism in Doctrine and Deed,
the Chicago Haymarket Conspiracy and the Detection and Trial of the Conspirators*
(Chicago: F. Schulte, 1889), 80; *Milwaukee DS*, April 29, 1885, 2.

5. "Vive la Commune! . . . Blow it up with dynamite": *CT*, April 29, 1885, 2;
"the robbers' roost": *LE*, May 16, 1885; William Holmes, "Reminiscences," *ME*
(November 1907): 290–291; "permitted to make": *Philadelphia Inquirer*, April
30, 1885; "unreasoning": *CT*, April 30, 1885, 4; *NYT*, April 30, 1885, 1.

6. "it was only a matter of time": testimony of Marshall H. Williamson, vol.
J, 7–8, CHS, HADC.

7. "to show me": testimony of Marshall H. Williamson, vol. J, 8, CHS,
HADC; "Their manner": ibid., 9.

8. Testimony of Thomas L. Treharn, vol. J, 246–248, CHS, HADC; testimony of Jeremiah Sullivan, vol. J, 255–266, ibid.; Timothy Messer-Kruse, *Trial of the Haymarket Anarchists: Terrorism and Justice in the Gilded Age* (New York: Palgrave Macmillan, 2011), 119; Timothy Messer-Kruse, *The Haymarket Conspiracy: Transatlantic Anarchist Networks* (Urbana: University of Illinois Press, 2012), 3, 125.

9. "I love clamor": *Alarm*, November 19, 1887; "force . . . revolt!": Lucy E. Parsons, ed., *Life of Albert R. Parsons with Brief History of the Labor Movement in America* (Chicago: Mrs. Lucy E. Parsons, 1889), 65, 68. The Burke quotation: "I love clamor when there is abuse. The alarm bell disturbs the inhabitants, but saves them from being burnt in their beds."

10. Bruce Nelson, "'We Can't Get Them to Do Aggressive Work': Chicago's Anarchists and the Eight-Hour Movement," *ILWCH* 29 (Spring 1986): 9; John R. Commons, David J. Saposs, Helen L. Sumner, E. B. Mittelman, H. E. Hoagland, John B. Andrews, and Selig Perlman, eds., *History of Labour in the United States*, vol. 2 (New York: Augustus M. Kelley, 1966 [1921–1935]), 378–381.

11. *Alarm*, October 4, 1884.

12. Ibid.

13. Ibid.

14. "bloodthirsty woman": *WP*, January 11, 1885, 2.

15. *LE*, April 4, 1885.

16. *Alarm*, August 8, 1885.

17. Ibid., September 18, 1885.

18. Ibid., December 26, 1885.

19. *LE*, March 27, 1886.

20. "Lucy E. Parsons handbill": *Cleveland Leader*, February 20, 1885; "the gospel . . . Chicago": ibid., February 9, 1885, and *Canton (OH) Repository*, February 11, 1885, and February 26, 1885; "Dynamite": *ISJ*, February 14, 1885; "little . . . terrors for her": *Chicago Herald*, reprinted in *WP*, January 11, 1885, 2.

21. "a negro . . . country": *NYT*, January 26, 1885, 1; Messer-Kruse, *Haymarket Conspiracy*, 71, 114–116.

22. "Bombs!": *Alarm*, May 2, 1885; ibid., May 16, 1885; "One man": ibid., October 18, 1884; "the equilibrium . . . impossible": Parsons, ed., *Life*, 181; "Gunpowder brought": *Alarm*, November 15, 1884.

23. Paul Avrich, *The Haymarket Tragedy* (Princeton, NJ: Princeton University Press, 1984), 165–166; "We believe": *Alarm*, January 13, 1885.

24. *LE*, April 25, 1885.

25. Floyd Dell, "Bomb-Talking" in David Roediger and Franklin Rosemont, eds., *Haymarket Scrapbook* (Chicago: Charles H. Kerr, 1986), 74; "the dear stuff": Schaak, *Anarchy and Anarchists*, 76.

26. Parsons, ed., *Life*, xxii–xxiii.

27. Edith Abbott, "Wages of Unskilled Labor in the United States, 1850–1900," *JPE* 13 (June 1905): 361–367; Herbert G. Gutman, "Alarm: Chicago and New York, 1884–1889," in Joseph R. Conlin, ed., *The American Radical Press, 1880–1960*, vol. 2 (Westport, CT: Greenwood Press, 1974), 380–386.

28. Ad: *Alarm*, February 1, 1885; "Let every dirty": *CT*, May 7, 1885, 3; Carolyn Ashbaugh, *Lucy Parsons: American Revolutionary* (Chicago: Haymarket Books, 2013 [1976]), 63.

29. "lady liberty . . . stood beneath": *Alarm*, February 21, 1886; "Brave . . . society": ibid., August 22, 1885; "Mrs. Parsons": *CT*, July 27, 1885, 5; "no other class": ibid., July 28, 1885, 4.

30. Schaak, *Anarchy and Anarchists*, 77.

31. "Wives and children . . . assemblies": *CT*, August 10, 1885, 8; "sour-headed . . . country": ibid., July 28, 1885, 4; "go arm . . . substance and form": testimony of Clarence P. Dresser, vol. J, 236, CHS, HADC.

32. "like whipped curs . . . company has got": *CT*, July 9, 1885, 2.

33. I. D. Roes in *Christian Recorder*, March 7, 1889.

34. See, for example, the following issues of *Alarm*: February 7, 1885, May 16, 1885, May 30, 1885, September 5, 1885, October 31, 1885, November 28, 1885. The format for the Wednesday evening meetings was a thirty- to fifty-minute presentation followed by respondents, each limited to ten minutes.

35. "memorable incidents": Parsons, ed., *Life*, 191.

36. *CT*, August 9, 1888, 1.

37. Parsons, ed., *Life*, 62.

38. Ibid., 59; "conservative workingmen": ibid., 31–32; ibid., 33; *Alarm*, December 26, 1885; Messer-Kruse, *Haymarket Conspiracy*, 125.

39. Parsons, ed., *Life*, 39; "cold": ibid., 56; "very dangerous . . . damnation": *Canton (OH) Repository*, February 11, 1886; ibid., October 15, 1887.

40. "the existing social order": *Canton (OH) Repository*, October 15, 1887, 26; "Here in Cleveland": *Alarm*, December 26, 1885.

41. "Dynamiters": Albert R. Parsons Papers, 1876–1893 (MSS 15A, Microfilm 523), Library Archives Division, Wisconsin Historical Society, Madison, Wisconsin (ARP Papers hereafter); "He Counsels": clipping, *Cleveland LH*, December 20, 1885, in ibid.; *Dallas WH*, March 26, 1885; "the final outbreak . . . negress": *NYT*, March 19, 1885, 5; *CT*, March 19, 1885, 6.

42. "whose whole being": Parsons, ed., *Life*, 60.

CHAPTER 6: HAYMARKET

1. Steve Fraser, *The Age of Acquiescence: The Life and Death of American Resistance to Organized Wealth and Power* (Boston: Little, Brown, 2015).

2. *NYT*, September 8, 1885, 2; "To the Employes [*sic*] of Chicago [1885], Convention of the Federation of Organized Trade and Labor Unions of the U.S.," signed by the Trades Assembly of Chicago, ARP Papers; "meaningless affair . . . free republic": *Alarm*, September 10, 1885; ibid., October 17, 1885; "The Voluntary Slaves": ibid., September 19, 1885.

3. Richard Schneirov, *Labor and Urban Politics: Class Conflict and the Origins of Modern Liberalism in Chicago, 1864–1897* (Urbana: University of Illinois Press, 1998), 173; Bruce Nelson, "'We Can't Get Them to Do Aggressive Work': Chicago's Anarchists and the Eight-Hour Movement," *ILWCH* 29 (Spring 1986): 4–6; Paul Avrich, *The Haymarket Tragedy* (Princeton, NJ: Princeton University Press, 1984), 83–86.

4. Carolyn Ashbaugh, *Lucy Parsons: American Revolutionary* (Chicago: Haymarket Books, 2013 [1976]), 49.

5. "if you started talking": Box 1, Memos and Drafts on Motivation Folder, audio cassette #2 (Interview with Irving Abrams), Carolyn Ashbaugh Papers—Lucy Parsons Research Papers—The Newberry Library, Chicago, Illinois (Ashbaugh Papers hereafter).

6. "Now printing": quoted in Eric L. Hirsch, *Urban Revolt: Ethnic Politics in the Nineteenth-Century Chicago Labor Movement* (Berkeley: University of California Press, 1990), 104–105.

7. *Alarm*, January 13, 1885; Albert Parsons, *Anarchism: Its Philosophy and Scientific Basis as Defined by Some of Its Apostles* (Chicago: Mrs. A. R. Parsons, 1887), 100; Michael J. Schaak, *Anarchy and Anarchists: A History of the Red Terror, and the Social Revolution in America and Europe, Communism, Socialism, and Nihilism in Doctrine and Deed, the Chicago Haymarket Conspiracy and the Detection and Trial of the Conspirators* (Chicago: F. Schulte, 1889), 108.

8. "God has a grudge": *Alarm*, May 30, 1885; Lucy E. Parsons, ed., *Life of Albert R. Parsons with Brief History of the Labor Movement in America* (Chicago: Mrs. Lucy E. Parsons, 1889), 40–41; Bruce Nelson, "Revival and Upheaval: Religion, Irreligion, and Chicago's Working Class in 1886," *JSH* 25 (Winter 1991): 235–238; William A. Mirola, *Redeeming Time: Protestantism and Chicago's Eight-Hour Movement, 1866–1912* (Urbana: University of Illinois Press, 2015); *Alarm*, January 9, 1886; Herbert G. Gutman, "Protestantism and the American Labor Movement: The Christian Spirit in the Gilded Age," *AHR* 72 (October 1966): 74–101.

9. "Thankless Day": *Alarm*, December 12, 1885; "You are to give": Schaak, *Anarchy and Anarchists*, 77; *CT*, November 30, 1884, 4; "a lie": *Alarm*, December 12, 1884; *CT*, November 28, 1885, 4; Parsons, ed., *Life*, 73, 77.

10. "twin relics": *Alarm*, June 18, 1885; *KL*, September 18, 1886, 2; *Alarm*, January 13, 1885; "the dregs": *Alarm*, April 4, 1885; "Her brother slaves": *Alarm*, November 14, 1885.

11. "rancid reform": *Alarm*, April 4, 1885; "brave and humane": *Alarm*, April 18, 1885.

12. "silly and vain": Albert Parsons, *Anarchism*, 109; *CT*, February 9, 1885, 1; "the dynamite assassins": *CT*, March 2, 1885, 8.

13. "The employers used . . . distress of the workers": Mary Field Parton, ed., *The Autobiography of Mother Jones* (Chicago: Charles H. Kerr, 1925), 12–13; "Such speakers": Schaak, *Anarchy and Anarchists*, 124; *Alarm*, April 4, 1885.

14. John R. Commons, David J. Saposs, Helen L. Sumner, E. B. Mittelman, H. E. Hoagland, John B. Andrews, and Selig Perlman, eds., *History of Labour in the United States*, vol. 2 (New York: Augustus M. Kelley, 1966 [1921–1935]), 366–374; Bureau of Labor Statistics of Illinois, *Fourth Biennial Report* (Springfield: H. K. Rokked, 1886), 446–453.

15. Sidney H. Kessler, "The Organization of Negroes in the Knights of Labor," *JNH* 37 (July 1952): 252, 259; Warren C. Whatley, "African-American Strikebreaking from the Civil War to the New Deal," *SSH* 17 (Winter 1993): 525–558; George B. Cotkin, "Evictions, Strikebreakers, and Violence: Industrial Conflict in the Hocking Valley, 1884–1885," *OH* (Spring 1978); John H. Keiser, "Black Strikebreakers and Racism in Illinois, 1865–1900," *JISHS* 65 (1972): 313–326.

16. David Roediger and Franklin Rosemont, eds., *Haymarket Scrapbook* (Chicago: Charles H. Kerr, 1986), 81–83.

17. "Two Soul-Saving Sams": Nelson, "Revival and Upheaval," 246–247.

18. Jeffrey S. Adler, "Shoot to Kill: The Use of Deadly Force by the Chicago Police, 1875–1920," *Journal of Interdisciplinary History* 38 (Autumn 2007): 233–254; Sam Mitrani, *The Rise of the Chicago Police Department: Class and Conflict, 1850–1894* (Urbana: University of Illinois Press, 2013), 166, 182; Schneirov, *Labor and Urban Politics*, 143; "The club today": quoted in Roediger and Rosemont, eds., *Haymarket Scrapbook*, 82; "socialism places": Schaak, *Anarchy and Anarchists*, 74; Ashbaugh, *Lucy Parsons*, 61.

19. "Mrs. Lucy Parsons": *Alarm*, March 6, 1886; "contemplates making": *Alarm*, April 3, 1886.

20. *CT*, March 19, 1886, 5; "Who but a devoted . . . economic system": *Alarm*, April 3, 1886; Rick Ward, "The Carrol County Court House Massacre, 1886: A Cold Case File," Mississippi History Now, May 2012, http://mshistorynow.mdah.state.ms.us/articles/381/the-carroll-county-courthouse-massacre-1886-a-cold-case-file.

21. *Alarm*, April 3, 1886.

22. "And to the negro himself . . . incendiary": ibid.; *WP*, March 21, 1886, 4; ibid., March 25, 1886, 2; "every conceivable": *NYT*, March 19, 1886, 1.

23. "the infernal machine": *LE*, January 2, 1886; *CT*, May 1, 1886, 8; "anarchists": Schaak, *Anarchy and Anarchists*, 122–123.

24. "stood for": *Alarm*, March 20, 1886.

25. "personally responsible": *Mail* quoted in Avrich, *Haymarket Tragedy*, 187; Roediger and Rosemont, eds., *Haymarket Scrapbook*, 13; *AZ*, May 1, 1886.

26. The following account is based on the eyewitness testimony of Lizzie Swank Holmes, in Parsons, ed., *Life*, 190–193, as well as her Haymarket trial testimony; Albert Parsons, CHS, HADC, www.chicagohistory.org/hadc/transcript/volumen /101-150/N108-143.htm; and secondary accounts provided by defense attorney William P. Black in Parsons, ed., *Life*, 100–109; Avrich, *Haymarket Tragedy*, 197–214; Timothy Messer-Kruse, *The Haymarket Conspiracy: Transatlantic Anarchist Networks* (Urbana: University of Illinois Press, 2012), 177–178.

27. "Good speakers . . . full force": handbill in Haymarket Trial evidence, CHS, HADC, www.chicagohistory.org/hadc/transcript/trialtoc .htm#EXHIBITS.

28. "shouting Amazons . . . *Zeitung*": CT, May 4, 1886, 1; Schneirov, *Labor and Urban Politics*, 197.

29. "I think we ought": Speech of Albert R. Parsons, in *The Accused, the Accusers: The Famous Speeches of the Eight Chicago Anarchists in Court When Asked If They Had Anything to Say Why Sentence Should Not Be Passed upon Them. On October 7th, 8th and 9th, 1886, Chicago, Illinois* (Chicago: Socialistic Publishing Society, 1886), 30 (also available online at CHS, HADC), 186; *CT*, May 5, 1886, 2; Mitrani, *Rise*, 190; *CT*, May 5, 1886, 2; *LE*, May 1, 1886; "American Group meets": quoted in Timothy Messer-Kruse, *The Trial of the Haymarket Anarchists: Terrorism and Justice in the Gilded Age* (New York: Palgrave Macmillan, 2011), 87; ibid., 177; *KL*, October 23, 1886, 2; Parsons, ed., *Life*, 201.

30. "Have you any . . . isn't he": testimony of Edgar E. Owen, vol. K, 214, CHS, HADC; testimony of Henry E. O. Heinemann, vol. I, 244–245, ibid.

31. Persons attending the meeting included Mr. and Mrs. Timmons, John Waldo, Thomas Brown, William Snyder, William Patterson, Michael Schwab, Samuel Fielden, Lucy Parsons, Albert Parsons, Lizzie Swank Holmes, and two men named Owens and Myers.

32. "go over . . . yes": testimony of Heinemann, vol. K, 252–253, CHS, HADC; "to write . . . milder": testimony of G. P. English, vol. K, 296, 300, 306, ibid.

33. "keep your eye upon it . . . peaceable": quoted in Avrich, *Haymarket Tragedy*, 215–216.

34. "slender tail": *NYT*, May 6, 1886, 1.

35. "many other arguments . . . took place": Parsons, ed., *Life*, 193.

36. "Spies, Parsons": *New York Tribune*, May 6, 1886, 5; *CT*, May 7, 1886, 4.

37. Messer-Kruse, *Trial*, 193n.56. The quotations are from Oscar Neebe in *The Accused, the Accusers*, 30; "brass cartridge": *Denver RMN*, May 12, 1886, 1.

38. "to shadow": *Cleveland PD*, May 6, 1886, 2; *CT*, May 8, 1886, 2; ibid., May 7, 1886, 2; *New York Tribune*, May 10, 1886, 1.

39. "minions . . . contempt": Gail Ahrens, ed., *Lucy Parsons: Freedom, Equality and Solidarity. Writings and Speeches, 1878–1937* (Chicago: Charles H. Kerr, 2004), 51–53.

40. "levanted": *Dallas MN*, May 6, 1886; "His Early Career . . . worded": *Waco Day*, May 6, 1886.

41. "mongrel": *Galveston DN*, May 16, 1886; *Dallas MN*, May 7, 1886; "an ordinary": *Cleveland PD*, May 18, 1886; "a single family": *Dallas MN*, May 6, 1886, 8.

42. "reticent . . . ability": *Dallas MN*, May 11, 1886, reprinted from the *Chicago DN* of May 8, 1886.

43. "My ancestors": *Atchison DG*, November 4, 1886.

Chapter 7: Bitter Fruit of Braggadocio

1. "poetry, music": *LE*, February 20, 1886; "or stay": ibid., April 24, 1886; testimony of Lizzie Swank Holmes, vol. M, 305–306, CHS, HADC; "there will be . . . beginning of the end": *LE*, February 26, 1886.

2. Sigmund Zeisler, *Reminiscences of the Anarchist Case* (Chicago: Literary Club, 1927), 19; Lucy E. Parsons, ed., *Life of Albert R. Parsons with Brief History of the Labor Movement in America* (Chicago: Mrs. Lucy E. Parsons, 1889), 193–195 (see the drawing of Albert in disguise between pages 185 and 186); Letter No. 2: "To A. R. Parsons, from his Friend and Brother, Simon B. Needham; also Letters from A. R. Parsons to his Friends at Waukesha," ARP Papers; *Firebrand*, August 25, 1895.

3. "liberty, fraternity . . . fragrant bloom": "To A. R. Parsons," August 12, 1880, ARP Papers; Parsons, ed., *Life*, 212.

4. "The theory of anarchy": testimony of Lizzie Mae Holmes, vol. M, 304, CHS, HADC.

5. Sam Mitrani, *The Rise of the Chicago Police Department: Class and Conflict, 1850–1894* (Urbana: University of Illinois Press, 2013), 192–194; *KL*, September 25, 1886, 4; "Anarchy's Red Hand . . . and Fielden": *NYT*, May 6, 1886, 1.

6. "Public justice . . . murder": quoted in Paul Avrich, *The Haymarket Tragedy* (Princeton, NJ: Princeton University Press, 1984), 233.

7. "well-educated": Zeisler, *Reminiscences*, 19, 22–23; Parsons, ed., *Life*, 100–116; Carl Smith, *Urban Disorder and the Shape of Belief: The Great Chicago Fire, the Haymarket Trial, and the Model Town of Pullman* (Chicago: University of Chicago Press, 1994), 128–129.

8. "stalking up and down . . . know him": *CT*, June 22, 1886, 1; Parsons, ed., *Life*, 136, 197; *KL*, October 23, 1886, 3.

9. "not only most ungracious": Zeisler, *Reminiscences*, 22–23; Parsons, *Life*, 103; "I thought" clipping, n.d. [c. August 22, 1886], ARP Papers.

10. "jauntily attired": *CT*, June 26, 1886, 4.

11. "in a pleasant . . . rather sympathizers": *Cleveland PD*, June 23, 1886, 6; *Dallas MN*, June 26, 1886.

12. Carolyn Ashbaugh, *Lucy Parsons: American Revolutionary* (Chicago: Haymarket Books, 2013 [1976]), 92.

13. "falsely sailing": *Liberty*, May 22, 1886; ibid., June 19, 1886; Richard Schneirov, *Labor and Urban Politics: Class Conflict and the Origins of Modern Liberalism in Chicago, 1864–1897* (Urbana: University of Illinois Press, 1998), 222; "to defend . . . without a cause": *LE*, May 8, 1886; ibid., May 15, 1886.

14. "the core of conspiracy . . . utterances": Michael J. Schaak, *Anarchy and Anarchists: A History of the Red Terror, and the Social Revolution in America and Europe, Communism, Socialism, and Nihilism in Doctrine and Deed, the Chicago Haymarket Conspiracy and the Detection and Trial of the Conspirators* (Chicago: F. Schulte, 1889), 133.

15. "she was doing": testimony of Clarence Dresser, vol. J, 226, CHS, HADC.

16. "by general addresses": Joseph E. Gary, "The Chicago Anarchists of 1886: The Crime, the Trial, and the Punishment," *Century Magazine* 45 (April 1893): 812. For a rebuttal to Messer-Kruse, who argues that the trial was fair by the standards of the day, and that the defendants were indeed conspirators and to varying degrees guilty of the charges, see Richard Schneirov, "Still Not Guilty," *Labor* 9 (2012): 29–33.

17. Smith, *Urban Disorder*, 143–145.

18. *LE*, July 24, 1886; *Chicago Times*, September 26, 1886; Parsons, ed., *Life*, 213–215.

19. "practiced bomb-maker": Zeisler, *Reminiscences*, 28; testimony of August Spies, vol. N, 57–58, CHS, HADC.

20. "boldness and eloquence": Parsons, ed., *Life*, 207.

21. Smith, *Urban Disorder*, 153; Timothy Messer-Kruse, *The Haymarket Conspiracy: Transatlantic Anarchist Networks* (Urbana: University of Illinois Press, 2012), 2–3; Timothy Messer-Kruse, *The Trial of the Haymarket Anarchists: Terrorism and Justice in the Gilded Age* (New York: Palgrave Macmillan, 2011), 118–121. See also Timothy Messer-Kruse, James O. Eckert Jr., Pannee Burkel, and Jeffrey Dunn, "The Haymarket Bomb: Reassessing the Evidence," *Labor* 2 (Summer 2005): 39–52; "Braggadocio": Schaak, *Anarchy and Anarchists*, 535; Parsons, ed., *Life*, 100–106.

22. "People's Exhibits," CHS, HADC; "Dynamite": *Alarm*, June 27, 1885.

23. "war with all means": *Alarm*, May 30, 1885; "get dynamite": ibid., February 6, 1886; "One man armed": ibid., October 21, 1884; ibid., January 13, 1885; "We rejoice": ibid., January 24, 1885.

24. "former assistant": testimony of LMS, vol. M, 280–307, CHS, HADC; Messer-Kruse, *Trial*, 89–90; Parsons, ed., *Life*, 100–101.

25. "Mr. and Mrs. . . . Yes": testimony of LMS, vol. M, 109, CHS, HADC; "I left my house": testimony of ARP, vol. N, 109, ibid.; testimony of Samuel Fielden, vol. M, 312, ibid.

26. The speech is included in testimony of ARP, vol. N, 117–135, CHS, HADC ("compulsory idleness"), and Parsons, ed., *Life*, 117–127; "was the original": vol. N, 140, CHS, HADC; testimony of G. P. English, vol. K, 298, ibid.; *LE*, August 14, 1886; Avrich, *Haymarket Tragedy*, 193–194.

27. See, though, his recounting of the day in *KL*, October 23, 1886, 2–3; Messer-Kruse, *Trial*, 86–90.

28. "At least I wrote": testimony of ARP, vol. N, 109, CHS, HADC; Parsons, ed., *Life*, 191; Messer-Kruse, *Trial*, 83, 177; cf. Ashbaugh, *Lucy Parsons*, 73.

29. Testimony of William Snyder, vol. M, 98, CHS, HADC; testimony of Samuel Fielden, vol. M, 310–311, ibid.; Messer-Kruse, *Trial*, 86–87.

30. "many innocent": "Albert R. Parsons autobiography, 1886" (written in jail for publication in *KL*, October 23, 1886); "he said he had": testimony of Thomas Brown, vol. M, 135, CHS, HADC.

31. "to be near . . . disowned": *CT*, August 11, 1886, 1; *CT*, November 27, 1880, 7; *DI-O*, May 20, 1875, 2; *Galveston DN*, December 1, 1880.

32. Messer-Kruse, *Trial*, 226; "disconsolate": *Galveston DN*, August 21, 1886; *CT*, August 21, 1886, 2; "sharing . . . haggard": *Lansing (MI) Sentinel*, August 28, 1886. For the judge's instructions to the jury, see vol. O, 1–10, 24–38, CHS, HADC ("consummation").

33. "a profound": Parsons, ed., *Life*, 110; ibid., 129; "against anarchy": *Galveston DN*, August 21, 1886.

34. *Philadelphia Inquirer*, August 21, 1886, 1; "Why not . . . of course be arrested": clipping, n.d. [c. August 23, 1886], ARP Papers; *Fort Worth DG*, August 21, 1886; "Secret Meeting": *Austin WS*, August 26, 1886.

35. *St. Louis G-D*, September 15, 1886; Waco City Directories for 1887–1888; John Dennis Anderson, "Cooper, Madison Alexander, Jr.," Handbook of Texas Online, Texas State Historical Association, n.d., www.tshaonline.org /handbook/online/articles/fco59; *London Anglo American Times*, October 9, 1886.

36. "step-father . . . drawing her away": *St. Louis G-D*, September 15, 1886.

37. "there is nothing": *St. Louis G-D*, September 15, 1886; "'Ostler Joe . . . women of the town": "The Poem Which Shocked Washington Society," *Daily Alta-California*, March 13, 1886.

38. FMC for McLennan County, Texas, for 1880, 1900, 1910.

39. "wife and ally . . . Oliver now": *St. Louis G-D*, September 15, 1886.

40. "the radical scalawag . . . tony clothes": ibid., September 18, 1886, 3.

41. "and have all . . . near Waco": ibid.

42. "carefully scanning . . . child unborn": *St. Louis G-D*, September 19, 1886, 6; "not accountable . . . in her veins": *CT*, September 20, 1886, 3.

43. "as a dusky . . . her environments": *Kansas City Star*, September 15, 1886.

CHAPTER 8: "THE DUSKY GODDESS OF ANARCHY SPEAKS HER MIND"

1. "You I bequeath . . . lay it down": Lucy E. Parsons, ed., *Life of Albert R. Parsons with Brief History of the Labor Movement in America* (Chicago: Mrs. Lucy E. Parsons, 1889), 211; *KL*, November 20, 1886; "The boy": *NYT*, October 17, 1886, 9.

2. *The Accused, the Accusers: The Famous Speeches of the Eight Chicago Anarchists in Court When Asked If They Had Anything to Say Why Sentence Should Not Be Passed upon Them. On October 7th, 8th and 9th, 1886, Chicago, Illinois* (Chicago: Socialistic Publishing Society, 1886).

3. "stump speaking": *DI-O*, October 10, 1886; *Accused, Accusers*, 95; "Your honor": ibid., 188.

4. "advised murder . . . dead": *DI-O*, October 10, 1886, 7; "vehemently": *Muskegon (MI) Chronicle*, October 12, 1886; Carolyn Ashbaugh, *Lucy Parsons: American Revolutionary* (Chicago: Haymarket Books, 2013 [1976]), 98–100.

5. Ashbaugh, *Lucy Parsons*, 105; Gail Ahrens, ed., *Lucy Parsons: Freedom, Equality and Solidarity. Writings and Speeches, 1878–1937* (Chicago: Charles H. Kerr, 2004), 56–57; "upon this all-important . . . dying for": *Rockford DR*, October 11, 1886, 4; *NYT*, October 17, 1886, 9; Carlotta R. Anderson, *All-American Anarchist: Joseph A. Labadie and the Labor Movement* (Detroit: Wayne State University Press, 1998), 138–139.

6. "Resistance to tyranny . . . unrewarded": *Wheeling (WV) Register*, September 6, 1886, 1.

7. "mercy": *KL*, September 11, 1886, 4; Edward P. Mittelman, "Chicago Labor Politics, 1877–1896," *JPE* 28 (May 1920): 418; *Baltimore Sun*, November 1, 1886.

8. William Scharnau, "Thomas J. Morgan and the United Labor Party of Chicago," *JISHS* 66 (Spring 1973), 41–47.

9. "freaks . . . offer was refused": *NYT*, October 18, 1886, 2.

10. *Dallas MN*, November 16, 1886; clipping, n.p., n.d., ARP Papers.

11. "no more consideration . . . even by a woman": *CT*, September 10, 1886, 4; "feared this one": *HW*, November 20, 1886; "Lucy Parsons, you": *Peoria Transcript* quoted in *Wichita (KS) Globe*, October 8, 1887; "dusky representative": *NYT*, October 17, 1886, 9; "sanguinary Amazon": clipping, n.d., n.p., ARP Papers; "quadroon": *NYT*, November 5, 1886, 2; "one of the most": clipping, n.p. [Saint Joseph, MO], January 31, 1887, 1; "The Dusky": Box 2, folder "Reproduced Copies of Materials Re the Parsons and Haymarket," Ashbaugh Papers.

12. *DI-O*, November 1, 1886, 4; *NYT*, November 1, 1886, 1; Albert Clark Stevens, *Cyclopedia of Fraternities* (New York: Hamilton Printing and Publishing Company, 1899), 144.

13. "Alles ist": undated handwritten letter in ARP Papers (translated by Matthew Bunn); *KL*, November 13, 1886.

14. Timothy Messer-Kruse, *The Haymarket Conspiracy: Transatlantic Anarchist Networks* (Urbana: University of Illinois Press, 2012), 117–119; *Milwaukee Sentinel*, December 30, 1886, 3; *DI-O*, January 4, 1887, 8; Edward O'Donnell, *Henry George and the Crisis of Inequality: Progress and Poverty in the Gilded Age* (New York: Columbia University Press, 2015); Armond Fields, *Lillian Russell: A Biography of "America's Beauty"* (Jefferson, NC: McFarland, 1999).

15. *DI-O*, October 16, 1886, 3; *CT*, January 16, 1887, 11; "like thieves": *CT*, November 8, 1886; "committee . . . their names": clipping, n.p. [Buffalo], January 31, 1887, 1, ARP Papers; *NYT*, October 16, 1886, 5; Richard Oestreicher, *Solidarity and Fragmentation: Working People and Class Consciousness in Detroit, 1875–1900* (Urbana: University of Illinois Press, 1989), 201.

16. *NYT*, October 16, 1886, 5; "everybody should": handbill dated December 20, 1886, ARP Papers; "Mrs. Lucy E. Parsons": handbill dated November 17, 1886, ibid.; "She is a very fluent . . . language": handbill dated May 5, 1887, ibid.

17. "Do you think": *New York Herald*, October 18, 1886; "Is that the way": clipping, n.p. [New Haven, CT], n.d. [November 17, 1886], ARP Papers. For perhaps the fullest rendering of her standard speech, see *Kansas City Journal*, December 21, 1886, 1.

18. *Kansas City Journal*, December 21, 1886, 1; "Free speech": *Detroit FP*, January 23, 1887.

19. "But the red flag": *Kansas City Journal*, December 21, 1886, 1; "This is our color": clipping, n.p. [Allegheny, Pennsylvania], November 22, 1886, ARP Papers; "conservative trade unionists": Ahrens, ed., *Lucy Parsons*, 57; "bloodthirsty": clipping, n.p. [Philadelphia], n.d. [c. November 1, 1886], 1, ibid.; *New York World*, c. November 6, 1886, ibid.

20. "Bartholdi's big girl": clipping, n.p. [New York], n.d. [c. November 5, 1886], ARP Papers; clipping, n.p. [*New York World*], n.d. [c. November 1, 1886], ibid.; clipping, n.p. [Cincinnati], n.d. [c. October 11, 1886], ibid.; *Cincinnati T-S*, October 18, 1886; Paul Avrich, *The Haymarket Tragedy* (Princeton, NJ: Princeton University Press, 1984), 142.

21. "Mrs. Lucy E. Parsons": *Milwaukee Journal*, February 14, 1887; "taking sides": *Philadelphia Inquirer*, October 18, 1886, 4; "gained the enmity": *Galveston DN*, October 19, 1886; *Dallas MN*, October 19, 1886, 6.

22. "I don't": *NYT*, October 18, 1886, 8; "would rend": *Detroit Advance and Labor Leaf*, January 26, 1887.

23. *CT*, January 23, 1887, 9; *DI-O*, November 5, 1886, 2; *NYT*, November 8, 1886, 5; "the missiles of today . . . advantage of it": *DI-O*, October 15, 1886, 5; "as a waltzing": *Detroit FP*, January 23, 1887; "a slaughterer": *Omaha Republican*, December 22, 1886, 1; "that chief": *DI-O*, October 15, 1886; "the scum": *Cincinnati T-S*, October 18, 1886; "dumb as oysters": clipping, n.p. [Detroit], January 22, 1887, ARP Papers; "she would have no more compunction": clipping, n.p. [Omaha], December 22, 1886, ibid.; "I will take the red flag": *NYT*, October 16, 1886, 5.

24. "damnable": *NYT*, October 16, 1886, 5; "at times . . . shame": *Cincinnati Enquirer*, October 13, 1886.

25. "as it bothered": *NYT*, October 18, 1886, 8; "Keep quiet": clipping, n.p., n.d., ARP Papers; "My dear sir": clipping, *New York CA*, n.d., ibid.; "remarked that smoking": *Detroit FP*, January 23, 1887.

26. The examples are from her appearance in Allegheny, Pennsylvania (November 21, 1886), recorded in the *Pittsburgh Dispatch*, November 22, 1886, ARP Papers; *KL*, November 13, 1886.

27. "the detective": clipping, n.p. [Buffalo], January 31, 1887, 1, ARP Papers; "fear-laden": clipping, *Bismarck DT*, November 7, 1886, ibid.

28. *DI-O*, October 25, 1886, 1; *Philadelphia Inquirer*, October 25, 1886, 8; *NYT*, October 25, 1886, 2; clipping, n.p. [Orange], n.d. [c. October 25, 1886], ARP Papers.

29. See the article "Lucy Parsons' Pluck," in *National Police Gazette*, November 6, 1886; clipping, n.p. [Orange], n.d. [c. October 25, 1886], ARP Papers.

30. "a woman of commanding": *Milwaukee DJ*, February 14, 1887; "She has a handsome . . . South": *NYT*, October 18, 1886, 8.

31. See, for example, "quadroon": *NYT*, November 5, 1886, 2; "light": clipping, n.p. [Philadelphia], n.d. [c. November 1, 1886], ARP Papers; *NYT*, October 17, 1886, 9; *Atchison DG*, November 4, 1886; clipping, n.p. [Buffalo], January 31, 1887, ARP Papers.

32. "there is no trace . . . Indian origin": *NYT*, October 17, 1886, 9.

33. "Her dense": *Cincinnati Enquirer*, October 11, 1886; "intelligence . . . interference": clipping, n.p. [Buffalo], January 31, 1887, ARP Papers; "Negro-Mexican": *Cincinnati Star*, October 13, 1886.

34. "the biggest demonstration . . . feathers": *NYT*, November 1, 1886, 1; "Her nose": *Bismarck DT*, November 7, 1886; "a modern Cleopatra": *Cincinnati Enquirer*, October 13, 1886.

35. "an unusually": *Detroit ALL*, January 26, 1887; "strange-looking": *Cincinnati Enquirer*, October 11, 1886; "the tangle-haired": clipping, n.p. [New York], November 5, 1886, ARP Papers.

36. "roughly clad": *Omaha Republican*, December 22, 1886; "sharp-featured . . . force of character": clipping, n.p. [Buffalo], January 31, 1887, ARP Papers.

37. Peter Rachleff, *Black Labor in Richmond, 1865–1890* (Urbana: University of Illinois Press, 1989).

38. "She addresses": clipping, n.p. [Omaha], n.d. [c. December 19, 1886], ARP Papers; "loud-mouthed": clipping, n.p. [Kansas City], December 20, 1886, ibid.; "she has a tongue": clipping, n.p. [Omaha], n.d., ibid.

39. "dangerous classes": "The Labor Vote," *HW*, November 20, 1886, 742; "peaceful means . . . repair it": *Labor Tribune*, quoted in *KL*, December 4, 1886, 10; *The Congregationalist*, November 4, 1886; clipping, *Omaha Republican*, n.d., ARP Papers; "She is doing": *Detroit Tribune*, January 27, 1887; "give her a fair hearing": *Omaha Truth*, December 18, 1886; "it greatly admire[d]": *Kansas City Times*, December 21, 1886.

40. *CT*, November 1, 1886, 5; "red-mouthed anarchist . . . ruins": clipping, n.p. [Cincinnati], n.d. [March 1887], ARP Papers.

41. "in a beautiful . . . labor": *DW*, March 11, 1942.

Chapter 9: The Blood of My Husband

1. William Salisbury, *The Career of a Journalist* (New York: B. W. Dodge, 1908), 107–108.

2. "disgrace to your Sex . . . same ills": Rattler to LP, Chicago, January 28, 1889, ARP Papers.

3. "most affectionate": clipping, n.p., n.d., ARP Papers; "They think": clipping, *CT*, March 29, 1887, ibid.

4. "furnish first-page . . . poetry": Salisbury, *Career*, 109–110.

5. "completely broken": *Los Angeles Times*, quoting *Chicago Herald*, October 30, 1887; *CT*, September 24, 1887, 2.

6. *New York Herald*, June 29, 1886, 3; "the amorous . . . Zandt": clipping, n.p. [Detroit], January 23, 1887, ARP Papers; clipping, "They Worship Spies: Women Kissing His Portrait," n.p., n.d., ibid.; "could only": Michael J. Schaack, *Anarchy and Anarchists: A History of the Red Terror, and the Social Revolution in America and Europe, Communism, Socialism, and Nihilism in Doctrine and Deed, the Chicago Haymarket Conspiracy and the Detection and Trial of the Conspirators* (Chicago: F. Schulte, 1889), 159; Carl Smith, *Urban Disorder and the Shape of Belief: The Great Chicago Fire, the Haymarket Trial, and the Model Town of Pullman* (Chicago: University of Chicago Press, 1994), 164–165; *San Francisco Bulletin*, October 10, 1887.

7. "She is with the kindest": Lizzie Swank Holmes to ARP, December 23, 1886, ARP Papers; Lum to ARP, December 25, 1886, ibid.

8. *New York World*, June 10, 1887; James R. Buchanan, *The Story of a Labor Agitator* (New York: Outlook, 1903), 373; "bright . . . brainless": Clarence Darrow, *In the Clutches of the Law: Clarence Darrow's Letters* (Berkeley: University

of California Press, 2013), 58–59; "a very impulsive . . . claim relation": *Chicago News*, June 10, 1887.

9. "cheery manner": Buchanan, *Story of a Labor Agitator*, 379; "is destructive": *Chicago Times*, August 25, 1886; Lucy E. Parsons, ed., *Life of Albert R. Parsons with Brief History of the Labor Movement in America* (Chicago: Mrs. Lucy E. Parsons, 1889), 107, 213–214, 218; *Alarm*, November 17, 1888.

10. "His anarchist arms": *Chicago News* story reprinted in *Baltimore Sun*, December 2, 1886, Supplement, 2; "and have every comfort": *Chicago MN*, November 29, 1886; clipping, "Cook County's Big Jail," n.p., n. d., ARP Papers; *Frank Leslie's Illustrated Newspaper*, October 1, 1887, 1; Timothy Gilfoyle, "'America's Greatest Criminal Barracks': The Tombs and the Experience of Criminal Justice in New York City, 1838–1897," *JUH* 29 (July 2003): 525–534.

11. "What Parsons Thinks": *Chicago Times*, September 26, 1886; "but they can't keep us": *CT*, March 9, 1887, 4; William Scharnau, "Thomas J. Morgan and the United Labor Party of Chicago," *JISHS* 66 (Spring 1973): 45–48; David Roediger and Franklin Rosemont, eds., *Haymarket Scrapbook* (Chicago: Charles H. Kerr, 1986), 86.

12. Scharnau, "Morgan," 52–55; Richard Schneirov, *Labor and Urban Politics: Class Conflict and the Origins of Modern Liberalism in Chicago, 1864–1897* (Urbana: University of Illinois Press, 1998), 205, 213, 218, 229–230.

13. "Mrs. Lucy Parsons": *Knights of Labor*, November 13, 1886, 4; ibid., November 20, 1886, 4; "Parsons be let out": ibid., November 13, 1886, 4.

14. Quotations in Gail Ahrens, ed., *Lucy Parsons: Freedom, Equality and Solidarity. Writings and Speeches, 1878–1937* (Chicago: Charles H. Kerr, 2004), 61–68, and Parsons, ed., *Life*, 235–241.

15. "Your liberty": *Columbus Capital*, March 13, 1887; *NYT*, March 10, 1887, 1; *DI-O*, March 10, 1887.

16. "acted more like": *CT*, March 10, 1887, 1; "Arrested to prevent": telegram in ARP Papers; "unnecessary arrest . . . Mahomedanism": *Columbus Capital*, March 13, 1887.

17. "Have you not sworn . . . Columbus, Ohio?": clipping, n.p., May 7, 1887, ARP Papers; "secret circular": *New York Herald*, October 10, 1887, 3; Roediger and Rosemont, eds., *Haymarket Scrapbook*, 136; "My answer is because": October 1887 correspondence, reel 23, Papers of Terence V. Powderly, 1864–1924, and John William Hayes, 1880–1921, American Catholic History Research Center and University Archives University, Catholic University of America, Washington, DC (available on microfilm).

18. "press of admirers": *Chicago Herald*, November 29, 1886, 1; "I will bow down": *Chicago MN*, November 29, 1886; "I am an anarchist": *AG*, March 20,

1888; "Dance for the Doomed": ibid.; "bloodthirsty": *CT*, February 14, 1887, 1; "a dangerous woman . . . others of this fact": *Chicago Herald*, November 30, 1886.

19. "Mind what . . . where you came from": *Chicago DN*, July 18, 1887; *Dallas MN*, July 19, 1887.

20. "I stand before you . . . speech": *Chicago Herald*, August 29, 1887.

21. "Am I tired . . . papa": *Alarm*, August 30, 1887; Paul Avrich, *The Haymarket Tragedy* (Princeton, NJ: Princeton University Press, 1984), 360.

22. *Alarm*, June 23, 1888; *CT*, September 24, 1887, 2; "To the American People . . . or give me death!": *CT*, September 22, 1887, 1.

23. "Sorrow and care": *Chicago Mail*, September 27, 1887; "There is not the slightest": *CT*, September 25, 1887, 11; *Milwaukee Sentinel*, September 25, 1887; "I am the last": *CT*, September 28, 1887, 2.

24. "talented and beautiful": *Galveston DN*, September 26, 1887, 1; *CT*, October 12, 1887, 4.

25. "O, my God!": *CT*, September 24, 1887, 2; *NYT*, September 24, 1887, 1; *DI-O*, September 24, 1887, 6.

26. "throw me off": *CT*, September 26, 1887, 1; "most implacable": *St. Paul DG*, September 10, 1887.

27. "the reporter . . . in their place": *CT*, October 1, 1887, 6; "only served": *St. Paul DG*, September 10, 1887.

28. "hope and fear . . . So have I": *Chicago Mail*, October 27, 1887, 1; "Workingmen and their friends": *Decatur HD*, October 29, 1887; "the catastrophe": Albert R. Parsons: *Anarchism: Its Philosophy and Scientific Basis as Defined by Some of Its Apostles* (Chicago: Mrs. A. R. Parsons, 1887), 52; "He was free": ibid., 15.

29. "the idea": *Oregonian*, October 29, 1887; *Caspar's Directory of the American Book, News, and Stationery Trade* (Milwaukee: C. N. Caspar's Book Emporium, 1889), 32f.

30. "a very bright girl . . . unusual intelligence": *Los Angeles Times*, October 30, 1887, 1; "pretty children": *Atchison DG*, October 17, 1887; *Canton (OH) Repository*, October 15, 1887, 5.

31. "enemies of labor": *CT*, November 7, 1887, 1.

32. "the greed, cruelty": *Alarm*, November 5, 1887; *NYT*, November 6, 1887, 3; "intoxicated": Melville E. Stone, *Fifty Years a Journalist* (Garden City, NY: Doubleday, Page, 1920), 176; "good (Medium)": ibid., 175; "cried out . . . his fate": ibid., 176.

33. *Dallas MN*, November 9, 1887, 2.

34. "his wife . . . perverseness": Parsons, ed. *Life*, 113; "I am innocent": *NYT*, November 9, 1887, 5; "Darling, Precious . . . obey her": images in Parsons, ed., *Life*, between 248 and 249.

35. "on the ground": *Baltimore Sun*, November 11, 1887, 1; "If he ... terrible": Buchanan, *Story*, 393–394.

36. "for the pearly": Salisbury, *Career*, 110; "to beg ... trick": William Holmes, "Reminiscences," *ME* (November 1907), 290; "Die, Parsons": Lum quoted in Avrich, *Haymarket Tragedy*, 364–365.

37. "he had never": Parsons, *Anarchism*, 8.

38. "scene ... dead faint": *Baltimore Sun*, November 11, 1887, 1.

39. *CT*, November 11, 1887, 2; ibid., November 12, 1887, 2; "Caesar kept": *Alarm*, November 19, 1887; "his efforts": *Baltimore Sun*, November 11, 1887, 1.

40. "were poorly dressed ... if you will": *DI-O*, November 12, 1887, 1; *Columbus DE*, November 12, 1887; "I don't want": *DI-O*, November 12, 1887, 1.

41. "Instead of being": *CT*, November 12, 1887, 2; Parsons, *Anarchism*, 194–200.

42. "I really feel": *DI-O*, November 12, 1887, 1; "wrought himself ... gallows picture": *Dallas MN*, November 12, 1887; "Will I be allowed ... heard, O": *NYT*, November 12, 1887, 1; "No proxy": *CT*, November 12, 1887, 2; "Justice Is Done": *DI-O*, November 12, 1887.

43. "the dark skinned ... business over": *St. Paul Globe*, November 13, 1887, 1; "My God!": *CT*, November 12, 1887, 2; "Full account": *Bismarck Tribune*, November 12, 1887, 1; *DI-O*, November 12, 1887, 1.

44. "Oh papa ... his life!": *NYT*, November 12, 1887, 1.

45. *Dallas MN*, November 13, 1887; "Every little": *NYT*, November 12, 1887, 2.

46. "She was not": *LE*, November 19, 1887.

47. Hartmut Keil and John B. Jentz, eds., *German Workers in Chicago: A Documentary History of Working-Class Culture from 1850 to World War I* (Urbana: University of Illinois Press, 1998), 190–194; "Let the voice": *DI-O*, November 14, 1887, 1; *Alarm*, November 19, 1887.

48. Carolyn Ashbaugh, *Lucy Parsons: American Revolutionary* (Chicago: Haymarket Books, 2013 [1976]), 137; "It is a duty": *CT*, November 16, 1887, 3; "Most bravely ... Parsons": *Alarm*, November 19, 1887.

49. *CT*, December 18, 1887, 10.

50. "Our Papa ... Freunde": *New Orleans T-P*, December 19, 1887, 2; "Mrs. Parsons Getting": *CT*, December 18, 1887, 10.

Chapter 10: The Widow Parsons Sets Her Course

1. "The sordid": *Debs: His Life, Writings, and Speeches* (Chicago: Charles H. Kerr, 1908), 285–286; "the most decisive ... birth and growth": Emma Goldman, *Living My Life*, eds. Richard Drinnon and Anna Maria Drinnon (New York: New American Library, 1977), 508; Shelley Streeby, "Looking at State Violence: Lucy Parsons, Jose Marti, and Haymarket," in Russ Castronovo, ed.,

The Oxford Handbook of Nineteenth-Century American Literature (New York: Oxford University Press, 2011), 115–136; " the chief tragedy": Lucy E. Parsons, ed., *Life of Albert R. Parsons with Brief History of the Labor Movement in America* (Chicago: Mrs. Lucy E. Parsons, 1889), xxvi; Paul Avrich, *The Haymarket Tragedy* (Princeton, NJ: Princeton University Press, 1984), 401–414; Kristin Boudreau, *The Spectacle of Death: Populist Literary Responses to American Capital Cases* (New York: Prometheus, 2006), 67–104.

2. "Look at me": *Cincinnati Gazette*, October 11, 1886, as quoted in *KL*, November 20, 1886.

3. *CT*, December 30, 1887, 8; "innocent women . . . professor": *Alarm*, January 28, 1888; *Liberty*, June 7, 1890, 93.

4. Michael R. Johnson, "Albert R. Parsons: An American Architect of Syndicalism," *MQ* (Winter 1968): 196–205; David DeLeon, *The American as Anarchist: Reflections on Indigenous Radicalism* (Baltimore: Johns Hopkins University Press, 1978), 93.

5. Benedict Anderson, *Under Three Flags: Anarchism and the Anti-Colonial Imagination* (London: Verso, 2005).

6. Bessie Louise Pierce, *A History of Chicago*, vol. 3, *The Rise of a Modern City, 1871–1893* (Chicago: University of Chicago Press, 1957), 300–500; Edith Abbott, "Wages of Unskilled Labor in the United States, 1850–1900," *JPE* 13, no. 3 (June 1905): 361–363.

7. William Scharnau, "Thomas J. Morgan and the United Labor Party of Chicago," *JISHS* 66 (Spring 1973): 60; Richard Schneirov, *Labor and Urban Politics: Class Conflict and the Origins of Modern Liberalism in Chicago, 1864–1897* (Urbana: University of Illinois Press, 1998), 241–267.

8. "Chicago's White Slaves": *Chicago Times*, February 12, 1888; "My lords": *Alarm*, September 15, 1888.

9. *Alarm*, September 22, 1888; "to encourage": *DI-O*, December 27, 1888, 4.

10. "Let the voice . . . children's children": *CT*, June 21, 1888, 4; "You should have": *CT*, June 21, 1888, 5; "anxious to catch": *CT*, June 23, 1888, 8.

11. *Milwaukee DJ*, August 9, 1888; "that a powerful": *Alarm*, August 25, 1888.

12. Sigmund Zeisler, *Reminiscences of the Anarchist Case* (Chicago: Literary Club, 1927), 36; *Alarm*, November 24, 1888.

13. "When Columbus": *Alarm*, December 8, 1888; *CT*, November 19, 1888, 5; *Birmingham (UK) Daily Post*, November 12, 1888; *Reynolds's Newspaper* (London), November 18, 1888.

14. *Evening Telegraph and Star and Sheffield (UK) Daily Times*, November 16, 1888, 4; "she is a curious": *The Collected Letters of William Morris*, ed. Norman Kelvin, vol. 2, Part B: "1885–1888" (Princeton, NJ: Princeton University Press, 1988), 837–839; "She has the full lips": *Alarm*, December 8, 1888; *London*

American Register, July 7, 1888; *Echo-London Middlesex*, November 6, 1888; Rosemary Taylor, "'The City of Dreadful Delight': William Morris in the East End of London," *Journal of William Morris Studies* 18 (Winter 2009): 9–28.

15. *DI-O*, December 11, 1888; *Milwaukee DJ*, December 11, 1888; "an infernal lie": *CT*, December 12, 1888, 1; "chain of unmitigated . . . our movement": *New York EW*, December 11, 1888; "it would be a strange": *CT*, December 12, 1888, 1; *CT*, December 11, 1888, 1.

16. *CT*, December 5, 1888, 3; *CT*, December 18, 1888, 7; "revolutionary gatherings": *CT*, December 9, 1888, 9; "boarder": *DI-O*, December 18, 1888, 7.

17. *Chicago Herald*, May 27, 1890; "on account": *DI-O*, December 27, 1888; *Milwaukee DJ*, May 16, 1887; *Wisconsin State Register*, December 29, 1888; "an exceptionally": *CT*, December 31, 1888. See Ancestry.com for marriage and birth records.

18. "black haired . . . accompany[ing] her": *DI-O*, June 17, 1889, 7.

19. "violent anarchistic . . . stars and stripes": ibid., December 27, 1888, 4; ibid., December 28, 1888; *Alarm*, January 5, 1889; "The truth": *CT*, January 23, 1889, 4; *CT*, February 3, 1890, 3.

20. *CT*, February 3, 1890, 3; *Centralia E and T*, September 20, 1890; *DI-O*, March 4, 1889, 7.

21. *CT*, October 17, 1889, 3; "Do you suppose . . . supreme": *Atchison DG*, November 18, 1889.

22. *CT*, October 28, 1889, 3; "O, my children": *Alarm*, November 17, 1888.

23. "queer little cottage . . . boy": *Milwaukee YN*, December 11, 1889.

24. "I do not want . . . keeping a boarder": *CT*, September 17, 1890, 2.

25. "a couple of houses . . . acquaintances": *CT*, September 15, 1890, 1; "Row Among the Reds": *CT*, January 10, 1891, 11; Minutes of the Pioneer Aid and Support Association, September 2, 14, and October 12, 1890, Records, 1888–1957, Joseph A. Labadie Collection, University of Michigan Special Collections Library, Ann Arbor, Michigan. The minutes are in German; the author would like to thank Matthew Bunn for his translation.

26. *Chicago Herald*, January 24, 1889; "the picture": *CT*, December 5, 1888, 3; "Let the children": *CT*, March 21, 1892, 2; "a kind of human": *DI-O*, August 6, 1888; *Chicago Herald*, January 24, 1890; "for dramatic . . . baby show": *St. Paul DG*, April 6, 1888.

27. "humble home . . . Lucy Wanted Blood": *Chicago Mail*, c. December 29, 1888, ARP Papers; "her life would be devoted": *Wisconsin State Register*, December 22, 1888; "You bloody old . . . little fellow": *CT*, August 9, 1888, 1; *CT*, December 31, 1888, ARP Papers.

28. *CT*, April 28, 1891, 3; *CT*, May 23, 1891, 3.

29. "malicious trespass": *CT*, July 16, 1891, 3.

30. *Wheeling (WV) Register,* July 20, 1891, 6; "for the past three . . . kill you": *DI-O,* July 17, 1891, 7.

31. *CT,* December 3, 1881, 1.

32. "only hush money": *Chicago Herald,* January 24, 1889; *CT,* March 10, 1890, 7.

33. Jane Addams, *Twenty Years at Hull-House,* ed. Victoria Bissel Brown (Boston: Bedford/St. Martin's, 1999), 114, 117.

34. "sweater [boss]": "The New Slavery: Investigation into the Sweating System as Applied to the Manufacture of Wearing Apparel by the Chicago Trade and Labor Assembly" (Chicago: Detweiler, 1891), 4; Addams, *Hull-House,* 101–102, 127, 128, 254.

35. Kathryn Kish Sklar, "Hull House in the 1890s: A Community of Women Reformers," *Signs* 10 (Summer 1985): 658–677.

36. *World* article reprinted in *Indianapolis Freeman,* January 3, 1891, 3.

37. "election crowd . . . was her failing": *Waco EN,* April 3, 1889.

38. "the only English": quoted in Ernesto A. Longa, *Anarchist Periodicals in English Published in the United States (1833–1955): An Annotated Guide* (Lanham, MD: Scarecrow Press, 2010), 95; *Freedom,* November 11, 1890; "it is a mere trick": ibid., May 1892; *CT,* May 23, 1889, 3; *CT,* April 18, 1892, 3; *Freedom,* October 1, 1891; *Denver RMN,* July 5, 1897.

39. *Wheeling Register,* March 25, 1889; *CT,* October 27, 1890, 3; Mari Jo Buhle, *Women and American Socialism, 1870–1920* (Urbana: University of Illinois Press, 1983), 75–78; clipping, n.p. [Chicago], February 11, 1889, ARP Papers.

40. "folly . . . revolutionary gatherings": *CT,* December 9, 1888, 9.

41. "the anarchistic element . . . crush it out": *Bismarck DT,* November 9, 1890; *NYT,* November 8, 1890, 1; ibid., November 11, 1890, 3.

42. *CT,* May 30, 1892, 3; "buy yourselves . . . conservative Socialists": Michael J. Schaak, *Anarchists and Anarchy: A History of the Red Terror, and the Social Revolution in America and Europe, Communism, Socialism, and Nihilism in Doctrine and Deed, the Chicago Haymarket Conspiracy and the Detection and Trial of the Conspirators* (Chicago: F. Schulte, 1889), 666; *CT,* June 15, 1891, 3; "too much red": *CT,* May 2, 1892, 6.

43. *CT,* December 31, 1888, 3; *DI-O,* January 29, 1889, 4; *Salt Lake City Herald,* January 1, 1889; *CT,* January 7, 1889, 1; "and about a dozen . . . leading socialists": *DI-O,* June 17, 1889, 7; "indicates a low degree . . . use force": ibid., December 31, 1888, 1.

44. "Before we can have": *DI-O,* December 31, 1888; *NYT,* July 29, 1889, 1; "When the great": *CT,* March 21, 1892, 2; "In years to come": *DI-O,* November 12, 1892.

45. "A Just Blow . . . like Berkman": *Freedom,* August 1892; Paul and Karen Avrich, *Sasha and Emma: The Anarchist Odyssey of Alexander Berkman and*

Emma Goldman (Cambridge, MA: Belknap Press of Harvard University Press, 2012), 51–97; Beverly Gage, *The Day Wall Street Exploded: A Story of America in Its First Age of Terrorism* (New York: Oxford University Press, 2009), 57–64.

46. *McCook (NE) Tribune*, March 10, 1889; *Tacoma DN*, November 12, 1913.

47. "I will not tolerate": *CT*, November 10, 1891, 3; *CT*, November 11, 1888, 5; *CT*, November 10, 1890, 1; *CT*, November 9, 1891, 1; Henry David, *The History of the Haymarket Affair: A Study in the American Social-Revolutionary and Labor Movements* (New York: Collier Books, 1963), 403–404; "Hiss after hiss": *Aberdeen (SD) Sun*, November 13, 1891; "Hang the murderers . . . infamous lie": *Atchison DG*, November 12, 1891; *CT*, November 13, 1891, 1; *CT*, December 14, 1891, 3; "Every star": *DI-O*, December 14, 1891; "severely plain": *CT*, November 12, 1892, 1. See F. O. Bennett's poem "The Red Flag" ("emblem of treason and hate") in Paul Hull, *The Chicago Riot: A Record of the Terrible Scenes of May 4, 1886* (Chicago: Belford, Clarke, 1886), 5.

48. *NY Tribune*, June 21, 1888; "verbal pyrotechnics": *DI-O*, February 27, 1888, 4; "fiery": ibid., July 29, 1889, 2; "inflammatory": *Philadelphia Inquirer*, December 14, 1891; "incendiary": *Wheeling Register*, July 29, 1889; "fire-eating": *Los Angeles Times*, April 19, 1904; "red mouthed": *Charleston N and C*, August 25, 1893; "red hot": *DI-O*, February 27, 1893, 3; "I don't want to be respectable": *Milwaukee YN*, February 2, 1890.

49. "living . . . questioned by some": Parsons, ed., *Life*, xxvii; "more than ordinary . . . in which they live": George Schilling to Lucy Parsons, Springfield, December 1, 1893, George A. Schilling Collection, Box 1893–1894, Abraham Lincoln Library, Illinois State Historical Society, Springfield, Illinois (Schilling Collection hereafter).

50. Schilling to Lucy Parsons, December 1, 1893, Schilling Collection.

Chapter 11: Variety in Life, and Its Critics

1. "By force": *CT*, August 21, 1893, 2; "How long can this": *Freedom*, August 1892.

2. "men with that unsatiated": *Tacoma DN*, September 11, 1893; "lunacy": *CT*, August 22, 1893, 4; "she devil": *NYT*, August 21, 1893, 8; "murder and other": *Abilene TCN*, March 16, 1894; "an enraged tigress": *CT*, August 22, 1893, 4.

3. *CT*, June 26, 1893, 7; *NYT*, June 26, 1893, 1.

4. "Gov. John P. Altgeld's Pardon of the Anarchists and His Masterly Review of the Haymarket Riot" (Chicago: Lucy E. Parsons, 1915; orig. pub. in the 1903 edition of *Life of Albert R. Parsons*); Henry David, *The History of the Haymarket Affair: A Study in the American Social-Revolutionary and Labor Movements* (New York: Collier Books, 1963), 399–419.

5. "and I don't want . . . personal conduct": *Galveston DN*, December 2, 1894; *Canton (OH) Repository*, December 2, 1894; letter from Dyer Lum to Voltairine de Cleyre, [n.d., c. Lucy's arrest in Newark], Box 197 [bMS Am 1614 (197)]; Dyer Daniel Lum, letters to Voltairine de Cleyre, in Joseph Ishill Papers, Houghton Library, Harvard College Library (Ishill Papers hereafter).

6. Carolyn Ashbaugh, *Lucy Parsons: American Revolutionary* (Chicago: Haymarket Books, 2013 [1976]), 274.

7. Nick Salvatore, *Eugene V. Debs: Citizen Socialist* (Urbana: University of Illinois Press, 1982); Jane Addams, "A Modern Lear," *Survey* 29 (November 2, 1912): 131–137; Richard Drinnon, *Rebel in Paradise: A Biography of Emma Goldman* (Chicago: University of Chicago Press, 1982); Donald B. Smith, *Honoré Jaxon: Prairie Visionary* (Regina, SK, Canada: Coteau Books, 2007); "the father of labor": *CT*, September 18, 1915, 5.

8. "prosperity": *Firebrand*, May 1903; William Leach, *Land of Desire: Merchants, Power, and the Rise of a New American Culture* (New York: Pantheon, 1993), 27–30, 69, 75–78.

9. David Nasaw, *Going Out: The Rise and Fall of Public Amusements* (New York: Basic Books, 1993), 158, 191.

10. *CT*, July 29, 1892, 2; *Dallas MN*, December 2, 1894; "as principally of": *NYT*, August 2, 1891, 5; Edward P. Mittelman, "Chicago Labor Politics, 1877–1896," *JPE* 28 (May 1920): 423–426.

11. Rudyard Kipling, *American Notes*, online at Gutenberg, www.gutenberg.org/files/977/977-h/977-h.htm, chap. 5.

12. "liberty-loving": "New Slavery," 7–8; "at ease in Zion": William T. Stead, *If Christ Came to Chicago! A Plea for the Union of All Who Love in the Service of All Who Suffer* (Chicago: Laird and Lee, 1894), 258.

13. Nasaw, *Going Out*, 66; "an element": *Brattleboro (VT) Phoenix*, December 2, 1892; Margaret Garb, *Freedom's Ballot: African American Political Struggles in Chicago from Abolition to the Great Migration* (Chicago: University of Chicago Press, 2014), 138.

14. Nasaw, *Going Out*, 75; Ida B. Wells, Frederick Douglass, Irvine Garland Penn, and Ferdinand L. Barnett, *The Reasons Why the Colored American Is Not in the World's Columbian Exposition*, ed. Robert W. Rydell (Urbana: University of Illinois Press, 1999), xvii, xix.

15. "loiter around": Miller quoted in Ray Stannard Baker, *Following the Color Line: American Negro Citizenship in the Progressive Era* (New York: Harper and Row, 1964 [1908]), 130; *CT*, April 18, 1892, 3; Garb, *Freedom's Ballot*, 12; "the safety of woman": Frances E. Willard, "The Race Problem: Miss Willard on the Political Puzzle of the South," *Voice*, October 23, 1890; Jacqueline Jones

Royster, ed., *Southern Horrors and Other Writings: The Anti-Lynching Campaign of Ida B. Wells, 1892–1900* (Boston: Bedford Books, 1997), 138–148; Thomas Lee Philpott, *The Slum and the Ghetto: Immigrants, Blacks, and Reformers in Chicago, 1880–1930* (Belmont, CA: Wadsworth, 1991), 315, 332; *Freedom*, March 27, 1892.

16. Garb, *Freedom's Ballot*, 51, 54; "We ask to be known": Barrier Williams quoted in Wells et al., *Reason Why*, xxix.

17. "the better class": Royster, ed., *Southern Horrors*, 43; Paula Giddings, *Ida: A Sword Among Lions: Ida B. Wells and the Campaign Against Lynching* (New York: Amistad, 2008); Thomas C. Holt, "The Lonely Warrior: Ida B. Wells-Barnett and the Struggle for Black Leadership," in John Hope Franklin and August Meier, eds., *Black Leaders of the Twentieth Century* (Urbana: University of Illinois Press, 1982), 39–61.

18. David Squires, "Outlawry: Ida B. Wells and Lynch Law," *AQ* 67 (March 2015): 141–163; *San Antonio Express*, November 4, 1899; *CT*, July 26, 1896, 10.

19. Dennis B. Downey, "The Congress of Labor at the 1893 World's Columbian Exposition," *JISHS* 76 (1893): 131–138; "We want work": *CT*, August 22, 1893, 1.

20. "to mention no names": *Chicago Times*, September 23, 1895; *Milwaukee Journal*, November 13, 1896; *Denver EP*, June 14, 1897; *CT*, June 14, 1897, 11; "Liberty is dead": *Brownsville DH*, September 26, 1895.

21. *St. Paul Globe*, July 11, 1897; "leading anarchistress": *CT*, November 13, 1894, 6; "intemperate gall": *New Haven Register*, January 7, 1893; *CT*, May 21, 1894, 7; *Evansville C and P*, April 12, 1894; *CT*, April 24, 1894, 1; *New York Tribune*, April 24, 1894; "that they were belched": Donald L. McMurry, *Coxey's Army: A Study of the Industrial Army Movement of 1894* (Boston: Little, Brown, 1929), 232; Benjamin F. Alexander, *Coxey's Army: Popular Protest in the Gilded Age* (Baltimore: Johns Hopkins University Press, 2015), 42, 92; *CT*, April 28, 1894, 2.

22. *Firebrand*, December 15, 1895.

23. "You hideous murderers! . . . uproar": *CT*, November 12, 1896, 4; "Her appearance . . . lightly": Graham Taylor, *Pioneering on Social Frontiers* (Chicago: University of Chicago Press, 1930), 132.

24. "It had been like": A. J. Brigati, ed., *The Voltairine de Cleyre Reader* (Oakland, CA: AK Press, 2004), 106; *CT*, November 10, 1899, 4; Paul Avrich, *American Anarchist: The Life of Voltairine de Cleyre* (Princeton, NJ: Princeton University Press, 1978).

25. *Firebrand*, September 6, 1896; Ernesto A. Longa, *Anarchist Periodicals in English Published in the United States (1833–1955): An Annotated Guide* (Lanham, MD: Scarecrow Press, 2010); "the billows of discontent": *Rebel*, October 20, 1895.

26. "Nudity . . . considered immodest": *Lucifer* article reprinted in *Firebrand*, January 26, 1896; "Sex Ethics . . . false modesty": *Firebrand*, August 30, 1896; "The Sexual Organs . . . magnetism": ibid., October 18, 1896; "it is not greater":

ibid., August 30, 1896; "Objections to Variety . . . sweetest words": ibid., September 27, 1896.

27. "We love . . . not an Anarchist": *Firebrand*, September 27, 1896; "old prejudices": ibid., November 22, 1896; Jessica Moran, "The *Firebrand* and the Forging of a New Anarchism: Anarchist Communism and Free Love," Anarchist Library, http://theanarchistlibrary.org/library/jessica-moran-the-firebrand-and -the-forging-of-a-new-anarchism-anarchist-communism-and-free-lov.

28. March through September 1893 issues of *Lucifer*; Blaine McKinley, "Free Love and Domesticity: Lizzie M. Holmes, *Hagar Lyndon* (1893), and the Anarchist-Feminist Imagination," *JAC* 13 (Spring 1990): 55–62.

29. *CT*, March 22, 1898, 12; *CT*, April 15, 1899, 4; "the cancer of trade": Candace Falk, ed., *Emma Goldman: A Documentary History of the American Years*, vol. 1, *Made for America, 1890–1901* (Berkeley: University of California Press, 2003), 315.

30. "red-mouthed": *Omaha MWH*, January 20, 1898; "tattered creatures": Falk, ed., *Emma Goldman*, 1:310; "The success": ibid., 312–313, 12; Candace Falk, *Love, Anarchy, and Emma Goldman* (New Brunswick, NJ: Rutgers University Press, 1990), 65.

31. "not only denounced": *CT*, June 16, 1897, 8; "We believe in the ballot": *CT*, September 13, 1897, 1; "Herr Most": *Sacramento R-U*, September 7, 1897; "the anarchist negress . . . bloodthirsty followers": *CT*, September 19, 1897, 1; "there is not a fool . . . toads": ibid., September 20, 1897, 1; *El Paso DH*, June 30, 1897.

32. "fretful silence": *DI-O*, November 13, 1895, 6; *Philadelphia Inquirer*, April 3, 1898; *Boston Herald*, April 25, 1898; *Aberdeen WN*, November 19, 1896; *Columbus DE*, September 11, 1901.

33. Perry R. Duis, *Challenging Chicago: Coping with Everyday Life, 1837–1920* (Urbana: University of Illinois Press, 2006), 275–280; Christiane Harzig, "Chicago's German North Side, 1880–1900: The Structure of a Gilded Age Ethnic Neighborhood," in Hartmut Keil and John B. Jentz, eds., *German Workers in Industrial Chicago, 1850–1910: A Comparative Perspective* (DeKalb: Northern Illinois University Press, 1983), 127–144.

34. "blood-red garments . . . striking appearance": *Dallas MN*, December 2, 1894.

35. "Mrs. Parsons was trying": *DI-O*, February 20, 1895; *Washington (DC) Star*, August 5, 1896; *DI-O*, August 6, 1896; *CT*, August 6, 1896, 5; *Firebrand*, September 6, 1896.

36. "Every stripe": *CT*, July 17, 1899, 4; Benedict Anderson, *Under Three Flags: Anarchism and the Anti-Colonial Imagination* (London: Verso, 2005).

37. "fighting machines": *Firebrand*, September 15, 1895; *Milwaukee Sentinel*, July 19, 1899; *CT*, July 19, 1899, 12; "in a calm": *NYT*, July 28, 1899, 1; *DISR*, July 29, 1899; *CT*, July 28, 1899, 12; William Briska, *The History of the Elgin Mental*

Health Center: Evolution of a State Hospital (Carpentersville, IL: Crossroads Communications, 1997).

38. Ashbaugh, *Lucy Parsons*, 207–209.

39. FMC, Cook County, Illinois, Chicago (1900).

40. "a victim": "The Civic Outlook," *American Magazine of Civics* 8 (February 1896): 211–224. Thanks to Michael Parrish for this citation.

41. FMC, McLennan County, Texas, Waco (1900).

42. "the dominating figure . . . things lively": *Freeland (PA) Tribune*, October 17, 1900; *Philipsburg (MT) Mail*, October 5, 1900; "goes far to . . . a mulatto": *Cleveland Leader* article, republished in *Dallas MN*, October 27, 1901.

43. "an anarchist colony": Robert A. Pinkerton, "Detective Surveillance of Anarchists," *NAR* 173, no. 540 (November 1901): 614.

44. *NYT*, August 23, 1899, 2; *Denver Post*, August 2, 1900; "defiant manner": *Lucifer* 4 (September 8, 1900): 276; *Lucifer* 4 (September 29, 1900): 301; *New York DP*, August 27, 1900; "the democracy": *Boston Journal*, September 1, 1900.

45. "a renaissance": *CT*, August 2, 1900, 3; Jeffrey S. Adler, "Shoot to Kill: The Use of Deadly Force by the Chicago Police, 1875–1920," *Journal of Interdisciplinary History* 38 (Autumn 2007): 240–243; *McClure's Magazine* 28 (April 1907): 575; "First in violence": *McClure's Magazine* 21 (October 1903): 563.

46. "the enemies of": Lincoln Steffens, "Enemies of the Republic," *McClure's Magazine* 23 (August 1904): 395; *Free Society*, May 1, 1901; *CT*, April 20, 1901, 1; *CT*, April 19, 1901, 9; Jane Addams, *Twenty Years at Hull-House*, ed. Victoria Bissell Brown (Boston: Bedford / St. Martin's, 1999), 268.

47. "Their names . . . man's life": *CT*, April 22, 1901, 7; *Free Society*, May 5, 1901.

48. "undeniably . . . must be focused": *Los Angeles Times*, September 12, 1901; *Dallas MN*, September 11, 1901.

49. Steven Kent Smith, "Research Note: Further Notes on Abraham Isaak, Mennonite Anarchist," *MQR* 80 (2006): 83–94; *WP*, September 23, 1901; "beautiful soul": Falk, *Emma Goldman*, 1:77; Carlotta R. Anderson, *All-American Anarchist: Joseph A. Labadie and the Labor Movement* (Detroit: Wayne State University Press, 1998), 202; Sidney Fine, "Anarchism and the Assassination of McKinley," *AHR* 60 (July 1955): 777–799; "It is impossible": Addams, *Twenty Years*, 269.

50. *CT*, January 24, 1902, 5.

51. "I offered" . . . into liberty": Taylor, *Pioneering*, 133.

52. "Sympathetic with . . . finished": Ibid.

53. "We eat not": *Free Society*, August 3, 1902; ibid., March 1, 1903; "Friends, I am": ibid., August 23, 1903; Shelley Streeby, "Looking at State Violence: Lucy Parsons, Jose Marti, and Haymarket," in Russ Castronovo, ed., *The Oxford*

Handbook of Nineteenth-Century American Literature (New York: Oxford University Press, 2011), 128–129.

54. Linda J. Lumsden, *Black, White, and Red All Over: A Cultural History of the Radical Press in Its Heyday* (Kent, OH: Kent State University Press, 2014), 27, 31; "not revolutionary . . . 1887": *Free Society*, February 22, 1903.

55. Gail Ahrens, ed., *Lucy Parsons: Freedom, Equality and Solidarity. Writings and Speeches, 1878–1937* (Chicago: Charles H. Kerr, 2004), 29–38.

56. Ibid.

57. Ibid.; FBI Case Files, Case #8000-112789, Fold3.com.

CHAPTER 12: TENDING THE SACRED FLAME OF HAYMARKET

1. *CT*, June 28, 1905, 2; Melvyn Dubofsky, *We Shall Be All: A History of the Industrial Workers of the World* (Chicago: Quadrangle Books, 1969), 81–87; "The working class": "Minutes of the IWW Founding Convention: The 1905 Proceedings of the Founding Convention of the Industrial Workers of the World, Friday June 27 Through Saturday July 8, 1905," Industrial Workers of the World, www.iww.org/history/founding.

2. Elizabeth Gurley Flynn, "Lucy Parsons: Tribute to a Heroine of Labor," *DW*, March 11, 1942; "Fellow workers": "Minutes of the IWW Founding Convention"; "honored guest": Dubofsky, *We Shall Be All*, 82; "platform decoration": Joseph Robert Conlin, *Bread and Roses Too: Studies of the Wobblies* (Westport, CT: Greenwood Press, 1970), 43; "dramatic visual": Salvatore Salerno, *Red November, Black November: Culture and Community in the Industrial Workers of the World* (Albany: State University of New York Press, 1989), 206.

3. "Minutes of the IWW Founding Convention"; Gail Ahrens, ed., *Lucy Parsons: Freedom, Equality and Solidarity. Writings and Speeches, 1878–1937* (Chicago: Charles H. Kerr, 2004), 77–78.

4. Ahrens, ed., *Lucy Parsons*, 78–85.

5. Ibid.

6. Ibid.; *CT*, June 27, 1905, 1.

7. "Great Labor War": *Charlotte (NC) Observer*, May 22, 1905; Allan Spear, *Black Chicago: The Making of a Negro Ghetto, 1890–1920* (Chicago: University of Chicago Press, 1967), 39.

8. "misleaders": *CT*, June 27, 1905, 1; "when we go down":"Minutes of the IWW Founding Convention."

9. "typical . . . human material": Hutchins Hapgood, *The Spirit of Labor* (New York: Duffield and Company, 1907), 16, 12; Andrew Wender Cohen, *The Racketeer's Progress: Chicago and the Struggle for the Modern American Economy, 1900–1940* (Cambridge: Cambridge University Press, 2009).

10. "ordinary, everyday . . . acute": *Free Society*, March 29, 1903; Margaret Garb, *Freedom's Ballot: African American Political Struggles in Chicago from Abolition to the Great Migration* (Chicago: University of Chicago Press, 2014), 139–142.

11. Lillian Symes and Travers Clement, *Rebel America: The Story of Social Revolt in the United States* (New York: Harper and Brothers, 1934), 273–276; Conlin, *Bread and Roses*, 42, 51.

12. Salerno, *Red November*, 81–82; "Issued under . . . succeed": *Liberator*, September 3, 1905.

13. "Workingmen, the landlords": *Liberator*, September 17, 1905.

14. Ibid., April 19, 1906.

15. "Necktie Party . . . quadrille": ibid., March 11, 1906; Perry R. Duis, *Challenging Chicago: Coping with Everyday Life, 1837–1920* (Urbana: University of Illinois Press, 2006), 225–233.

16. Salerno, *Red November*, 80–82; *Liberator*, October 8, 1905; "the split": ibid., February 3, 1906; "the dirty": ibid., October 8, 1905; "personalities": ibid., March 4, 1906.

17. "who had recently": *Topeka SJ*, October 9, 1905; "Grand Yom Kippur": *CT*, October 9, 1905, 2; *Liberator*, October 15, 1905; *Minneapolis Journal*, October 9, 1905; "Rex . . . heard of": *Liberator*, October 15, 1905.

18. *Liberator*, September 3, 1905; "aristocrats . . . beg for work": ibid., October 29, 1905; ibid., March 8, 1906.

19. *Liberator*, September 17, 1905; "awakening": ibid., September 24, 1905; "hereditary": A. M. Simons, *The American Farmer* (Chicago: Charles H. Kerr, 1902), 14; Linda J. Lumsden, *Black, White, and Red All Over: A Cultural History of the Radical Press in Its Heyday, 1900–1917* (Kent, OH: Kent State University Press, 2014), 31; Louise de Koven Bowen, "The Colored People of Chicago: Where Their Opportunity Is Choked—Where Open," *Survey* 31 (November 1, 1913): 117–120.

20. "everything now . . . and be free": *Liberator*, October 8, 1905; "worn-out": ibid., January 28, 1906; ibid., November 5, 1905; ibid., November 22, 1905; ibid., October 15, 1905; "highest aim . . . be at rest": ibid., September 10, 1905.

21. "The Woman Question . . . poverty and despair": *Liberator*, October 8, 1905. For the series on famous women, see, for example, *Liberator*, October 22, 1905, and October 29, 1905.

22. "a small clique . . . little boils": *Liberator*, March 5, 1906.

23. "agitation tour": *Liberator*, March 11, 1906; "It was the Lehigh . . . blank faces": ibid., April 8, 1906; "the tall factories . . . wonderful city": ibid., April 15, 1906.

24. *NYT*, April 2, 1906, 18.

25. "too far . . . ideal": Ahrens, ed., *Lucy Parsons*, 130–131 (*Demonstrator*, November 6, 1907); "no line of action . . . without a rudder": *Liberator*, April 8, 1906; Lumsden, *Black, White*, 170.

26. Melvyn Dubofsky, *"Big Bill" Haywood* (New York: St. Martin's Press, 1987); Peter Carlson, *Roughneck: The Life and Times of Big Bill Haywood* (New York: W. W. Norton, 1984), 86–135.

27. "anarchistic doctrine": *CT*, February 18, 1907, 3; "The Proposed Slaughter . . . civilization": *Liberator*, March 4, 1906 (this issue is mistakenly labeled 1905); *Rockford (IL) Republican*, May 20, 1907; "moderation . . . Constitution": *Denver Post*, May 20, 1907.

28. "I know": Darrow quoted in Beverly Gage, *The Day Wall Street Exploded: A Story of America in Its First Age of Terrorism* (New York: Oxford University Press, 2009), 82; *CT*, August 1, 1907, 5; "the Pinkerton plague . . . represented": *Demonstrator*, September 4, 1907.

29. "The anarchist cause": *Demonstrator*, November 6, 1907; ibid., November 20, 1907; Paul Avrich, *The Modern School Movement: Anarchism and Education in the United States* (Oakland, CA: AK Press, 2005), 58, 92; "put their own . . . future": *Demonstrator*, November 20, 1907; *Ross Winn's Firebrand*, November 3, 1909; "I was thrilled": Elizabeth Gurley Flynn, *The Rebel Girl: An Autobiography. My First Life (1906–1926)* (New York: International Publishers, 1955), 79.

30. "a pioneer": *Demonstrator*, September 4, 1907; "Lessons . . . resistance": *CT*, November 11, 1907, 3; "there was no riot": *IW*, May 1, 1912; "a little florid . . . foam on it": Frank Harris, *The Bomb* (New York: Published by the author, 1920), 47; "far better": ibid., 78; "it was a lie . . . Cemetery": LP to Carl Nold, January 17, 1930, Carl Nold Papers, 1883–1934, Joseph A. Labadie Collection, University of Michigan Library Special Collections Library, Ann Arbor, Michigan (Nold Papers, Labadie Collection, hereafter); "Harris had not": Emma Goldman, *Living My Life*, eds. Richard Drinnon and Anna Maria Drinnon (New York: New American Library, 1977), 682–683; *Agitator*, November 15, 1911. See also Emma Goldman, "The Crime of November 11," *ME*, November 11, 1911.

31. *CT*, May 26, 1906, 3; *ME*, March 3, 1908, 36; "To lecture": de Cleyre quoted in Blaine McKinley, "'The Quagmires of Necessity': American Anarchists and Dilemmas of Vocation," *AQ* 34 (Winter 1982): 515; "kid glove": ibid., 519; *Agitator*, December 1, 1910.

32. "The free coffee": *Demonstrator*, January 16, 1908; *Charities and the Commons* (February 1908): 1613.

33. *Rockford (IL) Republican*, January 18, 1908.

34. "Red peril": *CT*, February 4, 1908, 1; "Never in the history . . . squad": *Wilkes-Barre TL*, February 4, 1908; "There's Lucy": *CT*, March 16, 1908, 1; Irving S. Abrams, *Haymarket Heritage: The Memoirs of Irving S. Abrams*, ed. David Roediger and Phyllis Boanes (Chicago: Charles H. Kerr, 1989), 19.

35. *NYT*, March 3, 1908, 1; "Queen of the Reds": *CT*, March 3, 1908, 1.

36. "steadily the anarchist": *CT*, March 3, 1908, 1; Candace Falk, ed., *Emma Goldman: A Documentary History of the American Years*, vol. 2, *Making Speech*

Free, 1902–1909 (Urbana: University of Illinois Press, 2008), 283–284; *Agitator*, November 15, 1910.

37. "The Use": *CT*, March 16, 1908, 1; "it must . . . about his": *Juneau DR-M*, April 1, 1908.

38. Gage, *Day Wall Street Exploded*, 88, 98.

39. Ibid., 84–91; Andrew Cornell, *Unruly Equality: U.S. Anarchism in the Twentieth Century* (Oakland: University of California Press, 2016), 36–38; Lumsden, *Black, White*, 159.

40. *CT*, October 18, 1908, 5; "Bill Haywood": Ralph Chaplin, *Wobbly: The Rough-and-Tumble Story of an American Radical* (Chicago: University of Chicago Press, 1948), 182; "anarchist freaks": Flynn, *Rebel Girl*, 203; Stewart Bird, Dan Georgakas, and Deborah Shaffer, eds., *Solidarity Forever: An Oral History of the IWW* (Chicago: Lake View Press, 1985), 3–4.

41. Conlin, *Bread and Roses*; David M. Rabban, *Free Speech in Its Forgotten Years* (Cambridge: Cambridge University Press, 1997), 77–128; "But still . . . believed in": Chaplin, *Wobbly*, 150; "To hell": *OBUM*, August 1920, 9; "jawsmiths": Bird et al., *Solidarity*, 7; Matthew S. May, *Soapbox Rebellion: The Hobo Orator Union and the Free Speech Fights of the Industrial Workers of the World, 1909–1916* (Tuscaloosa: University of Alabama Press, 2013).

42. "propaganda literature . . . fruit": *Agitator*, December 15, 1911.

43. "Mrs. Parsons": *Anaconda (MT) Standard*, May 27, 1909; ibid., May 22, 1910; ibid., June 5, 1910; *IC*, June 25, 1910; *Salt Lake City Telegram*, June 11, 1910; ibid., June 13, 1910.

44. The quotations are from *Firebrand* issues of August and October 1910.

45. "the apostle": *CT*, August 30, 1909; "Religions seem": ibid.; *Oregonian*, August 13, 1909; "Mrs. Parsons": ibid.

46. "young bloods": *Agitator*, March 1, 1911; "My first": Emma Gilbert interview by Paul Avrich, *Anarchist Voices: An Oral History of Anarchism in America* (Princeton, NJ: Princeton University Press, 1995), 127; "If a white": Carl Nold to Metzkow, August 21, 1911, folder 201.1 (folder "Nold, Carl, 156 Letters to Max Metzkow, 1903–1904"), Ishill Papers; *Regeneración*, July 1912.

47. *Demonstrator*, February 19, 1908; "The longer . . . face it": *ME*, April 7, 1912, 60; Shelley Streeby, "Labor, Memory, and the Boundaries of Print Culture: From Haymarket to the Mexican Revolution," *ALH* 19 (Summer 2007): 406–433; Claudio Lomnitz, *The Return of Comrade Ricardo Flores Magón* (New York: Zone Books, 2014).

48. *Regeneración*, April 15, 1916; Streeby, "Labor, Memory," 412–420; Paul Avrich, *An American Anarchist: The Life of Voltairine de Cleyre* (Princeton, NJ: Princeton University Press, 1978), 226; David Roediger and Franklin Rosemont, eds., *Haymarket Scrapbook* (Chicago: Charles H. Kerr, 1986), 179; 1910

FMC, Kane County, Illinois, Ancestry.com; Erin Dwyer, "From the Pen of a Kicker: The Life and Circle of Lizzie Swank Holmes," master's thesis, Tufts University, 2006, 124–34.

49. Randi Storch, *Red Chicago: American Communism at Its Grassroots, 1928–35* (Urbana: University of Illinois Press, 2007), 16; Roediger and Rosemont, eds., *Haymarket Scrapbook*, 199.

50. "body of theorists . . . bore from within": *Syndicalist*, January 1, 1913; "means whereby": ibid., July 1, 1913; "the workers must realize": ibid., January 15, 1913.

51. *Syndicalist*, February 15, 1913.

52. "barren": Earl C. Ford and William Z. Foster, "Syndicalism" (William Z. Foster: 1000 S. Paulina St., Chicago, 1912), 27; "militant minority": ibid., 47, 43; "every forward": ibid., 13.

53. *Cleveland PD*, February 3, 1913.

54. Ahrens, ed., *Lucy Parsons*, 141–149; "Direct Action": *Regeneración*, April 19, 1913; "Mrs. Parsons": ibid.; "two burly": *IW*, May 1, 1913; *Syndicalist*, May 1, 1913.

55. City directories and 1920 FMC, Illinois, Cook County; *New York DP*, March 6, 1906; *Omaha DB*, April 5, 1905.

CHAPTER 13: WARS AT HOME AND ABROAD

1. *Oregonian*, July 16, 1913; ibid., July 17, 1913; *New York DP*, August 4, 1913; ibid., August 24, 1913; "white with rage": ibid., August 24, 1913.

2. "very deplorable": *Final Report and Testimony Submitted to Congress by the Commission on Industrial Relations Created by the Act of Aug. 23, 1912*, vol. 5, *General Industrial Relations in Portland, Oregon* (serial set vol. 6933, sess. vol. 23, 64th Cong., 1st sess., S. Doc. 415), 4117; Heather Mayer, "Beyond the Rebel Girl: Women, Wobblies, Respectability and the Law in Oregon and Washington, 1905–1924," Ph.D. diss., Simon Fraser University, Canada; Greg Hall, "The Fruits of Her Labor: Women, Children, and Progressive Era Reformers in the Pacific Northwest Canning Industry," *OHQ* 109 (Summer 2008): 226–251.

3. "mental prostitutes . . . Oregon": *New York DP*, August 4, 1913; Stewart Bird, Dan Georgakas, and Deborah Shaffer, eds., *Solidarity Forever: An Oral History of the IWW* (Chicago: Lake View Press, 1985), 142; "Forty cents": quoted in Hall, "Fruits," 239; Paul Avrich, *Anarchist Voices: An Oral History of Anarchism in America* (Princeton, NJ: Princeton University Press, 1995), 14–16.

4. *CT*, October 3, 1913, 1; "Never mind . . . county jail": *Oregonian*, October 3, 1913.

5. "I am pretty": LP to C. V. Cook, San Francisco, February 27, 1914, Cassius V. Cook Papers, Joseph A. Labadie Collection, University of Michigan Library Special Collections Library, Ann Arbor, Michigan (Cook Papers, Labadie

Collection, hereafter); *Tacoma DN*, November 12, 1913; *San Francisco Chronicle*, January 3, 1914; "Imitates": *Boise Statesman*, January 21, 1914.

6. "representative . . . being hungry": *International Socialist Review* (*ISR* hereafter), March 1915.

7. Ibid.

8. Paul Avrich, *The Russian Anarchists* (Princeton, NJ: Princeton University Press, 1967); "I am a baker . . . boisterous": Ralph Chaplin, *Wobbly: The Rough-and-Tumble Story of an American Radical* (Chicago: University of Chicago Press, 1948), 168–169; *ISR*, March 1915; *Rockford (IL) Republic*, January 4, 1915.

9. *CT*, January 18, 1915, 1; "as the heroine": *Freedom* (UK), March 15, 1915; "clever Indian . . . city blocks": ibid.; *CT*, January 18, 1915, 1; "I.W.W.'s Start": *Washington (DC) Herald*, January 18, 1915.

10. *NYT*, January 18, 1915, 1; *CT*, January 18, 1915, 1; "I know": ibid., January 19, 1915, 13; ibid., January 29, 1915, 13.

11. "a splendid": *Rockford (IL) Republic*, February 1, 1915; "If you want": ibid.; *CT*, February 1, 1915, 1; "From now on": ibid., February 11, 1915.

12. Lillian Symes and Travers Clement, *Rebel America: The Story of Social Revolt in the United States* (New York: Harper and Brothers, 1934), 277–278; Joseph Robert Conlin, *Bread and Roses Too: Studies of the Wobblies* (Westport, CT: Greenwood Press, 1970), 129–130; *CT*, April 11, 1915, 5.

13. "bellyaching": *Why?*, January 1913; "Impractical dreamers . . . understand them": ibid., April 15, 1914.

14. *Syndicalist*, September 1–15, 1913; C. V. Cook to LP, November 17, 1913, Cook Papers, Labadie Collection; Elizabeth Gurley Flynn, *The Rebel Girl: An Autobiography. My First Life (1906–1926)* (New York: International Publishers, 1955), 203.

15. "Could wars ever": *Instead of a Magazine*, September 1915.

16. "War as a Great": *Chicago DB*, January 6, 1917; ibid., September 23, 1916; ibid., November 20, 1915; ibid., January 20, 1917; ibid., January 27, 1917.

17. Melvin G. Holli, "The Great War Sinks Chicago's German *Kultur*," in Melvin G. Holli and Peter d'A. Jones, *Ethnic Chicago: A Multicultural Portrait*, 4th ed. (Grand Rapids, MI: Eerdmans, 1995); "the sixth": *Literary Digest*, July 7, 1917, 22.

18. "a hazy notion": Richard Wright, *12 Million Black Voices* (New York: Thunder's Mouth Press, 2002 [1941]), xvi; James R. Grossman, *Land of Hope: Chicago, Black Southerners, and the Great Migration* (Chicago: University of Chicago Press, 1989); Allan Spear, *Black Chicago: The Making of a Negro Ghetto, 1890–1920* (Chicago: University of Chicago Press, 1967), 12.

19. Junius B. Wood, "The Negro in Chicago: A First-Hand Study," articles reprinted from the *Chicago DN*, December 11–27, 1916; "Hit Me": Andrew Wender Cohen, *The Racketeer's Progress: Chicago and the Struggle for the*

Modern American Economy, 1900–1940 (Cambridge: Cambridge University Press, 2009), 217; "I am quite": Emmett J. Scott, "More Letters of Negro Migrants of 1916–1918," *JNH* 4 (October 1919): 457; Spear, *Black Chicago*, 185; Emmett J. Scott, "Letters of Negro Migrants of 1916–1918, *JNH* 4 (July 1919): 291; Ethan Michaeli, *The Defender: How the Legendary Black Newspaper Changed America* (Boston: Houghton Mifflin Harcourt, 2016).

20. "I would have . . . creep": Lum quoted in David Roediger and Franklin Rosemont, eds., *Haymarket Scrapbook* (Chicago: Charles H. Kerr, 1986), 95; "unions cannot": *Defender* quoted in Christopher Robert Reed, *The Rise of Chicago's Black Metropolis, 1920–1929* (Urbana: University of Illinois Press, 2011), 124; Linda J. Lumsden, *Black, White, and Red All Over: A Cultural History of the Radical Press in Its Heyday, 1900–1917* (Kent, OH: Kent State University Press, 2014), 236–239.

21. "plans were completed": *Broad Ax*, May 15, 1915; "I shall not": *CT*, March 4, 1913, 3; "perhaps not": Ovington quoted in Thomas C. Holt, "The Lonely Warrior: Ida B. Wells-Barnett and the Struggle for Black Leadership," in John Hope Franklin and August Meier, eds., *Black Leaders of the Twentieth Century* (Urbana: University of Illinois Press, 1982), 53.

22. Chaplin, *Wobbly*, 178–179; Irving S. Abrams, *Haymarket Heritage: The Memoirs of Irving S. Abrams*, ed. David Roediger and Phyllis Boanes (Chicago: Charles H. Kerr, 1989), 19–20; Carolyn Ashbaugh, *Lucy Parsons: American Revolutionary* (Chicago: Haymarket Books, 2013 [1976]), 234; "We tell": *ME* 10 (1915/1916): 88; "Thanks to our": *Freedom* (UK), February 1917, 9; *Why?*, September 1913; Benedict Anderson, *Under Three Flags: Anarchism and the Anti-Colonial Imagination* (London: Verso, 2005); Shelley Streeby, "Looking at State Violence: Lucy Parsons, Jose Marti, and Haymarket," in Russ Castronovo, ed., *The Oxford Handbook of Nineteenth-Century American Literature* (New York: Oxford University Press, 2011).

23. Shelley Streeby, "Labor, Memory, and the Boundaries of Print Culture: From Haymarket to the Mexican Revolution," *ALH* 19 (Summer 2007): 421–422; C. V. Cook to LP, July 31, 1914, Cook Papers, Labadie Collection.

24. "My First Impressions . . . comrades": *ME*, November 1916, 674–675.

25. Carlotta R. Anderson, *All-American Anarchist: Joseph A. Labadie and the Labor Movement* (Detroit: Wayne State University Press, 1998), 225; "Everything that we": Flynn, *Rebel Girl*, 283–284; "industrial freedom . . . limit": Chaplin, *Wobbly*, 213.

26. "while the army": Chaplin, *Wobbly*, 166–167.

27. Eric Thomas Chester, *The Wobblies in Their Heyday: The Rise and Destruction of the Industrial Workers of the World During the World War I Era* (Santa Barbara, CA: Praeger, 2014).

28. Chester, *Wobblies*, viii; "dangerous Red": Symes and Clement, *Rebel America*, 299.

29. "Their words": Haywood quoted in Beverly Gage, *The Day Wall Street Exploded: A Story of America in Its First Age of Terrorism* (New York: Oxford University Press, 2009), 115; Chester, *Wobblies*, 170–172; Chaplin, *Wobbly*, 231.

30. "Thou shalt": Flynn, *Rebel Girl*, 241; Lumsden, *Black, White*, 276–283.

31. "I would rather": Debs quoted in Flynn, *Rebel Girl*, 239–240; "the red flag": ibid., 252; Bird et al., *Solidarity*, 142; David M. Rabban, *Free Speech in Its Forgotten Years* (Cambridge: Cambridge University Press, 1997), 248–298; *ME* 1 (April 1918); Mark Leier, *Rebel Life: The Life and Times of Robert Gosden, Revolutionary, Mystic, Labour Spy* (Vancouver: New Start Books, 2013), 35–36.

32. "anarchic scum": quoted in Louis Adamic, *Dynamite: The Story of Class Violence in America* (New York: Viking Press, 1931), 211; Rebecca N. Hill, *Men, Mobs, and Law: Anti-Lynching and Labor Defense in U. S. Radical History* (Durham, NC: Duke University Press, 2008), 21, 141–143, 149, 159–160, 233 (Joe Hill); 147, 182 (Frank Little); 147–148 (Wesley Everest); 114, 143, 181, 184, 198, 215, 219 (Tom Mooney).

33. Ernesto A. Longa, *Anarchist Periodicals in English Published in the United States (1833–1955): An Annotated Guide* (Lanham, MD: Scarecrow Press, 2010), 241.

34. "from the other . . . I think": *Regeneración*, April 15, 1919.

35. "War, class war": "Plain Words" flyer in Paul Avrich, *Sacco and Vanzetti: The Anarchist Background* (Princeton, NJ: Princeton University Press, 1981), 81; Gage, *Day Wall Street Exploded*, 207–228.

36. "The anarchists will": *Edwardsville (IL) Intelligencer*, June 16, 1919; "grafter . . . out of the way": *CT*, June 6, 1919, 3; *NYT*, June 6, 1919, 1.

37. "holiness": *CT*, June 13, 1915, VIII, 1.

38. "Shall we": Chicago Commission on Race Relations, *The Negro in Chicago: A Study of Race Relations and a Race Riot* (Chicago: University of Chicago Press, 1922), 118.

39. "he was put": Ashbaugh, *Lucy Parsons*, 208–209 (nn. 21, 22), 276.

CHAPTER 14: FACTS AND FINE-SPUN THEORIES

1. "poorly dressed . . . Wobbly:" "Conversation with Studs Terkel about May Day . . ." Democracy Now, May 1, 1997, www.democracynow.org/1997/5/1/conversation_with_studs_terkel_about_may; "Studs Terkel Recalls Lucy Parsons," YouTube, posted October 9, 2012, www.youtube.com/watch?v=TFdKTIbBGbI.

2. "because I wanted": LP to Carl Nold, Chicago, February 27, 1934, Nold Papers (1883–1934), Labadie Collection; "From the *Tribune's*": *CT*, February 1,

1925, 8; ibid., August 6, 1925, 8; Vanzetti to Debs, September 29, 1923, in J. Robert Constantine, ed., *Letters of Eugene V. Debs*, vol. 3, *(1919–1926)* (Urbana: University of Illinois Press, 1990), 405.

3. "My daddy": *Studs Terkel's Chicago* (New York: New Press, 1985), 41; Lizabeth Cohen, *Making a New Deal: Industrial Workers in Chicago, 1919–1939* (Cambridge: Cambridge University Press, 2008), 3, 102; "No strike": Dunne quoted in Andrew Wender Cohen, *The Racketeer's Progress: Chicago and the Struggle for the Modern American Economy, 1900–1940* (Cambridge: Cambridge University Press, 2009), 236; Ku Klux Klan entry in Encyclopedia of Chicago, www.encyclopedia.chicagohistory.org/pages/696.html.

4. Cohen, *Making a New Deal*, 49; "turn the world": Mother Jones quoted in Elliott J. Gorn, *Mother Jones: The Most Dangerous Woman in America* (New York: Hill and Wang, 2002), 264; Randi Storch, *Red Chicago: American Communism at Its Grassroots, 1928–35* (Urbana: University of Illinois Press, 2007), 19.

5. "pineapple primary": Laurence Bergreen, *Capone: The Man and the Era* (New York: Simon and Schuster, 1994), 280; Gus Russo, *The Outfit: The Role of Chicago's Underworld in the Shaping of Modern America* (London: Bloomsbury, 2001); Michael Lesy, *Murder City: The Bloody History of Chicago in the Twenties* (New York: W. W. Norton, 2007).

6. Cohen, *Racketeer's Progress*, 233, 260.

7. Jackson Lears, "The Managerial Revitalization of the Rich," in Steve Fraser and Gary Gerstle, eds., *Ruling America: A History of Wealth and Power in a Democracy* (Cambridge, MA: Harvard University Press, 2005), 206, 211.

8. "more and more": Robert S. Lynd and Helen Merrell Lynd, *Middletown: A Study in Modern American Culture* (New York: Harcourt, Brace, 1929), 80–81.

9. "the dreams . . . setting sun": LP to C. V. and Sadie Cook, August 16, 1921; Cassius V. Cook letters, 1908–1950, Cook Papers, Labadie Collection.

10. David DeLeon, *The American as Anarchist: Reflections on Indigenous Radicalism* (Baltimore: Johns Hopkins University Press, 1978), 98–99; Kenyon Zimmer, "Premature Anti-Communists? American Anarchism, the Russian Revolution, and Left-Wing Libertarian Anti-Communism, 1917–1939," *Labor* 6 (2009): 45–71; Fred Thompson, "They Didn't Suppress the Wobblies," *RA* 1 (1967): 1–5.

11. Steve Nelson, *Steve Nelson, American Radical* (Pittsburgh: University of Pittsburgh Press, 1992), 72.

12. "I had high hopes": Carl Sandburg, *Billy Sunday and Other Poems*, eds. George Hendrick and Willene Hendrick (New York: Harcourt, Brace, 1993), 56; Franklin Rosemont, ed., *The Rise and Fall of the Dil Pickle: Jazz-Age Chicago's Wildest and Most Outrageously Creative Hobohemian Nightspot* (Chicago: Charles H. Kerr, 2004).

13. "looking for bums . . . outside": Rosemont, ed., *Rise and Fall*, 89.

14. "Near North Side": Ralph Chaplin, *Wobbly: The Rough-and-Tumble Story of an American Radical* (Chicago: University of Chicago Press, 1948), 170–171; "Heckling Is": Rosemont, ed., *Rise and Fall*, 45; "There are all": ibid., 67.

15. "Field Marshal": Albert Parry, *Garretts and Pretenders: A History of Bohemianism in America* (New York: Cosimo Classics, 2005), 204; "Women Are": *WST*, May 19, 1919; "prove the majority": Rosemont, ed., *Rise and Fall*, 31; Roger A. Bruns, *The Damndest Radical: The Life and World of Ben Reitman, Chicago's Celebrated Social Reformer, Hobo King, and Whorehouse Physician* (Urbana: University of Illinois Press, 1986), 271; "included almost": Frank O. Beck, *Hobohemia: Emma Goldman, Lucy Parsons, Ben Reitman and Other Agitators and Outsiders in 1920/30s Chicago* (Chicago: Charles H. Kerr, 2000), 77.

16. "Little Hell . . . World Ills": *DN*, April 29, 1930; ibid., July 30, 1929; ibid., August 6, 1929; Beck, *Hobohemia*, 81; Ben R. Reitman, *Sister of the Road: The Autobiography of Boxcar Bertha* (Oakland, CA: AK Press, 2002), 59.

17. "We had to harden": Chaplin, *Wobbly*, 258; "I have seen": ibid., 260; Joseph Robert Conlin, *Bread and Roses Too: Studies of the Wobblies* (Westport, CT: Greenwood Press, 1970), 140–145.

18. "Bolshevism is rotten . . . workers": Goldman quoted in *CT*, June 18, 1920, 1; ibid., May 7, 1920, 3; "a delusion": Emma Goldman to Debs, May 28, 1926, in Constantine, ed., *Letters*, 3:559; "severely": William Haywood, "An Anarchist on Russia: A Reply to Emma Goldman," *Communist Review* 3 (August 1922), Marxist Internet Archive, www.marxists.org/history/international/comintern/sections/britain/periodicals/communist_review/1922/04/emma_goldman.htm; Sander Garlin, "Lucy Parsons Carried Out Bequest of Her Husband, a Hero of American Labor," *Daily Worker*, March 11, 1942.

19. Elizabeth Gurley Flynn, *I Speak My Own Piece* (New York: Masses and Mainstream, 1955), 274; Paul Avrich, *Kronstadt, 1921* (New York: Norton, 1970); "nothing new": LP to Carl Nold, May 30, 1932, Nold Papers, Labadie Collection; Paul Avrich, *The Russian Anarchists* (Princeton, NJ: Princeton University Press, 1967), 205, 222, 227, 233, 245.

20. "the progress": Melville E. Stone, *Fifty Years a Journalist* (Garden City, NY: Doubleday, Page, and Co., 1920), 174; "substantial": Gail Ahrens, ed., *Lucy Parsons: Freedom, Equality and Solidarity. Writings and Speeches, 1878–1937* (Chicago: Charles H. Kerr, 2004), 151–152; *Voice of Labor*, March 10, 1922; folder "Ashbaugh File: Melville Stone on George A. Schilling," Box 3, Ashbaugh Papers.

21. "Grand Old": Constantine, ed., *Letters*, 3:557–558; "Over in Valhalla": "Eugene V. Debs," in Sandburg, *Billy Sunday*, 97.

22. See, for example, the quotations in the folder "Memos and Drafts on Motivation," Box 1, Ashbaugh Papers.

23. "Is Anarcho-Syndicalism . . . sympathizer": Dolgoff in Paul Avrich, *Anarchist Voices: An Oral History of Anarchism in America* (Princeton, NJ: Princeton University Press, 1995), 226; "turncoat . . . large doses": Sam Dolgoff, *Fragments: A Memoir* (Cambridge, UK: Refract, 1986), 42.

24. Bryan D. Palmer, *James P. Cannon and the Origins of the American Revolutionary Left, 1890–1928* (Urbana: University of Illinois Press, 2007); Ashbaugh interview with Cannon, Box 1, Ashbaugh Papers.

25. Rebecca N. Hill, *Men, Mobs, and Law: Anti-Lynching and Labor Defense in U. S. Radical History* (Durham, NC: Duke University Press, 2008), 198; Paul Avrich, *Sacco and Vanzetti: The Anarchist Background* (Princeton, NJ: Princeton University Press, 1996).

26. Vanzetti to Debs, September 29, 1923, in Constantine, ed., *Letters*, 3:405; "America shows": Cannon quoted in Hill, *Men, Mobs*, 198; Beverly Gage, *The Day Wall Street Exploded: A Story of America in Its First Age of Terrorism* (New York: Oxford University Press, 2009), 211–263.

27. *NYT*, November 13, 1927, 3; *Cleveland PD*, November 3, 1928; Palmer, *Cannon*, 311; Cora Meyer to Mother Jones, Milwaukee, January 9, 1928, in Edward M. Steel, ed., *Correspondence of Mother Jones* (Pittsburgh: University of Pittsburgh Press, 1985), 338.

28. "the electric chair": *Equal Justice*, July 1929, 139.

29. "political differences": Nelson, *American Radical*, 63; Storch, *Red Chicago*, 19, 76; DeLeon, *American as Anarchist*, 107.

30. "100 percent": Travis in Richard R. Guzman, ed., *Black Writing from Chicago: In the World, Not of It?* (Carbondale: Southern Illinois University Press, 2006), 135; St. Clair Drake and Horace R. Cayton, *Black Metropolis: A Study of Negro Life in a Northern City* (New York: Harcourt, Brace, 1945), 83.

31. Drake and Cayton, *Black Metropolis*, 69–97; Darlene Clark Hine and John McCluskey Jr., *The Black Chicago Renaissance* (Urbana: University of Illinois Press, 2012); Gareth Canaan, "'Part of the Loaf': Economic Conditions of Chicago's African-American Working Class During the 1920s," *JSH* 35 (Autumn 2001): 160–161; E. Franklin Frazier, "Chicago: A Cross-Section of Negro Life," *Opportunity* 7 (March 1929): 70–73; Chicago Commission on Race Relations, *The Negro in Chicago: A Study of Race Relations and a Race Riot* (Chicago: University of Chicago Press, 1922); Jacqueline Jones, *Labor of Love, Labor of Sorrow: Black Women, Work and the Family from Slavery to the Present* (New York: Basic Books, 2010), 131–162.

32. Christopher Robert Reed, *The Rise of Chicago's Black Metropolis, 1920–1929* (Urbana: University of Illinois Press, 2011), 129, 135, 144; Oscar Berland, "The Emergence of the Communist Perspective on the 'Negro Question' in America: 1919–1931, Part One," *Science and Society* 63 (Winter 1999/2000): 411–432.

33. *NYT*, May 2, 1930, 18; Storch, *Red Chicago*, 73–74; Ahrens, ed., *Lucy Parsons*, 155–159.

34. "go on and on . . . dead": Ahrens, ed., *Lucy Parsons*, 155–159.

35. *Cleveland PD*, September 3, 1931; Robert W. Rydell, *World of Fairs: The Century of Progress Expositions* (Chicago: University of Chicago Press, 1993), 111; "Old Timers": LP to Nold, January 17, 1933, Nold Papers, Labadie Collection.

36. "Baskets of fried": *Studs Terkel's Chicago*, 32–33; Michael J. Dennis, *The Memorial Day Massacre and the Movement for Industrial Democracy* (New York: Palgrave MacMillan, 2010); Ahmed White, *The Last Great Strike: Little Steel, the CIO, and the Struggle for Labor Rights in New Deal America* (Berkeley: University of California Press, 2016); "Police Repulse": *CT*, May 31, 1937, 1.

37. "They are very good": Michael Boda, "An Unpublished 1934 Letter from Lucy Parsons," *Pittsburgh GE*, October 13, 2009; David M. Rabban, *Free Speech in Its Forgotten Years* (Cambridge: Cambridge University Press, 1997), 344–379; David Roediger and Franklin Rosemont, eds., *Haymarket Scrapbook* (Chicago: Charles H. Kerr, 1986), 178; Audio Cassette #3, Ashbaugh Papers.

38. "I tell the world": Kwando M. Kinshasa, ed., *The Scottsboro Boys in Their Own Words: Selected Letters, 1931–1950* (Jefferson, NC: McFarland, 2014), 88; *CT*, March 19, 1932, 6.

39. "wind that has blown . . . speed": LP to Carl Nold, February 27, 1934, Nold Papers, Labadie Collection; Audio Cassette #1, Ashbaugh Papers; Anne M. Kornhauser, *Debating the American State: Liberal Anxieties and the New Leviathan, 1930–1970* (Philadelphia: University of Pennsylvania Press, 2015); *OBUM*, April 1937, 33; ibid., February 1938, 3–8; Jacqueline Jones, *American Work: Four Centuries of Black and White Labor* (New York: Norton, 1998), 339–345; Andrew Cornell, *Unruly Equality: U.S. Anarchism in the Twentieth Century* (Oakland: University of California Press, 2016), 126.

40. "tactically flexible": DeLeon, *American as Anarchist*, 109; "a girl might": Drake and Cayton, *Black Metropolis*, 572.

41. "We couldn't": Nelson, *American Radical*, 78; "the long wait": Weisbord quoted in Susan Ware, ed., *Notable American Women: A Biographical Dictionary Completing the Twentieth Century*, vol. 5 (Cambridge, MA: Harvard University Press, 2004), 675; Powell quoted in Charles H. Martin, "The ILD and the Angelo Herndon Case," *JNH* 64 (Spring 1979): 139. See also Lashawn Harris, "'Running with the Reds': African American Women and the Communist Party During the Great Depression," *JAAH* 94 (Winter 2009): 21–43.

42. *DW*, April 28, 1934.

43. LP to "Mr. Schilling," September 19, 1935, folder "Reproduced Copies of Various Articles by LP—1884 Through 1937," Box 1, Ashbaugh Papers;

"checked out . . . conditions": LP to Carl Nold, September 25, 1930, Nold Papers, Labadie Collection.

44. "get together": LP to Carl Nold, January 31, 1934, Nold Papers, Labadie Collection; "anarchism has not . . . today": LP to Carl Nold, February 27, 1934, ibid.

45. "This great . . . depraved mind": LP to Carl Nold, May 30, 1932, Nold Papers, Labadie Collection.

46. "dragged a man . . . asylum": Richard and Anna Maria Drinnon, *Nowhere at Home: Letters from Exile of Emma Goldman and Alexander Berkman* (New York: Schocken, 1975), 94–95, 170; Alice Wexler, *Emma Goldman in Exile: From the Russian Revolution to the Spanish Civil War* (Boston: Beacon Press, 1992), 154–155.

47. "kissed me": Carl Nold to Max Metzkow, February 12, 1931, Box 201.8, Ishill Papers; "well and happy": Carl Nold to Max Metzkow, August 8, 1933, Box 201.11, ibid. (translations provided by Matthew Bunn); interviews with Irving Abrams, James P. Cannon, Joseph Gigante, and Eugene Jasinksi, Box 1 and cassette tapes, Ashbaugh Papers; *CT*, May 4, 1938, 12.

48. *DW*, March 11, 1942; Beck, *Hobohemia*, 81–82; Eugene Jasinski and Abe Feinglass interviews, Box 1 and cassette tapes, Ashbaugh Papers; *Socialist Call*, December 9, 1939.

49. "Investigation of Un-American Propaganda Activities in the United States: Hearings Before a Special Committee on Un-American Activities, House of Representatives, 78th Cong., 2nd sess. (Washington, DC: US Government Printing Office, 1938–1944), vol. 10, Appendix, xxi; "Lucy Parsons was led": Note cards, Group 10, Box 3, Ashbaugh Papers; "When I croak . . . fare thee well": *Chicago DN*, March 11, 1942.

50. "he who died . . . being 'jealous'": *Chicago DN*, March 11, 1942.

51. *CT*, May 2, 1936, 4; "Labor to Honor . . . Race": *Chicago Defender*, May 2, 1936, 5.

52. "radical labor's": *CT*, May 2, 1937, 18; "Arise you . . . stuff": Richard Wright, "I Tried to Be a Communist," *Atlantic Monthly* 174 (August 1944): 61–76; *Atlantic Monthly* 174 (September 1944): 48–56.

53. "fervent, democratic . . . faith": *Atlantic Monthly* 174 (September 1944): 48–56; Hazel Rowley, *Richard Wright: The Life and Times* (Chicago: University of Chicago Press, 2001), chap. 16.

54. "yearly Gethsemane": *DW*, October 24, 1937; Irving Abrams, *Haymarket Heritage: The Memoirs of Irving S. Abrams* (Chicago: Charles H. Kerr, 1989), 32; "Lucy stepped": Dolgoff in Roediger and Rosemont, eds., *Haymarket Scrapbook*, 246.

55. "The crackpots": Dolgoff, *Fragments*, 231; "Oh, Misery": *OBUM*, November 1937.

56. Alan Calmer, *Labor Agitator: The Story of Albert R. Parsons* (New York: International Publishers, 1937); Carolyn Ashbaugh, *Lucy Parsons: American Revolutionary* (Chicago: Haymarket Books, 2013 [1976]), 261; Keith Rosenthal, "Lucy Parsons: 'More Dangerous Than a Thousand Rioters,'" Joan of Mark, September 6, 2011, http://joanofmark.blogspot.com/2011/09/lucy -parsons-more-dangerous-than.html.

57. *CT*, February 23, 1941, C13; "a beautiful": Elizabeth Gurley Flynn, "Lucy Parsons: Tribute to a Heroine of Labor," *DW*, March 11, 1942.

58. "Investigation of Un-American Propaganda Activities," 654, 830, 1578.

EPILOGUE

1. Folder "Birth and Death Certificates of LP and Family," Box 2, Ashbaugh Papers; death certificate on Ancestry.com.

2. Interviews, Audio Cassettes #1 and #2, folder "Acquaintances of Lucy E. Parsons," Box 1, Ashbaugh Papers; William Morris, "'The Signs of Change: Seven Lectures,' Inscribed by Morris to Lucy E. Parsons," The Saleroom, www .the-saleroom.com/en-gb/auction-catalogues/stroud-auctions-ltd/catalogue -id-srstr10037/lot-9d411702–5901-43cd-8aa8-a5280092ffcd. Thanks to Mark Jacob and Stephen Keeble for bringing this sale to my attention.

3. "Lucy Parsons," in "'Lucy Parsons: A Tribute,' by Dr. Ben Reitman, Labadie Collection, University of Michigan Special Collections; *Chicago Sun*, March 12, 1942; *CT*, March 9, 1942, 16.

4. Reitman's letter to the editor of the *Chicago DN*, written on the day of Parsons's funeral (March 12, 1942), is contained in folder 245, Box 22, Ben Lewis Reitman Papers, University of Illinois at Chicago, Special Collections, Richard J. Daley Library; George Markstall to Ben Reitman, July 20, 1941, ibid.; Andrew Cornell, *Unruly Equality: U.S. Anarchism in the Twentieth Century* (Oakland: University of California Press, 2016), 283; *Studs Terkel's Chicago* (New York: New Press, 1985), 23; Irving Abrams, *Haymarket Heritage: The Memoirs of Irving S. Abrams* (Chicago: Charles H. Kerr, 1989), 35.

5. "until recently": Charles H. Dennis, "On the Passing of Dark Lucy," *Chicago DN*, March 11, 1942; "Lucy Parsons, participant": *ISJ*, March 17, 1942; Sander Garlin, "Lucy Parsons Carried Out Bequest of Her Husband, a Hero of American Labor," *Daily Worker*, March 11, 1942. See also *Rockford R-R*, March 11, 1942, which says she was "just a wisp of the fiery woman who 54 years ago struggled with policemen in an attempt to say farewell to her husband, soon to be hanged."

6. *Socialist Call*, March 28, 1942; "was proud": *DW*, March 10, 1942; "What a great": ibid., March 11, 1942.

7. Office of the Clerk of the Circuit Court of Cook County, Illinois, Probate Estate File #42-P-1836 (Estate of Lucy Parsons Markstall). See, especially, the bill submitted by Sademan and Finfrock, Funeral Directors, March 11, 1942. A copy of her short will is in the file "Anarchism—Parsons, Lucy," in Labadie Papers, University of Michigan Special Collections.

8. "Chicana socialist": Alma M. García, *Chicana Feminist Thought: The Basic Historical Writings* (London: Routledge, 1997), 224; Matt S. Meier, ed., *Mexican-American Biographies: A Historical Dictionary* (Westport, CT: Greenwood Press, 1988), 96–97; "the first Black woman": Darlene Clark Hine, Elsa Barkley Brown, and Rosalyn Torberg-Penn, eds., *Black Women in America* (New York: Carlson Publishing, 1993), 909–910.

9. Kathryn Rosenfeld, "Looking for Lucy (in All the Wrong Places)," *Social Anarchism*, January 31, 2005; "Lucy Ella Gonzales Parsons," Chicago Park District, n.d., www.chicagoparkdistrict.com/parks/Lucy-Ella-Gonzales -Parsons/#f8pk04x605.

10. This question is inspired by James C. Scott, *Two Cheers for Anarchism: Six Easy Pieces on Autonomy, Dignity, and Meaningful Work and Play* (Princeton, NJ: Princeton University Press, 2012).

11. "when labor . . . and be free": *Liberator*, October 8, 1905.

12. See, for example, Bryan Burrough, *America's Radical Underground, the FBI, and the Forgotten Age of Revolutionary Violence* (New York: Penguin, 2015).

13. See, for example, "Chicago Police Department Plagued by Systemic Racism, Task Force Finds," *NYT*, April 14, 2016, A1; "Excessive Force Is Rife in Chicago, U.S. Review Finds," *NYT*, January 14, 2017, A1. On Lucy Parsons Labs, see https://lucyparsonslabs.com.

Index

o

International Brewers and Maltsters
Union, 192
International Brotherhood of Teamsters (IBT), 267
International Labor Defense (ILD),
334–335
Lucy associated with, 316, 320, 326,
327, 328, 333
International Publishers, 341
International Socialist Review (paper),
259
International Working People's Association (IWPA)
American Group of, 111, 112, 131–133,
150, 151–152
Defense Association of, 204
and eight-hour-day movement, 99
ideals of, 92, 121–124
meetings of, 129
membership of, 90, 118
sponsors speaking tours, 93–94,
113–116, 168
and undercover detectives, 95–96,
98
women's roles in, 109–110, 111
interracial relationships, in Reconstruction Texas, 3, 5, 18, 37–38
Inter-State Industrial Exposition
(Chicago fair, 1873), 40
Irish Republican Brotherhood (Fenians), 105–106
Isaak, Abe (editor of *Free Society*),
245, 246, 254, 257, 259
Italian anarchists, 282, 316, 319, 327
Italy, assassination in, 255
IWPA. *See* International Working
People's Association
IWW. *See* Industrial Workers of the
World

Jackson, Amos (alias of Albert Parsons), 140
James, C. L. (anarchist), 269
Jasinski, Eugene (Lucy's neighbor),
337
Jaxon, Honoré (labor radical),
236–237, 249, 295–296, 323
Jefferson, Thomas (American president), 92, 121, 164
Johnson, James (freedman), 30
Jones, Jack (proprietor of Dil Pickle
Club), 320–321
Jones, Jenkin Lloyd (minister), 258
Jones, Mary "Mother" (labor radical),
279
on anarchists' tactics, 124
on communists, 318
death of, 325–326
and IWW, 264, 268
on poverty in Chicago, 49
jury, prejudiced
in Haymarket trial, 143–144,
154–155, 235
in Sacco and Vanzetti case, 327
in textile workers' strike trial, 328

Kansas City Star, 159
Kansas City Times, 179
Kerr, Charles H. (founder of *Interna-
tional Socialist Review*), 259
Kinnard, David C. (minister), 31
Kipling, Rudyard (writer), 239
Klemencic, Andrew "Al" (labor orga-
nizer), 269
Knights of Labor
Chicago local assemblies, 59, 88,
188, 189
criticisms of, 83, 129
decline of, 212–213

BRIAN BIRZER

Jacqueline Jones is the Ellen C. Temple Chair in Women's History and the Mastin Gentry White Professor of Southern History at the University of Texas at Austin. A MacArthur Fellow (1999–2004), winner of the Bancroft Prize for *Labor of Love, Labor of Sorrow,* and Pulitzer Prize finalist for that book and also *A Dreadful Deceit,* Jones lives in Austin, Texas.